Michael Price

Windows 8 for Seniors

in easy steps

In easy steps is an imprint of In Easy Steps Limited
4 Chapel Court · 42 Holly Walk · Leamington Spa
Warwickshire · United Kingdom · CV32 4YS
www.ineasysteps.com

In Easy Steps Limited supports The Forest Stewardship Council (FSC), the leading international forest certification organisation. All our titles that are printed on Greenpeace approved FSC certified paper carry the FSC logo.

FSC
www.fsc.org
MIX
Paper from responsible sources
FSC® C020837

Printed and bound in the United Kingdom

ISBN 978-1-84078-539-5

Contents

3 Windows 8 Desktop 43

4 Personalize Your System 61

7 Windows 8 Apps 121

Sources for Apps 122
Supplied with Windows 8 123
Reader 124
SkyDrive 126
Windows Store Categories 128
Books & Reference 129
Search Windows Store 130
Installing Apps 131
Your App Account 132
Updates 133
Desktop Apps 134
Desktop Apps Available 136

8 Email and Calendar 137

Electronic Mail 138
Windows 8 Mail App 139
Add Email Account 140
The Mail Window 142
View Message 143
People 144
Viewing Contacts 146
Managing Contacts 147
Create a Message 148
Calendar 150
Instant Messaging 152
Windows Live Mail 154
Newsgroups 156

9 Internet 157

Internet Connection 158
Browse the Web 160
Right-click Menu 162
Desktop Internet Explorer 164
Tabbed Browsing 166
Close Tabs 168
Add to Favorites 170
Pin Websites 171
Zoom Web Page 172
RSS Feeds 174

10 Windows Games 175

Games in Windows 8 176
Games App 177
Minesweeper 178
Games at the Windows Store 180
Microsoft Solitaire Collection 182
Microsoft Mahjong 184
Word Games 186

11 Music and Pictures 187

Sound Card and Speakers 188
Recording 190
Play Audio CD 192
Copy Tracks 194
Media Library 195
Music App 196
Digital Pictures 198
Viewing Pictures 200
Photos App 201

Windows Photo Viewer 203
Photo Gallery 204
Movie Maker 206

12 Networking 207

Create a Network 208
Network Classification 209
Create HomeGroup 210
Connect to Wireless Network 212
Join the HomeGroup 213
View Network Devices 214
View HomeGroup 215
Network and Sharing Center 216
PC Settings 218

13 Security & Maintenance 219

Windows Help 220
More Support Options 222
Product Solution Centers 223
Windows Action Center 224
Program Compatibility 225
Windows Firewall 226
Windows Defender 227
Windows Update 228
System Restore 230
File History 232

Index 233

1 Get Windows 8

This chapter explains how Windows 8 has evolved from previous releases, identifies the new features and helps you recognize what's needed to upgrade your existing computer. It discusses the use of Microsoft accounts, to make your settings portable, and explains how to install Windows 8 apps on your system.

10 Windows 8
11 Which Release is Installed?
12 Features of Windows 8
14 What's Needed
15 Upgrade Assistant
16 Windows 8 Editions
17 Selecting your Edition
18 Upgrades
19 First Logon
20 Microsoft Account
21 Local Account
22 Install Applications
24 Install Windows 8 Apps
26 Activation

Windows 8

Don't forget

There have been other releases of Microsoft Windows, intended for business and server computers, including Windows NT, Windows 2000, Windows Server 2003, Windows Server 2008 and Windows Server 2012.

Hot tip

Windows RT is the version of Windows 8 that is designed for tablet PCs that use the ARM processor, as used in cell phones and other hand-held devices.

Hot tip

If you purchased a Windows 7 PC after May 30th 2012, you may be entitled to a reduced price upgrade to Windows 8 (see page 18).

Windows 8 is the latest release of Microsoft Windows, the operating system for personal computers. There has been a long list of Windows releases including:

- 1995 Windows 95
- 1998 Windows 98
- 2000 Windows Me (Millennium Edition)
- 2001 Windows XP (eXPerience)
- 2003 Windows XP MCE (Media Center Edition)
- 2007 Windows Vista
- 2009 Windows 7
- 2012 Windows 8 (and Windows RT)

When you buy a new computer, it is usually shipped with the latest available release of Windows. This takes advantage of the hardware features generally available at the time. Every year sees new and more powerful features being incorporated into the latest computers. In line with this, the requirements for Microsoft Windows have increased steadily. For example, the minimum and recommended amounts of system memory have increased from Windows 95 (4 MB to 8 MB), Windows 98 (16 MB to 24 MB), Windows XP (64 MB to 128 MB), Windows Vista (512 MB to 1024 MB), Windows 7 and Windows 8 (1 GB to 2 GB). There's a similar progression in terms of the processor power, the video graphics facilities and hard disk storage.

This means that your computer is likely to need upgrading or extending in order to use a later release of Windows, especially if you want to take advantage of new capabilities such as multi-touch. To take full advantage of new features, you may need a new computer, for example a "tablet" PC.

Each release enhances existing features and adds new facilities. Thus the new Windows 8 is able to support all the functions of Windows 7 and prior releases, often with enhancements, plus offer its own unique new features.

The value of all this is that you can use your computer to carry out tasks that would not have been possible with previous computers and operating system releases.

Which Release is Installed?

To check which release of Windows is currently installed on your system, you can look in System properties.

1. Press WinKey and the Break key (simultaneously) to display the System properties

2. The operating system details will be displayed (along with user, memory and processor information)

The layout varies between releases of Windows, but similar details are shown.

Windows XP

Windows 7

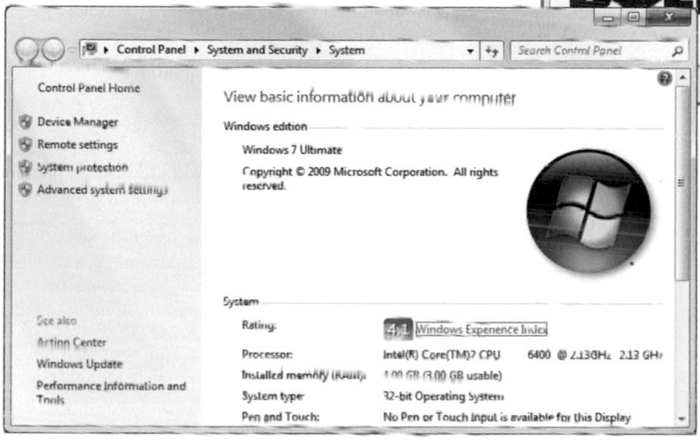

Windows 8

Hot tip

WinKey is used to represent the Windows Logo key or other designated Windows key on your system.

Don't forget

These images show the System properties for computers with Windows XP, Windows Vista and Windows 8.

Hot tip

There are other ways to open the System properties, but the method shown is supported in all the various releases.

Features of Windows 8

Hot tip

The Start screen replaces the Start menu of previous releases of Windows. The Desktop is used for traditional Windows applications.

Tile-based User Interface

Windows 8 features a tile-based user interface, similar to the interface for the Windows Phone and optimized for touch screens as well as mice and keyboards. The Start screen displays live application tiles which start Windows 8 apps. These run full-screen, or two can be displayed on higher resolution (1366×768 and larger) monitors by snapping one to the side of the screen. The Start screen also displays the user's name and picture.

Windows 8 also displays a new login/lock screen that shows the date and time and notifications, along with a customizable background.

Windows Store

Windows Store is a digital distribution application that is the only means of distributing Windows 8 apps to users. Microsoft will scan apps for security flaws and malware. Apps may be free or may carry a charge for download.

The Windows Store will also allow developers to publish traditional desktop applications, providing links to those applications on the developer websites.

Don't forget

There are some new Windows 8 apps and some traditional desktop applications provided with Windows 8 at installation, but you will need to visit the Windows Store for many functions that were previously included.

File Explorer

Access to files, folders and drives is provided by the new version of Windows Explorer, now known as File Explorer, which now includes a Ribbon interface to provide in-context access to commands.

Restore and Reset

With Windows 8 you can refresh your PC, which keeps all your documents, accounts, personal settings and modern apps but returns Windows to its original state. You can completely restore your PC to the state it was in when you first got it. You can create a recovery drive on a USB key with the files needed to refresh or reset your PC even if Windows 8 can't boot. Restoring from the USB drive is a good option if you have a tablet PC without a disc drive or you just want to save space.

Shorter Boot Times

Windows 8 has short boot times, because it saves the kernel's memory to the hard disk on shutdown (similar to the existing hibernate option) and reloads it on start up.

Internet Explorer 10

The latest version of the Windows web browser, Internet Explorer 10, dedicates the entire screen to your websites, giving a full edge-to-edge display. Only when you need them do the browser tabs and navigation controls appear and they quietly get out of the way when you don't want them anymore. By taking advantage of Windows 8 and your computer's hardware acceleration features, Internet Explorer makes browsing faster and more fluid and the security capabilities ensure that your access is safe.

Microsoft Account Integration

Your Windows User account can be linked up to your Microsoft account. This means that you will not lose your settings and files, as you move from your home computer to your work laptop or to any other computer also using Windows 8 and sign in via your Microsoft account.

Multiple Monitors

If you have multiple monitors, Windows 8 can span the taskbar across the desktop on each of the monitors. Similarly, you can show different wallpapers on different monitors, or the same wallpaper stretched across multiple monitors.

Removed Features

Several features that were present in Windows 7 are no longer available in Windows 8. The Start menu and the Start button have been removed, although there is a Start screen hotspot in the lower left corner of the screen. The Aero Glass themes have been replaced by Windows 8 themes. The Microsoft Gadgets Gallery has also been removed. Windows Media Center will not be included and Windows Media Player will not provide DVD playback.

Beware

Some features are only available in particular editions of Windows 8, or have specific hardware prerequisites.

Hot tip

The Windows Media Center will be available for purchase as an add-on and this will include DVD playback capability.

What's Needed

The minimum configuration recommended by Microsoft to install and run Windows 8 is as follows:

Processor	1 GHz 32-bit or 64-bit
System memory	1 GB (32-bit) or 2 GB (64-bit)
Graphics	DirectX 9 graphics device with WDDM 1.0 driver
Hard disk drive	16 GB (32-bit) or 20 GB (64-bit) free
Optical drive	DVD/CD (for installation purposes)

There may be additional requirements for some features, for example:

- SVGA display monitor with 1024x768 or higher resolution (1366×768 for snapping Windows 8 apps)
- Internet access for online services and features such as Windows Update
- TV tuner for Windows Media Center functions
- Five point Multi-touch hardware for touch functions
- A network and multiple PCs running Windows 8 for HomeGroup file and printer sharing
- An optical drive with rewriter function for DVD/CD authoring and backup function
- Trusted Platform Module (TPM) 1.2 hardware for BitLocker encryption
- USB flash drive for Windows to Go/BitLocker To Go
- An additional 1 GB memory, 15 GB extra hard disk space and a processor with Intel VT or AMD-V hardware features, for Hyper-V virtualiization
- Audio output (headphones or speakers) for music and sound in Windows Media Player

Don't forget

The terms 32-bit and 64-bit relate to the way the processor handles memory. You'll also see the terms x86 and x64 used for 32-bit and 64-bit respectively.

Beware

The product functions and the graphics capabilities may vary depending on the system configuration.

Upgrade Assistant

To have your computer assessed to see if it is able to support Windows 8, run the Windows 8 Setup program from the Windows 8 installation DVD (or from the Microsoft Web Installer site at www.microsoft.com/windows).

Windows 8 Upgrade Assistant
Here's what we found
You can get more info about each app and device in compatibility details.
34 of your apps and devices are compatible
6 items for you to review
You'll need to reinstall your compatible apps and devices in Windows 8
See compatibility details
I want to help make Windows 8 Upgrade Assistant better
Next

This program will assess your computer and generate a report to tell you if any changes are needed to support Windows 8 on your computer. It also identifies any incompatible software or accessories that you may have.

For example, when run on an Asus Eee PC netbook computer currently running Windows XP, the Upgrade Assistant says that this has insufficient resolution.

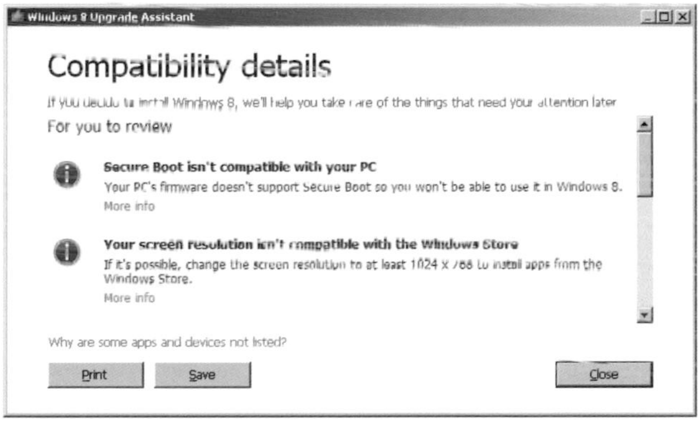
Windows 8 Upgrade Assistant
Compatibility details
For you to review
Secure Boot isn't compatible with your PC
Your PC's firmware doesn't support Secure Boot so you won't be able to use it in Windows 8.
More info
Your screen resolution isn't compatible with the Windows Store
Windows Store.
More info
Why are some apps and devices not listed?
Print
Save
Close

This machine has a resolution of 1024 x 600, but the minimum requirement to access the Windows Store to install apps is 1024 x 768. Netbooks are therefore effectively incompatible, even when it is possible to install Windows 8.

Hot tip

If your computer runs Windows 7 or Vista, it may already be able to run Windows 8, perhaps with a hardware upgrade. Computers running earlier versions of Windows are unlikely to have the necessary capabilities.

Beware

You can upgrade from Windows 7, Windows Vista and Windows XP, but you might not be able to keep all of your files, programs and settings.

Windows 8 Editions

There are three editions of Windows 8 for computers based on the x32/x64 Intel or AMD processors (until now the usual processors for Windows PCs), plus an edition called Windows RT for PCs based on the ARM processor.

Don't forget

The ARM processor is a RISC (reduced instruction set computer) processor with enhanced power-saving features, used for mobile phones, media players and tablet PCs. Currently, it is 32-bit only.

Windows 8

Windows 8 is the base edition, intended for consumers and containing the main features of Windows 8, including touch screen and keyboard/mouse support, Windows 8 apps, Windows Store, Internet Explorer 10, enhanced Task Manager and improved multi-monitor support.

Windows 8 Pro

Windows 8 Pro is the edition designed for advanced users and business/technical professionals and includes all the features in Windows 8 plus features for encryption, virtualization, PC management and domain connectivity. Windows Media Center is not included in any edition of Windows 8 but is available as a chargeable media pack add-on to Windows 8 Pro.

Don't forget

For the business user, the main choices are the Professional and the Enterprise editions.

Windows 8 Enterprise

Windows 8 Enterprise is the edition for customers with Software Assurance agreements and includes all the features of Windows 8 Pro plus features for IT organization, to enable PC management and deployment, advanced security, virtualization and new mobility scenarios. Unlike Windows 8 and Windows 8 Pro, it will not be supplied as a separate retail pack.

Windows RT

Windows RT will only be available pre-installed on PCs and tablets powered by ARM processors. It is designed to enable new thin and lightweight form factors with enhanced battery life.

Windows RT does not support conventional Windows desktop applications, though it does include touch-optimized desktop versions of the Microsoft Office applications – Word, Excel, PowerPoint and OneNote.

Selecting your Edition

If you are unsure which of these editions of Windows 8 is best for you, it may be useful to focus on those features that are excluded or restricted in particular editions.

The main selective features are:

Feature	B	P/E	R
Multi-touch capability (hardware req)	Y	Y	Y
Desktop support (restricted in RT)	Y	Y	Y
Storage Spaces	Y	Y	-
Upgrade from Win 7 Starter/Home	Y	Y	-
Windows Media Player	Y	Y	-
x32/x64 processor support	Y	Y	-
BitLocker and BitLocker To Go	-	Y	-
Boot from VHD	-	Y	-
Client Hyper-V	-	Y	-
Domain Join	-	Y	-
Encrypting File System	-	Y	-
Group Policy	-	Y	-
Remote Desktop (host)	-	Y	-
Upgrade from Win 7 Pro/Ultimate	-	Y	-
Windows Media Center (add-in)	-	Y	-
ARM support	-	-	Y
Device encryption	-	-	Y
Microsoft Office (included)	-	-	Y

If one of these features is a must have, this will dictate the editions that you need to investigate in more detail. In practice, the choice will often be dictated by the hardware characteristics of your computer, since Windows RT is the only option for the ARM-based systems.

For home use on x32/x64 computers, the choice is between the base and the professional editions, while business users will have either professional or enterprise, depending on their company's preferences.

For travelling, a computer based on the power-saving ARM processor may be the preferred choice, except where there are conventional (legacy) applications that must be used.

Don't forget

The four editions of Windows 8 are:

B	Base
P	Pro
E	Enterprise
R	RT

Hot tip

If you choose the base edition and discover you do need additional features, you have the opportunity to upgrade your edition to the higher level.

Upgrades

If you are planning to install Windows 8 on an existing computer running a previous version of Windows, you may be able to upgrade and retain your existing Windows settings, personal data and applications.

The upgrade paths available include:

- Upgrade to Windows 8 (base edition) from Windows 7 Starter, Home Basic or Home Premium and retain Windows settings, personal data and applications
- Upgrade to Windows 8 Pro from Windows 7 Starter, Home Basic, Home Premium, Professional or Ultimate and retain Windows settings, personal data and applications
- Upgrade to Windows 8 Enterprise from Windows 7 Professional or Enterprise and retain Windows settings, personal data and applications (volume licensees only)
- Upgrade to Windows 8 from Windows Vista (with SP1) and retain personal data and Windows settings
- Upgrade to Windows 8 from Windows XP (with SP3) or Vista (without SP1) and retain personal data only

There is no upgrade path offered for Windows RT.

You won't be able to upgrade or retain Windows settings, personal data and applications if you make a move between 32-bit and 64-bit configurations.

If you install from DVD or USB, rather than running Setup from your existing Windows, you are also unable to retain Windows settings, personal data and applications.

For installations before January 31st 2013, Microsoft priced the upgrade to Windows 8 Pro at only $39.99 (US price).

If you purchased a new Windows 7 PC between June 2nd 2012 and January 31st 2013, you could also register to buy an upgrade to Windows 8 Pro for only $14.99 (US price).

Hot tip

Check at the Microsoft website for your location, or with your software retail store, to find your prices for Windows 8 upgrades, during and after the promotions and for the prices for the full release of Windows 8.

Don't forget

If you prefer to install from DVD, you can purchase an upgrade for $69.99 (US price).

First Logon

When you upgrade your existing version of Windows to Windows 8, there are several actions that you may be asked to carry out.

Windows Setup
Windows 8
Install now
Repair your computer
© 2012 Microsoft Corporation. All rights reserved.

Personalize

1. Choose one of the 25 color schemes offered (or accept the default Blue scheme)

Personalize
Pick a color you like and give your PC a name–any name you want. You'll be able to personalize more later.
PC name
Dell
Next

2. Provide a descriptive name for the computer and click the Next button

Apply Settings

1. Customize settings for Windows updates and security, or choose to Use Express Settings

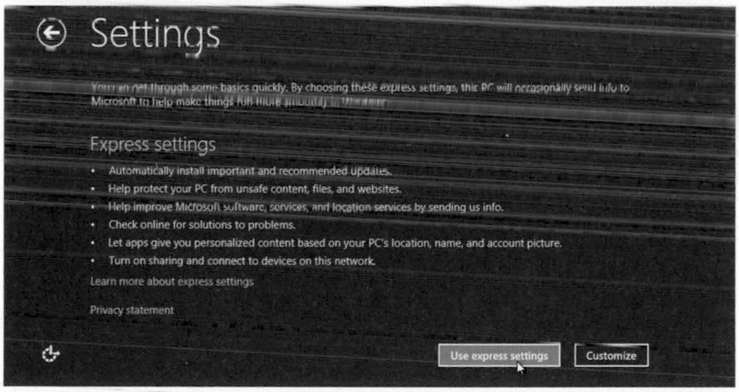
Settings
Express settings
Automatically install important and recommended updates.
Help protect your PC from unsafe content, files, and websites.
Help improve Microsoft software, services, and location services by sending us info.
Check online for solutions to problems.
Let apps give you personalized content based on your PC's location, name, and account picture.
Turn on sharing and connect to devices on this network.
Learn more about express settings
Privacy statement
Use express settings
Customize

Hot tip

The first time you start up a new computer with an edition of Windows 8 preinstalled, you'll also be prompted for these actions.

Don't forget

The Express Settings will enable Windows Update, Windows Firewall and Windows Defender, turn on network sharing and ensure that Windows 8 apps are personalized for your location.

Microsoft Account

You'll be asked to provide an email address to use as a Microsoft account, to let you access the Windows Store (see page 24), get online content and sync settings online.

Don't forget

You can choose to use a Local account (see page 21) that is not associated with a Microsoft account but you will not be able to download Windows 8 apps and your settings won't travel with you when you switch computers.

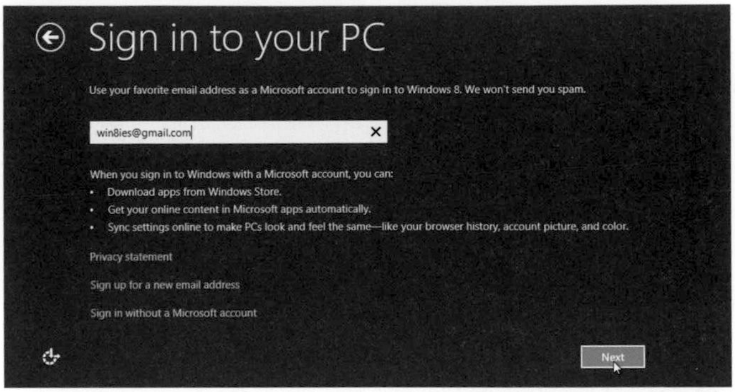
Sign in to your PC
Use your favorite email address as a Microsoft account to sign in to Windows 8. We won't send you spam.
win8ies@gmail.com
When you sign in to Windows with a Microsoft account, you can:
Download apps from Windows Store.
Get your online content in Microsoft apps automatically.
Sync settings online to make PCs look and feel the same—like your browser history, account picture, and color.
Privacy statement
Sign up for a new email address
Sign in without a Microsoft account
Next

1. Enter your preferred email address and click Next

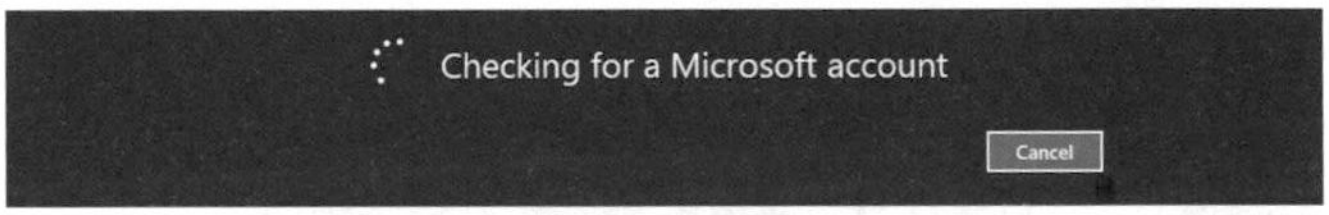
Checking for a Microsoft account
Cancel

2. Windows checks for the Microsoft account for that email address and prompts you for the password

Hot tip

If this email address is not recognized, you'll be prompted to provide personal details so that a Microsoft account can be created.

Enter your Microsoft account password
You already have a Microsoft account. It's the one you use with Messenger, Hotmail, Xbox LIVE or Windows Live services.
Email address
win8ies@gmail.com
Password
Sign up for a Microsoft account
Next
Cancel

3. Windows starts up with that account and its settings

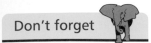

Start
Michael
Price

Local Account

If you'd prefer a local account, click the option to Sign in without a Microsoft account. Windows reminds you of the implications of this choice.

Privacy statement
Sign up for a new email address
Sign in without a Microsoft account

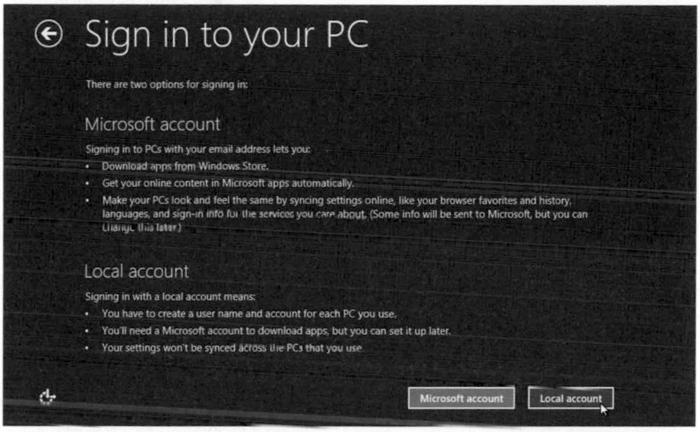
Sign in to your PC
There are two options for signing in:
Microsoft account
Signing in to PCs with your email address lets you:
Download apps from Windows Store.
Get your online content in Microsoft apps automatically.
Make your PCs look and feel the same by syncing settings online, like your browser favorites and history, languages, and sign-in info for the services you care about. (Some info will be sent to Microsoft, but you can change this later.)
Local account
Signing in with a local account means:
You have to create a user name and account for each PC you use.
You'll need a Microsoft account to download apps, but you can set it up later.
Your settings won't be synced across the PCs that you use.
Microsoft account
Local account

1. Select Local Account to confirm your wishes

Sign in to your PC
If you want a password, choose something that will be easy for you to remember but hard for others to guess.
User name
Michael Price
Password
Reenter password
Password hint
as it should be
Finish

2. Enter your user name and password, confirm the password, provide a password hint and click Next

3. Windows starts with a local account

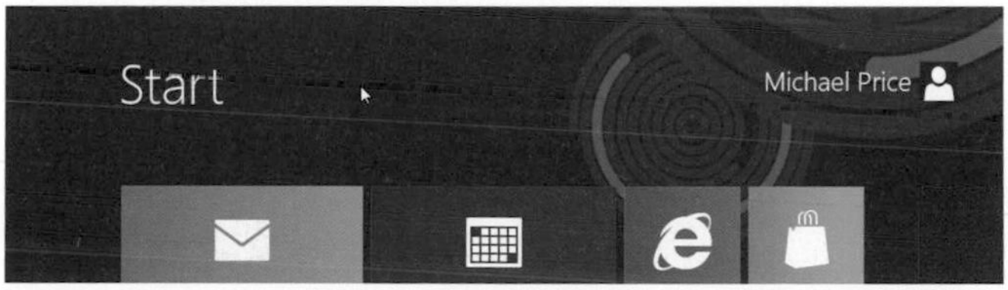
Start
Michael Price

Beware

You won't be able to access the Windows Store with a local account. However, you will be able to set up a Microsoft account later for that purpose.

Hot tip

Note the subtle change in the way the user name is displayed on the Start screen, for a local account versus a Microsoft account.

Install Applications

For the Desktop environment, you can start with Windows Essentials 2012. To install these programs:

Don't forget

Windows 8 doesn't include as many applications as previous releases. However, Microsoft provides additional apps for both Desktop and Windows 8 for you to download and install.

1. Go to the Desktop, select Internet Explorer from the Taskbar and go to windows.microsoft.com

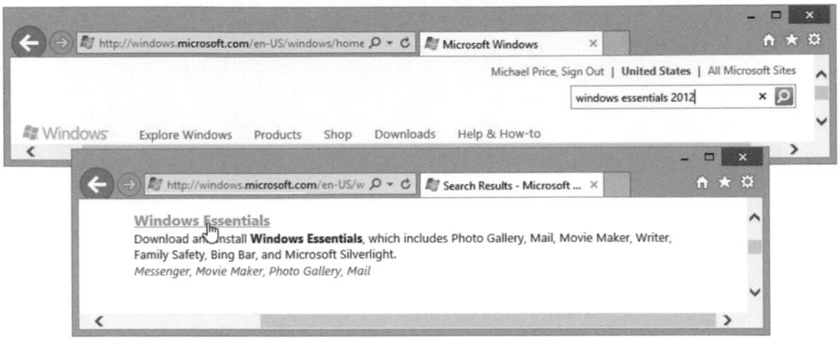

2. Type Windows Essentials 2012 in the Search box and press Enter to locate links to that product

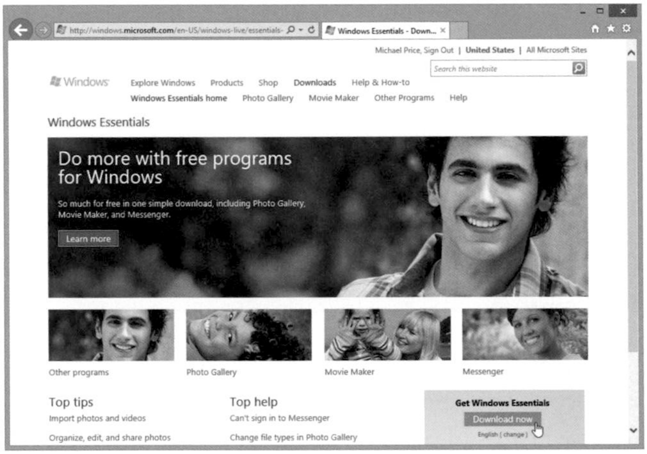

Hot tip

The link shown is for installation from the Web, but there is an alternative link that will allow you to download and install the programs offline.

3. Select the Microsoft Essential link, click Download Now and choose to Run the setup program

This installs the Windows Essential programs from the Web.

4 When prompted, you must authorize Windows Essentials to make changes to your system

User Account Control
Do you want to allow the following program to make changes to this computer?
Program name: Windows Essentials
Verified publisher: Microsoft Corporation
File origin: Hard drive on this computer
Show details
Yes
No
Change when these notifications appear

Windows Essentials 2012
What do you want to install?
Install all of Windows Essentials (recommended)
Windows Essentials includes Messenger, Photo Gallery, Movie Maker, Mail, Writer, Microsoft SkyDrive, and Outlook Connector Pack.
Choose the programs you want to install
By clicking an installation option, you agree to the Microsoft Services Agreement, and have reviewed Privacy & Cookies. You will get updates for this and other Microsoft software from Microsoft Update. This software may also download and install its updates automatically. At installation, you may receive updates to Windows.
Privacy & Cookies Microsoft Services Agreement Learn more

5 Choose to install all of Windows Essentials

6 The components of Windows Essentials are installed

Windows Essentials 2012
Installing Windows Essentials 2012
Hide Details
Cancel
44% complete
Installing: Messenger

7 Click Show Details to see the progress, program by program

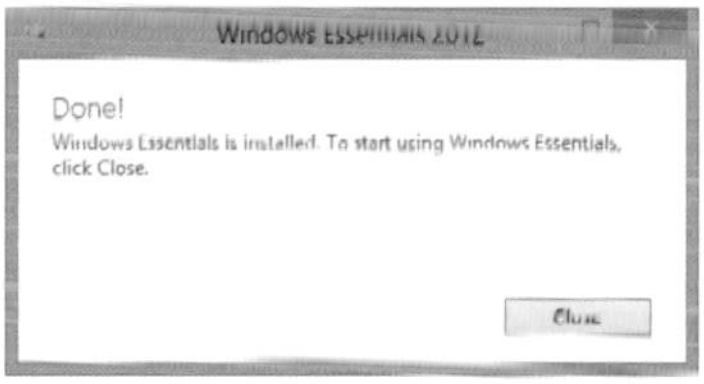
Done!
Windows Essentials is installed. To start using Windows Essentials, click Close.
Close

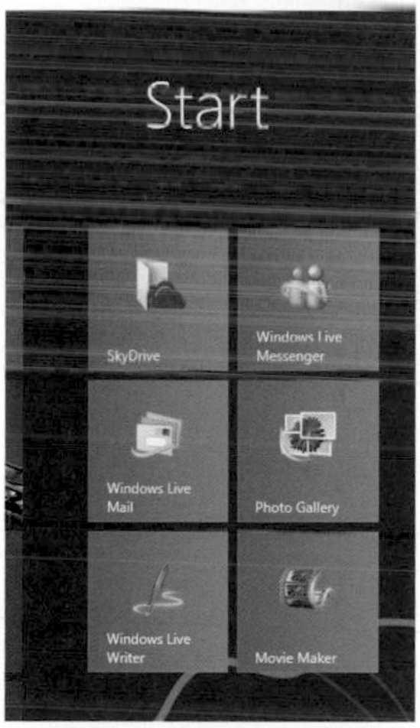
Start
SkyDrive
Windows Live Messenger
Windows Live Mail
Photo Gallery
Windows Live Writer
Movie Maker

8 The applications in Windows Essentials are Desktop programs, but they will still be added as a group of tiles on the Start screen

Hot tip

You may be prompted to allow additional Windows features such as Microsoft Net Framework, that may be needed to operate Windows Essentials.

Don't forget

Windows Essentials was previously identified as Windows Live Essentials. The terminology has changed, though the preview versions of the programs may still carry their old titles.

Install Windows 8 Apps

There are many Windows 8 apps in the Windows Store, but Microsoft spotlights sets of apps that can make good starting points. To install these:

1. From the Start screen, click Store, which opens as a full screen app

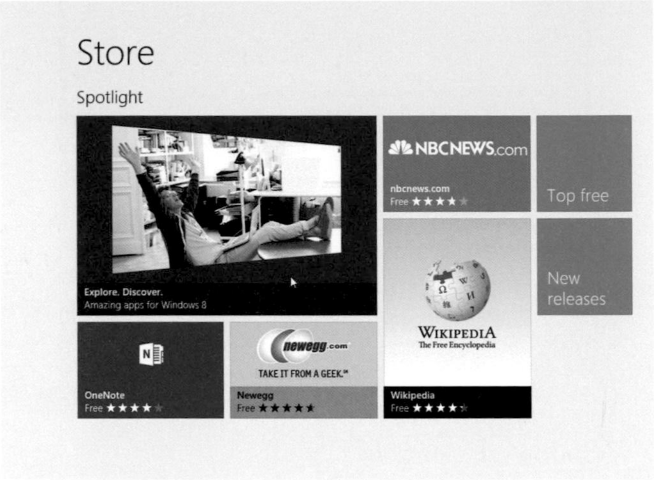

2. Select the Spotlight apps that have been selected to help you explore and discover apps for Windows 8

Don't forget

Applications designed for the Windows 8 environment can be downloaded and installed from the Windows Store, a procedure familiar to users of smartphones and tablet devices.

Hot tip

The Spotlight apps will be changed from time to time, but these illustrate some of the apps that are considered as useful for starting off with Windows 8.

3. Select an app, e.g. Cocktail Flow, to see the description

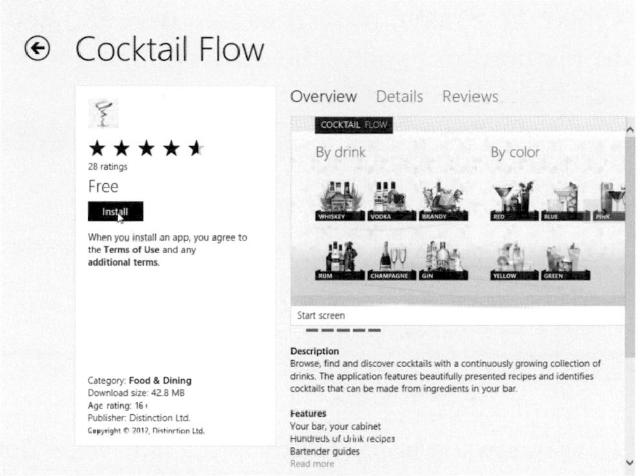

4. Click the Install button for that app, then select more from Spotlight or other areas

5. Go to the Start screen to see the additions

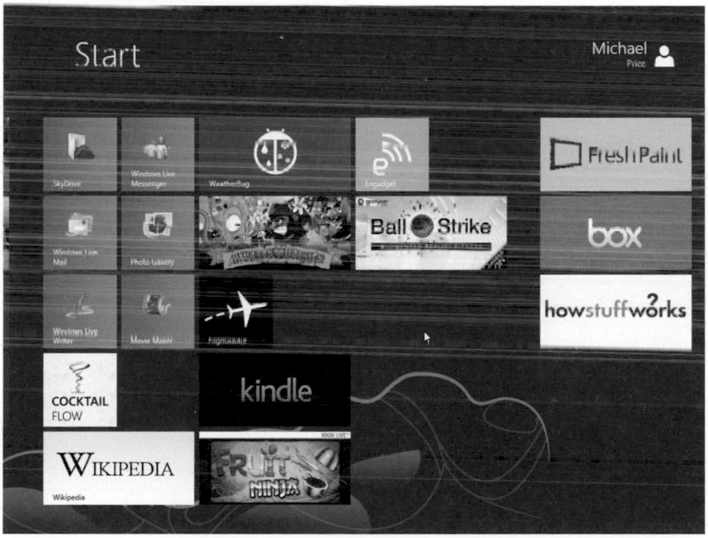

Hot tip

When you Install an app, the Store reappears and you see progress messages at the top right of the screen. You can select another app, even if previous installs are still pending.

Don't forget

Tiles for the apps that you install are added to the right-hand side of the Start screen, flowing on from the last group on the screen. You can regroup and reposition the tiles (see page 67).

Activation

Your copy of Windows 8 must be activated before you can apply an upgrade and in any event within 30 days of first using the system. To check the current status:

1. Open the System properties (see page 11) and scroll to the bottom to view the Activation status

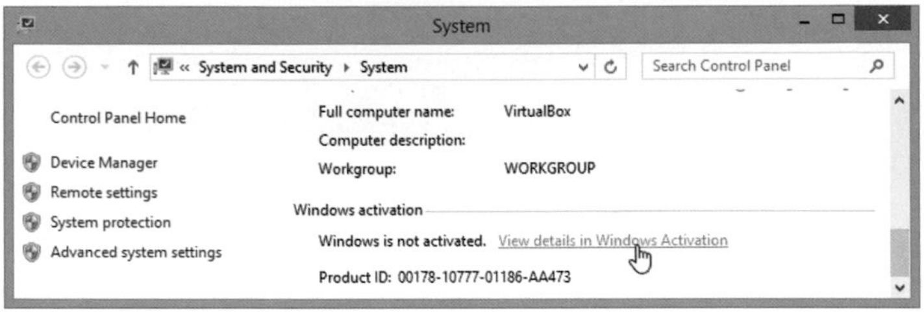

2. If Windows is not yet activated, click View details in Windows activation

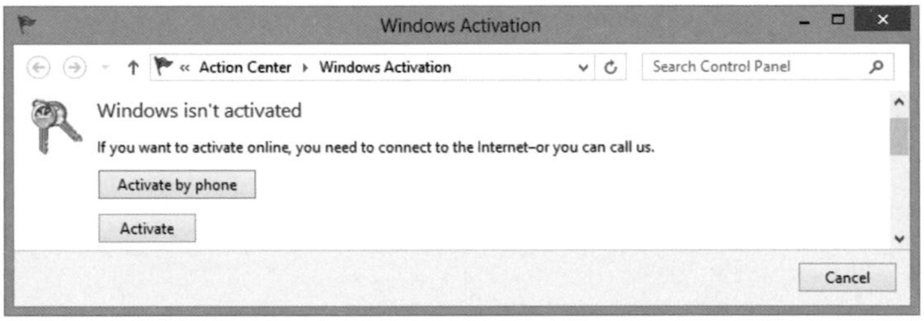

3. Connect to the Internet and click Activate, or you can activate by phone

4. System Properties will show the status as Activated

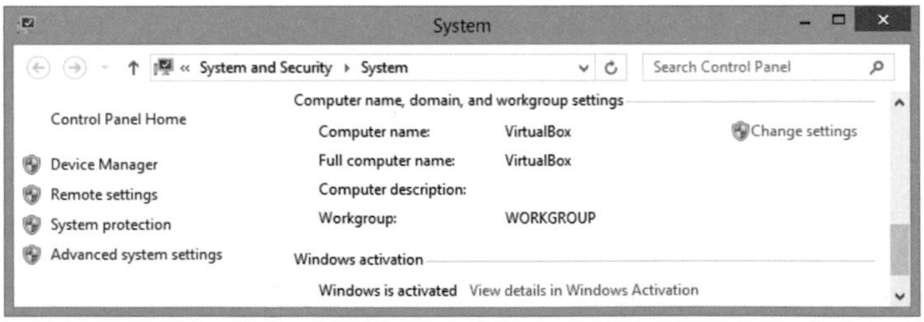

Hot tip

Activation is the process by which Microsoft associates your specific copy of Windows 8 with your computer.

Don't forget

If your system is connected to the Internet when you install Windows, or the first time that you run Windows, Activation will be completed automatically.

2 Windows 8 Interface

Windows 8 provides a new interface, with a tile-based Start screen that is designed for touch operation, while still supporting keyboard and mouse. It features Hotspots and Charms and new ways to start up apps and to close them down.

28 Start Windows 8
30 Logon Microsoft Account
31 Start Screen Layout
32 Hotspots and Charms
34 Power Users Menu
35 Moving Around
36 Start an App
38 Snap Apps
40 Close Apps
41 Close Windows 8

Start Windows 8

Hot tip

The start-up time depends on the configuration of your computer and on how it was previously closed, but usually it is less than a minute.

Switch on your computer to start up the operating system. The stages are as follows:

1. A simple Windows logo is displayed, with a rotating cursor to show that the system is being loaded

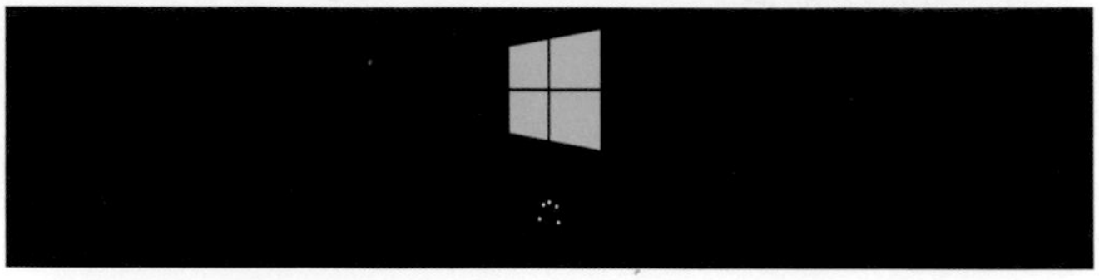

Don't forget

If there are multiple user accounts, the last used is shown on the Logon screen, but an arrow is added to indicate additional accounts. Click this arrow to choose a different account.

2. After a while, the Lock screen is displayed

3. Press a key or click a mouse button, or sweep up on a Touch monitor, to display the user Logon screen

Don't forget

Since there's no email address shown, you know the account is Local rather than Microsoft.

4. Type the password and click the arrow (or press the Enter key)

5. The Welcome message is displayed while the user account settings are being applied

6. The Windows 8 Start screen is displayed, showing the tile-based Windows 8 apps currently available

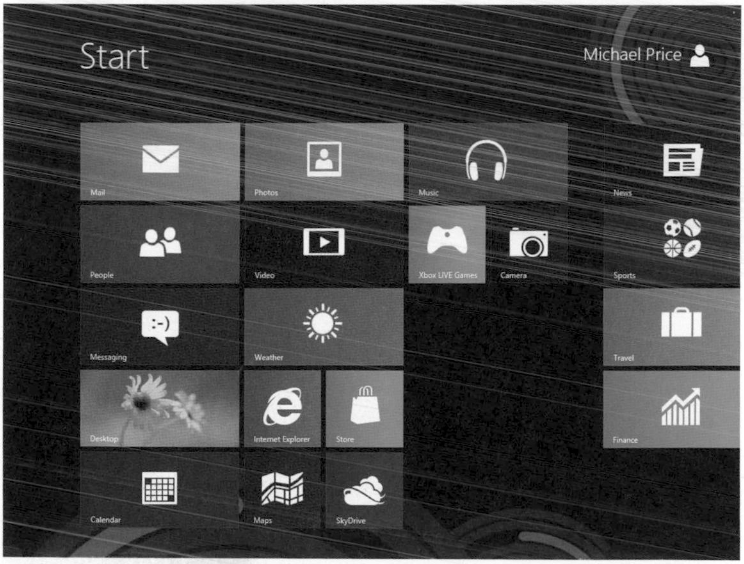

Hot tip

If there is only one user account and no password, Windows skips the Logon screen and goes straight to the Welcome message.

Hot tip

If you attempt to install apps from the Windows Store with a local account, you'll be prompted to sign in first with a Microsoft account.

Sign in with a Microsoft account
Email address
Password
Can't access your account?
Sign up for a Microsoft account
Read the privacy statement online
Sign in
Cancel

Logon Microsoft Account

When the user account is a Microsoft account, the Logon screen shows the associated email address:

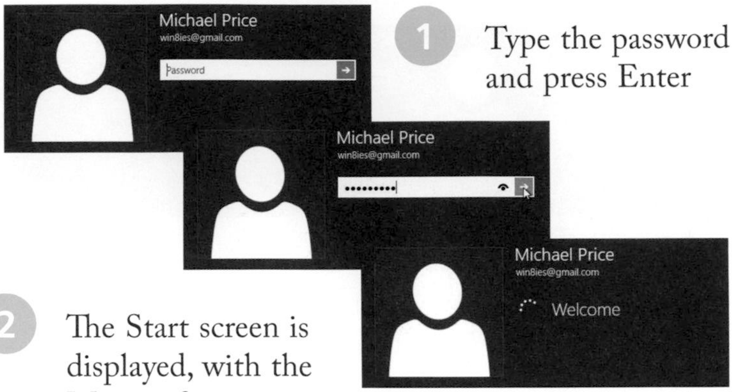

1. Type the password and press Enter

2. The Start screen is displayed, with the Microsoft account signed on and active

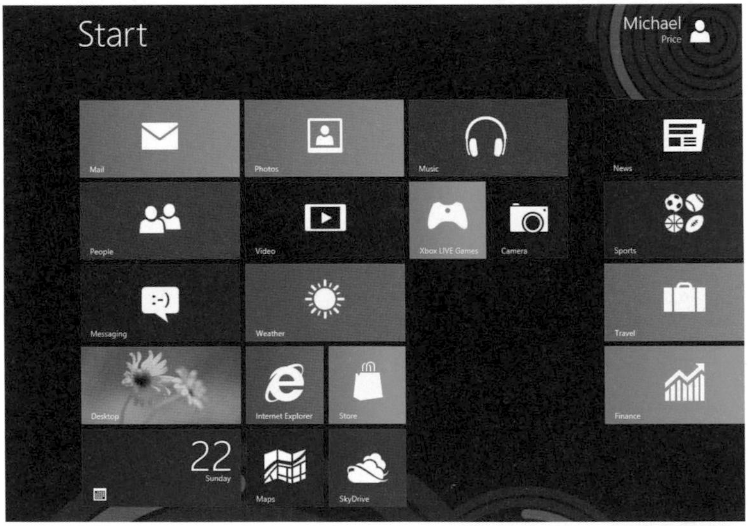

The appearance of this Start screen is much more akin to the smartphone, for example the Windows Phone, rather than the startup screens of previous versions of Windows. In particular, Windows 8 has no Start button.

You'll also find that the Start menu that is normally invoked from the Start button is also missing from Windows 8.

Hot tip

The use of a Microsoft account allows you to download and install apps directly from the Windows Store without the need for further logon.

Don't forget

You'll find Windows 8 involves new types of application and new ways of finding and invoking functions, whether you use a keyboard and mouse or a touch-enabled computer.

Start Screen Layout

The actual contents of the Start screen will depend on what customization and enhancements you (or your computer supplier) have applied. However, you can expect to find:

There is a Windows 8 app which displays the Desktop, used to run standard Windows applications, including those of Microsoft Office. See page 44 for more about the Desktop.

It is, however, the hidden items on the Start screen and the Desktop (see page 32) that are perhaps the most important.

Hot tip

Towards the top right of the Start screen is the User name and picture (which can be personalized – see page 66).

Hot tip

To display the Desktop, select the Desktop tile with the mouse or touch action, or use the WinKey + D keyboard shortcut.

Don't forget

The Desktop has many of the features you'd expect in previous releases of Windows, including background picture, desktop icons, taskbar, toolbars and the system notification area, but of course no Start button.

Hotspots and Charms

The corners of the Start screen are hotspots that help you navigate through Windows 8.

1. Hover the mouse pointer in the lower left corner and a miniature of the last accessed app is displayed. Click to switch there

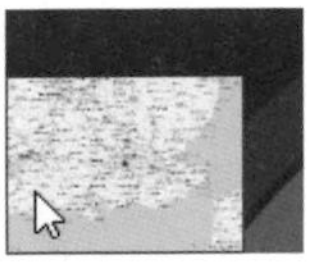

2. From an app, the lower left corner displays a miniature thumbnail Start screen. Click to switch there

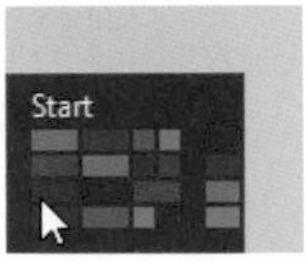

3. The Windows key acts as a toggle to switch back and forth between the Start screen and the last used app, or the Desktop if no app has been started

The top and bottom corners on the right will display what's known as the Charms bar (due to its appearance)

1. Move to either hotspot and the charms appear as overlays and not initially active

2. Move the pointer over any of the charms to activate the Charms bar and also display the time and date on the screen

Hot tip

If you have a Windows 8 compliant touch screen or tablet, you can swipe an edge of the screen to obtain the same effects.

Don't forget

Pressing WinKey + C is another way to display the Charms bar. You can display the Charms bar from any application screen, or from the Desktop.

The final hotspot, at the top left corner, allows you to display the active Windows 8 apps and switch to the one you want.

1. Move to the upper left corner and a miniature of the last accessed app is displayed. Click to switch there

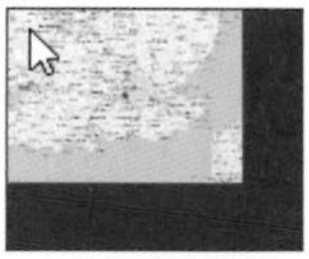

2. Move the mouse pointer down to display thumbnails for the full list of active apps

3. If you display the app list from an active app, it will show the remaining active apps, plus the Start screen thumbnail

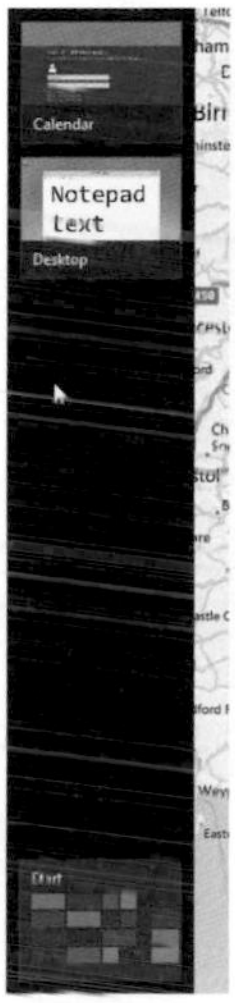

4. Hold down the Windows key and press Tab to display the App switcher and step to each app in turn, then release the Windows key to display the selected app

You can also hold down Alt and press Tab to cycle through the active apps in the conventional Windows fashion, showing each app screen in turn. In this case, Desktop-based Windows applications such as Notepad and the Office applications will be shown individually.

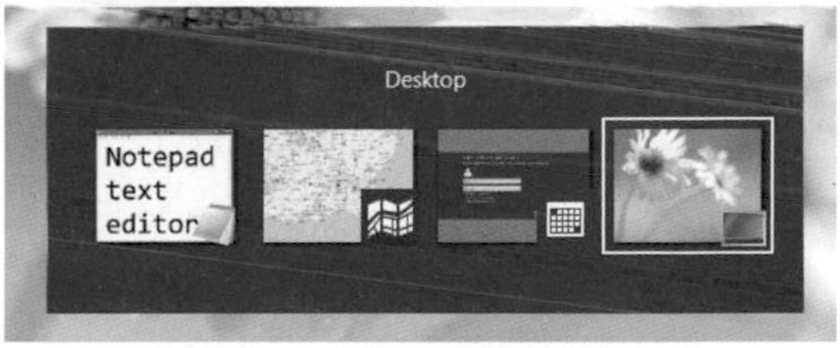

Hot tip

Conventional Windows applications that run on the Desktop are not included, though the Desktop itself appears as an app in its own right.

Don't forget

As always, you can use Touch gestures to display and select these lists, if you have the appropriate hardware.

Power Users Menu

There's a menu of useful shortcuts associated with the Start screen thumbnail (see page 32) at the lower left corner hotspot.

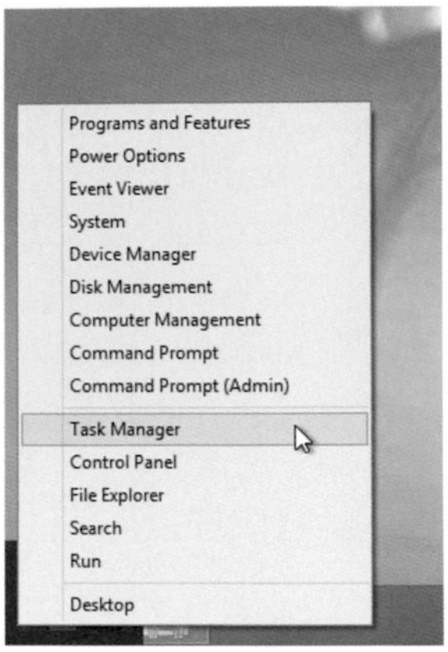

1. Display the thumbnail using mouse or touch, then right-click the thumbnail to display the menu

2. Alternatively, press WinKey + X to display that same menu

This allows you to access a set of functions that are often needed by the more advanced user, such as Task Manager, Control Panel, System properties, Computer Management and Command Prompt (Standard or Admin).

Make sure that the hotspot thumbnail is displayed before you right-click or you'll get the right-click action associated with the displayed app. On the Desktop, for example, you might get the Taskbar menu or the Screen menu.

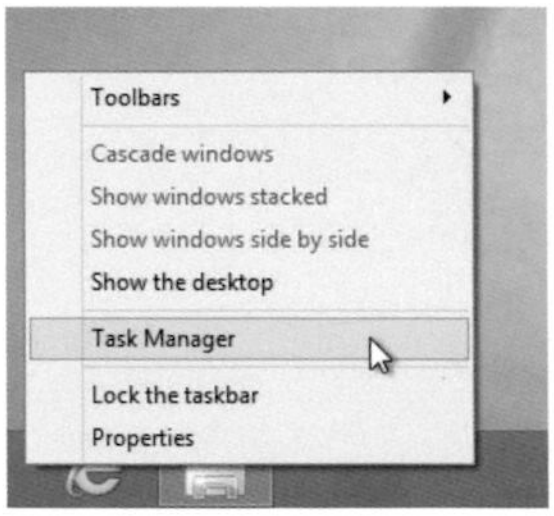
Toolbars
Cascade windows
Show windows stacked
Show windows side by side
Show the desktop
Task Manager
Lock the taskbar
Properties

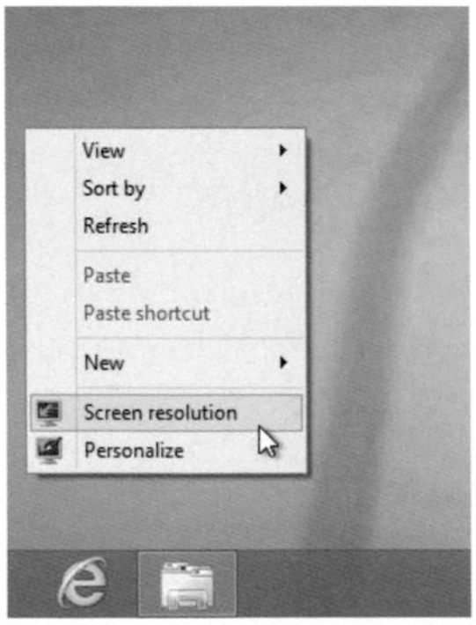

On the Start screen, you'll get the Apps bar (see page 53)

Don't forget

Though there's no longer a Start menu, there is a useful menu associated with the Start screen icon, providing power user functions.

Beware

The hotspot area at each corner is just a few pixels in size, so it is easy to click the wrong spot and get an unexpected result.

Moving Around

If the Windows 8 app you want is visible on the Start screen, you can left-click the tile with your mouse (or single touch the tile on a touch monitor). To see more tiles and groups of tiles, use the scroll bar that appears at the bottom of the screen when you when you move the mouse.

The screen also slides horizontally when you roll the mouse wheel up or down, or you can move the mouse pointer to the left or right edge to get the same effect.

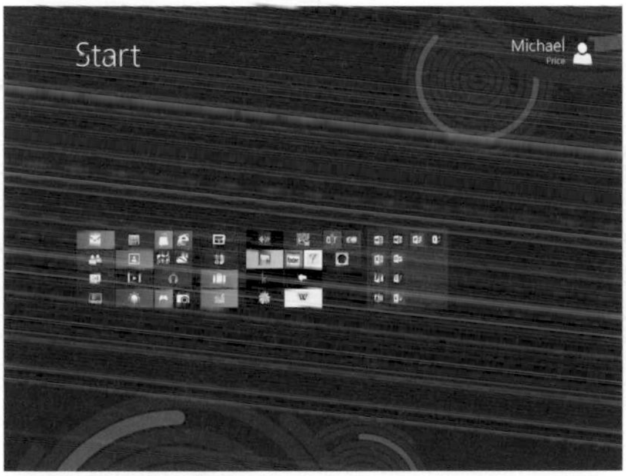

Click the Zoom button at the end of the scroll bar and the Start screen contents will be shrunk so you can see all the groups. Click on an app or a group to position the Start screen full size with that part of the screen centered on the display.

Don't forget

You can also use the four keyboard arrows to navigate through the Windows 8 apps, then press Enter when the one you want is selected.

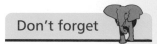

Hot tip

With a Multi-touch monitor or tablet PC, you simply drag the screen to the left or the right as necessary to display other tiles and groups of tiles.

Start an App

Windows 8 apps are represented on the Start screen by tiles. These can display dynamic information from the associated apps, even when they are not running.

1. To start an app, move the mouse pointer over the tile for the desired app and left-click to load it

2. The app loads up with a full screen image, in this case weather details for the current location

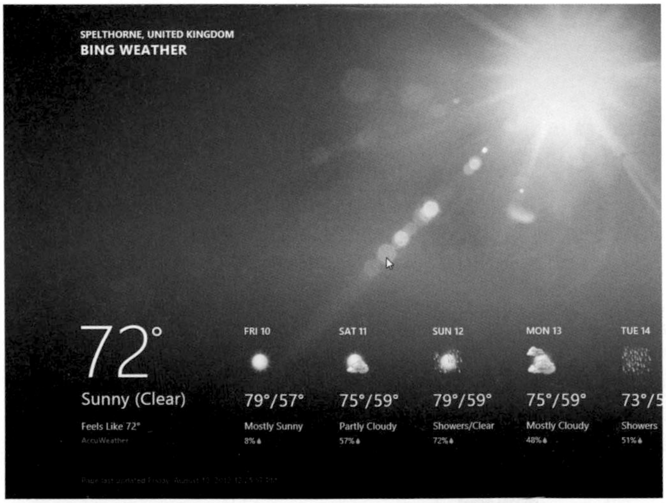

Hot tip

With a Windows 8 touch screen or tablet, tap the tile to start the app. With the keyboard, navigate to the required tile using arrow keys and then press Enter.

Don't forget

You may be prompted for a response, for example to allow the Weather app to use your actual location.

3. Switch back to the Start screen and choose another application, for example select Travel

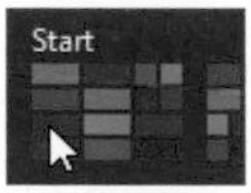

4. The new app opens full screen, taking over from the previous app

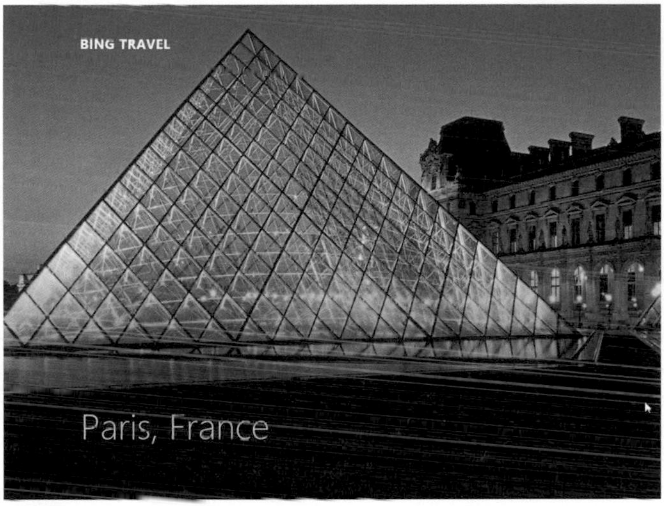

Don't forget

No matter what size screen you have, each Windows 8 app will normally take up the whole area. However, there is a Snap option that lets you display a second app on the screen (see page 38).

As you start more apps, the Desktop app included, each one will take over the whole screen, leaving all the other apps running in the background.

To switch between apps, press WinKey + Tab to display the Apps switcher and step through the list to select the required app

Alternatively, press Alt + Tab repeatedly to show Windows 8 apps and Desktop applications, and select the one you want.

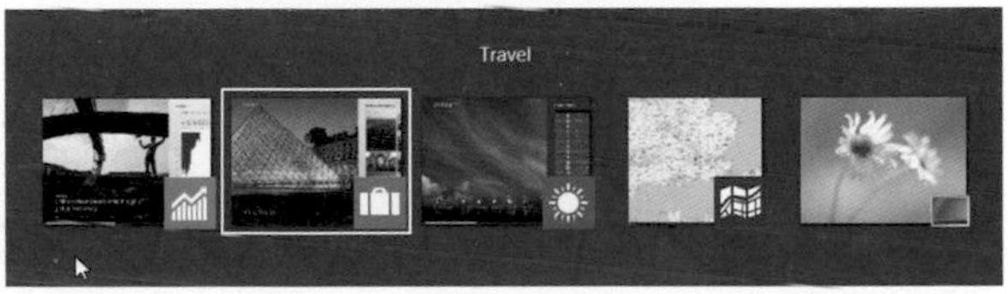

Snap Apps

Windows 8 apps can be persuaded to share the screen with the Desktop or another app, using the Windows 8 Snap feature, as long as you have a high resolution screen.

To display a background app alongside the current app:

1. Display the App switcher, right-click a background app and select Snap left or Snap right

2. The app is displayed in a narrow window alongside the current foreground app, left or right as selected

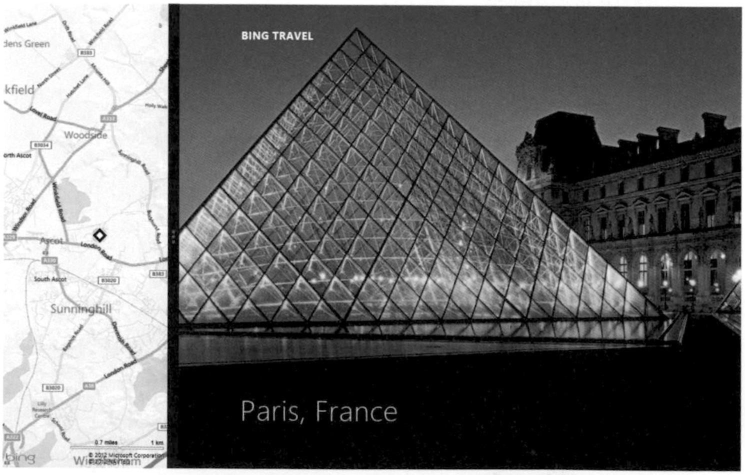

Don't forget

The minimum screen resolution to use the Windows 8 Snap feature is 1366 x 768.

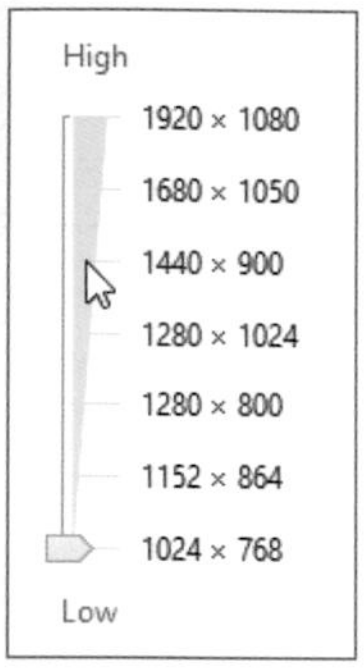

Hot tip

The snapped view is 320 pixels wide and the Snap bar is 22 pixels wide, while the Fill view is a minimum of 1024 pixels.

3 To Snap the current app, move the mouse pointer to the top edge of the app, drag the screen left or right and release when the Snap bar appears

4 To Snap with the keyboard, press WinKey + Period and the app snaps right, snaps left and back to full screen, changing each time you press those keys

5 Use the App switcher to select an app that will occupy the Fill view when you've set the Snap view

Hot tip

Using the mouse or touch, drag the Snap bar across the screen to expand the Snap view, or just double-click the Snap bar.

Don't forget

If you press WinKey + Shift + Period, the sequence becomes Left, Right, Full screen.

Close Apps

Applications that run on the Desktop are windowed, can be resized and feature the Close button at the top right.

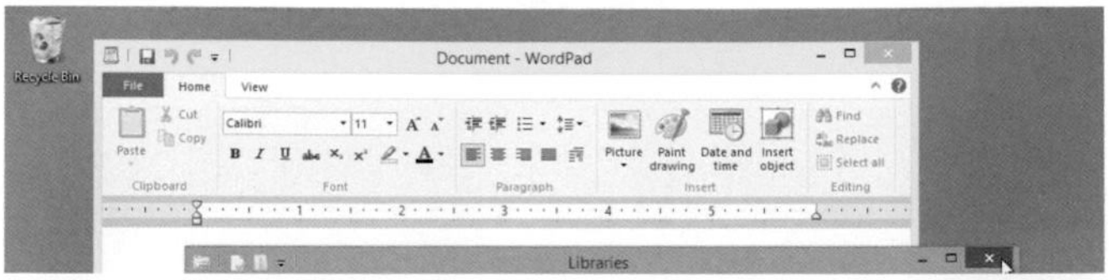

Windows 8 apps open in full screen, cannot be resized (except via Snap – see page 38) and have no obvious way to Close. Suspended apps don't use system resources, so that's no problem.

If you do want to close an app:

1. Display the Apps switcher (see page 37) for the list of active apps
2. Right-click the thumbnail for the app and select Close

Alternatively, from within the app:

1. Press the Alt + F4 keys
2. Alternatively, move the pointer to the top of the app until the pointer turns into the hand icon, then left click and drag the hand pointer down until the app shrinks and moves down to the bottom of the screen, then release the button

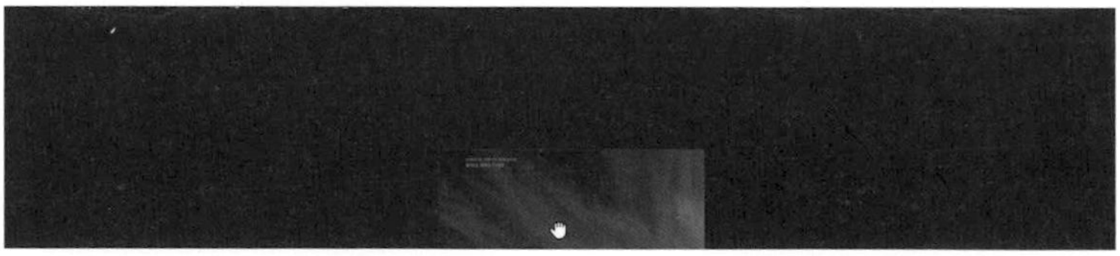

Another option is to delete the recently opened apps history. Open PC Settings, select General and click Delete history, to close all the active apps and remove them from memory.

Hot tip

When you switch apps Windows allows the current app to run in the background (if supported) or will suspend the app, which remains in the memory until the memory is needed. This allows apps to get restarted more quickly.

Don't forget

On a touch screen, click on the top of the app and drag the app down until the app shrinks and moves to the bottom of the screen and release.

Close Windows 8

With no Start button, there is no immediately obvious way to close Windows 8, but there are several options you can use, some familiar and some new.

Ctrl + Alt + Del

1. Press the Ctrl + Alt + Del key combination

2. Click the Power icon on the lower right and select the close option, e.g. Sleep, Shutdown or Restart

Charm Settings

1. Display the Charms bar (see page 32) and select the Settings icon to display Settings

2. Alternatively, you can press WinKey + I to display the Settings pane immediately

3. Click the Power icon to display the Close options and select the one that's appropriate

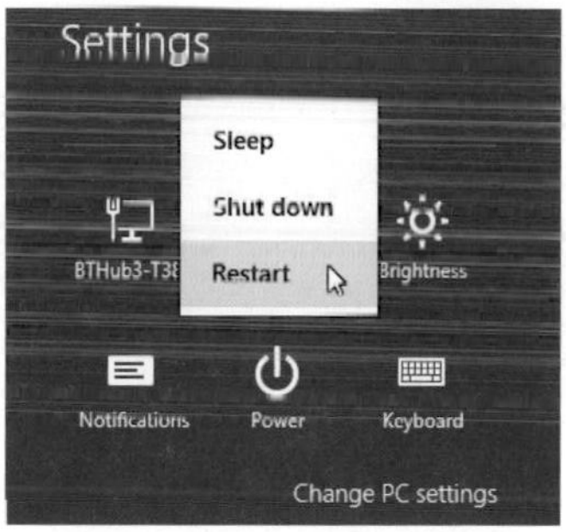

Hardware Shutdown

On a portable PC you can close the lid, or press the power button to suspend operations or close the system down.

Hot tip

Click the user name or picture on the Start screen to Lock or Sign out. Both take you to the Lock screen (see page 28) but Sign out also logs off the user account.

Don't forget

You can also Lock the system using the WinKey + L key combination.

...cont'd

Don't forget

If an application is selected, pressing Alt + F4 closes that application rather than the desktop.

From the Desktop

1. While at the desktop, select a clear area and press Alt + F4 to display Windows Shutdown

Beware

Before choosing Sign out or Shut down, make sure that you save your active apps or documents first.

2. Click OK to Shut down, or click the down arrow to list the options that are available

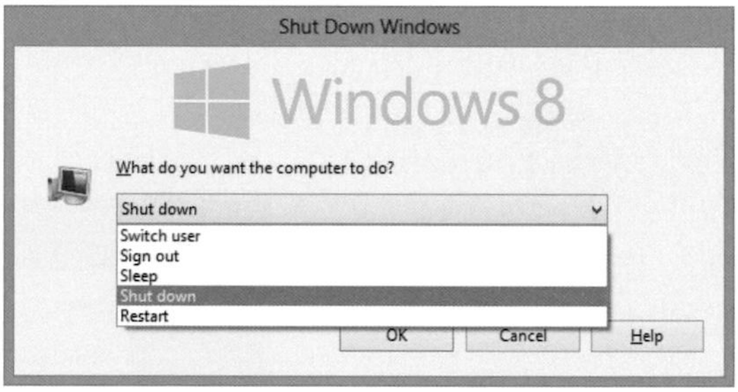

You can choose to:

- Switch User   keep current session and open new
- Sign out   end the current session
- Sleep   save session and set low-power mode
- Shut down   end the session and power off
- Restart   shut down and restart Windows

3 Windows 8 Desktop

Although the Start screen has replaced the Start menu, Windows 8 still supports the windowed Desktop environment, with taskbar, notification area and Desktop icons and the familiar windows structure, menus and dialogs, and functions for managing Desktop applications.

44 Display the Desktop

46 Taskbar

48 Taskbar Properties

50 Notification Area

51 Peek At or Show Desktop

52 Desktop Icons

55 Window Structure

56 Application Windows

57 Menus and Dialogs

58 Move and Resize Windows

59 Snap

60 Close Desktop Apps

Display the Desktop

Hot tip

You can Logon to a local account to get settings as defined on the specific computer, or to your Microsoft account to get transferable settings (see page 20).

Switch on your computer to start up Windows 8 and display the Lock screen (see page 28) and Logon to your user account to display the Start screen.

If you are running the Windows RT edition on a tablet PC, this will be your main starting point. For the conventional PC, especially with traditional applications installed, you may prefer to switch to Desktop mode.

There are a number of ways to display the Desktop, for example:

1. Click or touch the Desktop tile on the Start screen

2. Press the WinKey + D keys

The appearance of your Desktop will vary, depending on configuration and personalization, but you should find:

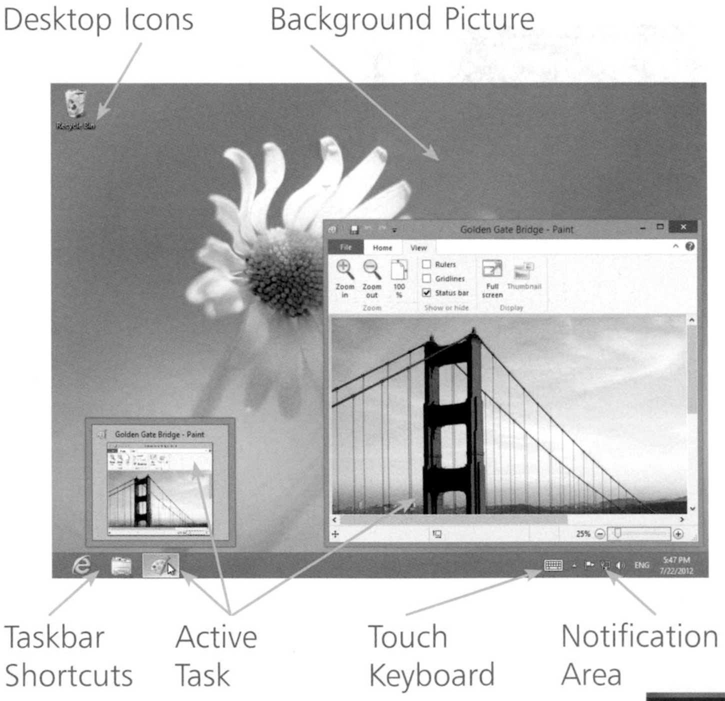

The Desktop also has the corner hotspots.

Don't forget

If you have previously displayed the Desktop, you can select it from the Apps switcher (see page 33).

Don't forget

Run a conventional application from the Start screen, e.g. Paint, and the Desktop will display with that application open.

If you are using mainly conventional applications, you may want to start up the computer with the Desktop. While you cannot actually bypass the Start screen, you can achieve a similar effect.

1. Move the Tile for the Desktop app so that it is the first on the Start screen (at the top left)

2. Restart the computer and, after entering your Logon password, press and hold the Enter key
3. The Desktop is displayed when Logon completes
4. If the Start screen does appear just press Enter to display the Desktop

Sleep from Desktop

If you make a habit of closing down your system while the Desktop is displayed, you'll automatically return to the Desktop when you restart the computer. From the Desktop:

1. Press WinKey + I to display Settings
2. Click the Power icon and select Sleep

Hot tip

When you Logon, the first tile on the Start screen is automatically selected. Therefore pressing Enter executes that app.

Don't forget

On a battery-powered PC, make a habit of switching to Desktop before closing the lid and be sure of restarting at Desktop.

Hot tip

You can display the Charms bar from the Desktop, via the corner hotspots on the right and select Settings.

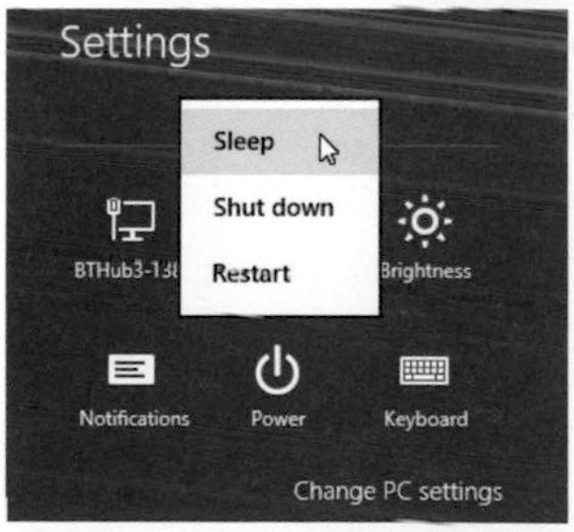

Taskbar

The contents of the Taskbar change dynamically to reflect the activities that are taking place on your Desktop.

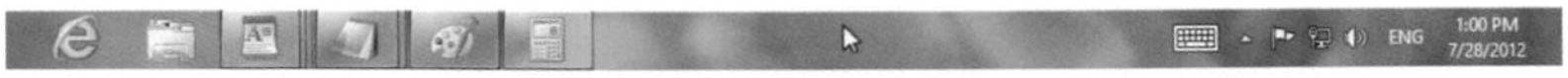

Taskbar Shortcuts

At the left on the Taskbar you'll find shortcuts that turn into task buttons when you select them to start a program. By default, there are shortcuts for Internet Explorer and File Explorer, but you can pin any applications here.

Task Buttons

There is a task button for each open window (program or file folder). The selected or foreground task, in this case the Calculator, is shown emphasized. The other tasks are shaded.

Touch Keyboard

If your system has touch support, you'll find the Touch toolbar which invokes the on-screen keyboard.

Notification Area

The portion of the bar on the right is known as the Notification Area and contains icons such as Action Center, Network, Speaker and Date/Time. These are system functions that are started automatically when Windows starts up.

If you have defined more than one input language on your system, you'll have a Language icon which lists the languages installed and makes it easier to switch between them.

Hot tip

The right edge of the frame around the task button tells you the number of windows:

Three or more
Two windows
One window

Don't forget

Click the button to show hidden icons, in this case for Safely Remove Hardware and Eject Media.

If you start more tasks, the Taskbar may become full and scrolling arrows will be added to let you select any task.

You can resize the Taskbar, but first it must be unlocked.

1. Right-click an empty part of the Taskbar and, if there's a check next to Lock the Taskbar, click the entry to remove the check and Unlock the taskbar

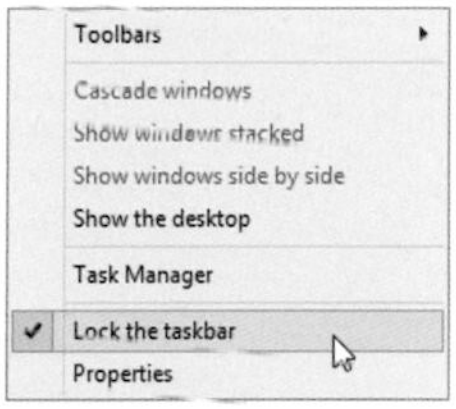
Toolbars
Cascade windows
Show windows stacked
Show windows side by side
Show the desktop
Task Manager
Lock the taskbar
Properties

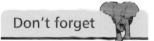

2. Move the mouse over the edge of the Taskbar until the pointer becomes a double-headed arrow, then drag the border up or down to resize the Taskbar

3. You can lock the Taskbar at the new size - reselect the Lock option from the Taskbar right-click menu

You can add other toolbars to the Taskbar:

1. Right-click an empty part of the Taskbar and select Toolbars

2. Select a toolbar and a tick will be added and the toolbar will be displayed on the Taskbar. Reselect a toolbar to remove it

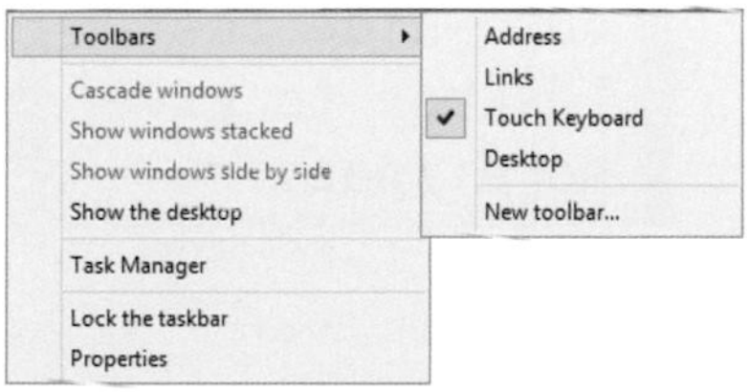
Toolbars
Cascade windows
Show windows stacked
Show windows side by side
Show the desktop
Task Manager
Lock the taskbar
Properties
Address
Links
Touch Keyboard
Desktop
New toolbar...

Hot tip

Taskbar Properties (see page 48) gives options for customizing the location, operation and appearance of the Taskbar.

Don't forget

This right-click menu is also used to arrange windows or to display the Taskbar Properties.

Taskbar Properties

Hot tip

See page 79 for more information about personalizing your Desktop.

To make changes to the Taskbar settings:

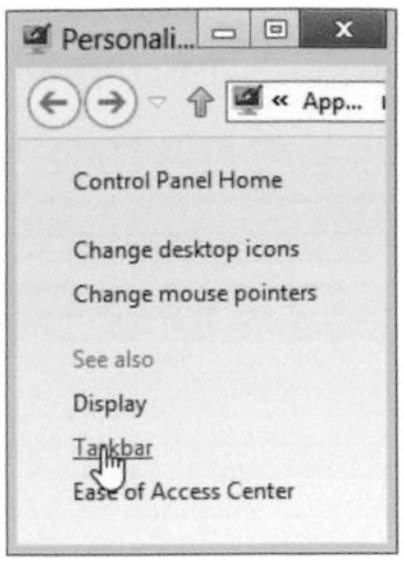

1. Select the Taskbar link from the list at the side of the Personalization dialog

2. Alternatively, right-click an empty part of the Taskbar and select Properties from the menu

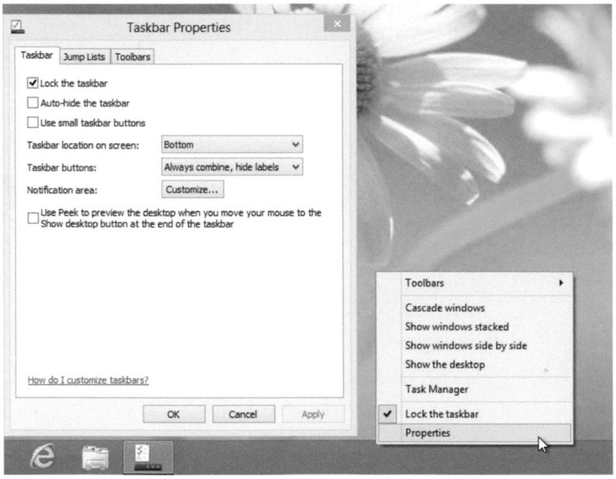

3. You can lock and unlock the Taskbar from Properties as well as from the right-click menu

4. Click the box labelled Auto-hide the Taskbar, to make the full area of the screen available

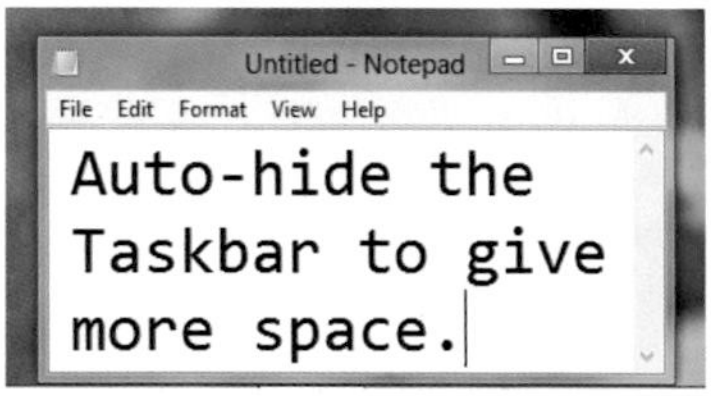

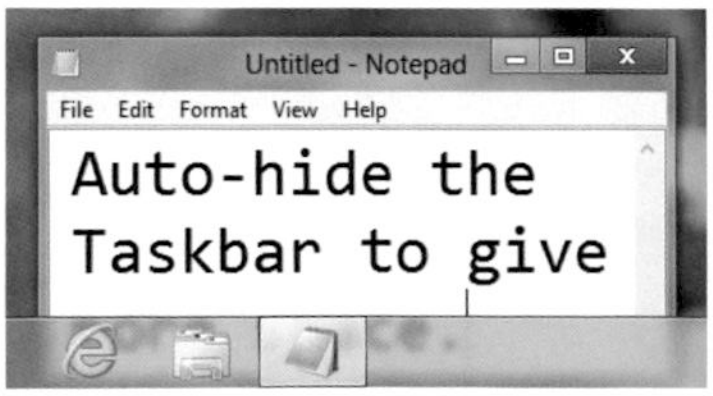

5. It reappears when you move the mouse to the part of the screen where the taskbar should be located

Don't forget

In the example, the taskbar is located at the bottom edge, but it can be located on any edge (see page 49) so you'd move the mouse pointer to the appropriate edge for your setup to reveal the taskbar.

Use Small Taskbar Buttons

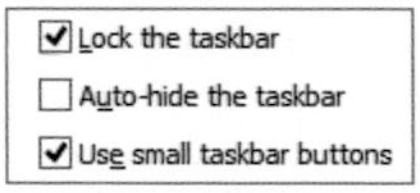
Lock the taskbar
Auto-hide the taskbar
Use small taskbar buttons

1. Click the box Use small taskbar buttons, so you can fit more items onto it

Taskbar Location

1. Click the bar labelled Taskbar location on screen, to replace the default Bottom with, e.g. Top

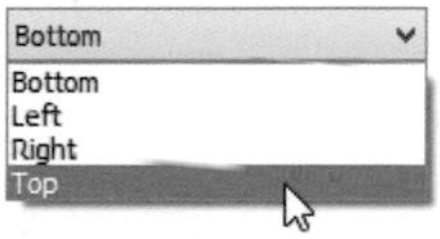

Combine Taskbar Buttons

The default in Windows 8 is to show the taskbar buttons without labels and to combine windows of the same type. However, you can keep things more separate.

1. Click the bar Taskbar buttons, to select Combine when taskbar is full and show the task labels

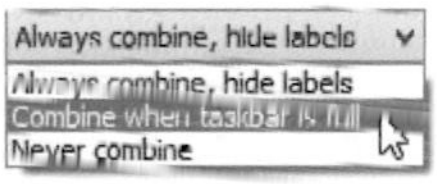
Always combine, hide labels
Always combine, hide labels
Combine when taskbar is full
Never combine

2. Extra tasks may get combined onto the same button

3. With Never combine, taskbar scrolling may be used

Hot tip

There is no need to Unlock the taskbar when you want to change the size or its location on the screen.

Don't forget

This style of taskbar works best with higher resolution screens or smaller numbers of active tasks.

Notification Area

The Notification Area (also called the System Tray) is at the right on the Taskbar. Some icons will appear by default and installed programs may add icons. To control what shows:

1. Click Customize in the Notification Area portion of Taskbar properties

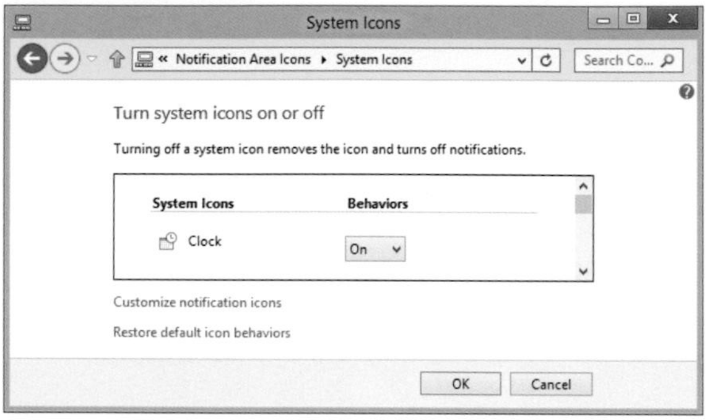

2. Select Turn system icons on or off and choose the appropriate setting for the icons listed

3. Select Customize notification icons

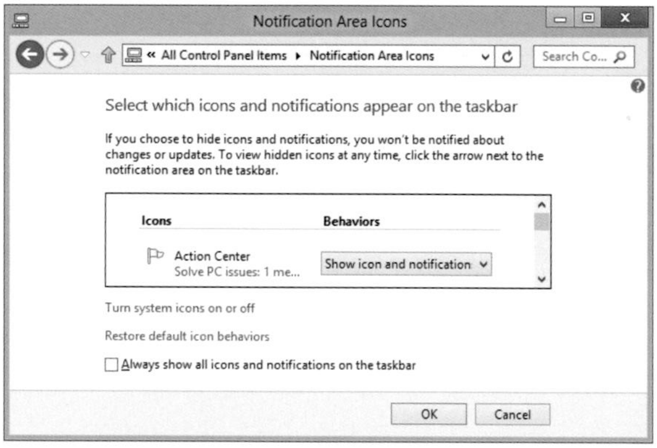

4. For each icon you can choose to Show icon and notifications, or Hide icon and notifications, or Only show notifications

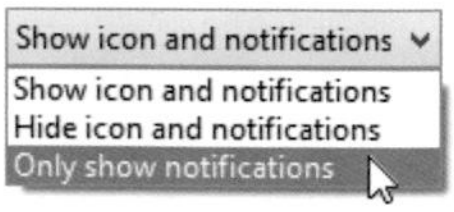

Hot tip

Clicking the Hidden icons button will also provide access to the Customize option.

Don't forget

The System icons that are offered depend on the configuration, for example Network requires some form of connection and Power is for laptop PCs only.

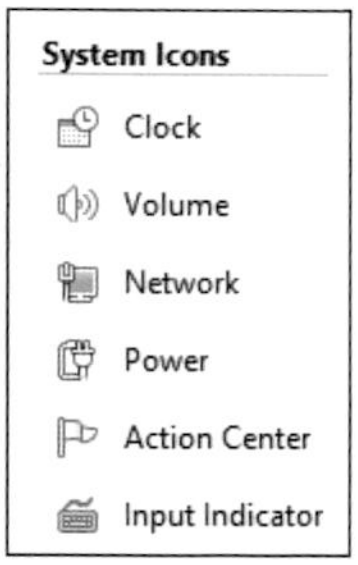

Peek At or Show Desktop

The Taskbar area to the right of the Notification area is the Show Desktop button. Starting with several open windows:

1. Hover over the Show Desktop button to see desktop, icons and outlines of all open windows

2. Click Show Desktop button to reveal the desktop

3. Click again to restore the desktop

Don't forget

Peek is active only when you select the option Use Peek to preview, from the Taskbar Properties.

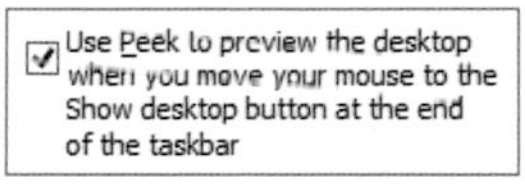

Hot tip

The desktop and the outlines are displayed only temporarily and the original window contents are redisplayed as soon as the mouse moves away from the Show Desktop button.

Hot tip

Here the desktop is fully cleared, allowing you, if required, to select one of the Desktop icons.

Desktop Icons

Shortcuts to standard Windows applications can be stored on the Desktop. To start there are standard system icons.

Don't forget

You can change the desktop icons from the default size Medium, to Large as shown here, or to Small.

1. To display or resize icons on the desktop, right-click an empty part of the desktop and select View

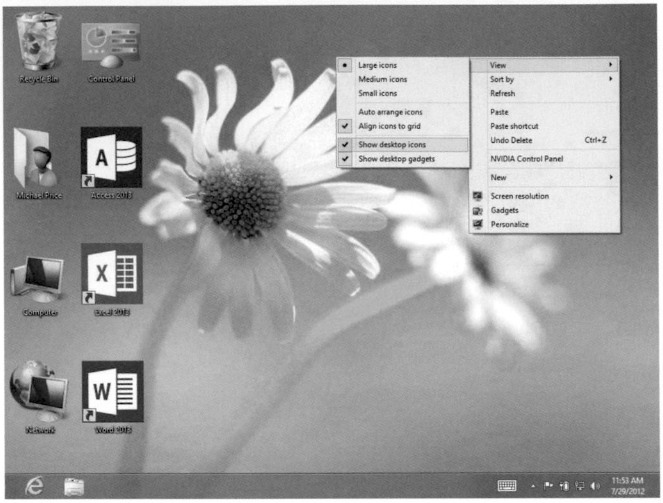

2. If the entry Show desktop icons is not already selected (ticked) then click to enable it

3. To specify which system icons to display, right-click the desktop and select Personalize

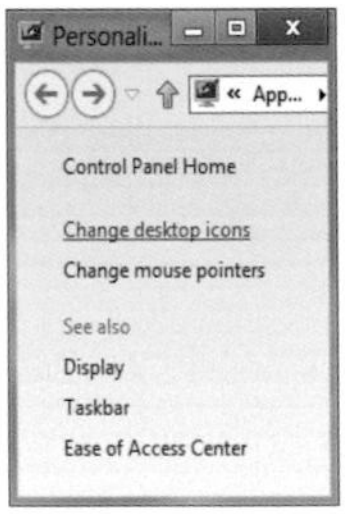

Don't forget

Click the Change Icon button to select alternative images for any of the system icons. Click Restore Default to revert to the original images.

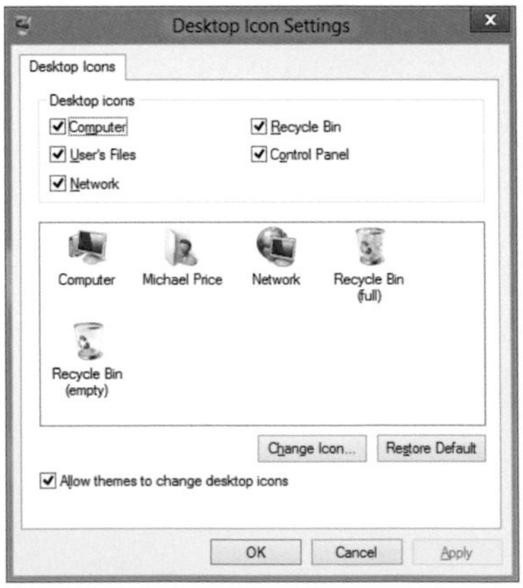

4. Click Change Desktop Icons

5. Select the icons that you wish to display then click OK to apply the changes

...cont'd

To add shortcuts to the Taskbar or the Desktop for an existing application:

1. Switch to the Start screen and type the application name, e.g. Notepad.exe

2. Right-click the result to display the Apps bar and click the button to Pin to Taskbar

3. Switch back to the Desktop and you'll see the shortcut for the application on the Taskbar

You can run the application from the Taskbar. However, if you prefer you can create a shortcut on the Desktop.

1. Right-click the shortcut, to display the Jump List for the entry

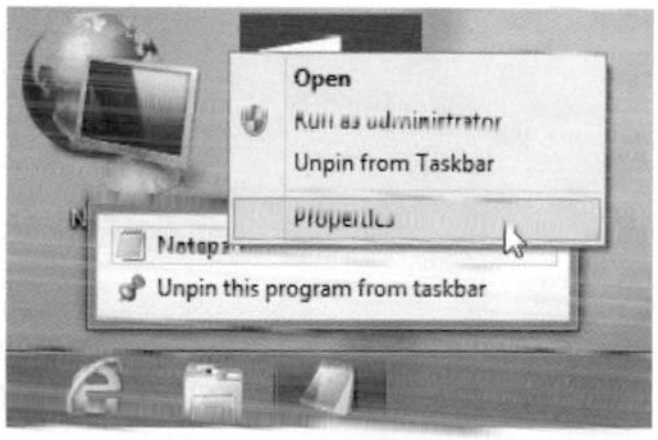

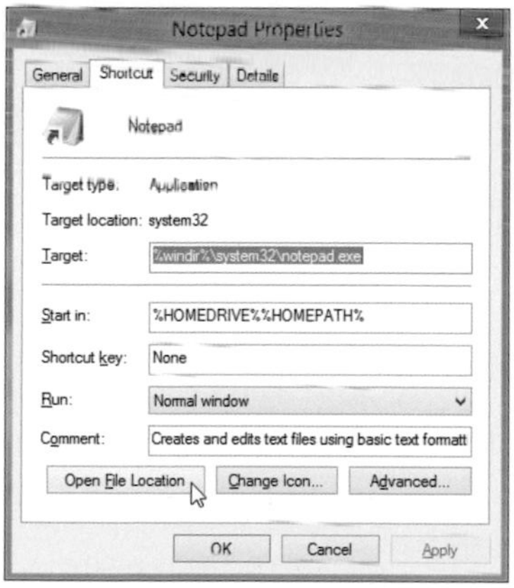

2. Right-click the program name and click Properties

3. Click the button to Open File Location

Don't forget

Since you have no Start menu, you could add shortcuts to the Taskbar for the standard Windows applications.

Don't forget

You can use the Taskbar entry to locate the program file and then create a shortcut on the Desktop

...cont'd

Don't forget

If the shortcut does get created within the folder, you can drag and drop it onto the Desktop.

4. Right-click the program file for the application and select Create Shortcut

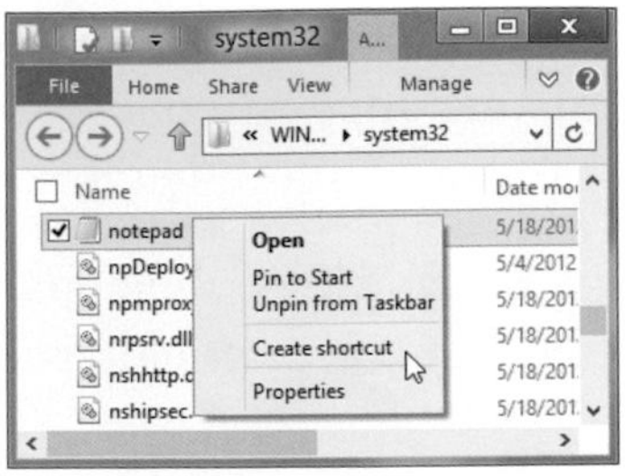

5. Confirm when prompted that you want the shortcut to be placed on the Desktop

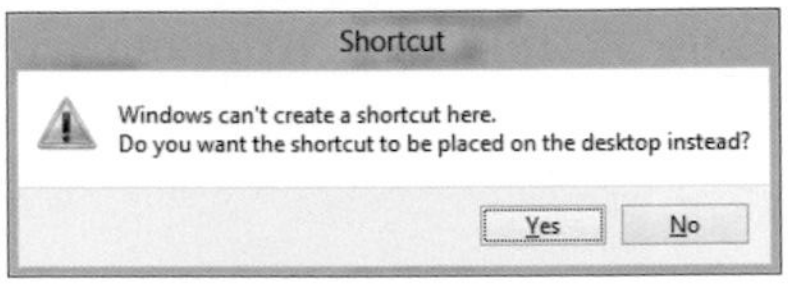

6. You can now run that application from the Desktop by double-clicking the shortcut

7. Right-click the Taskbar entry and select Unpin this program from taskbar

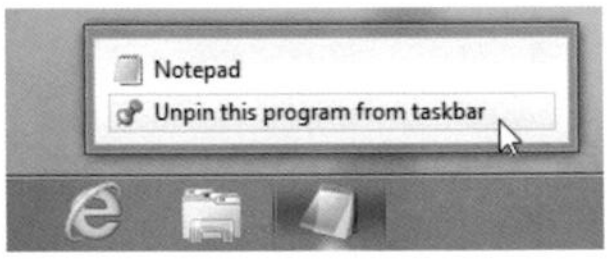

Hot tip

Of course, you can also pin Windows applications to the Start screen and select their tiles to run the programs on the Desktop.

You can add other Windows programs such as Paint or Calculator, or applications such as Word and Excel from the Microsoft Office suite. You may also find that some applications automatically get added to the Desktop when installed, for example Abobe Reader.

Window Structure

When you open a folder or start a Windows function or application program on the Desktop, it appears as a window that can be moved and resized. For example:

1. Click the File Explorer shortcut icon on the Taskbar

Features of the Window

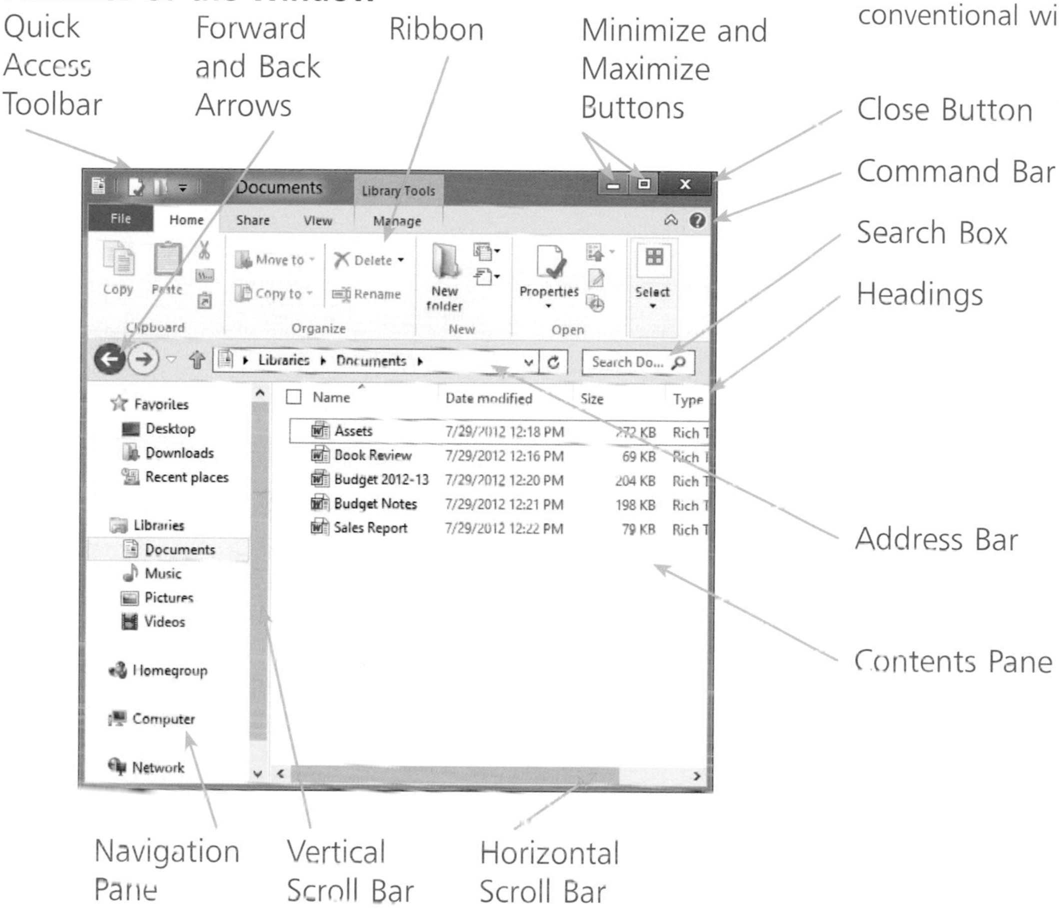

2. Click the Maximize button to view the window using the whole screen and the Restore button appears in its place

Don't forget

Not all the Windows applications use the ribbon style. See page 56 for Notepad, an example of a conventional window.

Application Windows

Application programs, even ones included in Windows 8, may use the traditional window structure, with Title bar and Menu bar. For example, the Notepad application window:

1. Select Start, All Programs, Accessories and Notepad then type some text (or open an existing file)

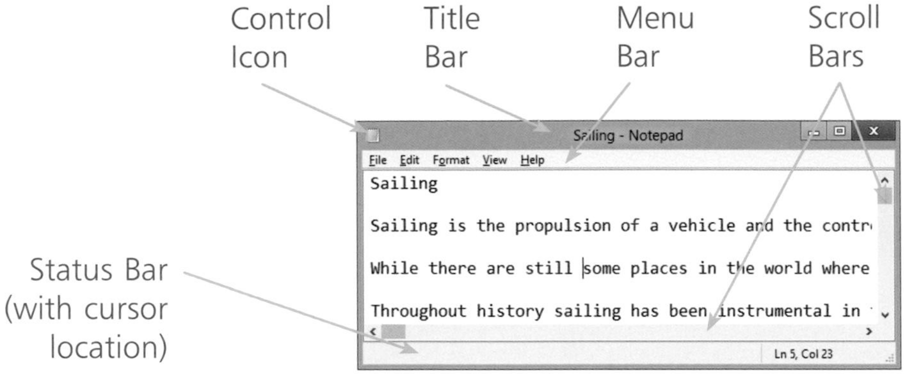

Other Windows 8 applications such as Paint and WordPad feature the Scenic Ribbon in place of menu bar and toobar.

1. Select Start, All Programs, Accessories and WordPad then open a file (or type some text)

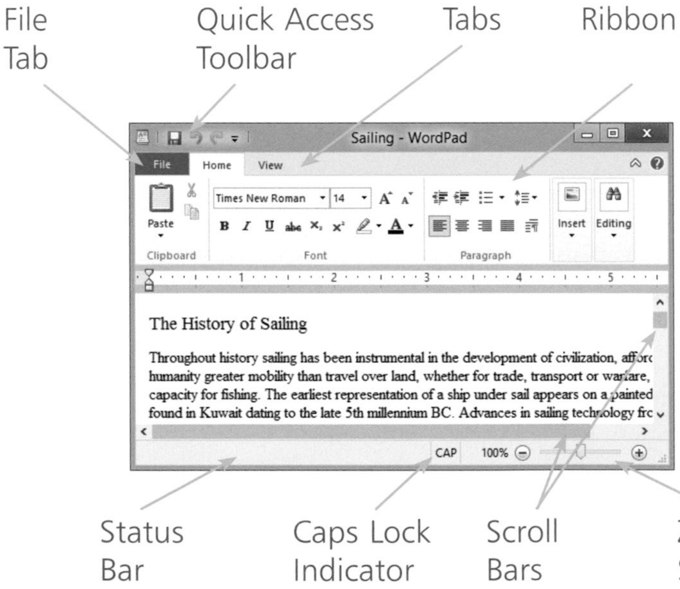

Don't forget

Some applications may not use all the features. For example the Calculator window has no scroll bars and also cannot be resized.

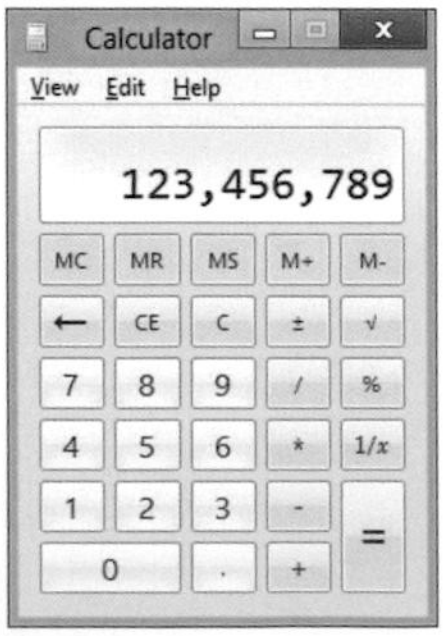

Menus and Dialogs

The entries on the Command bars, Menu bars and Ribbons expand to provide a list of related commands to choose. Some entries expand into a submenu, for example:

1. Open the Libraries folder, select Documents and click Manage, then click Set save location. Note the submenu for the Public save location

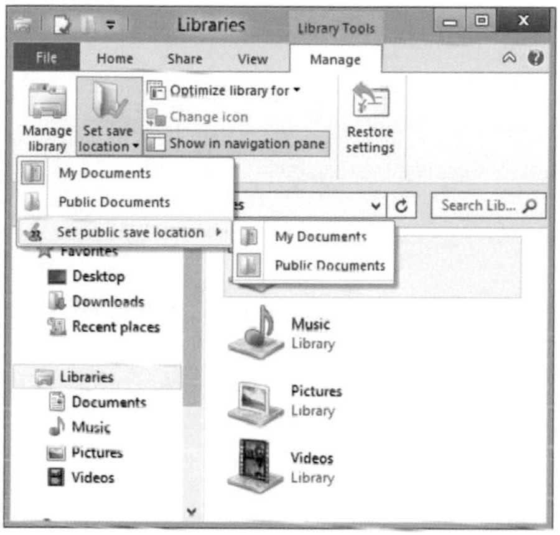

Other entries open dialog boxes that allow you to apply more complex configurations and settings. For example:

1. In the Libraries folder, select the Home tab then click the Properties button

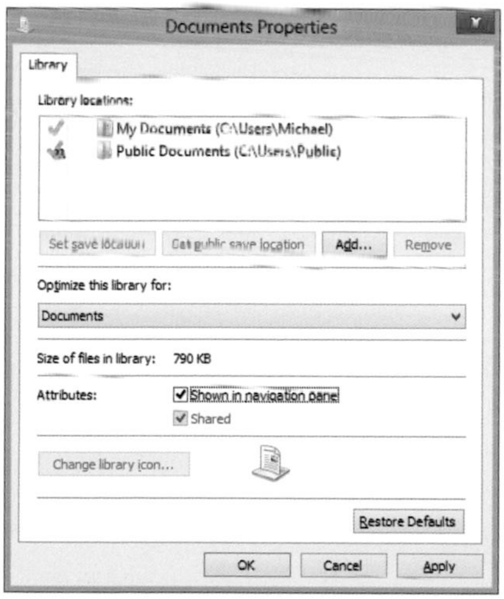

2. The Properties panel is displayed

3. Make changes and click OK to apply, or click Restore Defaults to undo

Don't forget

The black triangle opposite a menu entry indicates that there are additional options available to be displayed.

Hot tip

Some entries are toggles that switch on when selected, then switch off when reselected. For example, a ✓ symbol, may be added to or removed from a box.

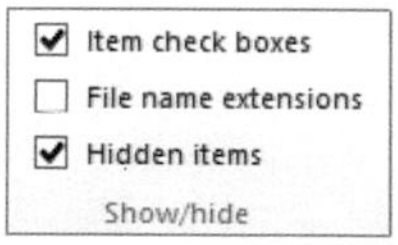

Move and Resize Windows

Hot tip

Double-clicking the title bar is an alternative to the Maximize and Restore buttons.

1. To maximize the window, double-click the title bar area (double-click again to restore the window)

2. To move the window, click the title bar area, hold down the mouse button and drag the window

3. To resize the window, move the mouse pointer over any border or any corner

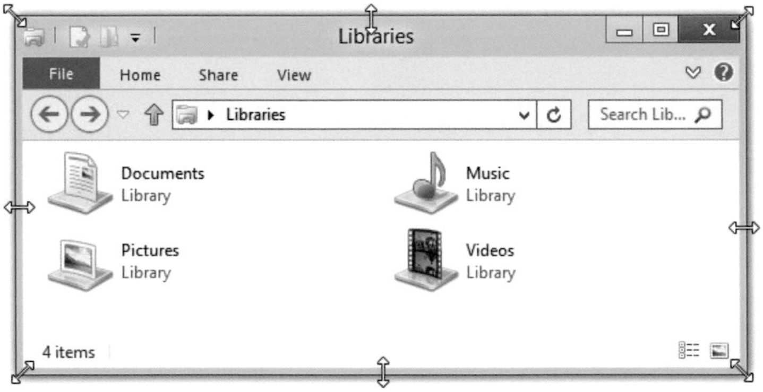

Hot tip

Dragging a corner of the window allows you to adjust the two adjacent borders at the same time.

4. When the double-headed resize arrow appears, click and drag until the window is the desired size

Snap

On the Windows 8 Desktop, the Snap feature offers ways to move and resize windows in one step.

Maximize the Window

1. Drag the title bar to the top of the screen
2. The window's outline expands to fill the whole desktop
3. Release the title bar to maximize the window

Expand Vertically

1. Drag the top border of the window to the top of the screen
2. The window's outline expands to the height of the desktop
3. Release the title bar to maximize the height but maintain the width of the window

Compare Two Windows

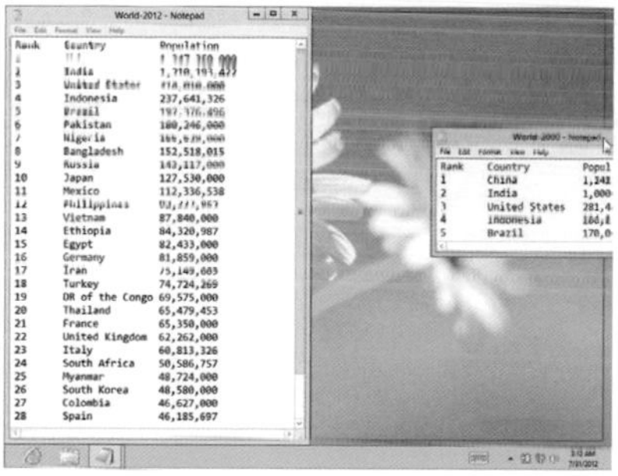

1. Drag the title bar to the left of the screen
2. Release and the window expands to fill half the desktop
3. Repeat with a second window, dragging the title bar to the right and you'll be able to view them side-by-side

Don't forget

There is also a Snap function for the Windows 8 apps, but this is a simpler function that allows you to view two of the normally full screen apps, side-by-side (see page 38).

Hot tip

You can also drag the bottom border to the bottom edge, to expand vertically.

Hot tip

To return a window to its original size, drag the title bar away from the top of the desktop and then release.

Close Desktop Apps

When you finish with your active Desktop applications, there are several ways you can close them.

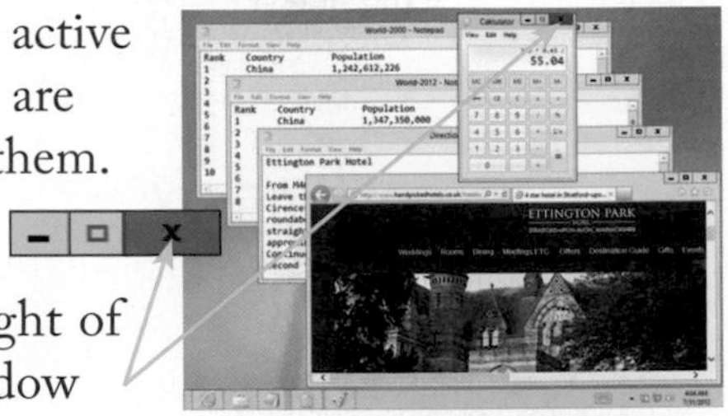

1. Click the Close button at the top right of the application window

2. Click the Control icon at the left of the title bar and select Close

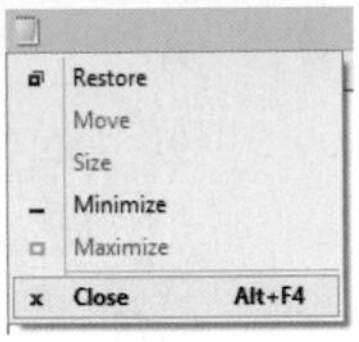

3. The application may include a File button that offers an Exit option

File Edit Format View Help
New Ctrl+N
Open... Ctrl+O
Save Ctrl+S
Save As...
Page Setup...
Print... Ctrl+P
Exit

There are a number of ways to close an application using the Taskbar button that's associated with it.

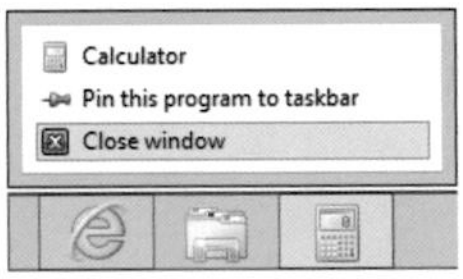

4. Right-click the Taskbar button for the application and select Close window

5. If there are multiple windows for the application select Close all windows

Recent
World-2000
World-2012
Directions
Sailing
Notepad
Unpin this program from taskbar
Close all windows

6. If any application has a modified document open you'll be prompted to Save changes, whichever method you choose to close your applications

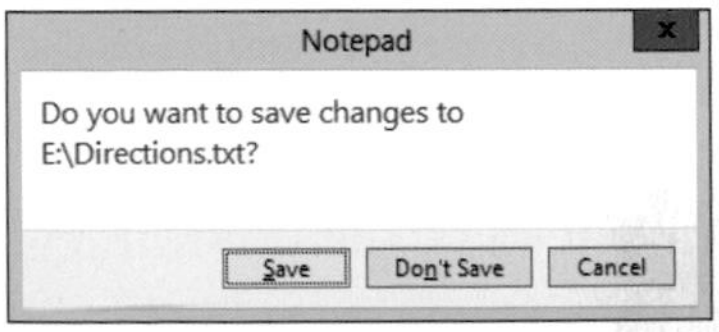

Hot tip

You can also select the application windows and press Alt + F4, or move the mouse over the Taskbar button and click the Close button on the thumbnail.

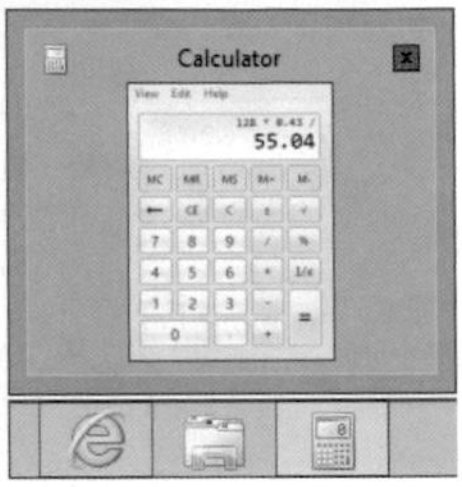

Beware

You cannot use the Apps switcher list of active apps (see page 37) to close Desktop apps, even if they were started from one of the Windows 8 tiles.

4 Personalize Your System

Change the appearance of the Windows 8 Lock screen and Start screen, add an account picture, organize the tiles and the apps, manage your user account, adding picture password or pin code and take advantage of ease of use features. You can also personalize the Desktop environment and manage the display options, including screen resolution and multiple displays.

62 PC Settings vs Control Panel
63 Personalize Lock Screen
65 Start Screen
66 Account Picture
67 Manage Tiles
69 Manage Apps
70 Create a Group
72 Name the Group
73 Change User Account
74 Picture Password
76 PIN Code
77 Ease of Use
78 Open Control Panel
79 Personalize via Control Panel
80 Display Settings
82 Ease of Access

PC Settings vs Control Panel

Windows 8 provides two main ways to make changes to your computer setup and (if you use a Microsoft account to sign on) you can take those changes with you when you sign on at other computers.

There is a Windows 8 function called PC Settings which is an easy way to apply the most often-required changes.

1. Select Settings from the Charms bar (or press WinKey + I) to display the Settings pane

2. Click the button to Change PC Settings

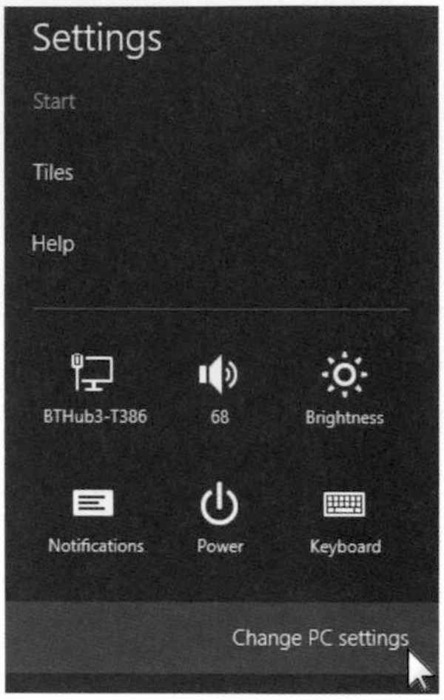

This provides a range of options for you to change the way your system appears or operates and to examine the components that make up your system.

For many users, in particular those with tablet PCs, this will be all that's needed. However, there's a complete set of functions provided via the Control Panel, as in prior releases of Windows, to allow in depth changes.

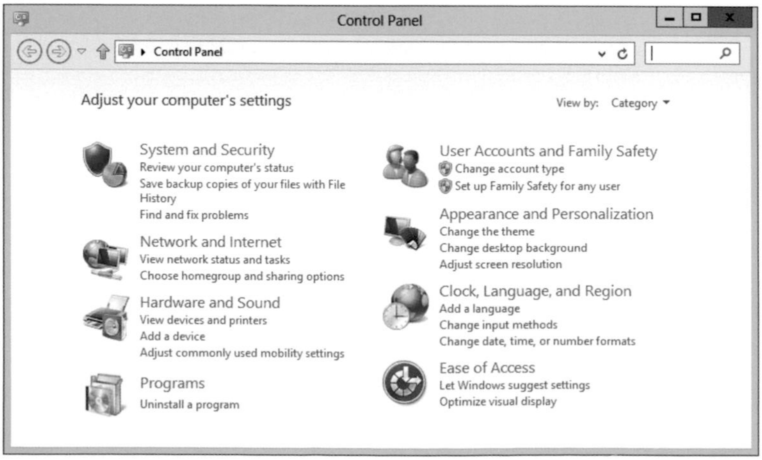

Hot tip

The PC Settings app allows you to make a variety of changes to your computer system.

Don't forget

Press WinKey + X for the Power Users menu (see page 34) to select Control Panel.

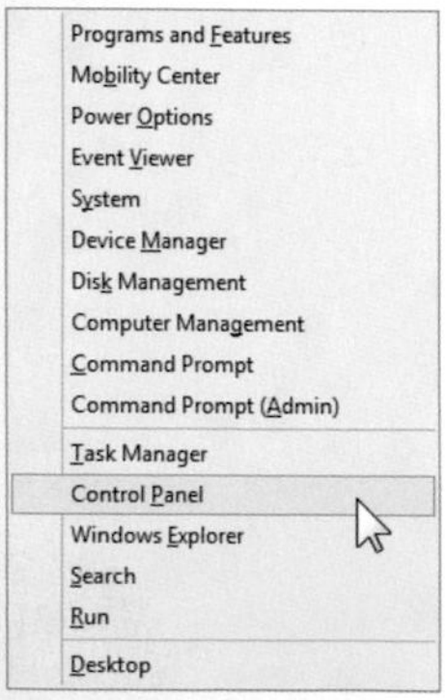

Personalize Lock Screen

The Lock screen appears when you start your Windows 8 computer or resume from Sleep. To customize this screen:

1. Select the option to Change PC Settings (see page 62), then click Personalize and the Lock screen tab

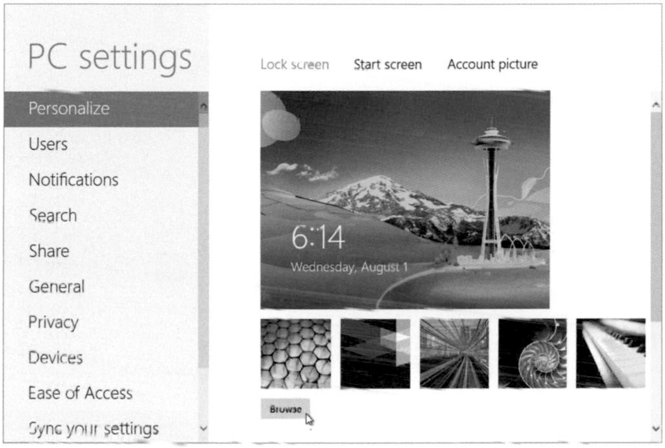

2. Click one of the supplied pictures to make it the background image

3. Click Browse to select an image from your Pictures library or another folder

4. Scroll down the Lock screen pane to choose Lock screen Apps to display notifications and updates

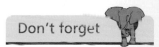

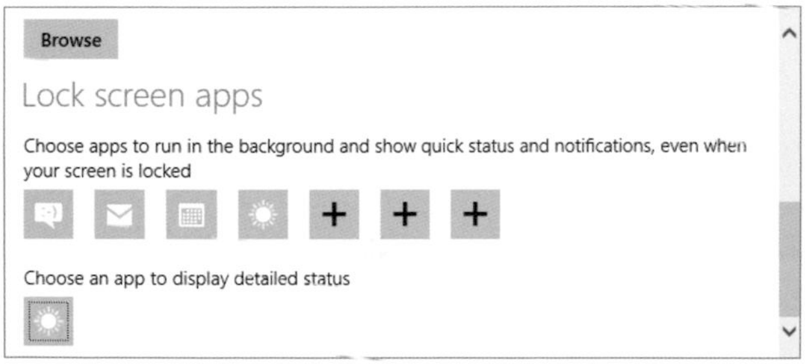

Don't forget

The Lock screen is full size and includes basic information, such as time and date, plus notifications from various apps.

Don't forget

You can have up to seven Windows 8 apps that provide simple status updates, plus a single app to provide more detailed updates.

...cont'd

Hot tip

You don't have to save the changes or close the Settings function. The updates will be applied immediately.

5. Click one of the seven existing App icons or Add icons and choose an app from the list (or select Don't show quick status here)

6. Similarly you can choose the single app that will display detailed status (or select the option Don't show detailed status on the Lock screen)

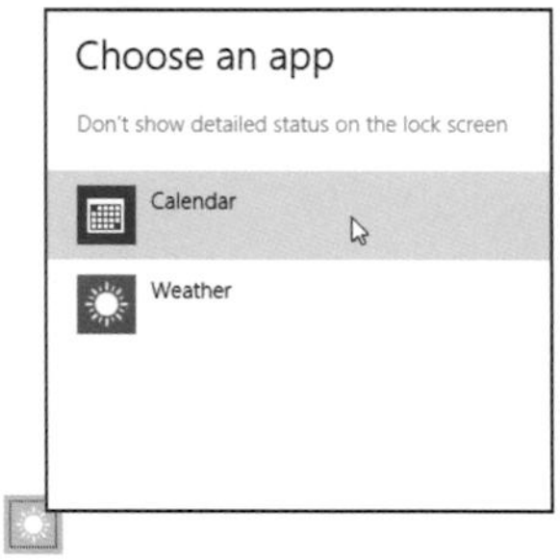

You can view the changes without having to wait until the next time you logon to the system. To do this:

1. Switch to the Start screen and right-click the user name or the user picture

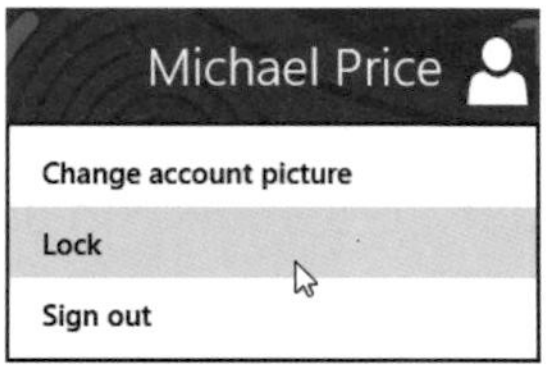

2. Select Lock to display the Lock screen

Don't forget

You may have status indicators in the form of icons, e.g. Network for connected PCs and Power for battery PCs.

Start Screen

1. Open Change PC Settings (see page 62), then click Personalize and the Start screen tab

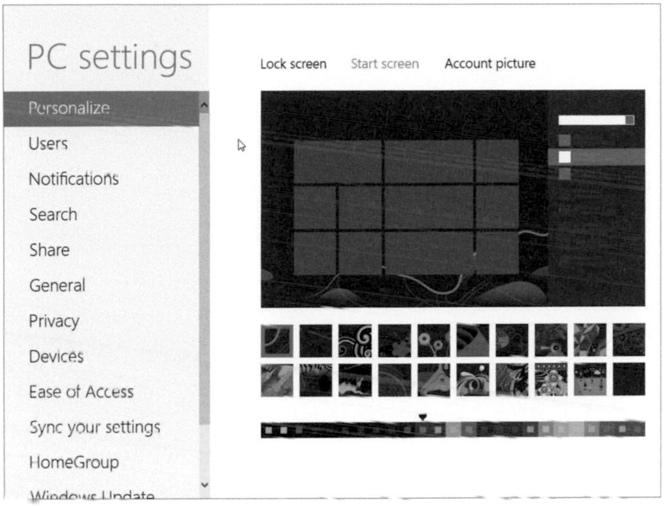

This offers the same color scheme selections as you see during installation and first run, giving you an opportunity to change your preference. However, it also offers a choice of background image for the Start screen.

1. Click one of the supplied patterns, to make that the background image

2. Drag the slider to choose a different foreground/background color set

3. View the effects on the Start screen illustration provided, which gets an instant update

4. Press the Windows key to toggle between Settings screen and Start screen, to see the full effects

If you are signed on with a Microsoft account, your final selection of color scheme and background image will be applied, not just to the current PC, but to any Windows 8 PC that you sign on to with the same Microsoft account.

Don't forget

The pattern is used only for the Start screen, while the Color set (a pre-defined pairing of foreground and background) will be used in all Windows 8 apps, as well as the Start screen.

Don't forget

Unlike the Lock screen and the Desktop, the Start screen does not give you the opportunity to choose your own images for the background.

Account Picture

1. Open Change PC Settings (see page 62), then click Personalize and the Account picture tab

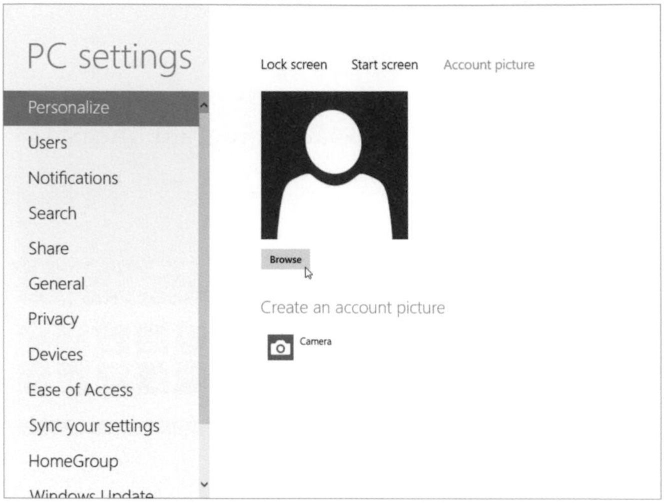
PC settings
Personalize
Users
Notifications
Search
Share
General
Privacy
Devices
Ease of Access
Sync your settings
HomeGroup
Lock screen
Start screen
Account picture
Browse
Create an account picture
Camera

You can specify a photo or image that will be used alongside your user name on the Start screen.

1. Click the Browse button to select an existing image from your Pictures library or another folder
2. Alternatively, if your computer has a webcam or built-in camera, select Camera to take a picture
3. You can take a still photo or a video, but the video is limited to five seconds
4. Press the Windows key to toggle between Settings screen and Start screen, to see the results

If you are signed on with a Microsoft account, the selected image will be displayed on the Start screen of any Windows 8 computer that you sign on to. It will also be displayed when you sign on to that account using Internet Explorer, or if you use that account for messaging.

Don't forget

You can select or create a picture of any size and it will be converted to the appropriate size for use with the Start screen or other functions related to the Microsoft account.

Beware

You can change the user image from any Windows 8 PC, but to remove it completely, you may need to sign on to your Microsoft account using Internet Explorer and amend your profile.

Manage Tiles

The Windows 8 app tiles displayed on your Start screen will depend on the choices made by your supplier and may be in no particular order or sequence, but you do have full control and can add, rearrange and remove as it suits you.

Select Tiles

The first task is to select a tile. You can't just click or touch it, since that will run the associated program. Instead:

1. To select a tile with the mouse, right-click the tile

2. On the App bar displayed, select the required action

The options depend on the app type selected. For Windows 8 apps you can Unpin from Start, Uninstall, Make smaller (or larger) and, if appropriate, Turn live tile off (or on).

There are two sizes of tile, the Large (oblong) and the Small (square). Note that only tiles for Windows 8 apps can be resized (see page 69 for the options available to Desktop apps).

3. For multiple tiles, just select the additional tiles (using your preferred methods). Reselect a tile to remove it from the selection

With multiple tiles selected, the only options offered are Unpin from Start and Clear selection.

Hot tip

With a touch screen, touch and drag down slightly. With the keyboard, use the arrow keys to locate the tile, then press the Spacebar.

Don't forget

If you select and hold a tile, you can drag it into a new position and tiles automatically reflow. This happens also when you Unpin or Resize tiles.

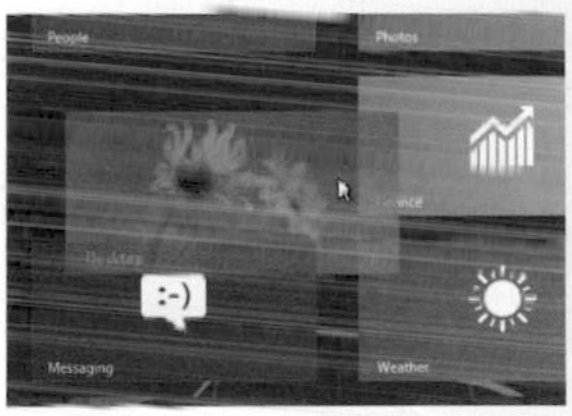

...cont'd

Don't forget

As always, the options offered vary depending on the type of entry selected and its current status.

4. Select a Desktop-based tile such as Internet Explorer to see the actions that are offered for such programs

The Apps bar displays to offer Unpin from Start, Unpin from Taskbar, Uninstall and Open new window. There's no option to Resize the tile - all Desktop apps have Small tiles.

Add Tiles

There are a number of ways to add tiles to the Start screen, but perhaps the easiest way is using the Apps bar.

Hot tip

If you've selected a tile and an Apps bar is currently displayed, you can click All Apps from that bar.

1. Go to the Start screen, press the WinKey + Z keys to display the Apps bar and click the All Apps button

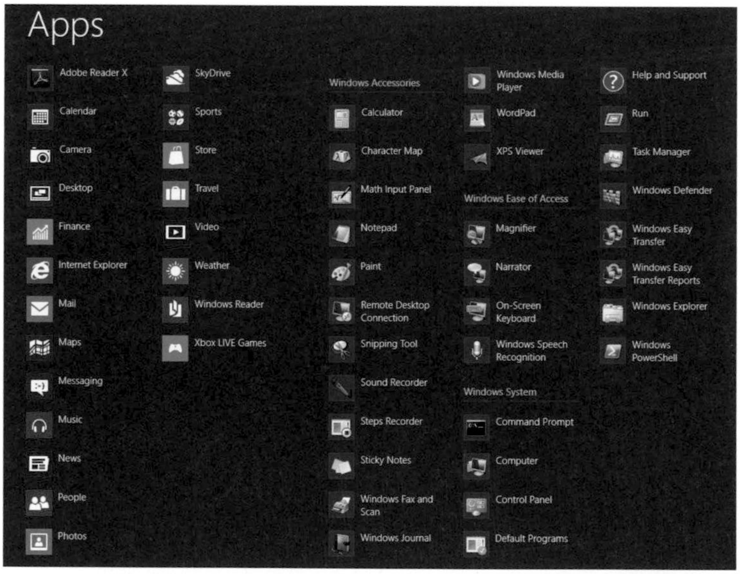

Don't forget

Applications that you have installed from the Microsoft Office suite would be shown in their own set.

You'll see all the apps that were installed with your system, listed as sets of Apps, Accessories, Ease of Access and System, plus any apps you have installed since. Some, Adobe Reader for example, are added to an existing set, while others have their own set.

Manage Apps

You select items on the Apps screen in the same ways as you select tiles. However, you can only select one at a time. Selecting a second app will deselect the previous one.

Select various apps to see what actions are available, for example:

1. Select an App, e.g. Weather, that's on the Start screen and you can Unpin from Start or Uninstall

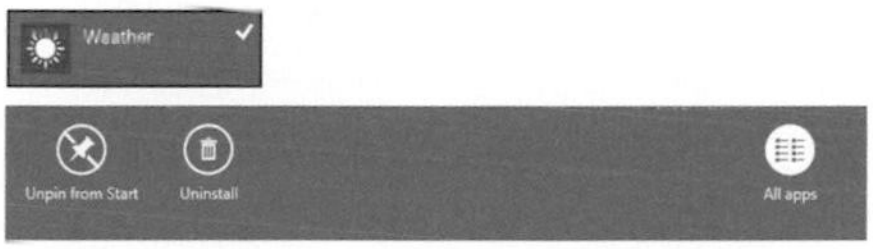

2. With an App such as Calendar, you can Unpin from Start, but the Uninstall option is grayed (disallowed)

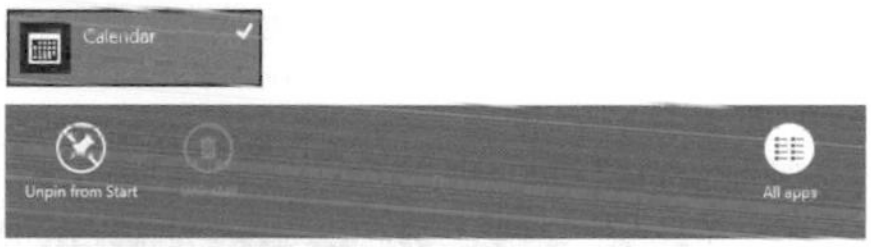

3. Select an accessory such as Paint and you can Pin to Start, Pin to Taskbar, Open in a window, Run as Administrator or Open file location

4. Internet Explorer is effectively two versions that run as a Windows 8 app and a Desktop application and its options include Unpin from Start, Unpin from Taskbar, Uninstall and Open new window

Hot tip

The Apps screen lists your applications and allows you to add them to the Start screen or the Taskbar (and create shortcuts on the Desktop – see page 53).

Don't forget

You can add items from the Desktop to the Start screen, such as disks, libraries and folders. Right-click the item in File Explorer and select Pin to Start from the menu.

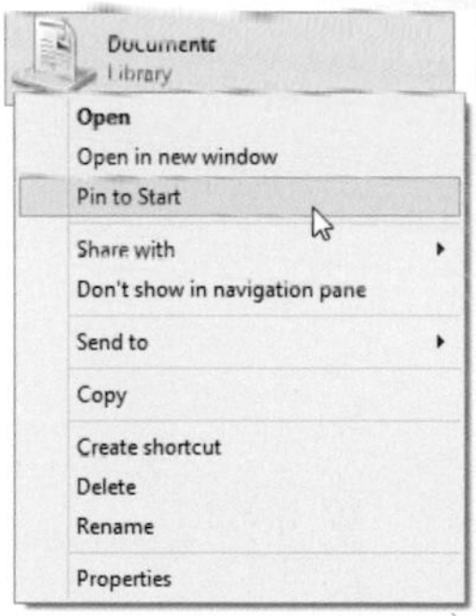

Create a Group

Suppose that you have just installed the Microsoft Office suite. You'll find that tiles for the applications will be added to the right of the Start screen, flowing on from the existing tiles.

1. To start a new group for the Office applications, drag one of the tiles from its current position

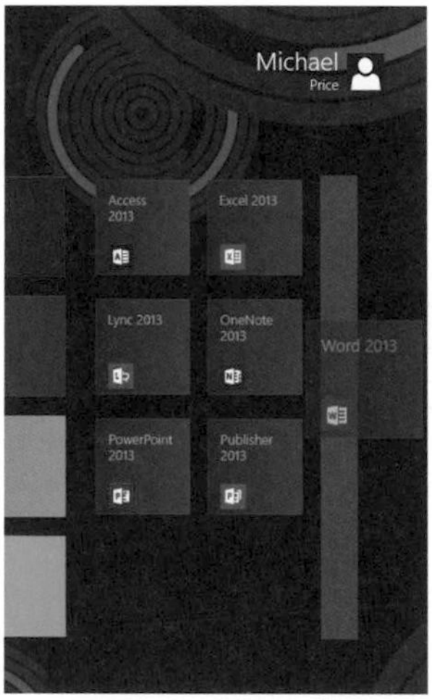

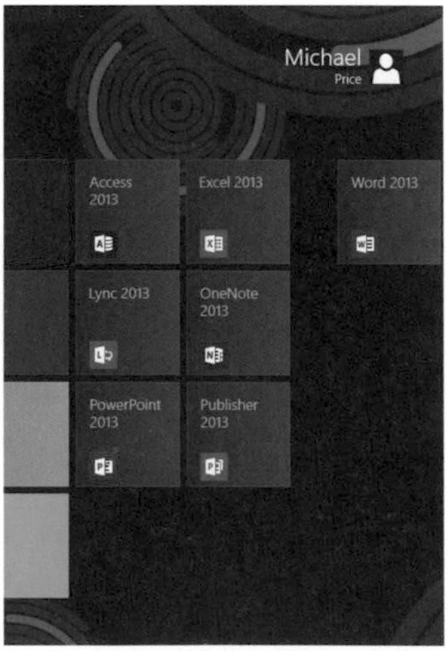

2. When the group separator bar comes into view, release the tile to initiate the new group

Don't forget

Start screen tiles can be arranged in groups, to bring together sets of related tiles, such as Games or Office applications.

Hot tip

As you drag the tile, a bar appears, to show you when to drop the tile to create a group location for that tile.

3. Drag each Office tile in turn across to the new group

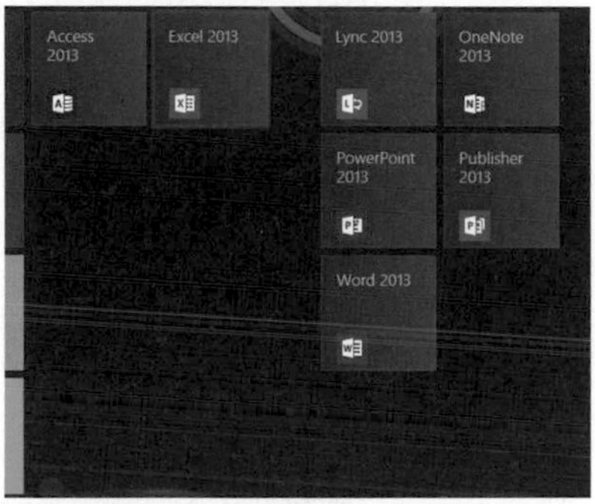

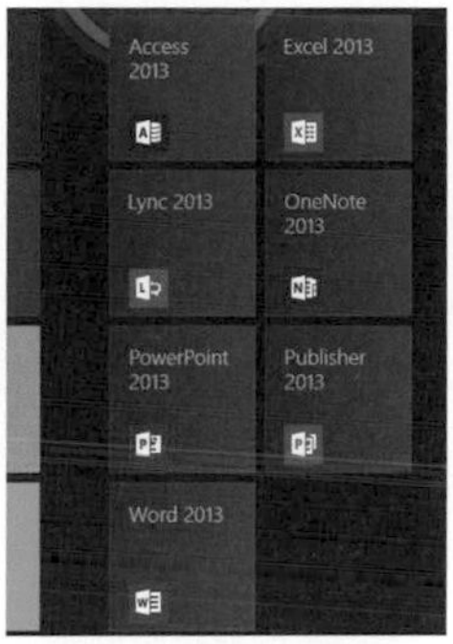

4. When all the tiles have been moved, the group moves adjacent to the previous group

5. Click the Zoom button at the bottom right of the Start screen, to see the overall view of the groups

From this view you can adjust the relative positions of groups and also assign names to them (see page 72).

Hot tip

You can drag tiles to the new group from anywhere on the Start screen, including tiles that are included in other groups.

Don't forget

To return to the normal view just left-click or touch any part of the zoomed screen.

Name the Group

Don't forget

If you left-click or just touch any part of the zoomed screen, it will return to normal size rather than select any group.

1. From the zoomed view of the Start screen, right-click (or touch and drag) to select the group you want to name

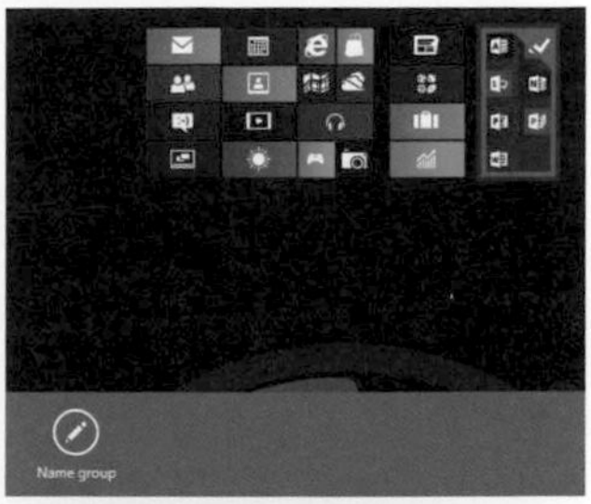

2. The Apps bar appears with the option Name Group

3. Click the Name Group button to display the Name panel

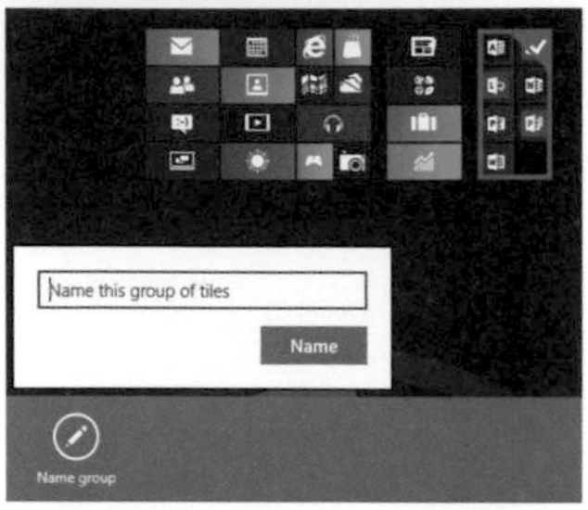

4. Type a name for the group, e.g. Microsoft Office, and click Name

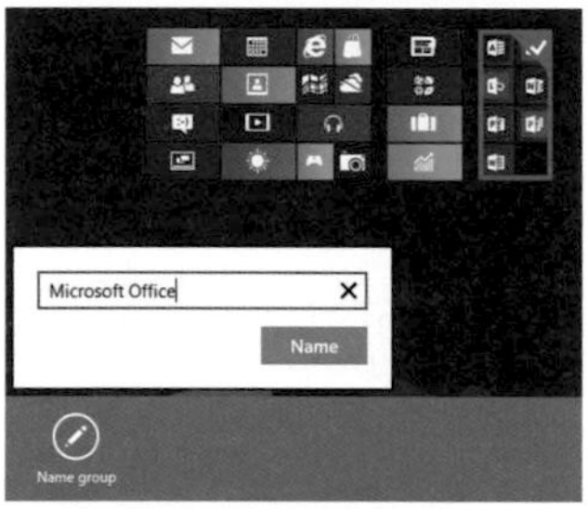

The group is named and the Start screen returns to its normal size.

Repeat this procedure to add or change the name for any other groups of tiles you have.

Hot tip

When you have selected a group, you can then left-click and drag that group to a new position on the Start screen.

Change User Account

1. Select the option to Change PC Settings (see page 62), then click Users

2. If you are signed on with a local account, you can switch to a Microsoft account

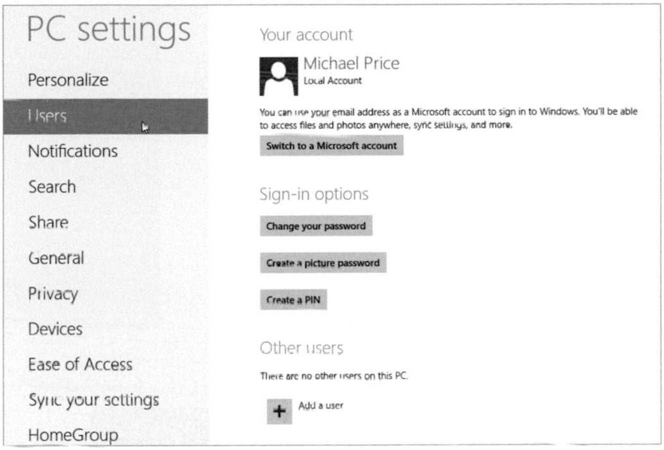
PC settings
Personalize
Users
Notifications
Search
Share
General
Privacy
Devices
Ease of Access
Sync your settings
HomeGroup
Your account
Michael Price
Local Account
You can use your email address as a Microsoft account to sign in to Windows. You'll be able to access files and photos anywhere, sync settings, and more.
Switch to a Microsoft account
Sign-in options
Change your password
Create a picture password
Create a PIN
Other users
There are no other users on this PC.
Add a user

3. If you are signed on with a Microsoft account, you can switch to a local account

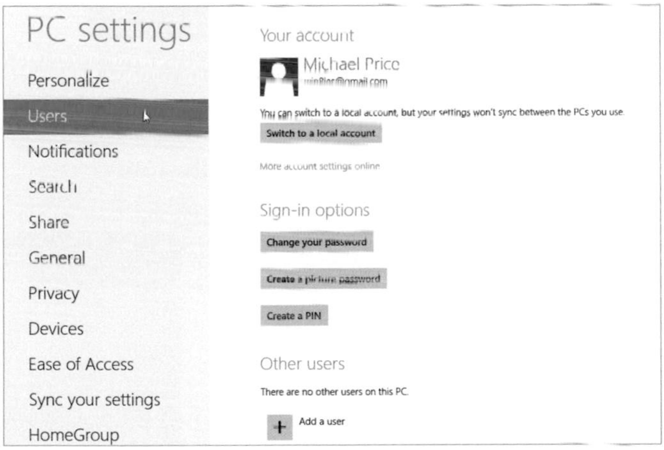
PC settings
Personalize
Users
Notifications
Search
Share
General
Privacy
Devices
Ease of Access
Sync your settings
HomeGroup
Your account
Michael Price
You can switch to a local account, but your settings won't sync between the PCs you use.
Switch to a local account
More account settings online
Sign-in options
Change your password
Create a picture password
Create a PIN
Other users
There are no other users on this PC.
Add a user

4. In either case, you can change your password, create a picture password, create a PIN or add a new user

Don't forget

You'll be asked to provide an email address which may be an existing Microsoft account, or can be used to create such an account (see page 21).

Don't forget

You must provide a user name, password and password hint (see page 21) for future use in signing on to this computer. Note that as a local account, it will not be synced to your global settings.

Hot tip

PIN is an acronym for Personal Identification Number.

Picture Password

Don't forget

The picture password consists of three gestures, applied in sequence at specific locations. You can choose one or more types of gesture - draw a circle, draw a straight line or tap the screen at a point.

1. In PC Settings, select Users and then Create a picture password

Sign-in options
Change your password
Create a picture password
Create a PIN

2. Enter your current password to confirm and click OK

Create a picture password
First, confirm your current password.
Michael Price
OK
Cancel

Welcome to picture password
Picture password is a new way to help you protect your touchscreen PC. You choose the picture — and the gestures you use with it — to create a password that's uniquely yours.
When you've chosen a picture, you "draw" directly on the touchscreen to create a combination of circles, straight lines, and taps. The size, position, and direction of your gestures become part of your picture password.
Choose picture
Cancel

3. Click on Choose picture then select the picture and click Open

Files
Pictures
Go up
Sort by name
Open
Cancel

Hot tip

If needed, you can start over to enter a new set of gestures, if you have trouble repeating your initial selection.

4. Follow the prompts to position the picture, draw the three gestures and confirm your gestures

How's this look?
Drag your picture to position it the way you want.
Use this picture
Choose new picture
Cancel

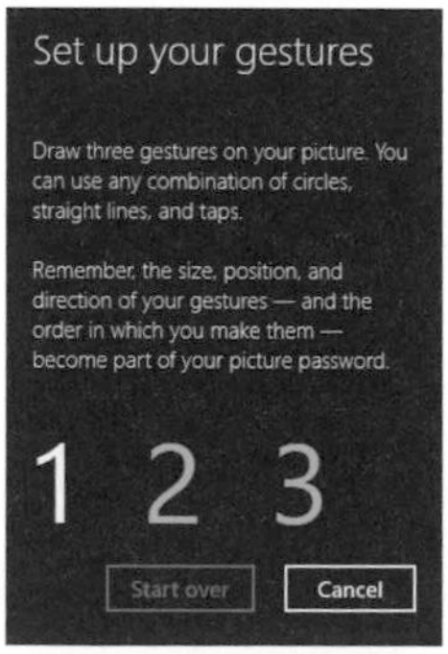
Set up your gestures
Draw three gestures on your picture. You can use any combination of circles, straight lines, and taps.
Remember, the size, position, and direction of your gestures — and the order in which you make them — become part of your picture password.
1 2 3
Start over
Cancel

Confirm your gestures
To finish setting up your picture password, just repeat your three gestures. (You can always start over by tapping the Start over button.)
1 2 3
Start over
Cancel

5. When you've successfully confirmed and your picture password is set up, click Finish

The next time the Lock screen appears and you sign on, you'll be able to use your picture password.

6. If you wish, click Switch to password to use the standard sign-in process

Don't forget

The selected gestures - a circle, a line and a tap - are shown here for interest, but such indicators will not normally appear on the display except when you are having problems during the initial definition.

Don't forget

You'd normally use picture passwords with a touch screen, but it is possible to use a mouse.

Hot tip

Click Sign-in options on the Password screen to display the methods available (see page 76).

PIN Code

Don't forget

The PIN code consists of exactly four digits and is mainly intended for tablet PCs, but can be defined on any type of computer running Windows 8.

1. In PC Settings, select Users and then select Create a PIN

2. Enter your current password to confirm and click OK

Hot tip

You always change or remove your Picture password or PIN code using PC Settings.

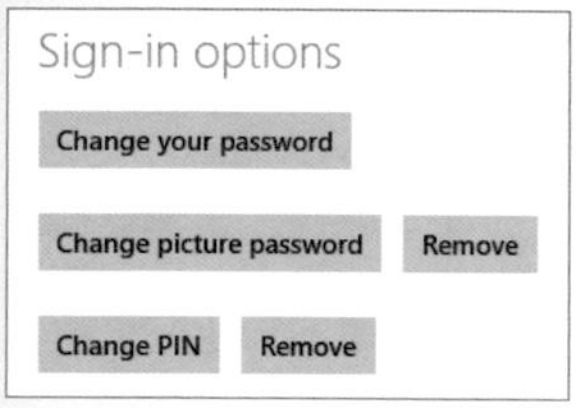

3. Touch the entry box for the PIN to display the touch keypad for numeric entry

4. Touch the keypad numbers in turn to enter the PIN and confirm the value

5. Select Finish when the values are entered

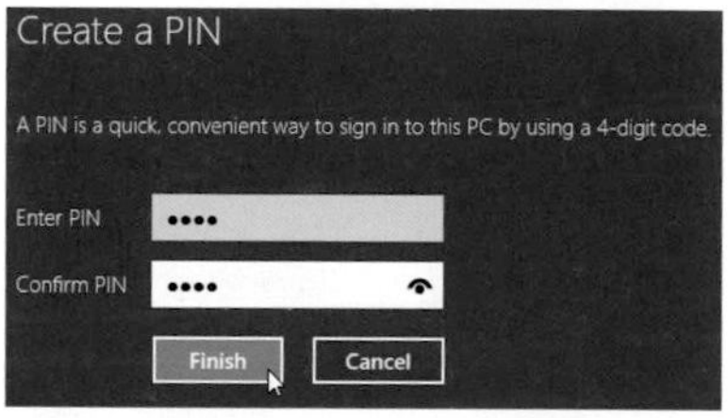

Beware

PIN codes (and Picture passwords) apply only to the specific computer on which they are defined and will not be shared with other computers that you may sign on to using your Microsoft account password.

When you next sign in, you'll be asked for the PIN, which you can enter by keyboard or touch.

Click Sign-in options to switch between the Picture password, the PIN code and your Microsoft account password.

Ease of Use

PC Settings also allows you to set up Ease of Use options on your computer, to improve accessibility.

1. In PC Settings, select the Ease of Use category

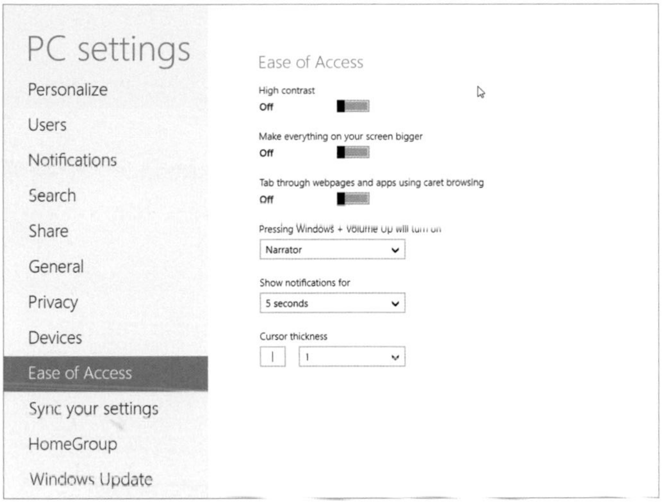

2. Click the appropriate button to turn On or Off:
   - High contrast
   - Make everything on your screen bigger
   - Tab through web pages and apps using caret browsing

3. Pick the action for Pressing WinKey + Volume Up. The default is Narrator

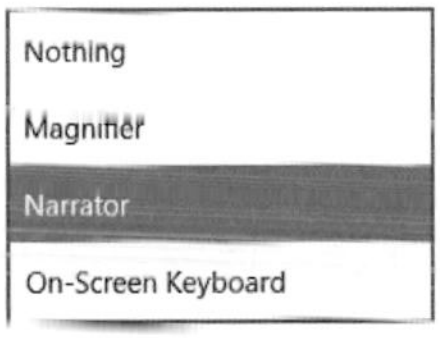

4. Choose the duration for which notifications will display. The default is 5 seconds, but you can set a time of up to 5 minutes

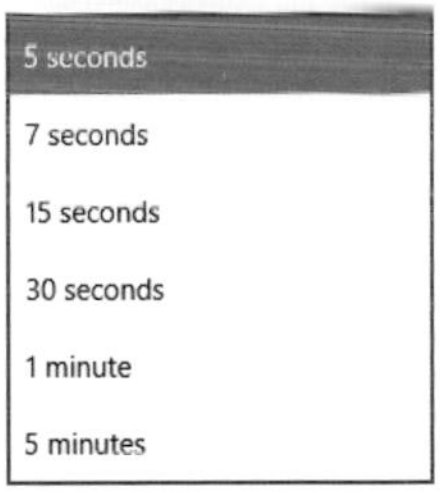

5. You can also increase the cursor thickness from the default of one to any value up to 20

Don't forget

There are fuller Ease of Use functions available in the Control Panel (see page 82).

Don't forget

With Caret Browsing you use the keyboard keys (including Home, End, Page Up, Page Down, arrow keys and Tab) to navigate through the buttons, content and text entry fields on most web pages.

Open Control Panel

For the more comprehensive options for customizing your system, you can use the Control Panel. There are several ways to invoke this:

1. From the Start screen, start typing Control Panel. When the Control Panel entry appears, press Enter

2. From the Desktop, with Show desktop icons enabled (see page 52), double-click the Control Panel icon (if present)

3. From the Desktop, click File Explorer on the Taskbar, select Computer, click the Computer tab and select Control Panel from the ribbon

4. From the Desktop, display the Charms bar (see page 32), click Settings and select the Control Panel entry

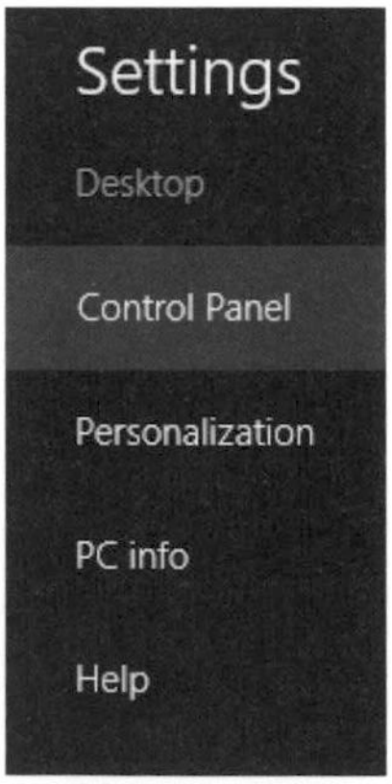

Note that there's no Control Panel entry for Settings when the Charms bar is displayed from the Start screen.

Hot tip

You can use the All Apps screen (see page 68) to select Control Panel, or use Search from the Charms bar.

Don't forget

You can also open the Control Panel from the Power Users menu (see page 34).

Personalize via Control Panel

When the Control Panel opens, you see the categories as displayed in previous versions of Windows. To personalize:

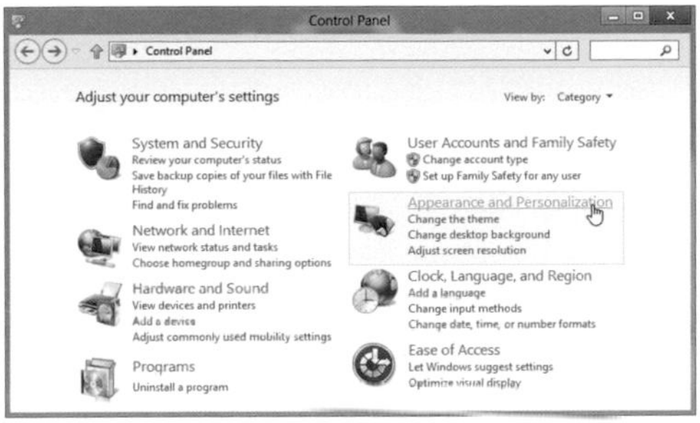

1. Select the Appearance and Personalization option

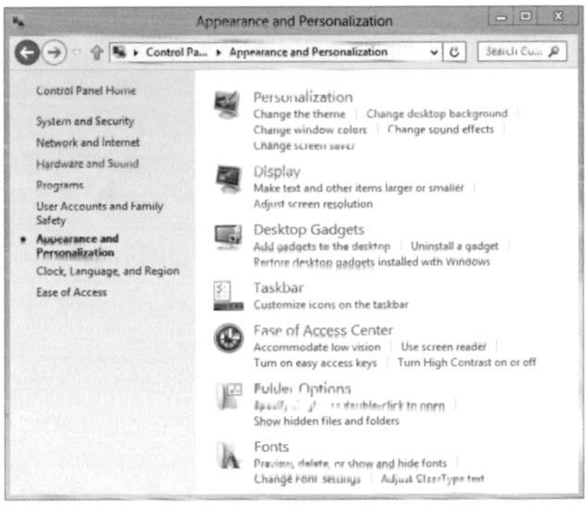

2. Select Personalization to adjust the Desktop

3. Choose a theme or change individual characteristics

Don't forget

Control Panel is a Desktop app and so will open as a window on the Desktop.

Don't forget

These options will be familiar to users of previous versions of Windows, particularly Windows 7 and Windows Vista. Note that the changes do not affect the Start screen or Windows 8 apps.

Display Settings

Don't forget

Display options other than resolution affect the PC in Desktop mode only and do not affect the Start screen and Windows 8 apps.

Hot tip

You can also right-click the Desktop and select Screen Resolution to show the panel to adjust resolution.

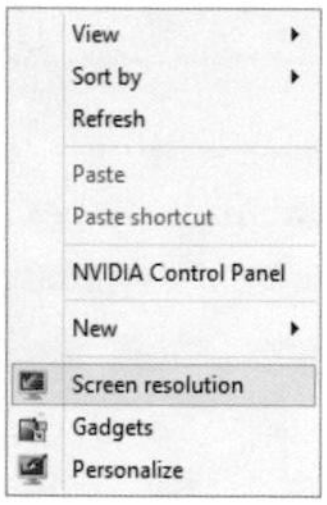

1. From the Control Panel select the Display option

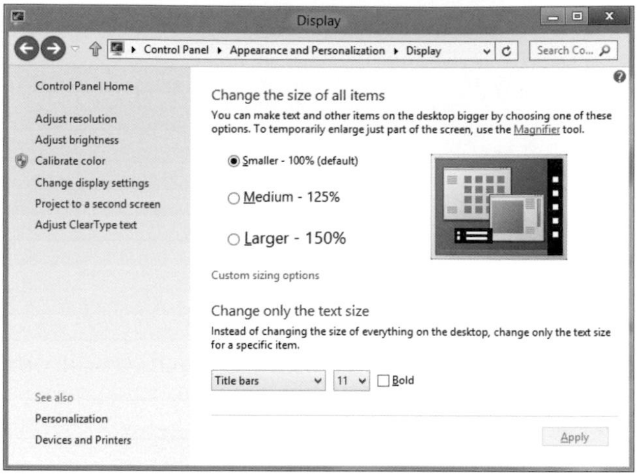

2. You can change the size of text and other items, or you can click Adjust Resolution

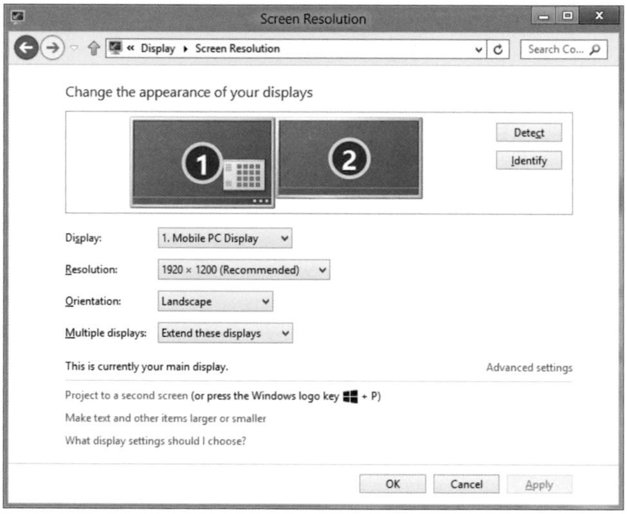

3. From here you can set the resolution for your screen, choose the orientation and manage multiple displays

4. Click the down arrow next to Resolution

5. Drag the slider to select a new resolution and click OK

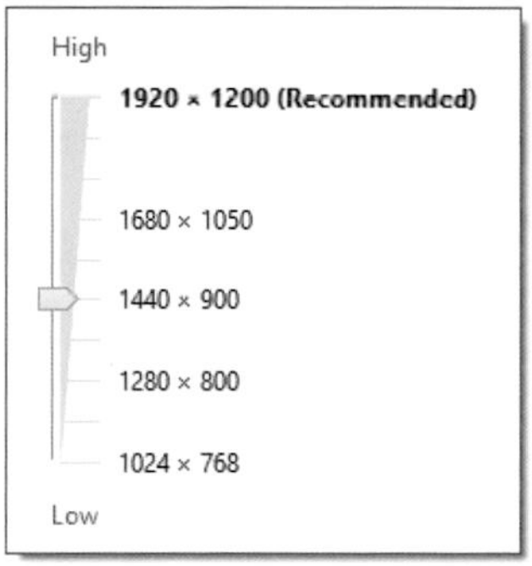

The higher the resolution, the more you can fit on the screen, but the smaller the text and images will then appear.

6. Click the down arrow next to Orientation to select Landscape or Portrait, flipped if desired

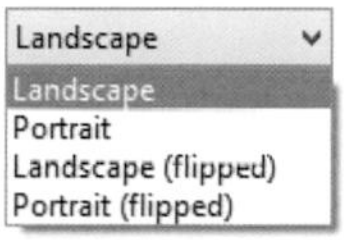

7. If you have multiple displays, choose how they'll be used

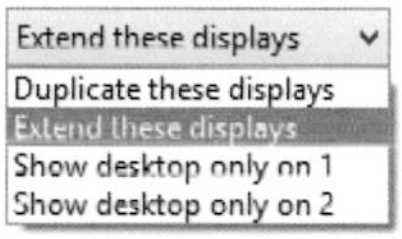
Extend these displays
Duplicate these displays
Extend these displays
Show desktop only on 1
Show desktop only on 2

You can duplicate the screen contents, extend to use both, one being the main display, or just use a single screen.

8. After any change, you are asked to confirm you want to keep the changes, or they'll automatically revert to their previous values

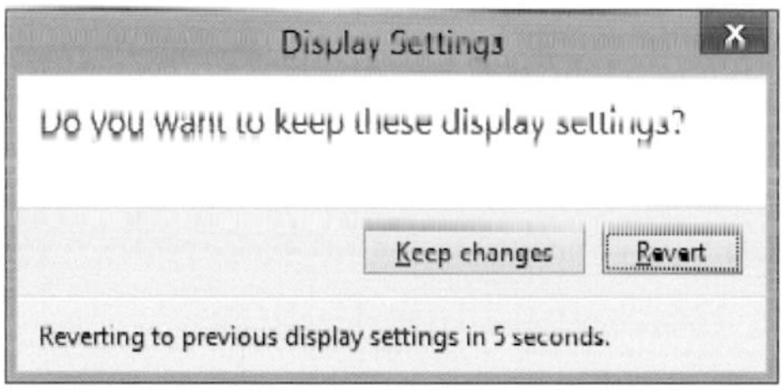

You can also control how a projector screen will relate to the PC screen. As with multiple displays, you have the options of duplicating the contents, using the two screens independently or having just one of the screens active.

Beware

The resolutions and color settings offered depend on the type of monitor and the type of graphics adapter that you have on your computer.

Don't forget

A projector can be handled in a similar way to multiple screens attached to the PC.

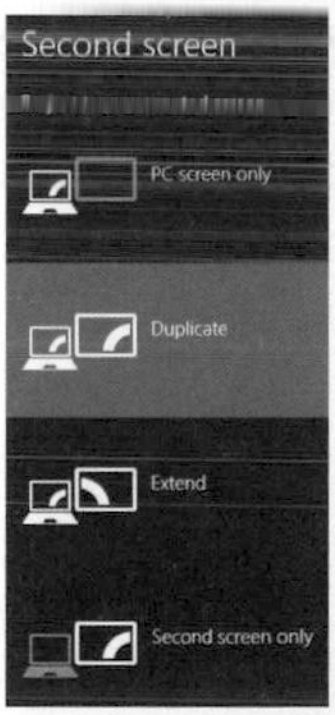

Ease of Access

Hot tip

If your PC has a microphone attached, you can use it to dictate to the computer or to issue commands to control the computer.

1. From the Control Panel select the Ease of Access option

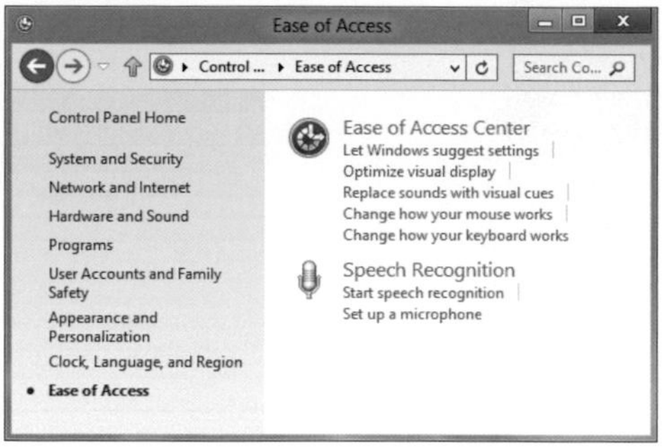

Don't forget

The magnifier is not just for text, it is also very useful for close-up views of images of all types, including graphics, buttons and pictures.

2. You can set up speech recognition with a microphone, or from the Ease of Access Center

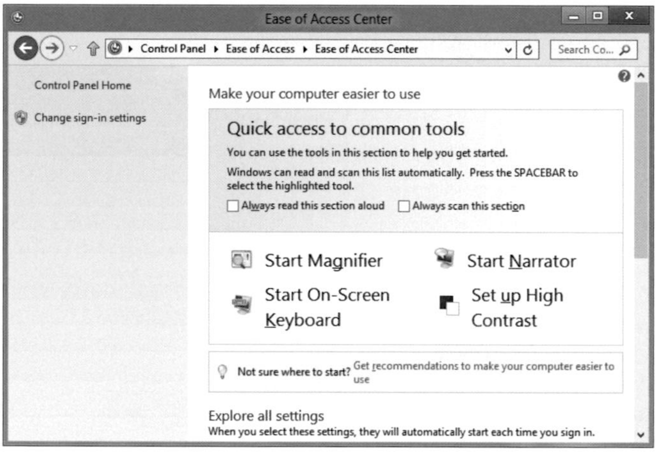

Don't forget

There are settings to Optimize the computer for blindness, set up alternative input devices, set up alternatives to sound and make touch and tablets easier to use.

3. Start the main tools – Magnifier, Narrator, On-Screen Keyboard, High Contrast
4. If you are unsure, you can ask for recommendations to make your computer easier to use
5. Scroll down to explore all the settings

5 Search and Organize

Windows 8 helps organize the files and folders on your hard disk. Data is stored by user name with separate folders for different types of files, or you can add new folders. Libraries allow you to work with a group of folders. Powerful instant search facilities help you find your way around the folders and the menus.

84 Files and Folders
86 New User Account
88 Change Account Type
90 User Folders
91 Libraries
92 Add Folder to Library
94 Working with Libraries
95 Folder Navigation
96 Create Folders and Files
97 Copy or Move Files
99 Delete Files
100 Folder Views
102 File Explorer Ribbon
104 File Explorer Layout
106 Search Box
107 Using the Search App
108 Settings for Search App

Files and Folders

The hardware components are the building blocks for your computer but it is the information on your disk drive that really makes your computer operate. There is a huge number of files and folders stored there. To get an idea of how many:

1. From the Start screen type Computer and press Enter when that option appears

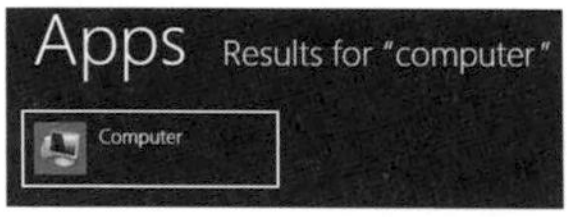

2. In the File Explorer windows that appears, double-click the system drive (C:) to open it

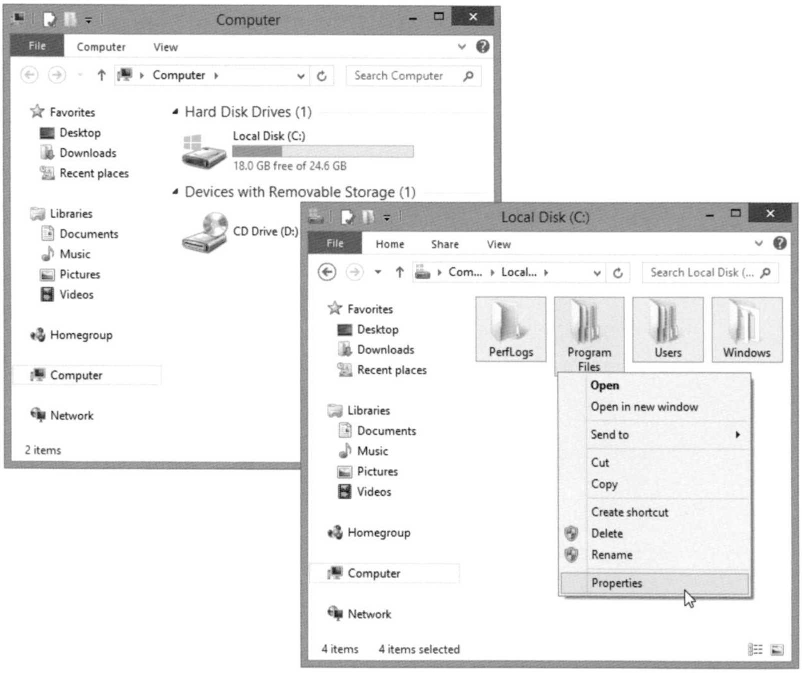

3. Press Ctrl + A to select all the items in the drive

4. Right-click the selection and click Properties

5. This example shows over 46,000 files and 10,000 folders

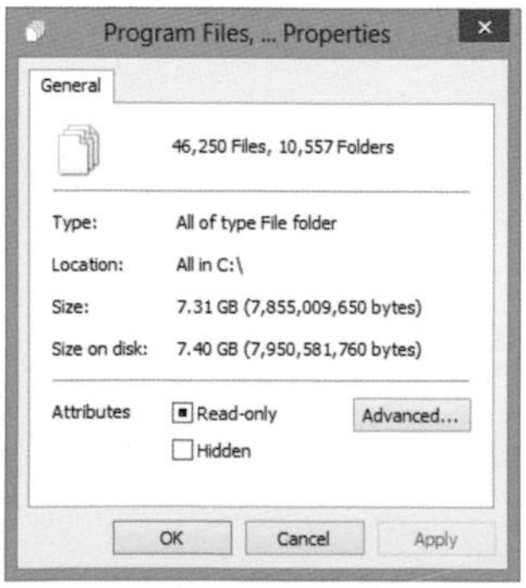

Hot tip

Alternatively, from the Desktop, click the File Explorer icon on the Taskbar and then select the Computer entry on the Navigation pane.

Hot tip

Select the View tab and click the box to Show Hidden items and you'll find there are even more folders on the system hard disk than had initially appeared.

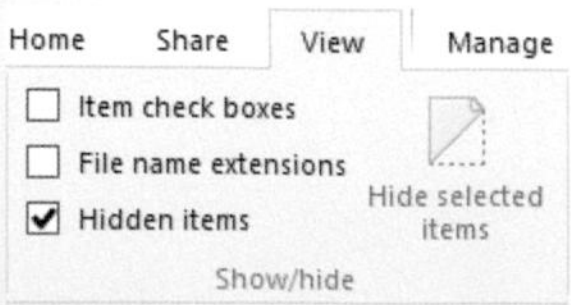

With so many files and folders to handle, they must be well organized to ensure that you can locate the documents, pictures and other data that you require. Windows helps by grouping the files into related sections, for example:

- Program Files — Application programs
- ProgramData — Application data files (usually hidden)
- Windows — Operating system programs and data
- Users — Documents, pictures, etc.

These are top-level folders on your hard disk and each one is divided into subfolders. For example, the Program Files folder is arranged by supplier and application.

1. Open the C: drive, then double-click Program Files, then Adobe and then the Reader subfolders

2. Move the mouse pointer over the Navigation pane and you'll see triangles against some folders

3. The white triangle (▷) shows there are subfolders within and the black triangle (◢) means it is an expanded folder

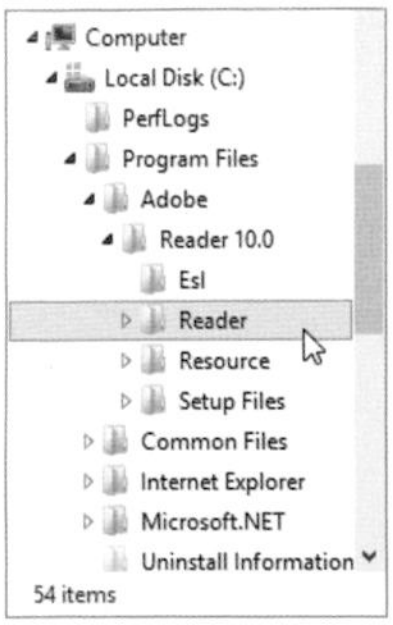

Hot tip

The Users folder contains Document, Pictures, Music and other folders for each user defined on the computer.

Don't forget

The Program Files, ProgramData and Windows folders are managed by the system and you will not normally need to access them directly.

Hot tip

The triangle symbols also appear when you select any of the folder names within the Navigation pane.

New User Account

Hot tip

Before sharing your PC with other users it is helpful to give them an account of their own with libraries and standard folders.

1. Open PC Settings (see page 62) and select Users, then click the button to Add a user

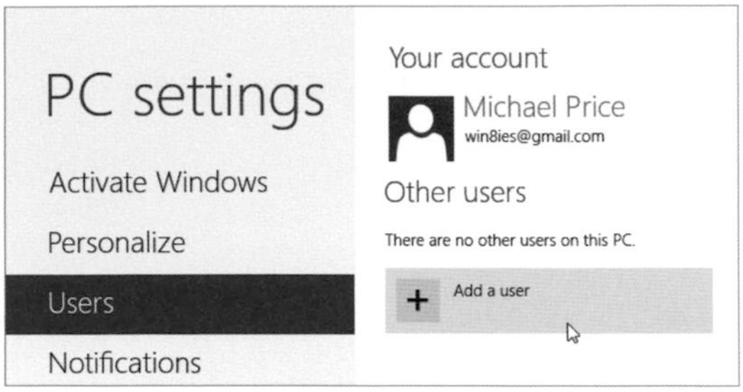
PC settings
Activate Windows
Personalize
Users
Notifications
Your account
Michael Price
win8ies@gmail.com
Other users
There are no other users on this PC.
Add a user

Don't forget

You can choose to use a local Windows account that is not associated with a Microsoft account (see page 20) but the new users will not be able to download apps and their settings won't travel with them when they switch computers.

2. Provide an email address for a Microsoft account

3. Click Next and follow the prompts to create the Microsoft account (or access an existing account)

4. The new user is defined to the system, ready for sign in

Add a user
The following user will be able to sign in to this PC.
Sue Price
sue.price2012@live.com
Is this a child's account? Turn on Family Safety to get reports of their PC use.
Finish
Cancel

Hot tip

For children's accounts you should turn on Family Safety to get reports of their PC usage.

Is this a child's account?

You can allow a new user to sign in while you are still logged on to the computer.

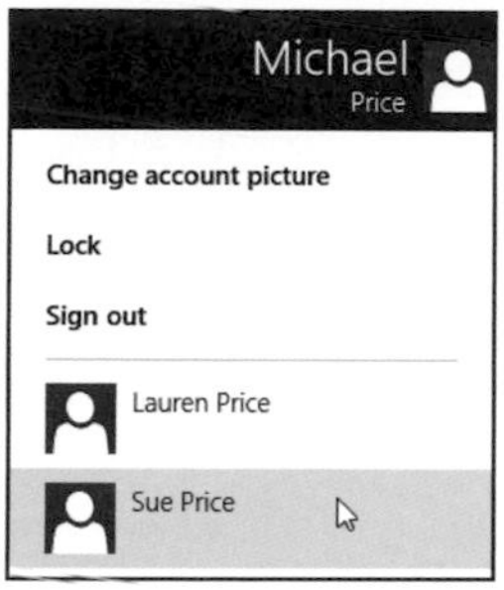

5. From the Start screen, right-click the user name or picture and select the user account required

Alternatively, if you have signed out or shutdown the system:

6. From the Logon screen, click the arrow next to the Last user signed in and select the required account

In each case, Windows creates the user libraries and folders (see page 92) and installs any necessary apps. There's a small tutorial presented while this is taking place.

7. When initialization completes, the Start screen appears with the new user account

Hot tip

Any new users that you create are added at the foot of the Users section of PC settings.

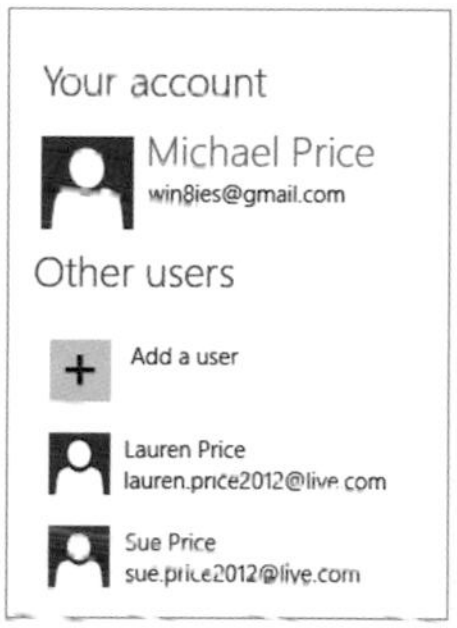

Don't forget

On any subsequent sign in, initialization isn't required and there is no tutorial, so the system goes straight to the Start screen.

Change Account Type

1 Select Start, Control Panel and in User Accounts and Family Safety click Change account type

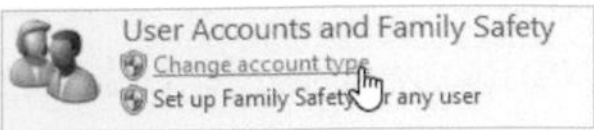

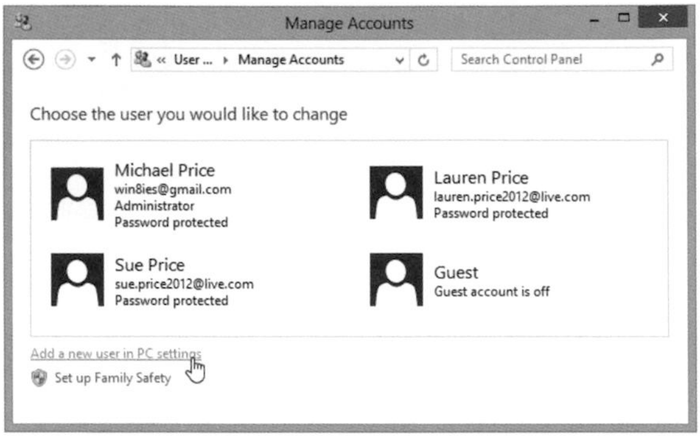
Manage Accounts
« User ... › Manage Accounts
Search Control Panel
Choose the user you would like to change
Michael Price
win8ies@gmail.com
Administrator
Password protected
Lauren Price
lauren.price2012@live.com
Password protected
Sue Price
sue.price2012@live.com
Password protected
Guest
Guest account is off
Add a new user in PC settings
Set up Family Safety

2 Click on one of the new accounts

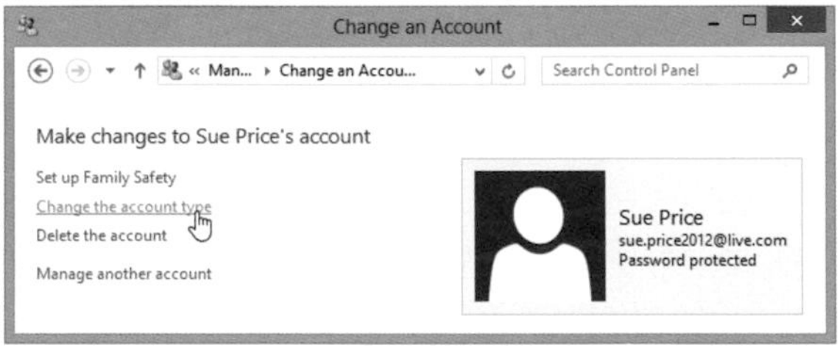

3 Click Change the account type and you'll see that it has been defined as Standard

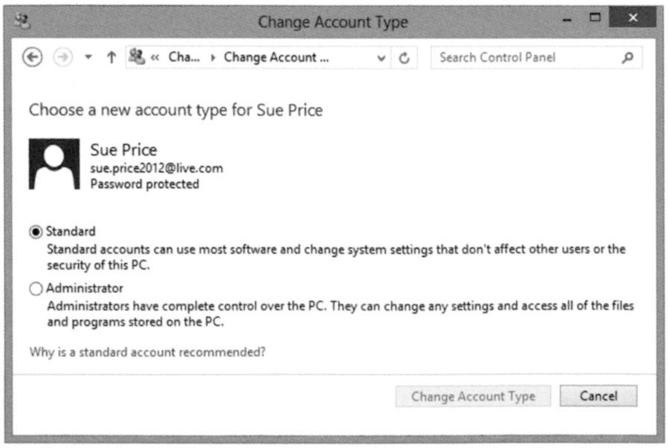

Don't forget

This displays details of all the accounts on your computer. You'll see that the first account created when the system was originally set up has been defined as Administrator.

Hot tip

Note that you cannot create new accounts from within Control Panel, but must select the link to Add a new user in PC Settings.

Hot tip

Standard user accounts are recommended for every user, even the administrator, to minimize the risk of unintended changes Windows will ask for the administrator password, when that level is needed.

...cont'd

Windows provides a Guest account for casual use, by visitors for example. By default this is turned off. To enable it:

1. Select Change account type from Control Panel and click on Guest

Guest
Guest account is off

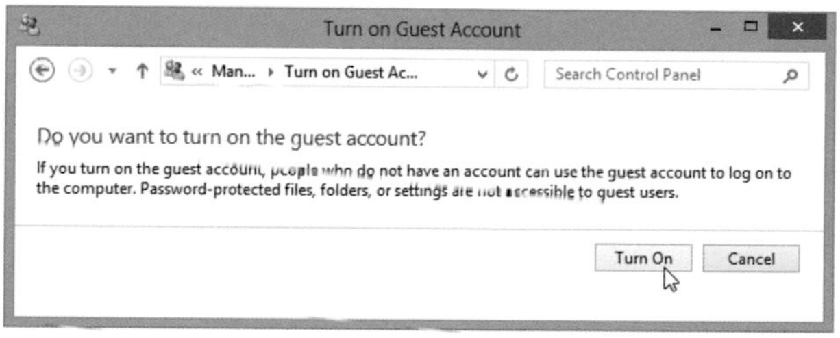
Turn on Guest Account
« Man... ▸ Turn on Guest Ac...
Search Control Panel
Do you want to turn on the guest account?
If you turn on the guest account, people who do not have an account can use the guest account to log on to the computer. Password-protected files, folders, or settings are not accessible to guest users.
Turn On
Cancel

2. Click the button to Turn On the Guest account

3. The Guest account is enabled as Local (with no access to the Store)

Guest
Local Account
Guest account

4. Click Set up Family Safety to see full details and to apply the family safety features to any account

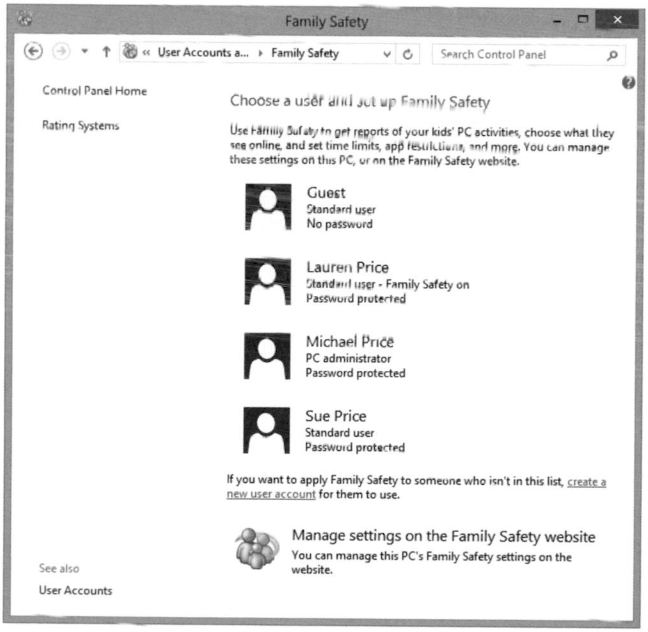
Family Safety
« User Accounts a... ▸ Family Safety
Search Control Panel
Control Panel Home
Rating Systems
Choose a user and set up Family Safety
Use Family Safety to get reports of your kids' PC activities, choose what they see online, and set time limits, app restrictions, and more. You can manage these settings on this PC, or on the Family Safety website.
Guest
Standard user
No password
Lauren Price
Standard user - Family Safety on
Password protected
Michael Price
PC administrator
Password protected
Sue Price
Standard user
Password protected
If you want to apply Family Safety to someone who isn't in this list, create a new user account for them to use.
Manage settings on the Family Safety website
You can manage this PC's Family Safety settings on the website.
See also
User Accounts

Hot tip

There is no password associated with the Guest account, so anyone with access to your computer can use it. However, they cannot view password protected files, folders or libraries.

Don't forget

Each account will have its own set of files and folders (see page 92) and also personal preferences such as color themes or backgrounds and password types.

User Folders

Documents and pictures that you create or save on your computer are kept in folders associated with your user name.

Don't forget

The Public folder is available to all user accounts and can be used to share files with other people using the same computer or using other computers on the same network.

1. Open Computer and the C: drive (see page 84) and double-click the icon for Users

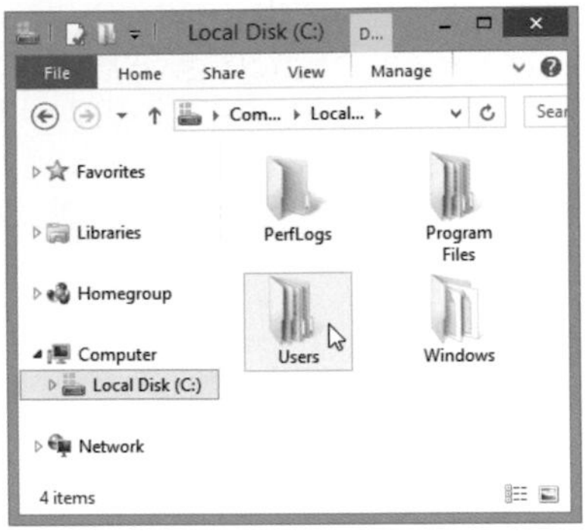

2. There's a subfolder for each user account name defined, plus the Public folder

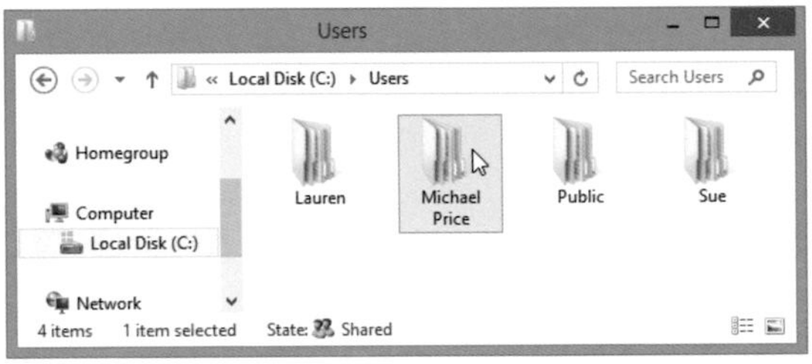

Hot tip

To see the hierarchical structure of the user folders, right-click the Navigation pane and select Expand to current folder.

3. Double-click the folder for the active user, in this case Michael Price

There's a set of subfolders with all the documents, pictures and settings belonging to that user.

Each user folder (including the Public folder) has a similar set of subfolders defined.

The Documents, Music, Pictures and Videos folders can also be accessed from Libraries in the Navigation pane – click the white triangle (▷) to expand the list.

Libraries

Libraries in Windows 8 provide a place where you can manage your documents, music, pictures and other files. There are four default libraries – Documents, Music, Pictures and Videos, which give you a combined view of the relevant folders for the current user and the Public folders.

To see the libraries:

1. Click the Libraries entry in the Navigation pane for any folder window

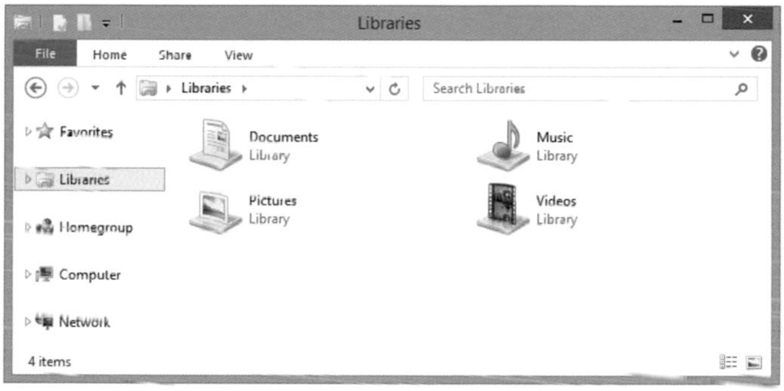

2. Double-click the Pictures library to open it

3. By default, the library is shown in Folder view, with all the files and subfolders in two locations – My Pictures and Public Pictures – with files shown as large icons

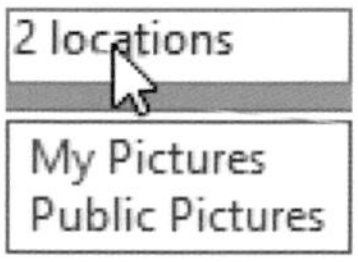

Hot tip

To display the libraries when there's no folder window open, switch to the Desktop and select File Explorer from the Taskbar.

Hot tip

Note how File Explorer provides tabs related to the specific file or folder types, in this case Library Tools and Picture Tools.

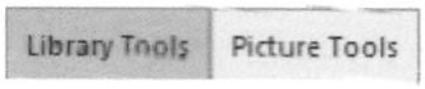

Don't forget

The libraries have links to all the files and subfolders in the locations defined for that library, but the actual files and subfolders remain where they were originally stored.

Add Folder to Library

Don't forget

Folders on your C: drive, on an additional hard drive, on a USB drive or on a network drive can be included in a library. However, you cannot include files from a removable drive such as CD/DVD.

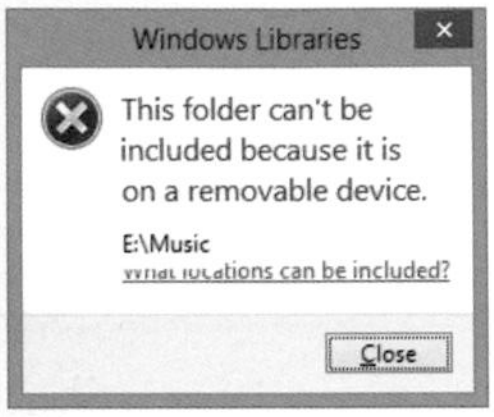

Hot tip

Select Create new library to use the folder as the basis for a new library.

1. Attach the device, if the folder is on a separate drive, open Computer and double-click the drive icon

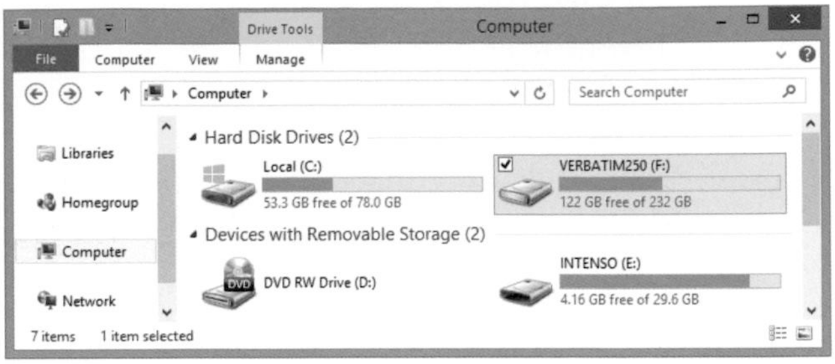

2. Locate the required folder then right-click the folder, select Include in library then pick an appropriate library, e.g. Pictures

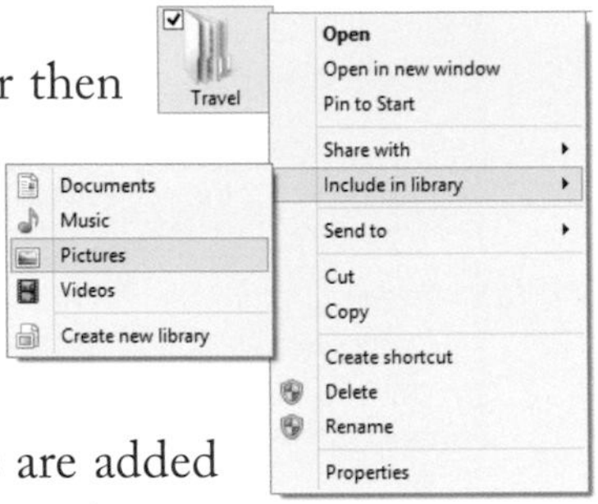

3. The folder and subfolders are added to the library as another location, and the library contents are grouped by location

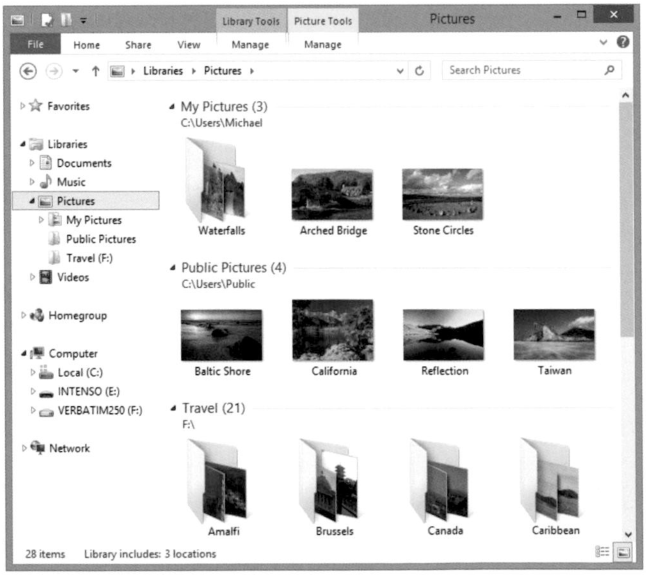

To display the contents of a library in a different arrangement:

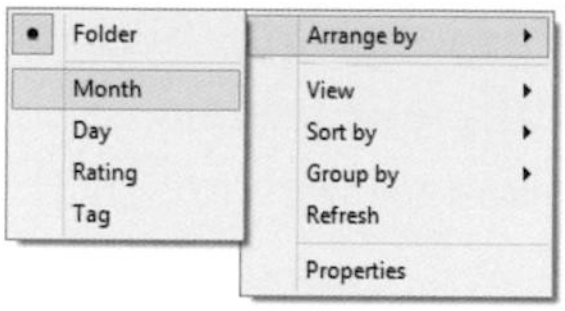
Folder
Month
Day
Rating
Tag
Arrange by
View
Sort by
Group by
Refresh
Properties

1. Right-click the library, click Arrange by action and select an attribute, for example Month

2. The files in the library's folders are re-organized by month of file creation (e.g. date photos imported)

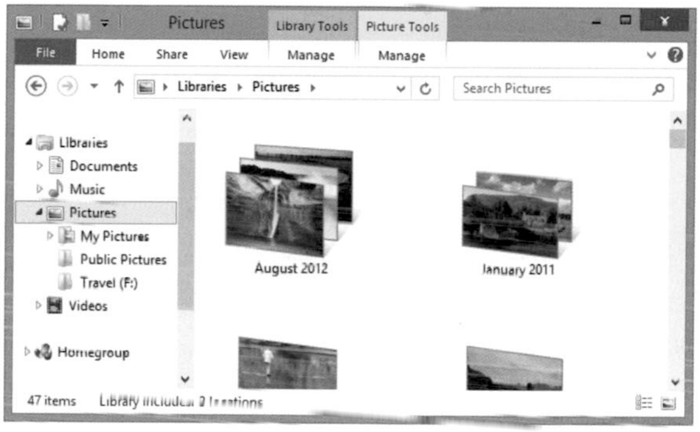

3. Double-click one of the stacks, for example August 2012, and the files are displayed (by day, newest first)

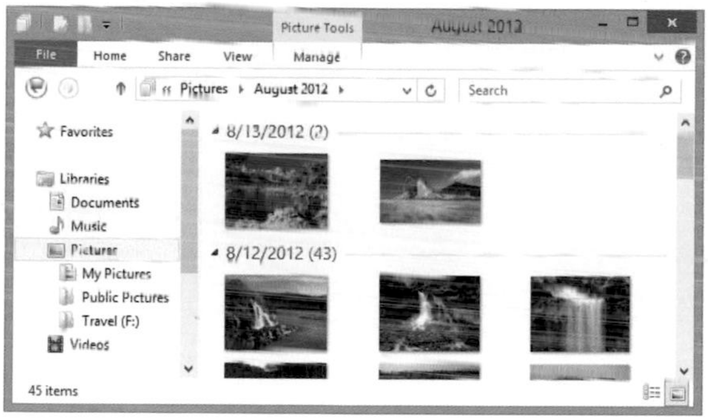

The files that are grouped together may come from any of the folders or subfolders in the library, even if they are on different drives. Select an individual location in the Navigation pane to see the specific contents. The arrangement will then be by folder, unless changed.

Hot tip

The attributes that are displayed for Arrange by function depend on the library type. For the Music or Document library you'd choose from:

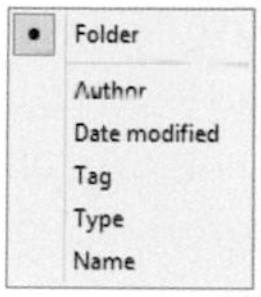
Folder
Author
Date modified
Tag
Type
Name

Don't forget

The icon for each of the monthly groups is created from a selection of the files in that group, set in a stack formation.

Hot tip

The contents of folders from an external drive can only be displayed while it is attached. If the drive is removed, the library shows the folders as Empty and unavailable.

Travel (Empty)
F:\
This folder is unavailable.

Working with Libraries

Don't forget

The first time you view images, you can specify the default program that's used when you open a picture file. The options depend on which programs you have installed. Windows Essentials, for example, adds several picture viewers.

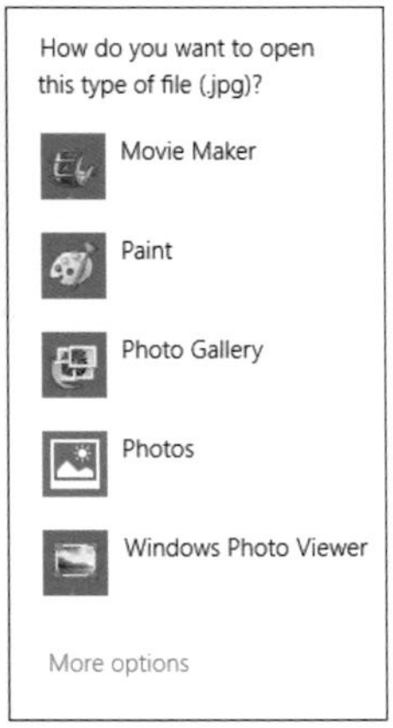

Although the files in the library collection are stored in different folders or drives, you can work with them as though they are in the same folder. For example:

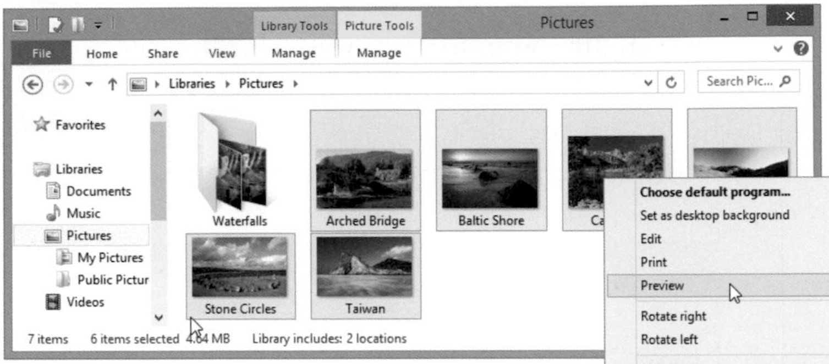

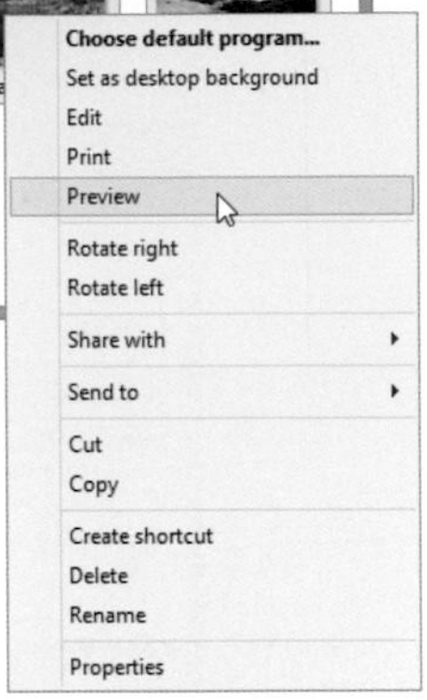

1. From a group of Picture library items, make a selection and click Preview to see them enlarged

2. Click Play to view the items as a slide show

3. Similarly, right-click a set of pictures and click Print from the menu to send them to the printer

Folder Navigation

When you open a drive or folder, you'll find a number of different ways to navigate among the folders on your disk.

1. Open the Documents folder in File Explorer

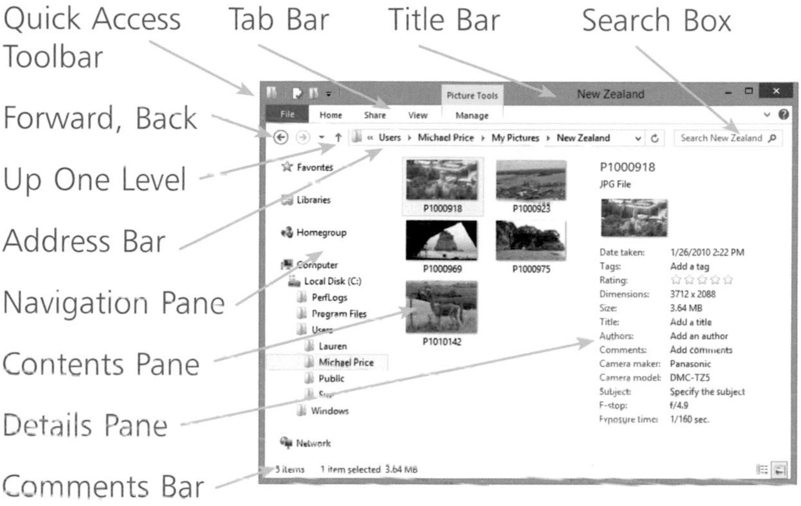

2. To go directly to a location on the Address bar, just click that location, for example the User folder (in this case Michael Price)

Users
Michael Price
My Pictures
New Zealand
Contacts
Desktop
Downloads
Favorites
Links
My Documents
My Music
My Pictures
My Videos
Saved Games
Searches
SkyDrive
Tracing

3. To go to a subfolder of a location on the Address bar, click the arrow at the right, and select a subfolder from the list

4. To type a location, click the blank space to the right of the current location, to display the current folder address, highlighted

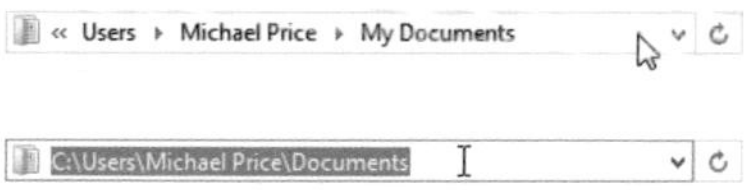
« Users › Michael Price › My Documents
C:\Users\Michael Price\Documents

5. Edit the folder address to the required location, e.g. C:\Users\Public\Documents and then press Enter

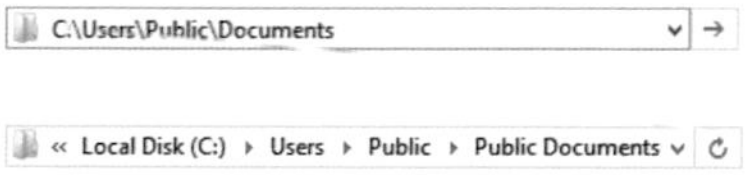
C:\Users\Public\Documents
« Local Disk (C:) › Users › Public › Public Documents

Hot tip

Click the Forward and Back buttons to navigate through locations you have already visited.

Don't forget

The address bar displays the current location as a series of links, separated by arrows. There's an Up arrow at the left, to go Up one level.

Hot tip

For common locations, you can type just the name, for example:

- Computer
- Contacts
- Control Panel
- Documents
- Pictures

Create Folders and Files

Hot tip

Create new folders to organize all your documents by use or purpose, or create files of particular types, ready for use.

1. Open the library or folder where the new folder is required, for example select Libraries, Documents

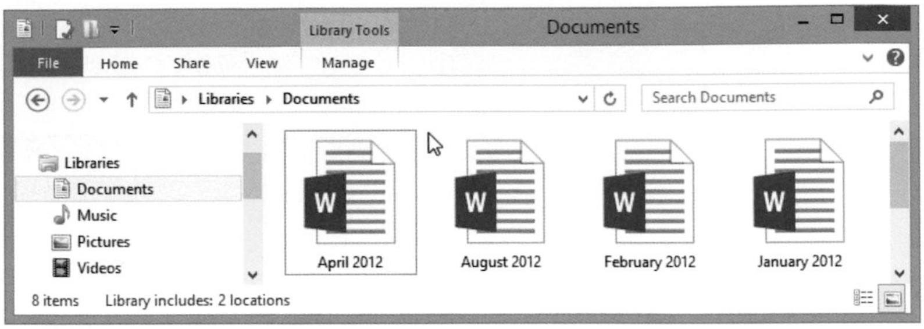

2. Right-click an empty part of the folder area and select New Folder (or choose a particular file type)

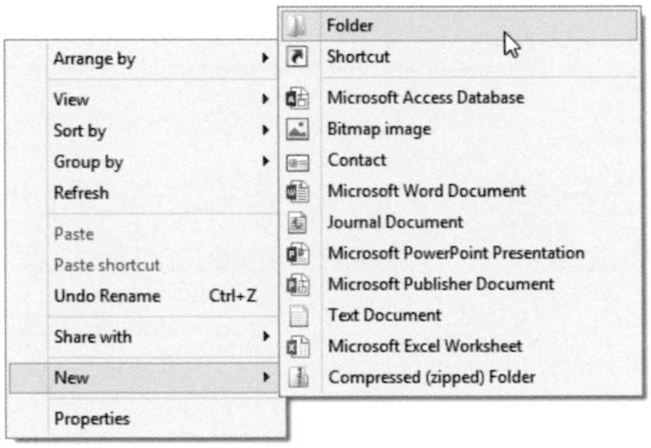

3. Overtype the name New Folder with the required name and press Enter (or click elsewhere)

If you create a folder or a file in a library such as Documents or Pictures, it will be created and stored within the library's default save location, for example the current user's My Documents or My Pictures.

Don't forget

Choose one of the file types, for example Microsoft PowerPoint Presentation, and it will be initially named as New Microsoft PowerPoint Presentation. Overtype this name, as shown for the New Folder.

Copy or Move Files

You can copy a file or files using the Windows clipboard.

1. Open the folder containing the file, right-click the file icon and select Copy (to record the file path)

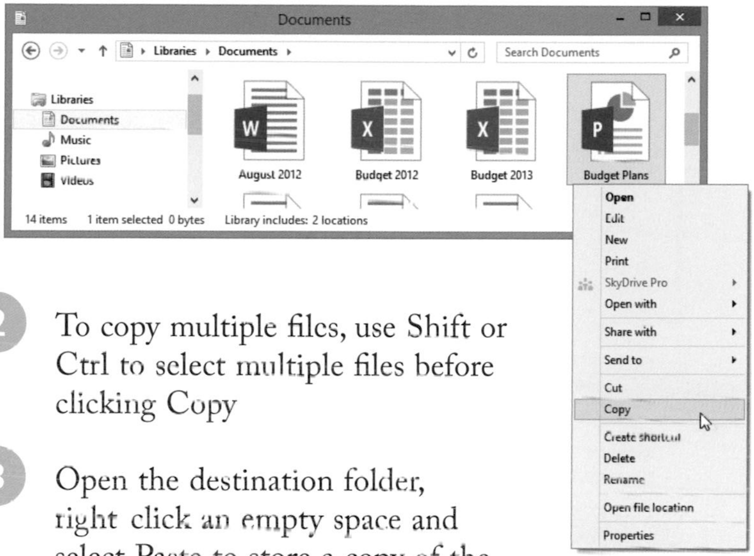

2. To copy multiple files, use Shift or Ctrl to select multiple files before clicking Copy

3. Open the destination folder, right click an empty space and select Paste to store a copy of the file in that folder

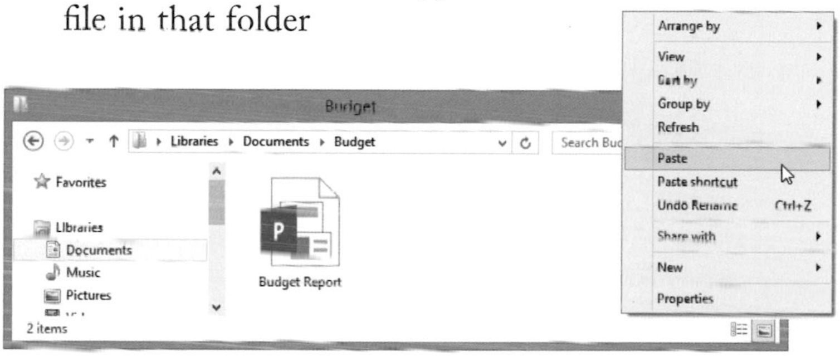

4. To move the file rather than make a copy, right-click and choose Cut

5. The original file icon will be dimmed until you select Paste, when it will be transferred in the new location

Hot tip

You could also select the file or files and then press the keyboard shortcut Ctrl + C for Copy.

Hot tip

Alternatively, select the folder and then press the keyboard shortcut Ctrl + V for Paste.

Hot tip

The keyboard shortcut is Ctrl + X to Cut the selected files.

...cont'd

To move or copy files using drag-and-drop operations:

1. Use File Explorer to locate and open the folder with the files you want to move

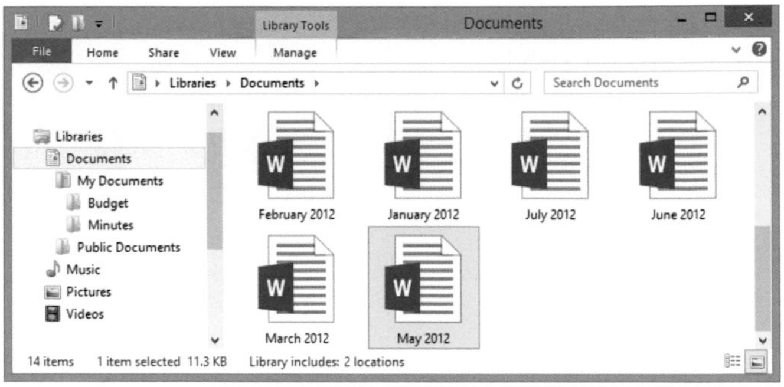

2. Select the first file then press the Ctrl key as you select the second and subsequent files

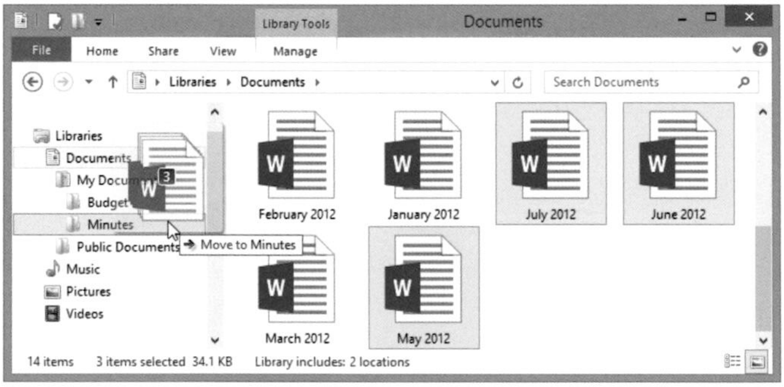

3. Click and hold any of the selected files, then drag the selection to the target folder and release there

4. To Copy rather than Move the files, hold down Ctrl as you drag and release the selection

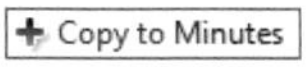

5. If the target folder is in a different drive, hold down Shift as you drag to Move, otherwise you will Copy

Hot tip

If the target folder isn't visible, locate it using the navigation pane, clicking the white triangles to expand the folders.

Don't forget

Drag using the Right mouse button rather than the Left. When you release the files, you get a menu to confirm the desired action (or Cancel).

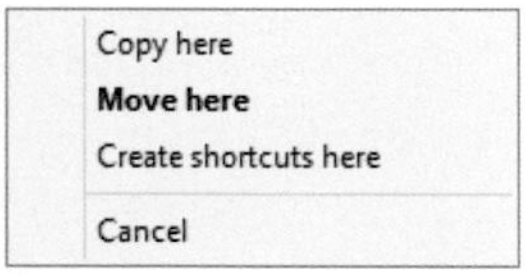

Beware

When the source and target folders are on different drives, the actions of the Ctrl and Shift keys are interchanged.

Delete Files

To remove files from a folder:

1. Select the file or files, right-click the selection and click the Delete command

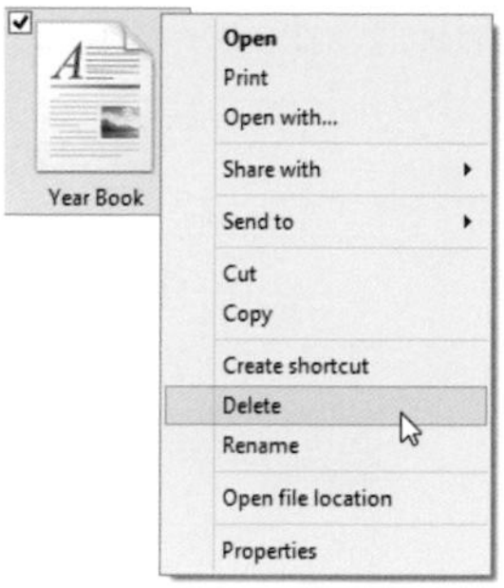

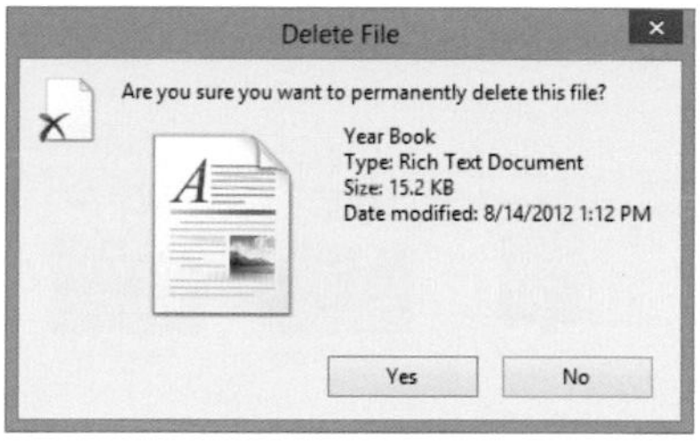

2. If the drive is other than your hard disk, you are asked to confirm permanent deletion

3. Files on the hard disk will be moved to the Recycle bin, with the warning message turned off

To recover a file deleted by mistake:

1. Right-click the Recycle bin and select Open (or just double-click)

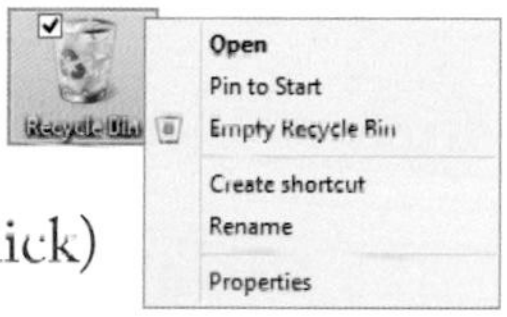

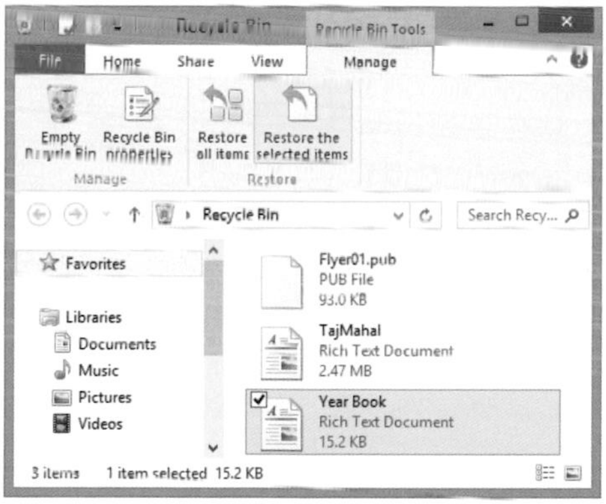

2. Select the file required and click Restore this item

Hot tip

Pressing the keyboard Delete key will have the same effect as selecting the Delete menu entry.

Don't forget

To remove hard disk files completely without using the Recycle bin as an interim store, hold down Shift as you select Delete.

Hot tip

If you'd prefer to turn on the warning message for hard disk files, click Recycle Bin Properties and select Display delete confirmation dialog.

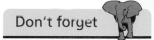

Folder Views

Hot tip

You can also change folder views using the File Explorer ribbon (see page 102)

File Explorer offers a variety of ways to view the files and subfolders contained in folders and libraries.

1. Open a library or folder, for example Documents and note the file list style in use (e.g. Large Icons)

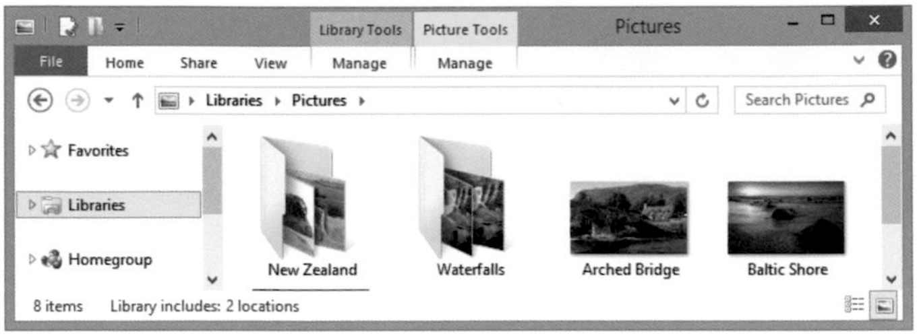

2. Right-click an empty part of the folder area and select the View command, to see the options with the current setting marked

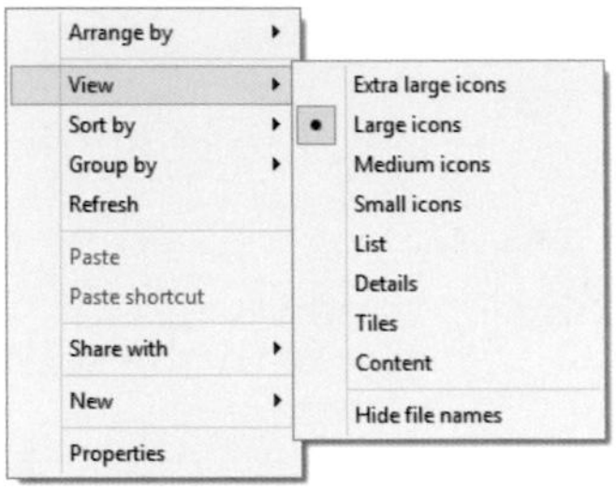
Arrange by
View
Sort by
Group by
Refresh
Paste
Paste shortcut
Share with
New
Properties
Extra large icons
Large icons
Medium icons
Small icons
List
Details
Tiles
Content
Hide file names

3. Choose any of the four icon sizes to see the effects

Extra Large icons

New Zealand
Pictures ▸ New Zealand
Search New Zealand
5 items

Large icons

Medium icons

Small icons

Don't forget

The folders illustrated here have their layouts changed (see page 105) to hide the navigation and details panes.

For icons sizes other than Small, you can Hide file names

Other views can offer more information about the files.

List

Details

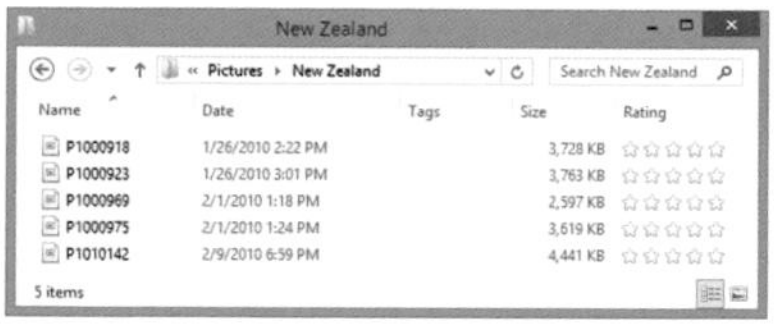

Tiles

Content

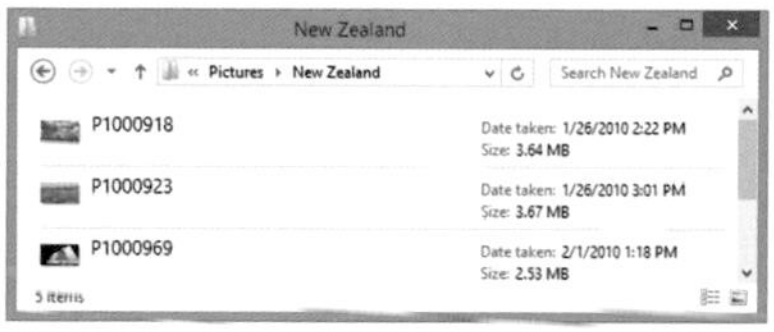

The details provided with the Content view depend on the file type and on the data provided when the file was created.

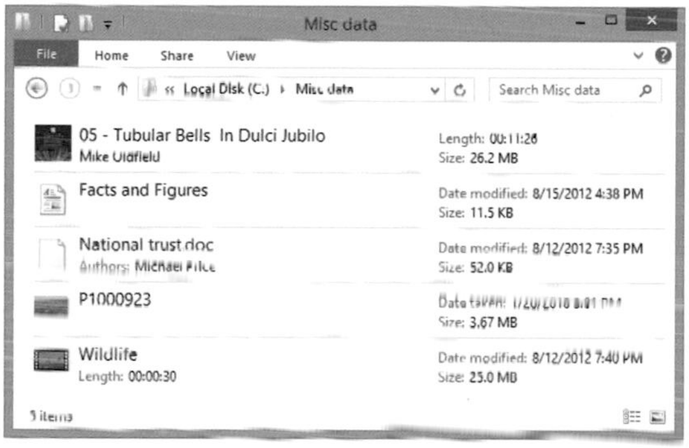

The right-click menu also offers Sort by and Group by, with attributes that depend on the type of file that the folder has been optimized for, i.e. Document, Music, Picture or Video.

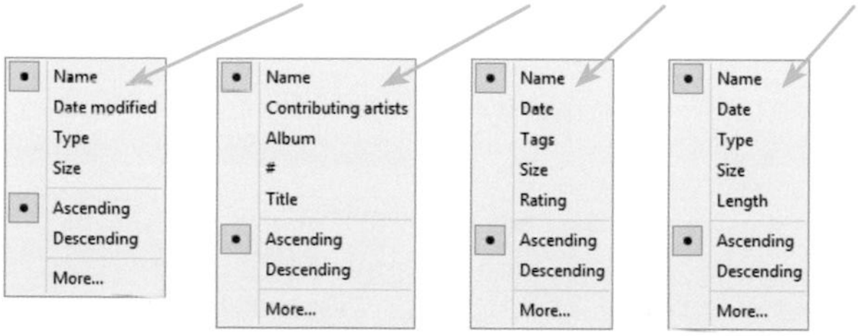

Don't forget

A file type icon rather than a thumbnail is used for the Small Icons, List and Details views.

Hot tip

As with Views, you can also change sort and group attributes using the File Explorer ribbon (see page 102).

File Explorer Ribbon

You can also manage the appearance of libraries and folders using File Explorer's Ribbon, a new feature in Windows 8.

Hot tip

The Ribbon can be set as Minimized, but it will be revealed whenever you select a tab (Home, Share, View or Manage).

1. Open File Explorer and select the Pictures library

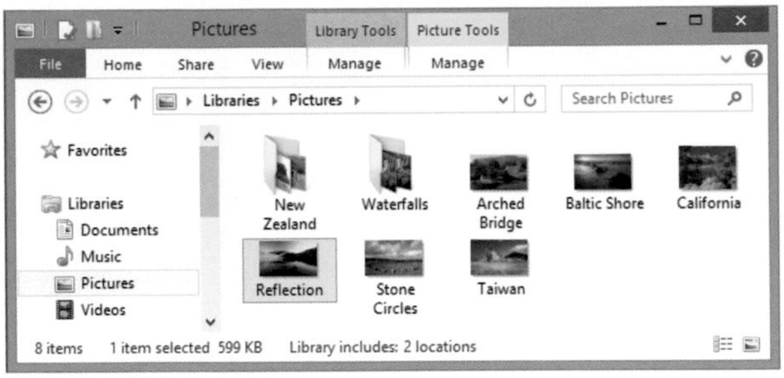

2. If there's no Ribbon, click a tab, e.g. the Home tab

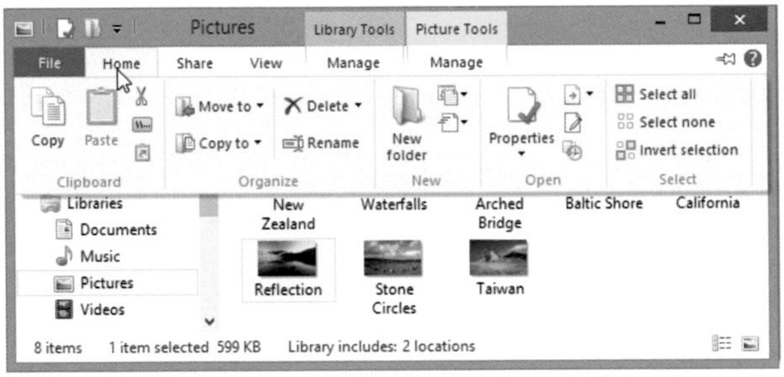

Don't forget

Where space permits, commands have icons with names. On the narrower window, some become icons only, or get put in drop-down boxes.

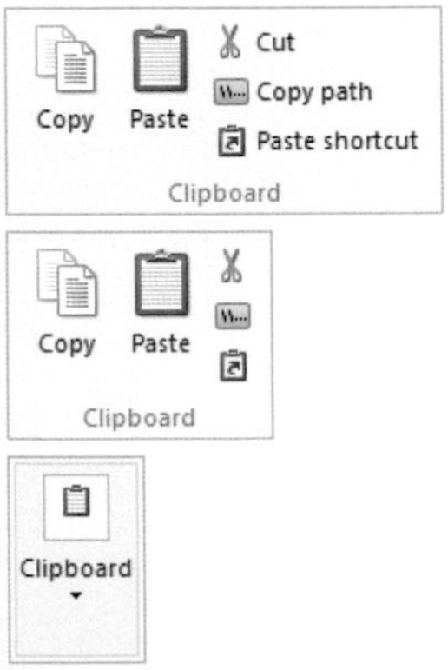

3. To always show the Ribbon, right-click the tab bar and select Minimize the Ribbon to untick

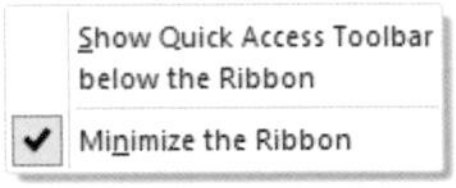

The Ribbon shows commands appropriate to the specific tab and grouped by function. Inactive commands are dimmed.

The Home Tab

The Ribbon has commands for handling items in the folder.

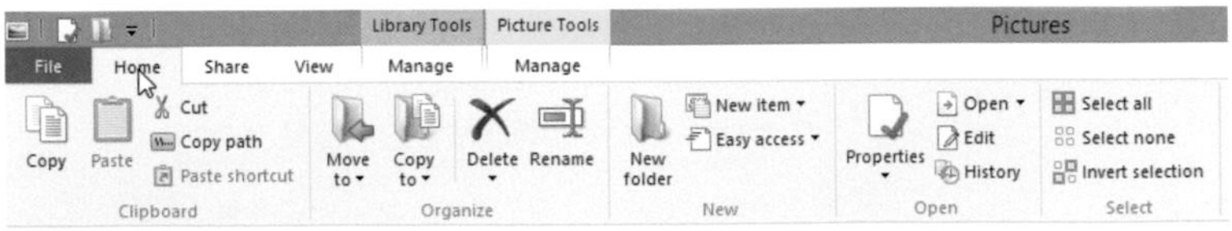

The Share Tab

These commands are to help you make files and folders available to other users.

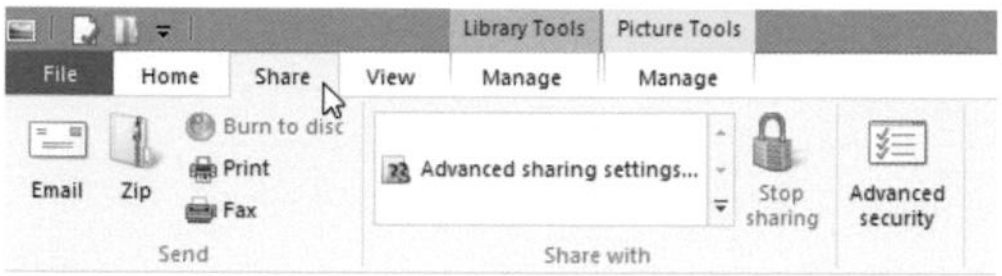
Library Tools
Picture Tools
File
Home
Share
View
Manage
Manage
Email
Zip
Burn to disc
Print
Fax
Send
Advanced sharing settings...
Share with
Stop sharing
Advanced security

The View Tab

With these commands you can control the layout of folders and the appearance of items in the folders.

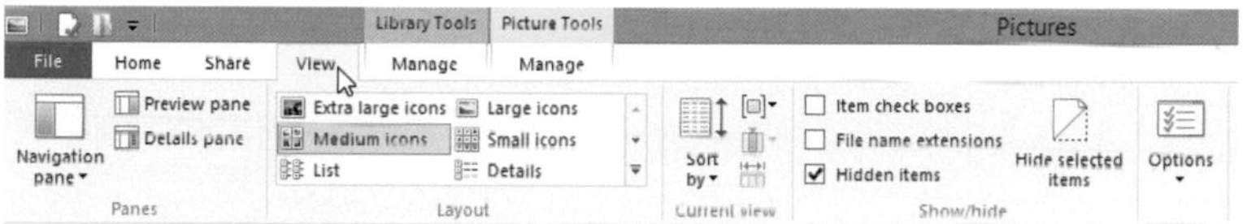
Library Tools
Picture Tools
Pictures
File
Home
Share
View
Manage
Manage
Navigation pane
Preview pane
Details pane
Panes
Extra large icons
Large icons
Medium icons
Small icons
List
Details
Layout
Sort by
Current view
Item check boxes
File name extensions
Hidden items
Hide selected items
Show/hide
Options

The Manage Tabs

These are commands that are specific to the type of folder – Library and Picture as shown and also Music and Video.

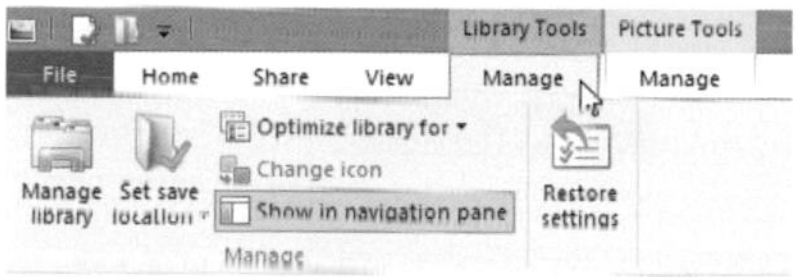

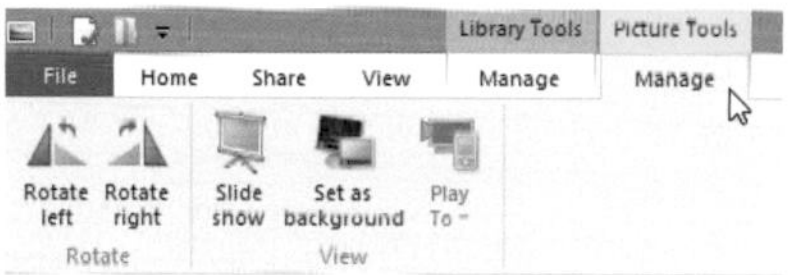
Library Tools
Picture Tools
File
Home
Share
View
Manage
Manage
Rotate left
Rotate right
Rotate
Slide show
Set as background
Play To
View

The File Menu

Select File to open new windows, access Help and Close File Explorer. If there's a folder (rather than a Library) displayed, you can open a Command Prompt at that location.

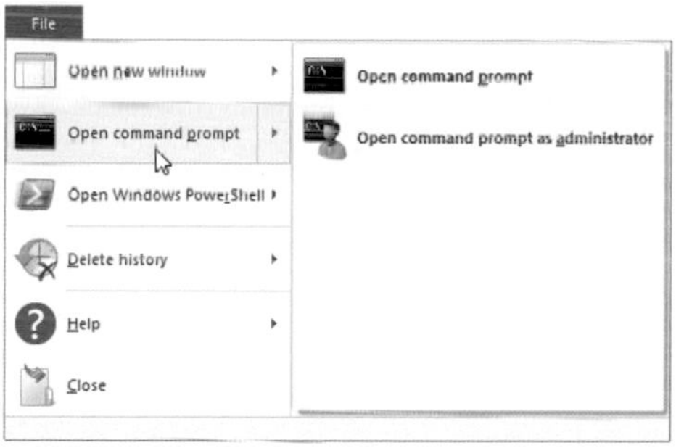

Don't forget

You can send files via email, burn files to CD or DVD and set up sharing across the network.

Hot tip

The Current view category includes Sort by and Group by and Show/hide allows you to reveal hidden files.

Don't forget

The Manage tools displayed are based on the type of file for which the library or folder has been optimized.

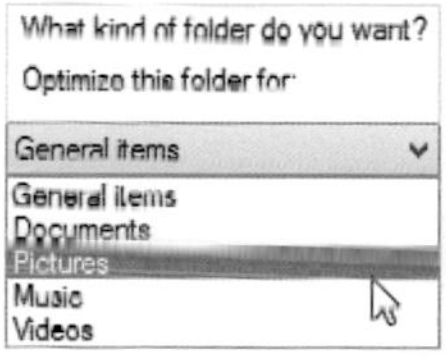
What kind of folder do you want?
Optimize this folder for:
General items
General items
Documents
Pictures
Music
Videos

File Explorer Layout

You can control how libraries, folders and files are displayed in the File Explorer window. To illustrate the options:

1. Open File Explorer and select the Pictures library

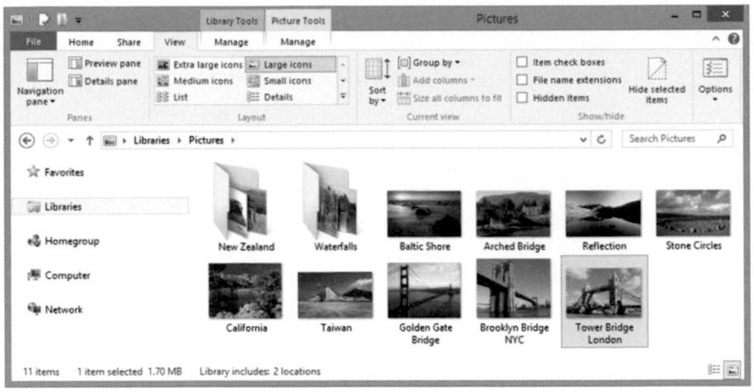

2. Click Preview pane and choose the Details view

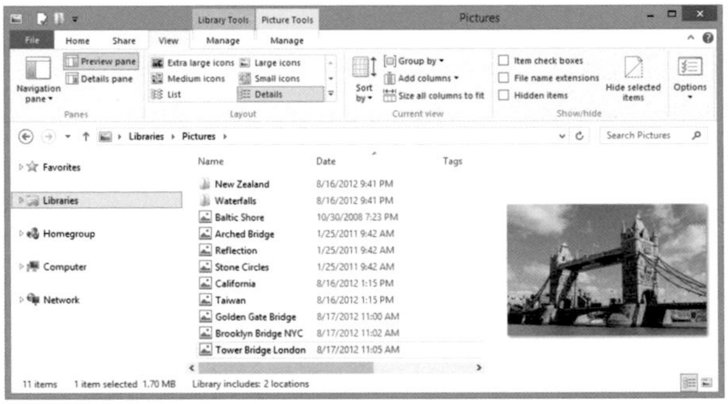

3. Click Details pane to switch and select List view

Don't forget

In this example, File Explorer shows the Ribbon, Navigation pane and Contents pane (with Large icons).

Hot tip

You can see a preview or extended details of the selected file, useful when you use list views rather than graphical icons for the folder contents.

Don't forget

Preview pane and Details pane act as toggles - select one to switch off the other, or reselect the active pane to turn both off.

4. Click the Navigation pane button to display or hide the Navigation pane and the Favorites entry on that pane

5. You can have the Navigation pane automatically expand to open folder

6. Show all folders puts the system folders, drives and network items in a hierarchical list starting at Desktop

7. To change the pane sizes, move the mouse pointer over the line separator and drag using the resize arrow, or resize the whole window

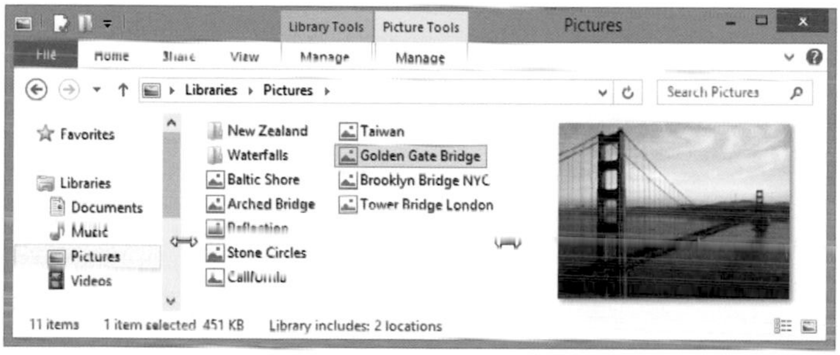

In the Documents library, if you select a Notepad or WordPad file, the text contents are shown in the Preview pane. For other file types, you will usually see the message No preview available.

To display just the folder contents in the File Explorer windows (as shown on page 100), clear all the Navigation pane options and deselect the Preview and Details panes.

Don't forget

By default, Favorites shows links for the Desktop, Downloads and Recent places.

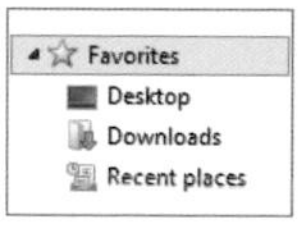

When you are at a folder you want to remember, right-click Favorites and select Add current location to Favorites.

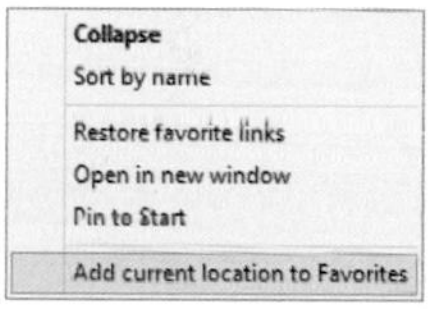

Hot tip

The preview image is automatically resized to make full use of the preview pane, while retaining the image proportions.

Search Box

If you want to access a file, but are not sure which subfolder it is in, you can start at the higher-level folder and use the Search box to find the exact location.

1. Open the Music library from File Explorer

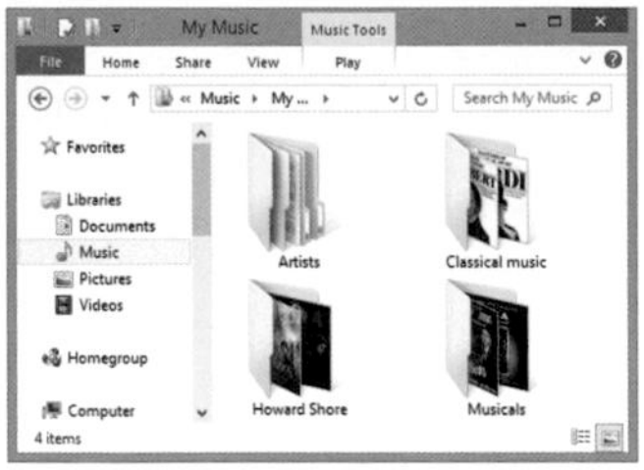

2. Click the Search box and start typing the search words, e.g. "love is all around"

3. As you type, matches so far are listed in the Search Results folder

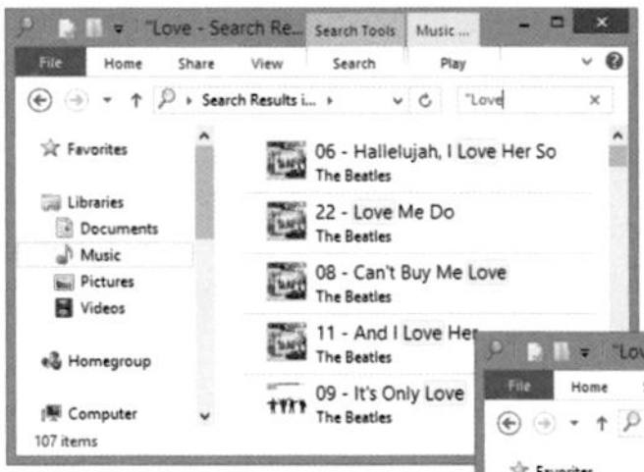

107 items

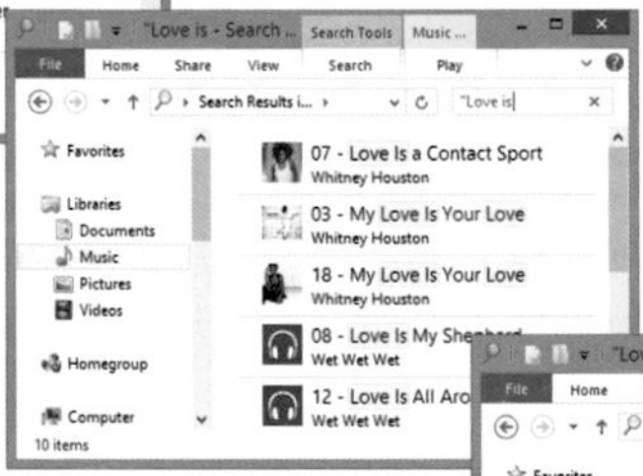

10 items

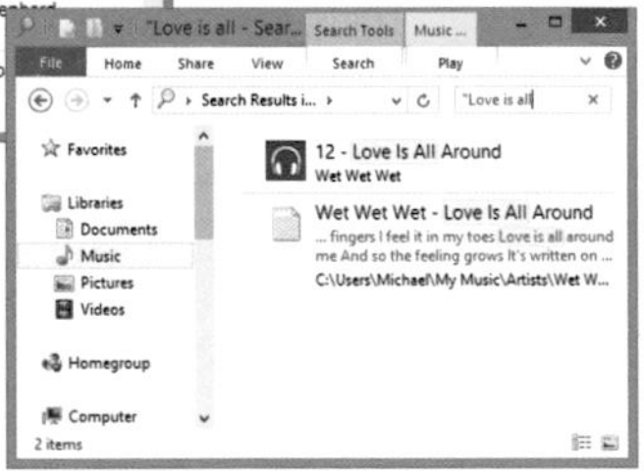

2 items

4. Stop typing when the results show the file you are seeking or when the full list fits in the window

In the example, the results include a song with the search text in its name and a document that contains the text.

Hot tip

Search looks for matches with file names, file types, text content, file tags and other file properties.

Hot tip

Start with a quotation mark to match a phrase rather than individual words. You don't have to worry about capitalization.

Don't forget

At any stage, you can select the required file from the list of results and double-click to open or run it.

Using the Search App

1. Display the Charms bar (see page 32) and select the Search App, click an appropriate category, e.g. Music and start typing text

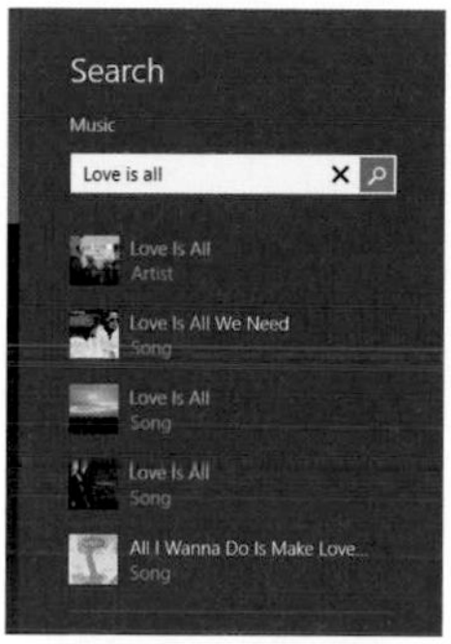

Don't forget

You can Search from the Start screen by typing the text, but it looks only at Apps, the default category.

2. Search looks in the Store as well as on the computer

Hot tip

Depending which category you choose, Search may look in multiple sources for matching items.

3. Click From all sources and select the local source, i.e. My music, to show the results on your computer only

Don't forget

There are keyboard shortcuts to start Search at a category: WinKey + F (Files) WinKey + Q (Apps) and WinKey + W (Settings).

Settings for Search App

Don't forget

You can control how the Search app operates, using the PC Settings (see page 62).

1. Press WinKey + I to display the Settings pane

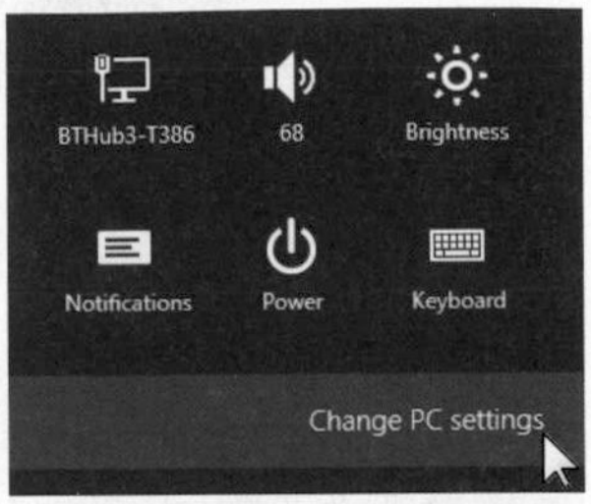

2. Click the button to Change PC Settings

3. Select the Search entry

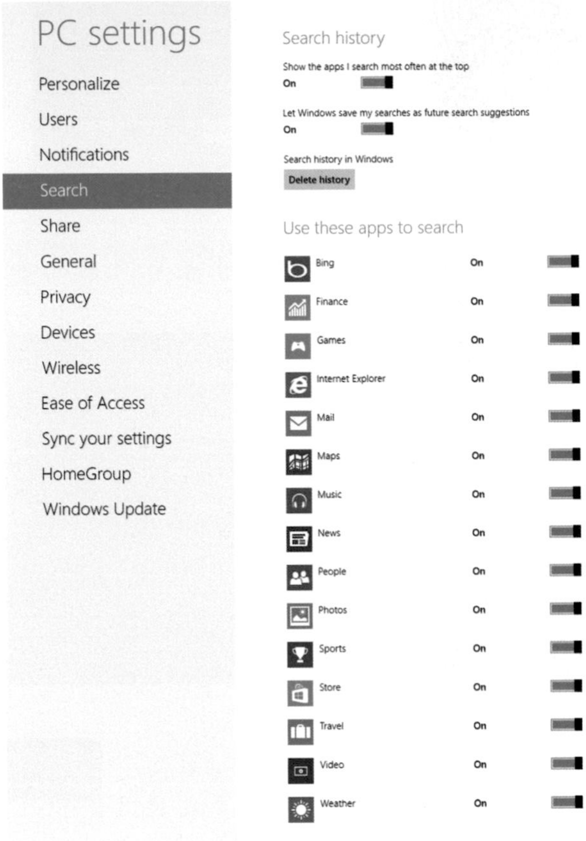
PC settings
Personalize
Users
Notifications
Search
Share
General
Privacy
Devices
Wireless
Ease of Access
Sync your settings
HomeGroup
Windows Update
Search history
Show the apps I search most often at the top
On
Let Windows save my searches as future search suggestions
On
Search history in Windows
Delete history
Use these apps to search
Bing On
Finance On
Games On
Internet Explorer On
Mail On
Maps On
Music On
News On
People On
Photos On
Sports On
Store On
Travel On
Video On
Weather On

Hot tip

Windows will show the apps you use most often at the top of the list and also save your searches as future suggestions. However, you can always choose to clear the search history.

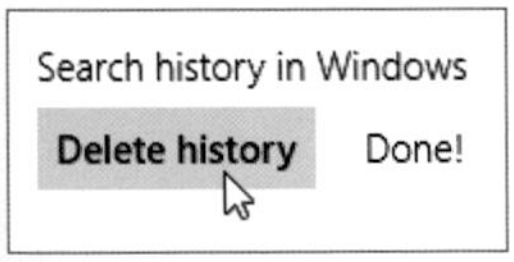

4. Click a button to turn off a search category. Click again to turn it back on

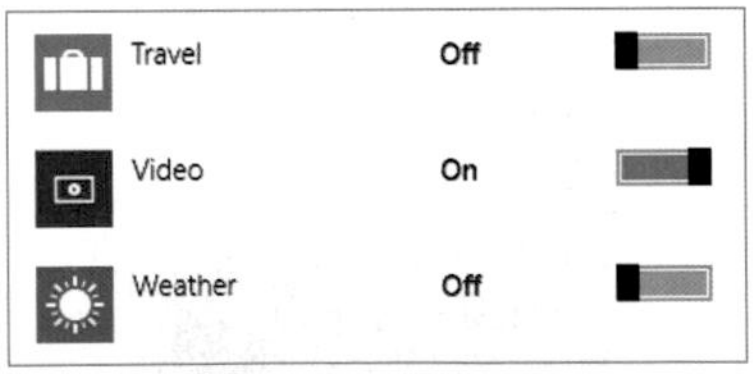
Travel Off
Video On
Weather Off

6 Desktop Applications

Windows 8 includes some useful Desktop applications for calculating, text editing, word processing and picture editing and you can search the Internet for external programs to handle other functions.

Conventional Applications

Windows 8 provides the operating environment for a variety of applications. In many cases, these are supplied as separate programs or suite of programs. However some of the desired functions may be in the form of small but potentially very useful programs included with Windows or Windows Essentials (see page 22). The main application areas and the related Windows programs are:

- Text processing — Notepad
- Word processing — WordPad
- Electronic mail — [see chapter 8]
- Drawing — Paint
- Spreadsheet — Calculator only
- Database — [no program]
- Multimedia — [see chapter 11]

For requirements that are not supported by the programs in Windows, you'll need to install separate programs or a suite of programs such as Adobe Acrobat or Microsoft Office. Even if you don't have these you may need readers and viewers, free programs that allow you to view the files created by those separate applications. You can also install Windows 8 apps from the Windows Store (see page 24).

Don't forget

These applications take advantage of Windows 8 features and can be pinned to the Start screen, but they do not operate as Windows 8 apps (see page 36).

Don't forget

We show you where you can find these applications and what's involved with downloading and installing them.

Calculator

While no substitute for a spreadsheet application, Windows Calculator provides quite powerful computational facilities.

1. Select Start, All Programs, Accessories, Calculator

2. Type or click to enter the first number, the operation symbol and the next number

3. Enter any additional operators and numbers and press = to end

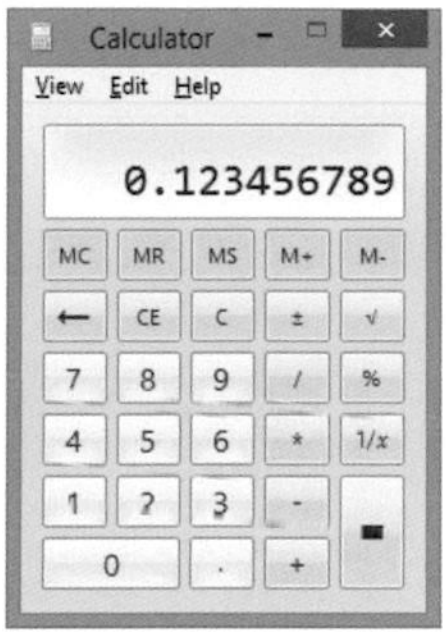
Calculator
View Edit Help
0.123456789
MC MR MS M+ M-
CE C ± √
7 8 9 / %
4 5 6 * 1/x
1 2 3 -
0 . + =

Click the calculator buttons or press the equivalent keyboard keys, to perform Add, Subtract, Multiply, Divide, Square Root, Percent and Inverse operations. You can also store and recall numbers from memory and the History capability keeps track of stages in the calculations.

Scientific, Programmer and Statistics views are also provided:

1. Open Calculator, select View and choose, for example, Scientific

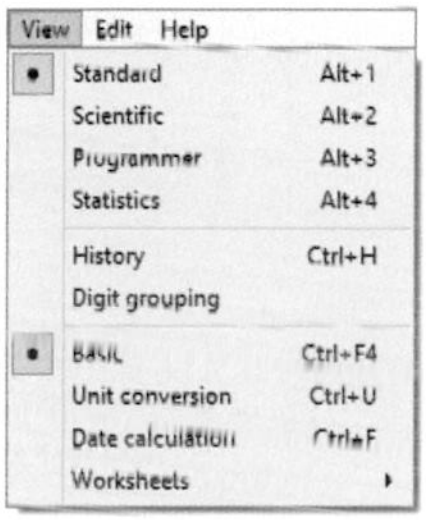
View Edit Help
Standard Alt+1
Scientific Alt+2
Programmer Alt+3
Statistics Alt+4
History Ctrl+H
Digit grouping
Basic Ctrl+F4
Unit conversion Ctrl+U
Date calculation Ctrl+E
Worksheets

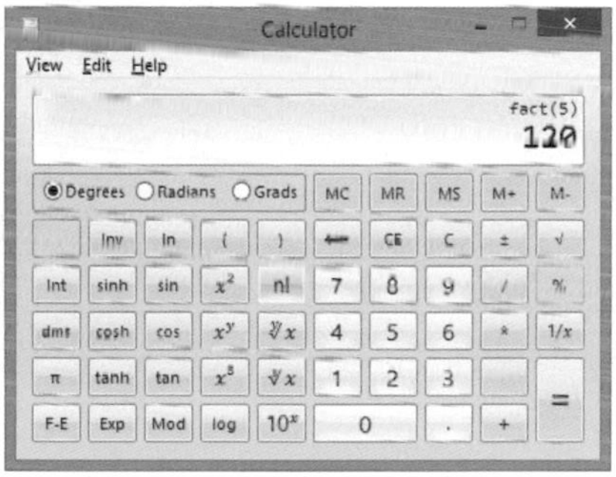

The Scientific calculator includes a variety of functions and inverse functions, including logarithms and factorials.

Windows Calculator also supports unit conversions, date calculations and some basic worksheet functions for mortgage, vehicle lease and fuel economy calculations.

Don't forget

You can also use the numeric keypad to type numbers and operators. Press Num Lock if it is not already turned on.

Don't forget

You will find other, specialized calculators in the Windows 8 App format, if you Search the Windows Store.

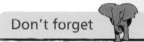

Notepad

Notepad is a text editor that you can use to create, view or modify text (.txt) files. It provides only very basic formatting and handles text a line at a time.

1. Search for Notepad at the Start screen and select the program, then type some text, pressing Enter for each new line

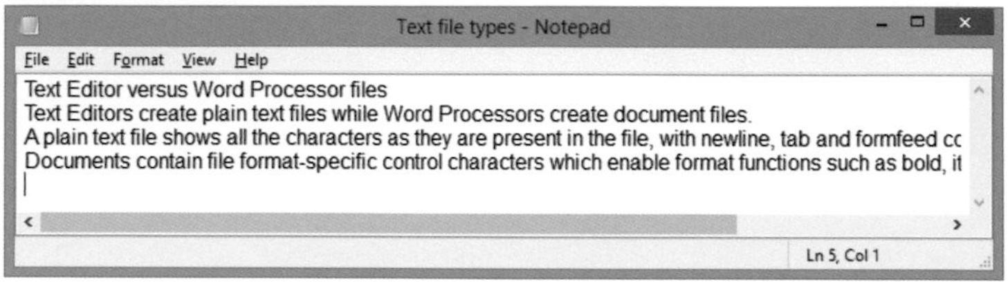

2. Select File, Save As and type the required file name (with file type .txt) then click Save

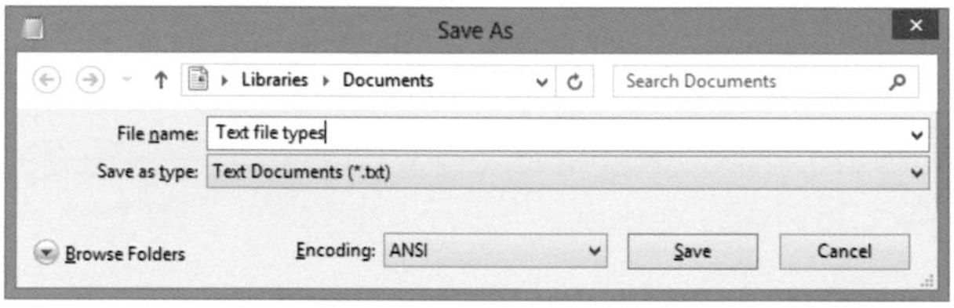

3. To show the whole of the long text lines in the window, select Format and click Word Wrap

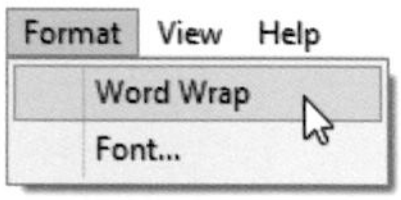

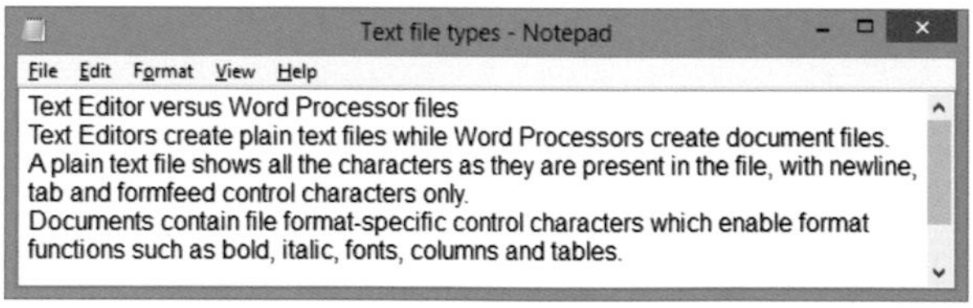

4. When you print the file, it will wrap according to the paper width, regardless of the word-wrap setting

Don't forget

The absence of formatting turns into a benefit when you are working with the source files for a program or the HTML code for a web page, since these require pure text.

Hot tip

Edit, Go To and type a line number to go to a specific line in the file (as shown in the Status bar).

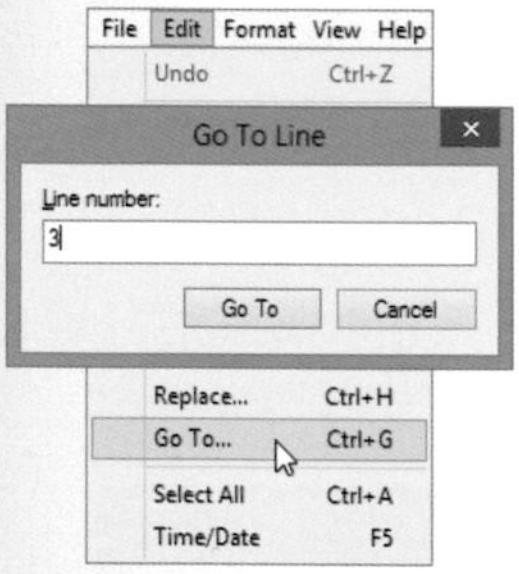

Beware

The Go To function is grayed and disabled and the Status bar is hidden, when you select the Word Wrap option.

WordPad

WordPad also offers text-editing, but adds tools and facilities for complex formatting of individual pieces of text.

1. Find and start the WordPad program and enter text, pressing Enter to start each new paragraph

WordPad

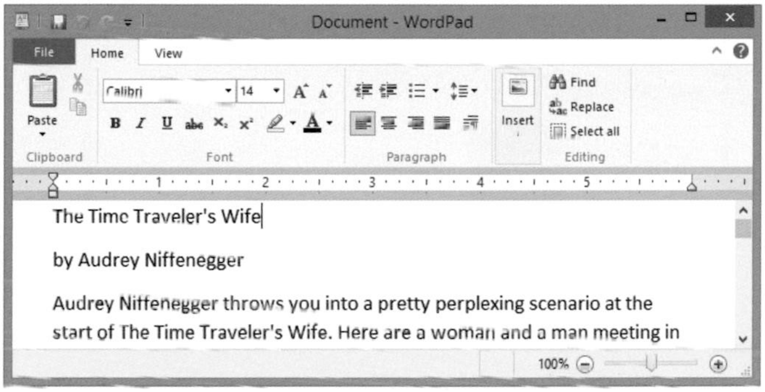

2. Use the formatting bar to change the font, size, style and color for selected (highlighted) text

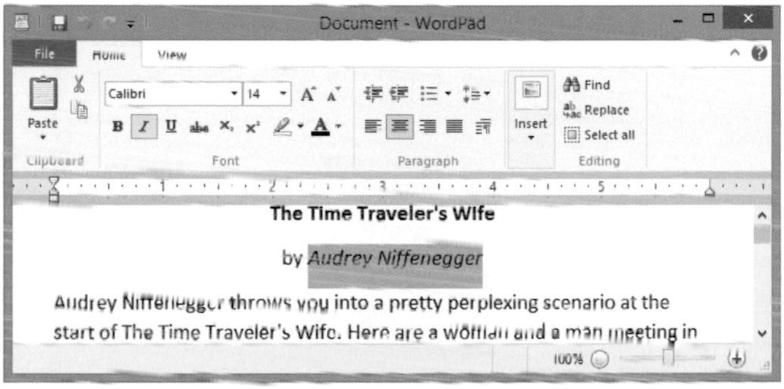

3. Click the Save button on the Quick Access Toolbar (or press Ctrl + S)

File
Home

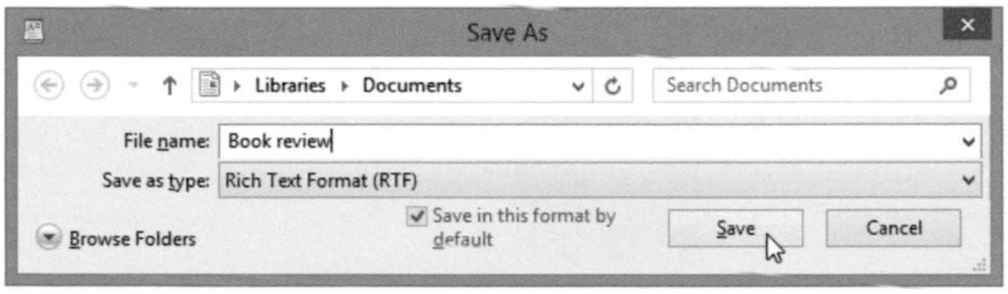
Save As
Libraries
Documents
Search Documents
File name:
Book review
Save as type:
Rich Text Format (RTF)
Save in this format by default
Browse Folders
Save
Cancel

Don't forget

WordPad uses the ribbon rather than a menu bar. There are two tabs: Home and View. The File button provides Save, Setup and Print functions.

Hot tip

Click the left, center or right alignment button to adjust the positioning of the selected paragraph or line of text.

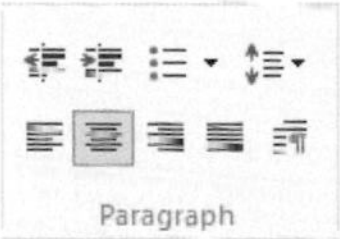

Don't forget

Save WordPad documents as .rtf (Rich Text Format) to retain the text formatting. Saving as .txt will remove the formatting (and images or links).

Insert Pictures

WordPad also allows you to include pictures in documents.

1. Position the typing cursor and click the Picture button in the Insert group on the Home tab

2. Locate and select the picture file then click Open

3. A copy of the image is added to the document and displayed at the cursor location

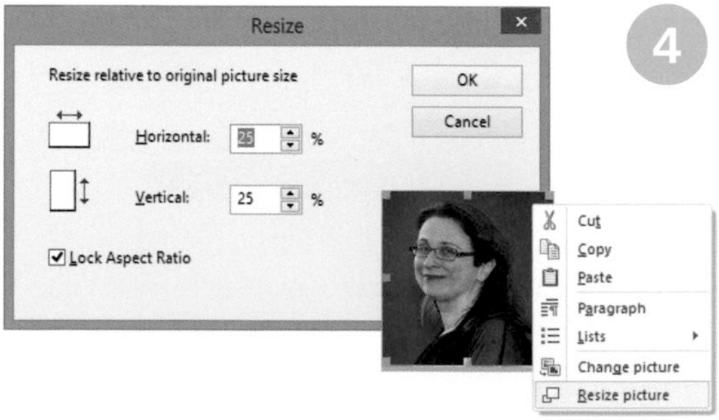

4. Right-click the picture and select Resize picture and choose the scale required

Hot tip

You can also click the Paint drawing button, to insert a drawing you create using Microsoft Paint.

Don't forget

WordPad can open text files in a variety of formats, including Open XML, Unicode Text and Microsoft Office .docx (but not the older .doc format).

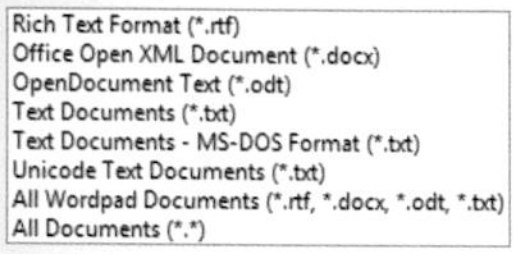
Rich Text Format (*.rtf)
Office Open XML Document (*.docx)
OpenDocument Text (*.odt)
Text Documents (*.txt)
Text Documents - MS-DOS Format (*.txt)
Unicode Text Documents (*.txt)
All Wordpad Documents (*.rtf, *.docx, *.odt, *.txt)
All Documents (*.*)

Paint

Paint is a digital sketchpad that can be used to draw, color and edit pictures. These can be images that you create from scratch, or you can modify existing pictures, such as digital photographs or a web page graphics. For example:

1. Find and Run the Paint program, to start with a blank canvas

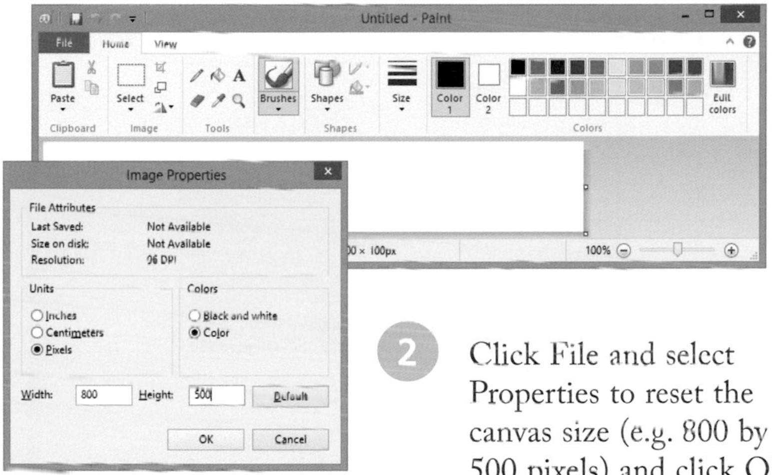

2. Click File and select Properties to reset the canvas size (e.g. 800 by 500 pixels) and click OK

3. Select the arrow below Paste, select Paste From, locate a picture to add to the canvas and click Open

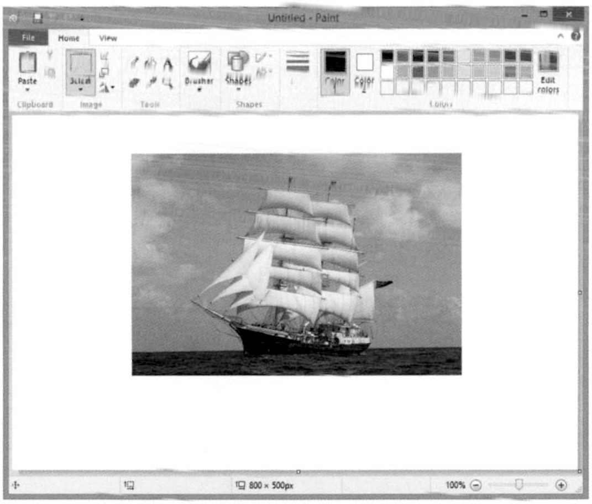

4. Drag the image to position it

Hot tip

Although it is a simple image editor, Paint can be used to create very complex images, a pixel at a time if required.

Don't forget

If the pasted image is larger than the canvas, the canvas will automatically be extended to hold the picture.

...cont'd

5 Select the Rounded Rectangle tool then click and drag to draw a frame around the picture

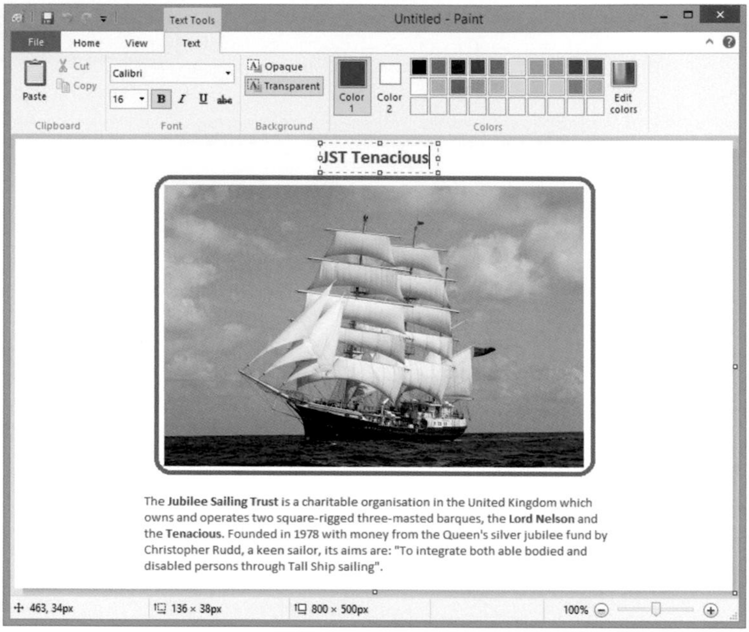

Hot tip

Draw a second frame and use the Fill tool to color the space between the frames.

6 Use the Text tool to draw a text box and add information such as a description of the contents

7 To make changes, select the View tab and the Zoom in button, or the View tab and the Magnifier

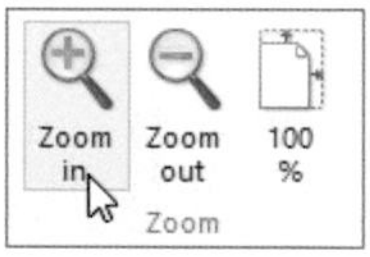

8 When you've finished changes, select File, Save, type the file name and click Save

Tools

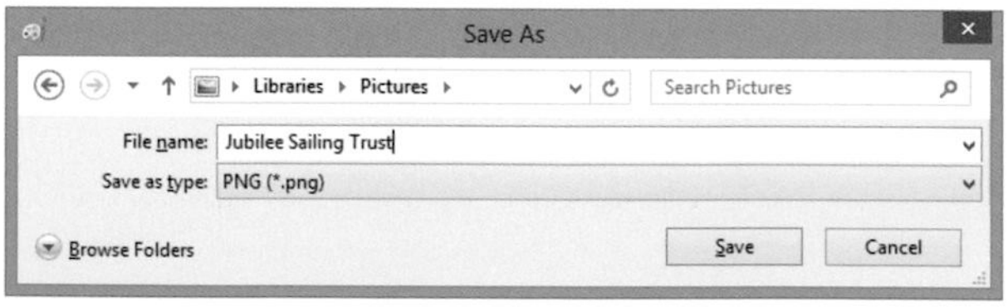
Save As
Libraries
Pictures
Search Pictures
File name:
Jubilee Sailing Trust
Save as type:
PNG (*.png)
Browse Folders
Save
Cancel

Don't forget

Choose a suitable file type such as .jpeg for pictures, or .png for documents, Paint also supports .bmp, .gif and .tif file formats.

Unknown File Types

Windows and its applications cannot help when you receive attachments or download files of unknown file types.

1. If there are unknown file types in your Downloads folder, the extensions (normally hidden) are displayed

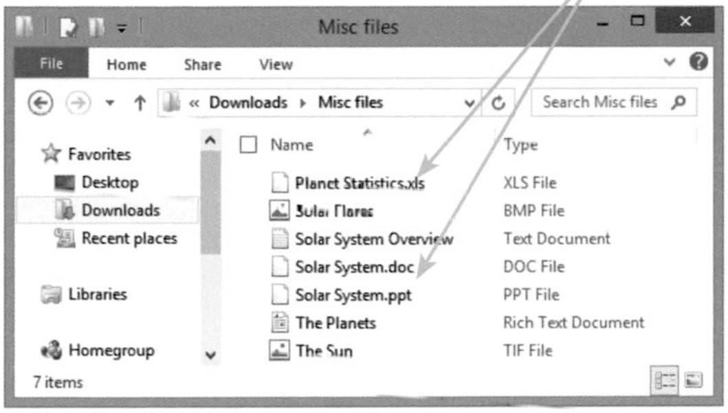

2. Double-click an unknown type e.g. Solar System.doc and you are asked how you want to open it

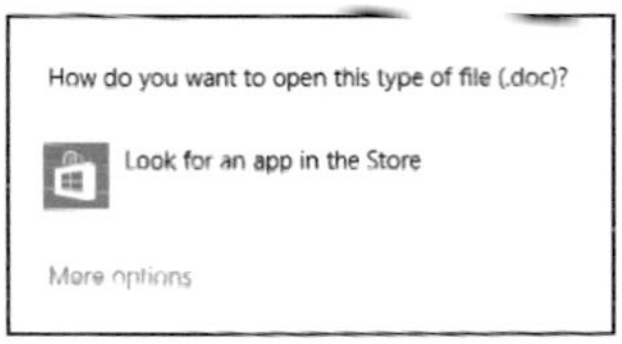

How do you want to open this type of file (.doc)?
Look for an app in the Store
More options

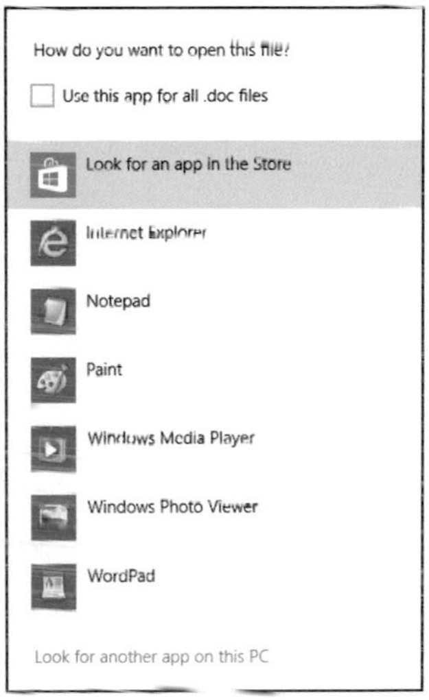

3. Click More options to view suggested programs. If none are suitable, select Look for another app on this PC or else select Look for an app in the Store, to see what's there

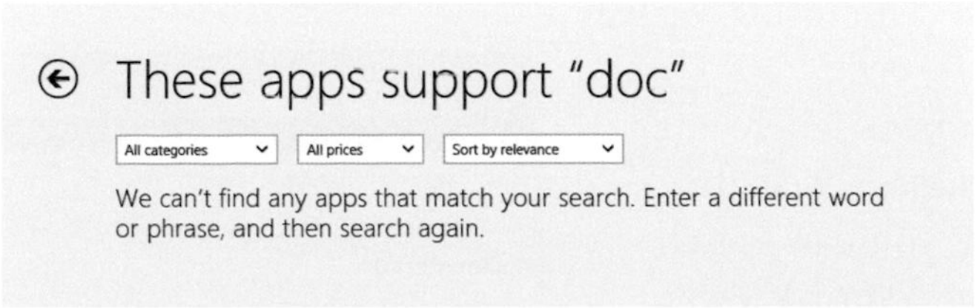

These apps support "doc"
All categories
All prices
Sort by relevance
We can't find any apps that match your search. Enter a different word or phrase, and then search again.

Don't forget

You can also right-click the file and select Open with, to get the list of suggestions.

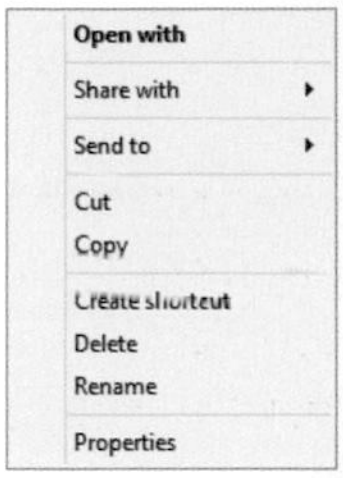

Open with
Share with
Send to
Cut
Copy
Create shortcut
Delete
Rename
Properties

Hot tip

If there's nothing suitable, just press Escape. Anything you choose gets remembered, even if it doesn't work for that file type.

Beware

In previous releases, Windows offered a Web service to look for suitable programs. The Store is less likely to find solutions, so you may want to search the Internet yourself (see page 118).

Search Web for Software

If there's no obvious choice from the Windows suggestions, you can search on the Internet for suitable software.

1. To get information about the use and purpose of an unknown file type go to FilExt at http://filext.com

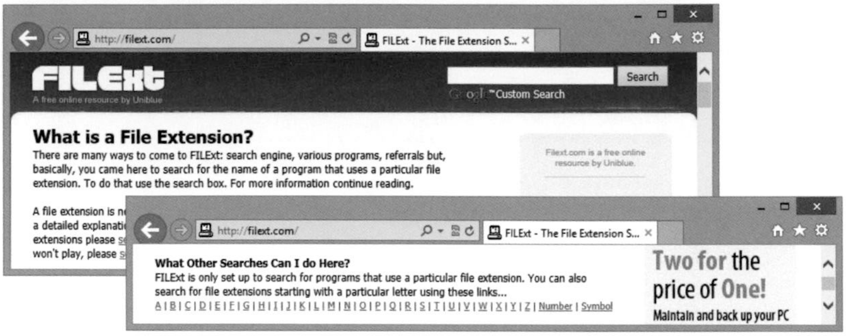

2. Scroll down to the alphabetic index and select a letter, e.g. D

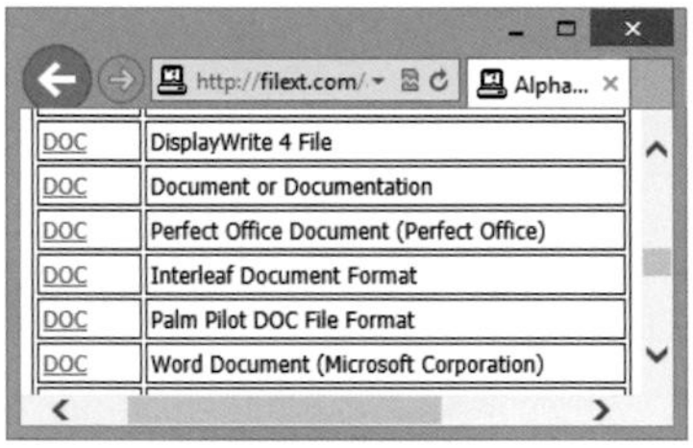

http://filext.com/
Alpha...
DOC DisplayWrite 4 File
DOC Document or Documentation
DOC Perfect Office Document (Perfect Office)
DOC Interleaf Document Format
DOC Palm Pilot DOC File Format
DOC Word Document (Microsoft Corporation)

3. Locate .DOC and click the best choice

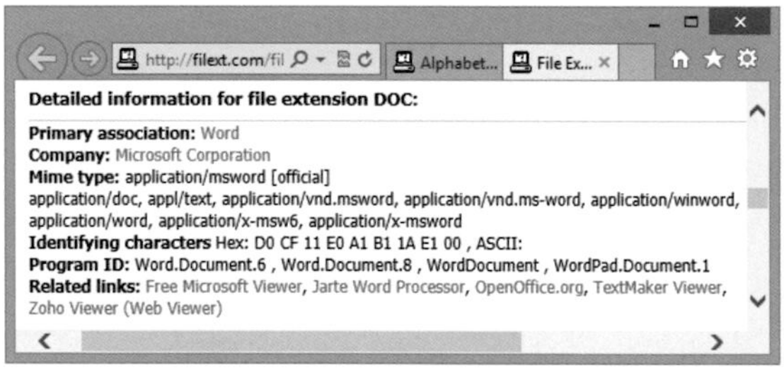

4. Select one of the Related links, for example Free Microsoft Viewer

This opens Microsoft's Downloads website, where you can search for the Word Viewer.

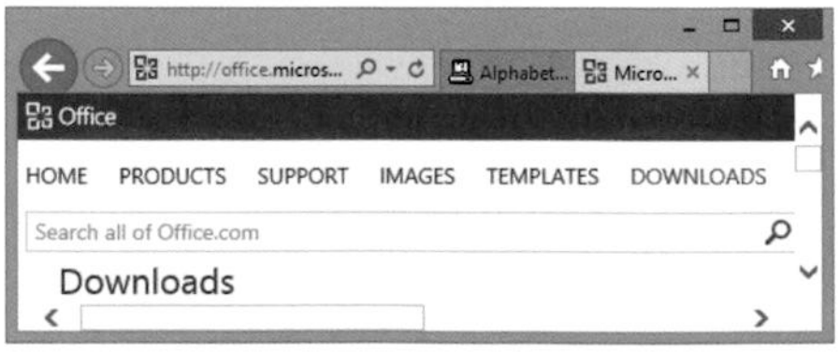

Don't forget

FilExt is a free online service by UniBlue, the PC Tools supplier. They, of course, take the opportunity to remind you about their products.

Don't forget

The .doc extension has been used by many programs over the years. Microsoft Word is the most likely entry in this case.

Hot tip

Microsoft also provides free viewers for other Office applications including Access, Excel, PowerPoint and Visio.

5 Type Word Viewer and click the Search button

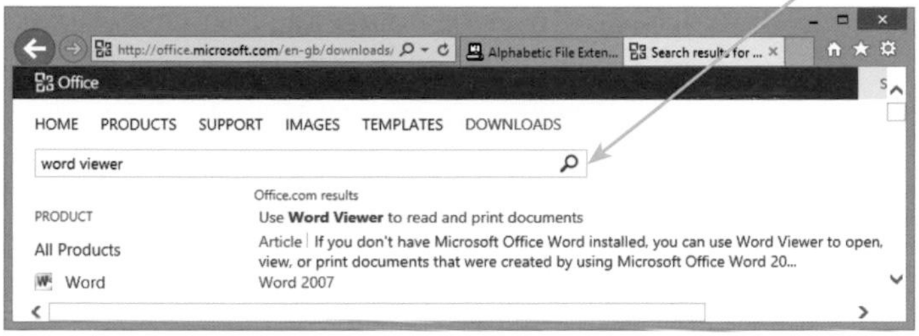

6 Follow the links to Download and Run the Setup program, accept the terms and Install Word Viewer

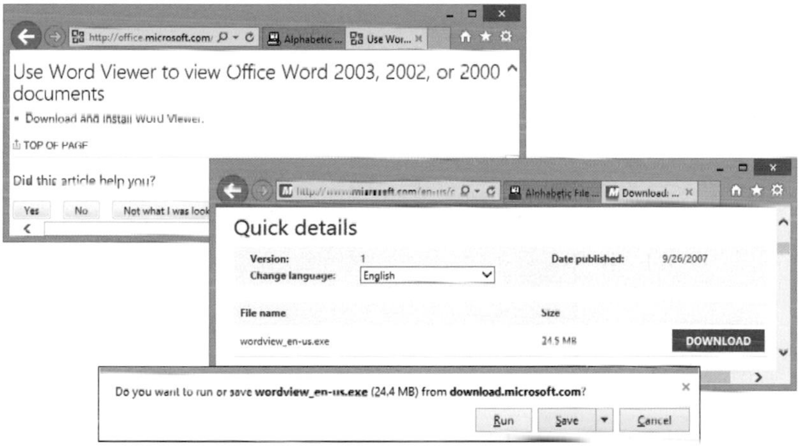

Don't forget

A tile for Microsoft Word Viewer will be added to the Start screen, in the next available space on the right hand side.

7 The .doc files are now recognized, file extension is hidden and the documents open in Word Viewer

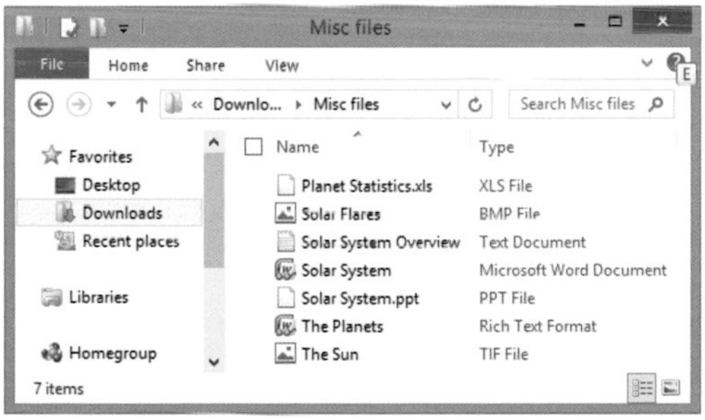

Beware

Word Viewer will also become the default program for the .rtf (Rich Text Format) files previously handled by WordPad.

Change Default Program

To restore WordPad as the default program for .rtf files:

1. Right-click any .rtf file and select Open With then Choose default program

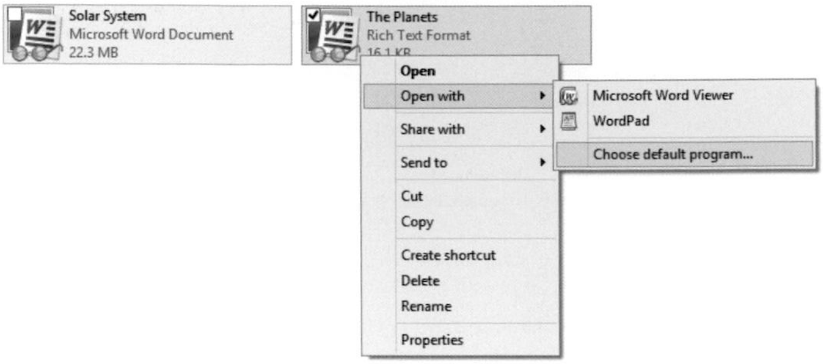

2. Select the option to Use this app for all .rtf files, then click WordPad

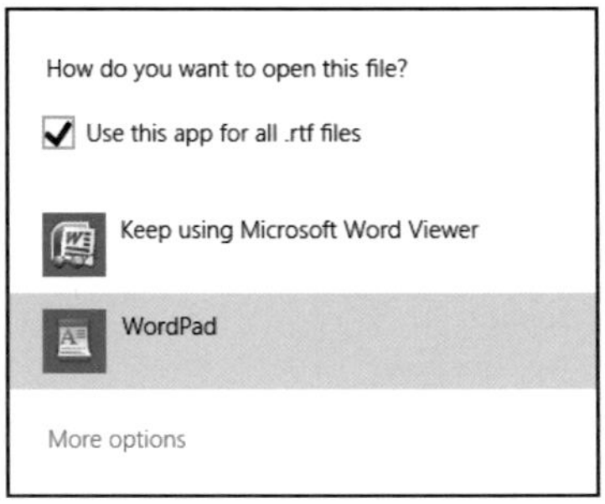

3. The .rtf files now have WordPad as the default, while .doc files still have Microsoft Word Viewer

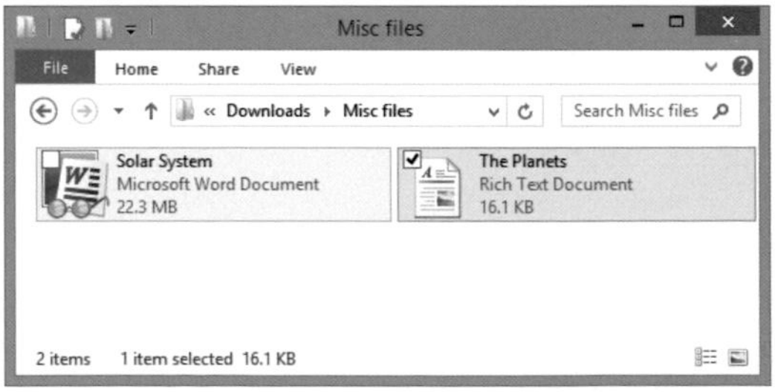

Hot tip

You may wish to change the default program that is associated with a particular file type.

Hot tip

To open a file with a particular program, without changing the default, clear the box then choose the program.

Don't forget

The icon that is associated with a file indicates which program is the default for that file type.

7 Windows 8 Apps

The emphasis is on the new full screen Windows 8 functions. Some, such as Reader and SkyDrive, are supplied at installation time. However, there are many Windows 8 apps at the Windows Store, where you search, review descriptions, then download and install apps on your system.

122 Sources for Apps

123 Supplied with Windows 8

124 Reader

126 SkyDrive

128 Windows Store Categories

129 Books & Reference

130 Search Windows Store

131 Installing Apps

132 Your App Account

133 Updates

134 Desktop Apps

136 Desktop Apps Available

Sources for Apps

Don't forget

In the past, Windows applications have been available from many sources, including supplier and enthusiast websites, as well as Microsoft. Sources for Windows 8 apps are much more limited.

Although desktop and conventional applications are supported (see page 44), the main functions are provided by the new-style Windows 8 apps. As already discussed these are full screen programs, except when Windows 8 Snap allows a second app to share the screen.

The primary design point for the Windows 8 apps is the touch screen as exemplified by the tablet PC, but all the apps can also be operated on a system with standard monitor, mouse and keyboard equipment.

The Window 8 apps that are available can be found in just two places:

1. Supplied and installed with Windows 8

This is a typical Start screen for a newly-installed Windows 8 system, showing some of the Windows 8 apps you may expect to find installed.

2. For Download from the Windows Store

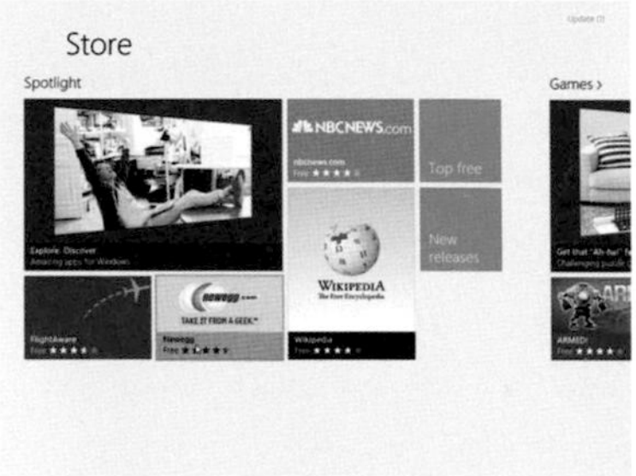

The range of Windows 8 apps and Desktop apps available at the Windows Store can be expected to change frequently, as new products are added and others removed or revised.

Beware

All Windows 8 apps must be submitted to Microsoft for certification before they are allowed in the Windows Store (or included on installation discs).

Programs submitted to Microsoft can also include Desktop apps. These are conventional applications that are listed at the Windows Store, but provided from the manufacturer's website, via a link that is included with the application description. These and other conventional apps may still be obtained directly, without visiting the Windows Store.

Supplied with Windows 8

The details may change with updates to Windows 8, but these are the Windows 8 apps that were initially included on the installation disc.

There are 21 Windows 8 apps shown on the All apps screen. Tiles for all except Reader can be found by default on the Start screen. These are all true Windows 8 apps. However, some of them (Camera, Internet Explorer, Maps, Reader and SkyDrive) are given Small tiles that cannot be resized (a restriction that's normally associated with Desktop apps). Other apps (Games, Music, Store and Video) have Small tiles but these can be resized.

Some of these apps, such as Mail, Internet Explorer, Music, Photos and Video, will be discussed in the relevant chapters on the specific topics.

On the following pages we will look more closely at the Reader and some of the other apps.

Don't forget

From the Start screen, press the WinKey + Z keys to display the Apps bar and click the All Apps button.

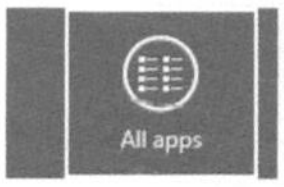

Hot tip

To resize a tile, right-click and from the Apps bar select Smaller or Larger as appropriate. There's no option provided for tiles that cannot be resized.

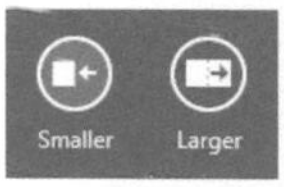

Reader

This is Microsoft's own app for reading Adobe PDF (Portable Document Format) files. It isn't normally added to the Start screen, but you can add it if you wish.

1. Display the Apps screen and right-click Reader

2. Select Pin to Start

3. The first time you start Reader, it tells you there's no recent history and suggests you browse for PDF or XPS files

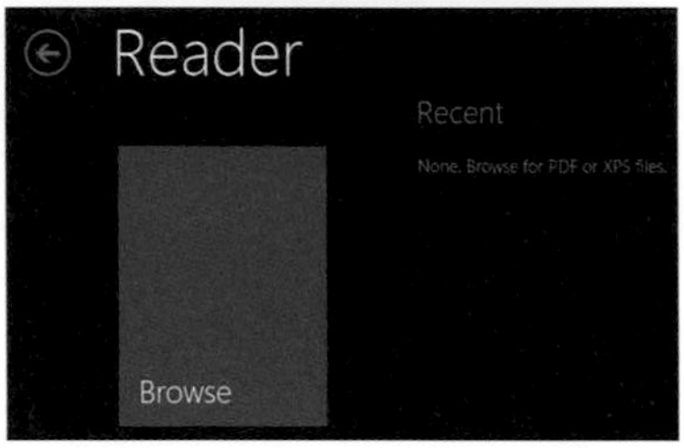

4. In future, it will remember the last document viewed and open that one

More typically, you might come across a PDF file while checking your folders and decide to view that file.

1. Double-click the PDF file (or select and press Enter)

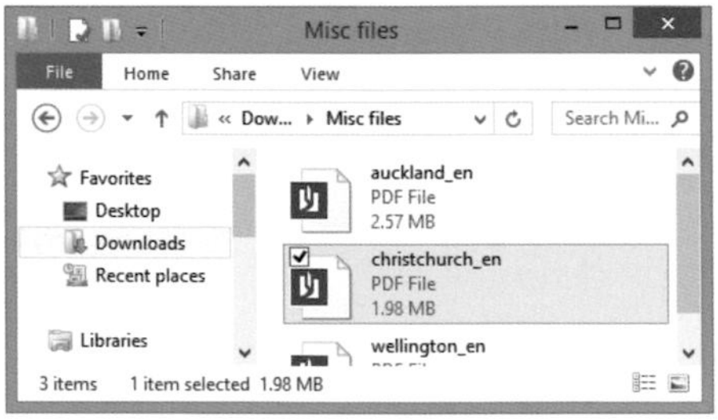

2. If not already active, the Reader app is launched

Don't forget

It is not considered necessary to have Reader on the Start screen, since it is usually launched from File Explorer where the required file is located.

Hot tip

Reader is designed to handle Adobe's PDF files and the Microsoft equivalent, XPS files.

3 The PDF is loaded with the first page displayed

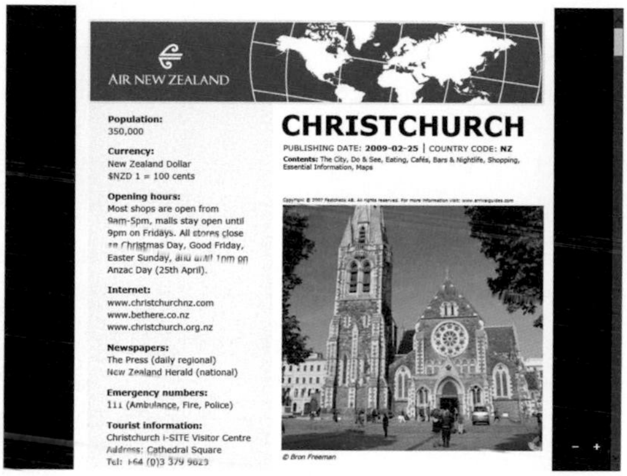

4 Right-click the screen to display the App bar

5 Find text, or select Two page or One page view

6 Click More to Rotate, get Info or Close

7 You can annotate the PDF and Save

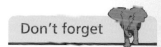

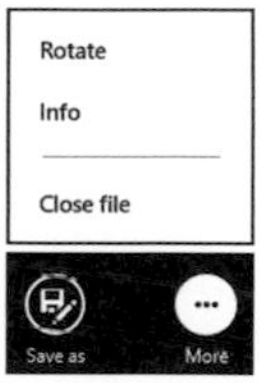

Hot tip

You can Zoom the picture by pinching on a touch system, using Crtl + - or Ctrl + =, with Ctrl + mouse wheel, or by clicking the - and + buttons.

Don't forget

By default, Reader uses continuous display and scrolls vertically, but you can select full page views and scroll horizontally.

Don't forget

Press Ctrl + P to Print, or open the Charms bar and select Devices and Printer.

SkyDrive

Microsoft SkyDrive is a file hosting service that allows you to upload and sync files to a cloud storage facility and then access them from a Web browser or your local computer (or other device). It allows you to keep your files private, or share them with your contacts, or make the files public.

The service offers 7 GB of free storage for new users. Additional storage is available for purchase. Files up to 300 MB can be uploaded via drag and drop into the web browser, or up to 2 GB via the Microsoft SkyDrive desktop app (see page 134). To access your SkyDrive:

1. Switch to the Start screen and click the SkyDrive tile

2. The application launches

3. If you are currently signed in with a local account, you are asked for your Microsoft account

4. The SkyDrive for your account is displayed showing the top level

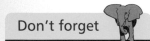

Hot tip

You need a Microsoft account to create a SkyDrive or to share another user's Skydrive, but publicly-shared files do not require a Microsoft account for access.

Don't forget

Right-click the App window to display the App bar with the options Refresh, New Folder, Upload, Details and Select All.

5. Click the Documents folder to see the contents

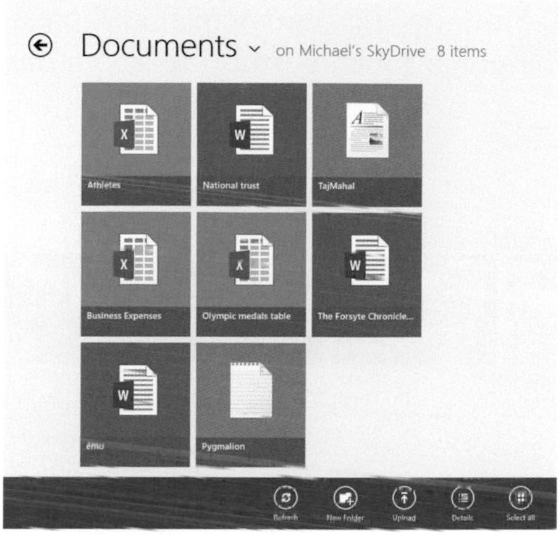

6. Again right-click the window to show the Apps bar
7. Click the Details button to switch the file view

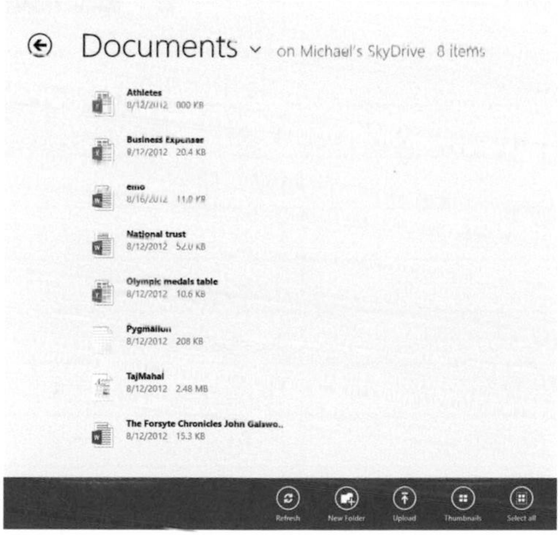

Click (or touch) a document to open it with the associated application for the file type, e.g. NotePad for .txt. However, in the case of Office documents, it uses the associated Office Web App, rather than an application on your computer.

Don't forget

There are just Details and Thumbnails views and switching at any level affects all the other folders.

Hot tip

To download, right-click to select the files and choose Download from the Apps bar. You can also Delete the selection, or choose Open with (for single files only).

Windows Store Categories

The Windows 8 apps in the Windows Store are grouped into a number of categories. To see what's offered:

1. Click Store on the Start screen and press Ctrl + - (or use the pinch touch gesture) to zoom out

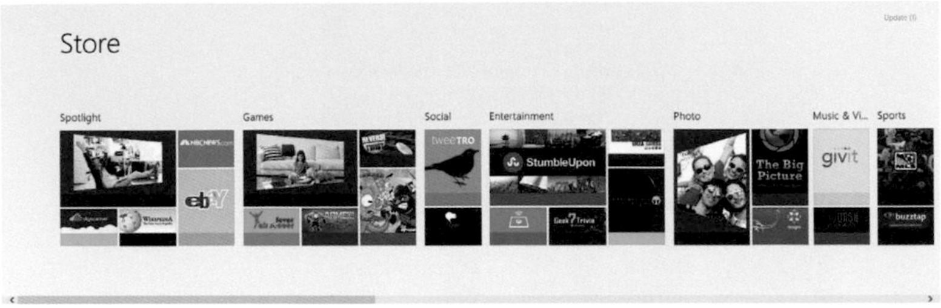

2. Scroll horizontally to identify all the categories

The Spotlight at the beginning includes apps from several categories and these are recommended to start you off using Windows 8 apps (see page 24). There are 20 categories covering the following areas:

Games	Lifestyle
Social	Shopping
Entertainment	Travel
Photo	Finance
Music & Video	Productivity
Sports	Tools
Books & Reference	Security
News & Weather	Business
Health & Fitness	Education
Food & Dining	Government

3. Click on a category, e.g. Books & Reference, (or press Ctrl + =, or use the stretch gesture) to zoom in and examine the category in more detail

Hot tip

The Zoom function provides two views, usually one close up and one wide angle to show more of the contents at once. This feature is available for all Windows 8 apps.

Don't forget

Each Windows 8 App is assigned to a specific category. It may also appear in Spotlight, but it won't be found under any other category. See page 130 for searching across categories.

Books & Reference

There are a number of ways to explore the content of the Windows Store, to make sure you find useful items.

1. Locate a category of interest in the Windows Store

2. Select Apps for bookworms, for example, and you'll find a collection of nine apps for readers

3. Press the back arrow and select Top free (21 apps) or New releases (12 apps)

Don't forget

For each category you can expect a special interest group, some individual apps and the main lists, Top free and New releases.

Beware

The specific groups and apps included for any category are highly likely to change frequently, so these steps are just to illustrate the process.

Hot tip

Top free contains all the apps highlighted, except for two apps in New releases, so there are 23 apps in total shown for Books & Reference.

Search Windows Store

You can use the Search app to find items of interest in the Windows Store and to check out its scope. For example, we could see if there are more apps in Books & Reference section than have already been identified.

1. Display the Charms bar, select the Search App, choose Store and type Books

2. The Windows Store opens and displays results for the search, in this case 41 apps, across several different categories

3. Click All categories and select Books & Reference and the number of apps listed drops to 27

The reason for this is that apps may not be classified under the category you'd expect, so it is always useful to search for apps using your terms of interest, to see what does turn up.

4. Many apps are free, but there is a charge for some. Click All prices and select Paid, to see those apps

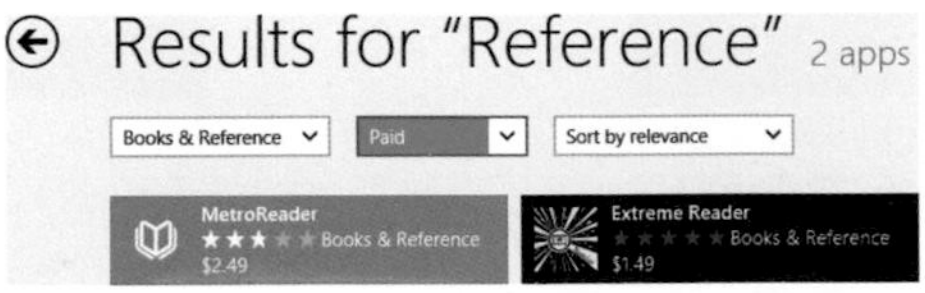

Don't forget

If you open the Store app before you open Search, it will automatically select the Store category.

Hot tip

You can filter search results by Category.

You can also filter by the Pricing method.

The results may be sorted to make them easier to review.

Installing Apps

1. Search the Store for items of interest, for example ebooks

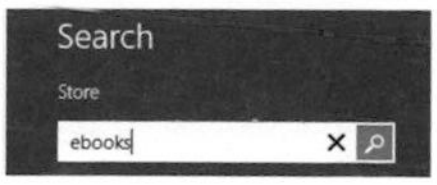

2. From the results, click an app you want to review, e.g. Free Books – 23,469 classics to go

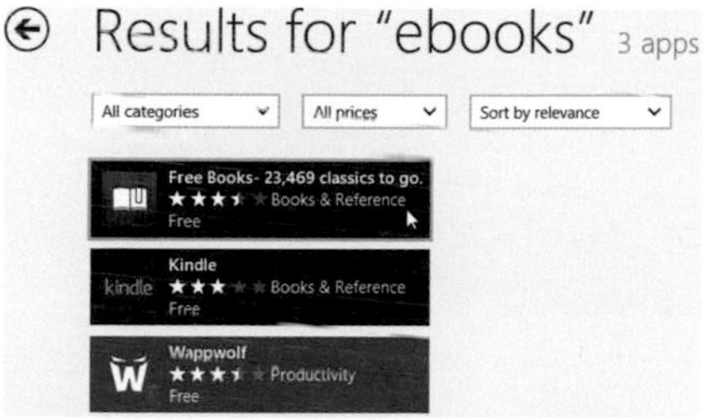
Results for "ebooks" 3 apps
All categories
All prices
Sort by relevance
Free Books- 23,469 classics to go.
Books & Reference
Free
Kindle
Books & Reference
Free
Wappwolf
Productivity
Free

3. Click the Install button if you want this app

4. Messages at the Store show you the installation in progress and completed

Installing Free Books- 23,469 classics to go....

5. Click the tile on the Start screen to run the app

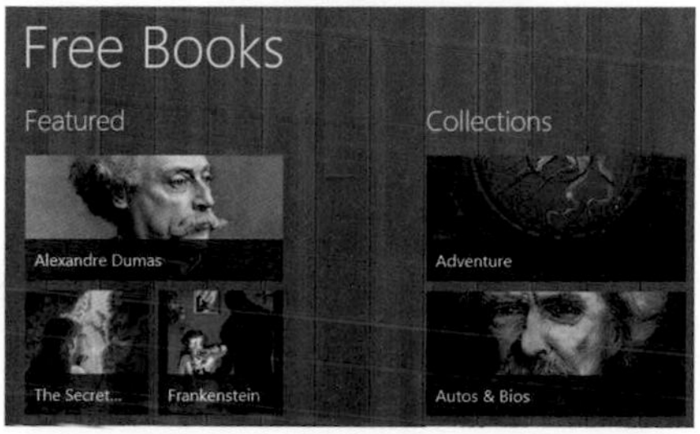

Don't forget

Searching for the topic "eBooks" locates Windows 8 apps in more than one category, in this case Books & Reference and Productivity.

Hot tip

If you've already installed the app on your PC, instead of the Install button you see a message saying that You own this app.

Your App Account

If you use your Microsoft account on multiple machines, it is possible that you'll get a warning while installing an app.

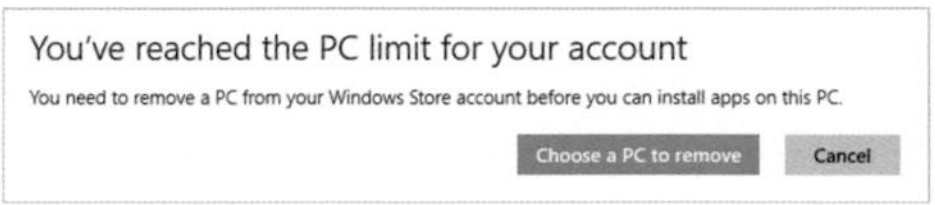

1. Click Choose a PC to remove, to view your account

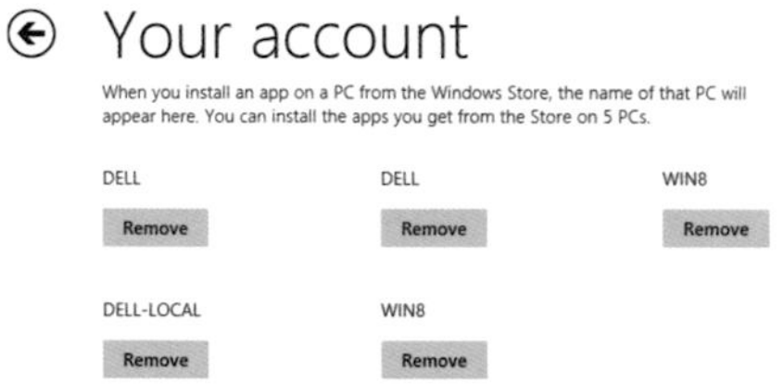

2. If there's an out of date computer defined, Remove it

3. To work with your account, right-click the Store screen and select Your apps from the bar that appears at the top

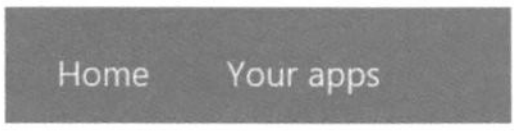

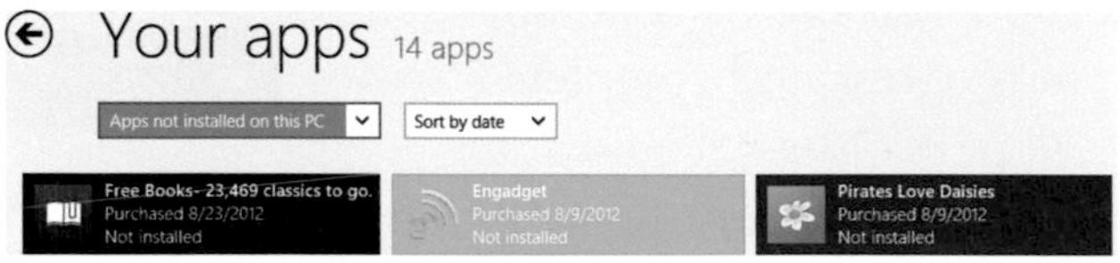

4. Click Select all, or right-click individual apps and then click Install, to add the selected apps to the current computer

Beware

You can install apps from the Store, free or charged, on up to five Windows 8 systems. If you install Windows 8 on more than one partition, or if you use Virtual PC software, each Windows 8 image counts as one of the five, even if you use duplicate names.

Don't forget

Your apps will show all apps installed on the machines defined to your Microsoft account and also lists Apps not installed on this PC.

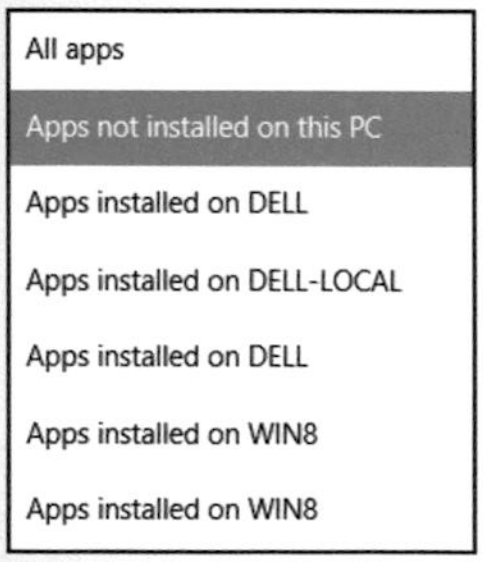

Updates

If any Windows 8 apps that you've installed get updated, you'll see an indicator on the Store tile, telling you how many updates you have waiting.

1. Click the tile to open the Windows Store and you'll see a message to the same effect at the top right

2. Click the Updates message and you'll see a list of the updates available

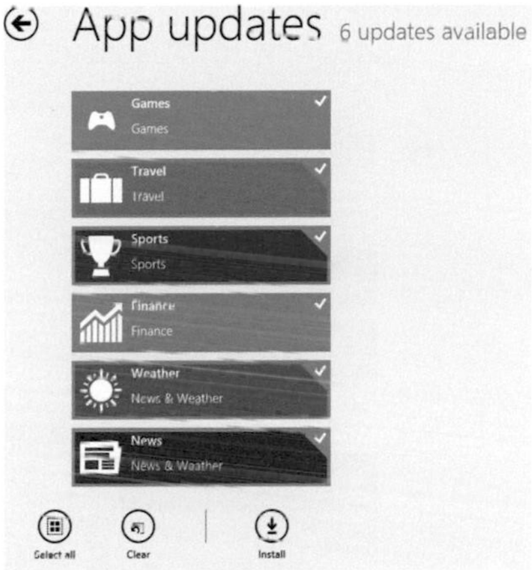

3. The updates are preselected, but you can right-click any you don't want to install at this time

4. Click Install to begin applying the selected updates

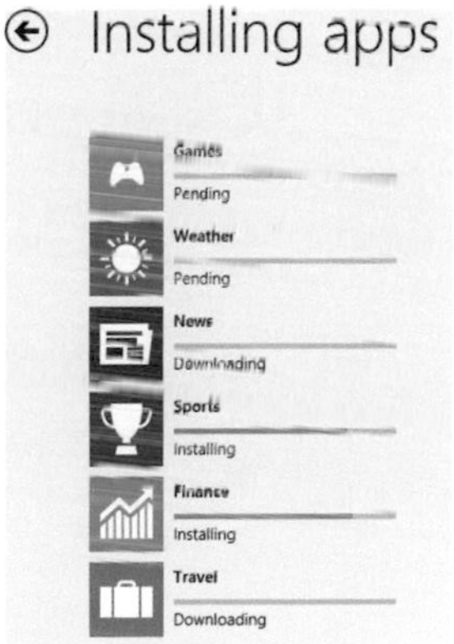

5. You'll see a progress report for each update:
   Pending
   Downloading
   Installing

6. When all stages are complete for each item, you are told "Your apps were installed"

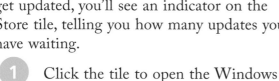

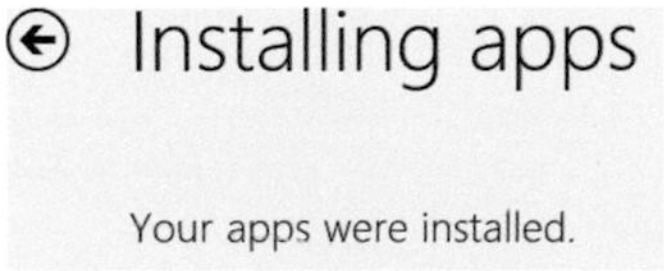

Hot tip

This includes those apps automatically installed when your Windows 8 system was initially set up.

Don't forget

You don't have to apply the updates immediately, or all at once. You can select which ones you want at any particular time.

Desktop Apps

Windows Store includes entries for Desktop apps, which are conventional Windows applications that run in the traditional desktop environment.

There's no specific search for such applications – you'll just come across them during your searches for Windows 8 apps. For example:

Hot tip

You cannot purchase Desktop apps from the Windows Store – it just provides a link to the publisher's website.

1. Search the Store for Productivity apps and limit the list to that category, in this case 55 apps

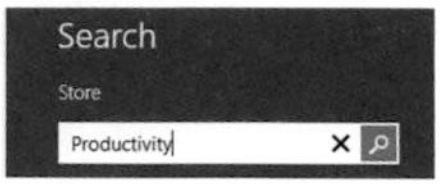

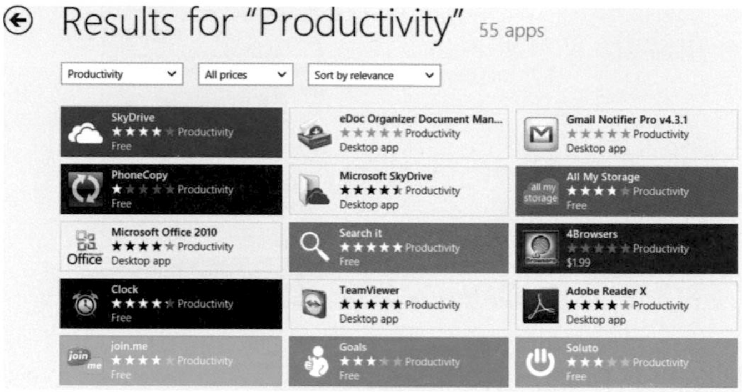

2. Examine the results and you'll see some that have Desktop app, rather than show the price (or Free)

3. Select the Microsoft SkyDrive

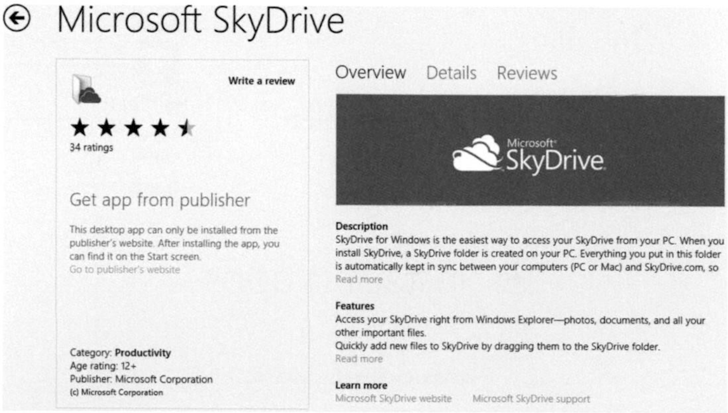

Hot tip

There's a Windows 8 App called SkyDrive, which provides direct access to your storage (see page 126). The Desktop version gives access via File Explorer.

4 Click the link Go to publisher's website

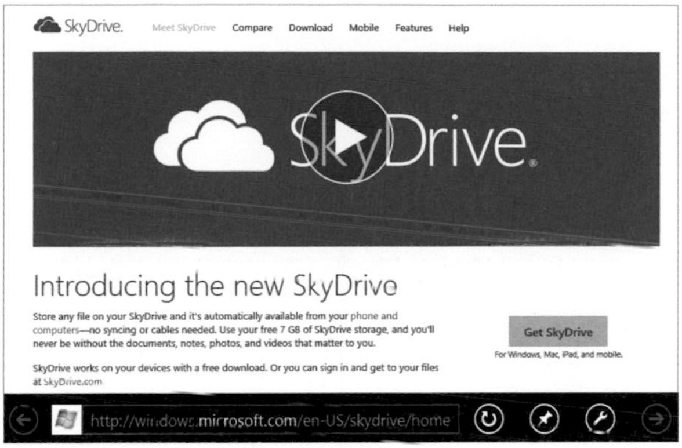

5 Click Get SkyDrive and follow the prompts to Run the SkyDriveSetup program

6 Click Get started to set up access to your SkyDrive

7 Your SkyDrive can now be accessed just like another folder in your User area

Don't forget

The SkyDrive website has a video to give you an overview of the SkyDrive system and how to make use of and share the storage that it provides.

Beware

The SkyDrive appears to be a local folder, but is actually at the Microsoft website. So data transfers and syncs will impact the data transfer allowance provided by your ISP.

Desktop Apps Available

Don't forget

There is no way to search explicitly for Desktop apps, but they will be included as appropriate whenever you search the Windows Store.

To get an idea of the range of Desktop apps available in the store, you could review other categories as described for Productivity (see page 134).

The contents of the Store can be expected to increase and change regularly, but at the time of writing the following Desktop apps were listed:

Games	*Tools*
Age of Empires Online	Duplicate File Detective 4
Entertainment	Foldersizes 6
Ultra Screen Saver Maker	Hypersnap
Photo	InSync
Crayola Art Studio	PDF Converter
Adobe PhotoshopLightroom	SyMON System Monitor
Corel Paintshop Pro	Visual Studio 2012
Instagrille	Visual Studio Express 2012
Serif PhotoPlus X5 Digital Studio	WinZip 16.5
Music & Video	*Security*
Audials One 9	mSecure for Windows Desktop
Moyea PPT to Video Conv	*Business*
Productivity	XLSTAT 2012
Adobe Reader X	*Education*
eDoc Organizer	Jumpstart Adv Preschool
Gmail Notifier Pro v4.3.1	Jumpstart Adv K-2 Training
Microsoft Office 2010	Jumpstart Adv K-2 Quest
Microsoft SkyDrive	Jumpstart Adv 3-5
Team Viewer	

Hot tip

The main categories for Desktop apps at this time are Photo, Productivity and Tools, plus several in Education, and individual items in other categories.

The Windows Store entries do not indicate if the Desktop apps are free or chargeable. You will have to check this out at the Publisher's website before deciding whether to download and install the app.

8 Email and Calendar

Windows 8 provides the Mail app for email communications, the People app to manage the details of your contacts and the Calendar app to keep track of events and meetings. Communicate instantly using the Messenger app. For functions such as Newsgroups, you can download the Windows Essentials Live Mail.

138 Electronic Mail
139 Windows 8 Mail App
140 Add Email Account
142 The Mail Window
143 View Message
144 People
146 Viewing Contacts
147 Managing Contacts
148 Create a Message
150 Calendar
152 Instant Messaging
154 Windows Live Mail
156 Newsgroups

Electronic Mail

Don't forget

An email address consists of a user name or nickname, the @ sign and the server name of your email provider, e.g. jsmith99@myisp.com or web service e.g. jsmith99@gmail.com.

Email or electronic mail is used to send and receive text messages. You can send an email message to anyone with an email address, you can receive messages from anyone who knows your email address and you can reply to those messages, or forward them to another email address. You can send your email message to more than one person at the same time and attach files such as documents or pictures.

Email is free, since no stamp or fee is required. However, before you can use email, you require:

- An account with an Internet Service Provider (ISP)
- An Internet connection such as telephone or cable
- A modem or router to make the connection
- An email address from your email service provider or from a web service such as Gmail or Hotmail
- An email program such as Mail or Windows Live Mail

Mail

This is the Windows 8 app that is installed with Windows 8, which provides full screen access to multiple email accounts.

Hot tip

You can also send and receive email using your web browser, or using the email client included with your office software, for example Outlook.

Windows Live Mail

This is one of the applications included with Windows Essentials (see page 22). It provides Windows 8 with an equivalent to the Windows Mail and Outlook Express applications found in previous releases of Windows. It runs on the Desktop and, in addition to email, it supports newsgroups. These are Internet-based discussion forums where members share information and opinions on topics of mutual interest. Windows Live Mail helps you read the messages posted by other members and add your own messages to the forum for others to read.

amazon.co.uk

nk you for shopping at Amazon.co.uk!

9 A2

ice for	**Billing Address**	**Shipping Address**
order of 26 May, 2013	**fiona hurst**	**fiona hurst**
r ID 204-3133881-6187516	greenbank cottage	greenbank cottage
ce number DpmqhxhxN	parkhill road	parkhill road
ce date 26 May, 2013	blairgowrie, perthshire ph107ds	blairgowrie, perthsire ph107ds
	United Kingdom	United Kingdom

Item	Our Price (excl. VAT)	VAT Rate	Total Price
Windows 8 for Seniors In Easy Steps Paperback. Price, Michael. 184078539X (** P-3-A122E105 **)	£8.79	0%	£8.79
Shipping charges	£0.00		£0.00
Subtotal (excl. VAT) 0%			£8.79
Total VAT			£0.00
Total			£8.79

ersion rate - £1.00 : EUR 1,17

This shipment completes your order.

You can always check the status of your orders or change your account details from the "Your Account" link at the top of each page on our site.

Thinking of returning an item? PLEASE USE OUR ON-LINE RETURNS SUPPORT CENTRE.

Our Returns Support Centre (www.amazon.co.uk/returns-support) will guide you through our Returns Policy and provide you with a printable personalised eturn label. Please have your order number ready (you can find it next to your order summary, above). Our Returns Policy does not affect your statutory rights.

Amazon EU S.a.r.L, 5 Rue Plaetis, L-2338, Luxembourg
VAT number : GB727255821

Please note - this is not a returns address - for returns - please see above for details of our online returns centre

mRhchDN/-1 of 1-//PF01/premium-uk/1875369/0526-19:00/0526-15:48 Pack Type : A2

Windows 8 Mail App

To define your Microsoft account email address to Mail:

1. On the Start screen select the tile for the Mail app

2. Enter the password for your Microsoft account and click Connect to add it

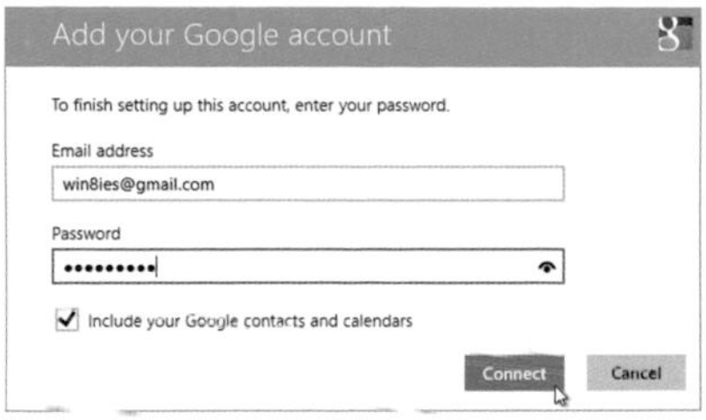

Add your Google account
To finish setting up this account, enter your password.
Email address
win8ies@gmail.com
Password
Include your Google contacts and calendars
Connect
Cancel

With higher resolution monitors, you'll see three panes Accounts, Folder, Reading.

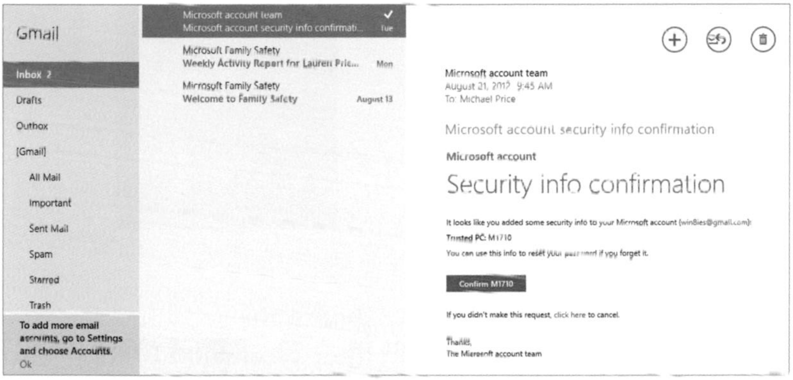

Gmail
Inbox 2
Drafts
Outbox
[Gmail]
All Mail
Important
Sent Mail
Spam
Starred
Trash
To add more email accounts, go to Settings and choose Accounts.
Ok
Microsoft account team
Microsoft account security info confirmati...
Microsoft Family Safety
Weekly Activity Report for Lauren Pric...
Mon
Microsoft Family Safety
Welcome to Family Safety
August 13
Microsoft account team
August 21, 2012 9:45 AM
To: Michael Price
Microsoft account security info confirmation
Microsoft account
Security info confirmation
Trusted PC: M1710
Confirm M1710
Thanks,
The Microsoft account team

With lower resolution monitors you'll see just Folder and Reading. Click the arrow to show Accounts and Reading.

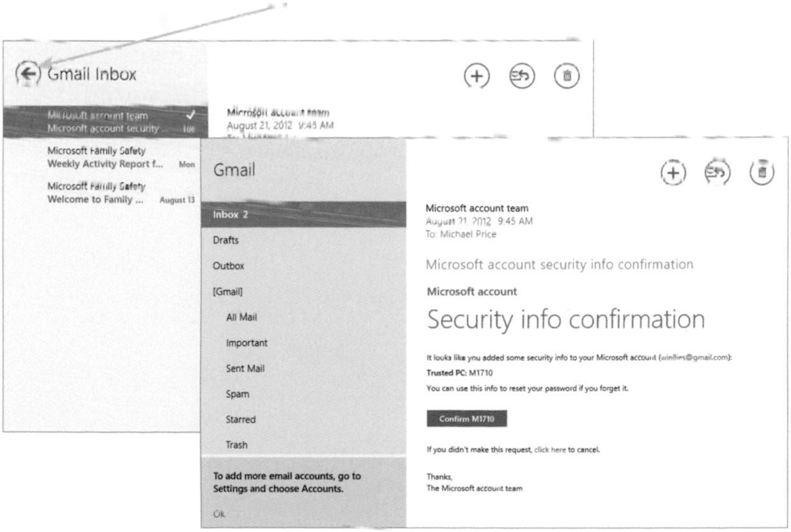

Gmail Inbox
Microsoft Family Safety
Weekly Activity Report f...
Mon
Microsoft Family Safety
Welcome to Family ...
August 13
Gmail
Inbox 2
Drafts
Outbox
[Gmail]
All Mail
Important
Sent Mail
Spam
Starred
Trash
To add more email accounts, go to Settings and choose Accounts.
Ok
Microsoft account team
August 21, 2012 9:45 AM
To: Michael Price
Microsoft account security info confirmation
Microsoft account
Security info confirmation
It looks like you added some security info to your Microsoft account (win8ies@gmail.com):
Trusted PC: M1710
You can use this info to reset your password if you forget it.
Confirm M1710
If you didn't make this request, click here to cancel.
Thanks,
The Microsoft account team

Hot tip

By default the Inbox for the email account is selected and the latest message will be displayed.

Hot tip

Note the reminder at the foot of the Accounts pane, to add more email accounts, go to Settings and choose Accounts. Click OK to remove the message.

Don't forget

See page 142 for more details of the parts of the Mail window.

Add Email Account

You can add multiple email accounts to your Mail app, using the Settings app.

1. From Mail, display the Charms bar and select Settings

2. From Settings, click the Accounts entry

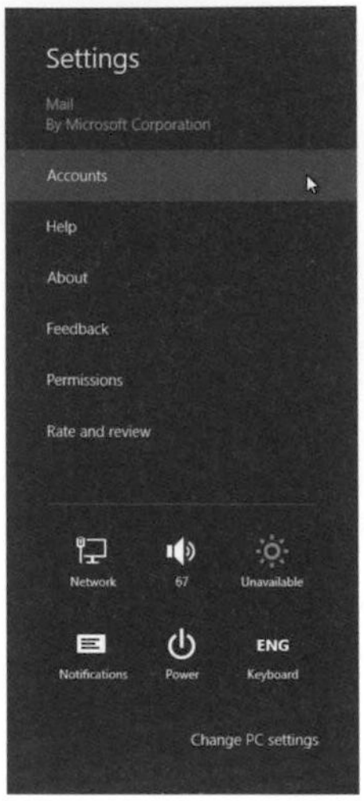

3. From the Accounts list select Add an account

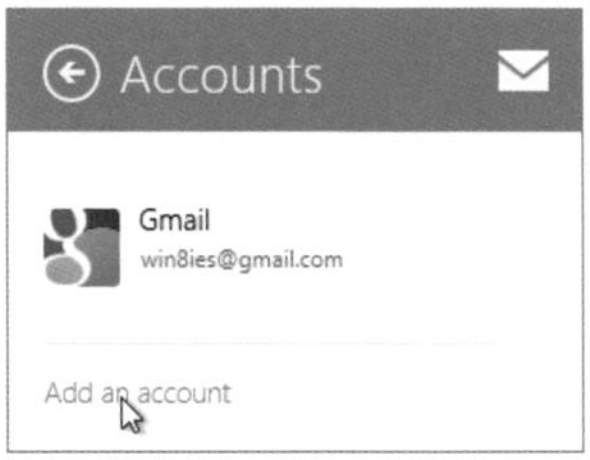

4. Choose the account type, either Hotmail, Outlook, Google or Other account

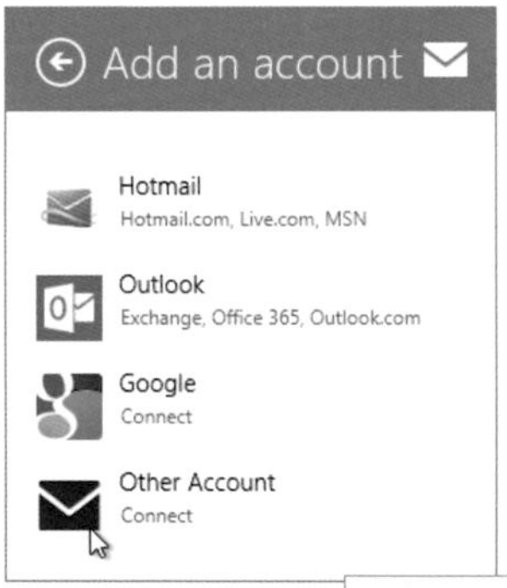
Add an account
Hotmail
Hotmail.com, Live.com, MSN
Outlook
Exchange, Office 365, Outlook.com
Google
Connect
Other Account
Connect

5. For example, select Other account and enter the email address and password, in this case a BT Internet account

6. Click Connect and mail will define the account and set up the appropriate folders

Don't forget

The commands displayed when you open Settings depend on where you issue the request. There's no Accounts unless you start from Mail.

Hot tip

The minimum amount of data required is the Email address and password. However, you may be asked for additional information in some cases.

For some accounts, Mail may require additional information.

1. Open Mail Account Settings and enter an email address for Dial.Pipex.Com

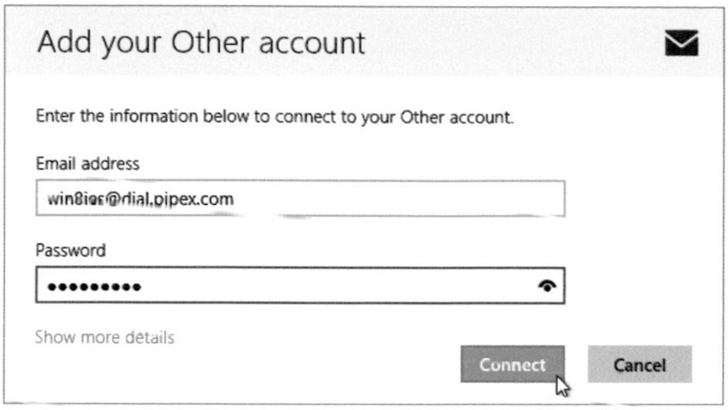
Add your Other account
Enter the information below to connect to your Other account.
Email address
win8ies@dial.pipex.com
Password
Show more details
Connect
Cancel

2. Mail attempts to set up the account, but is unable to find the settings, so asks for more information

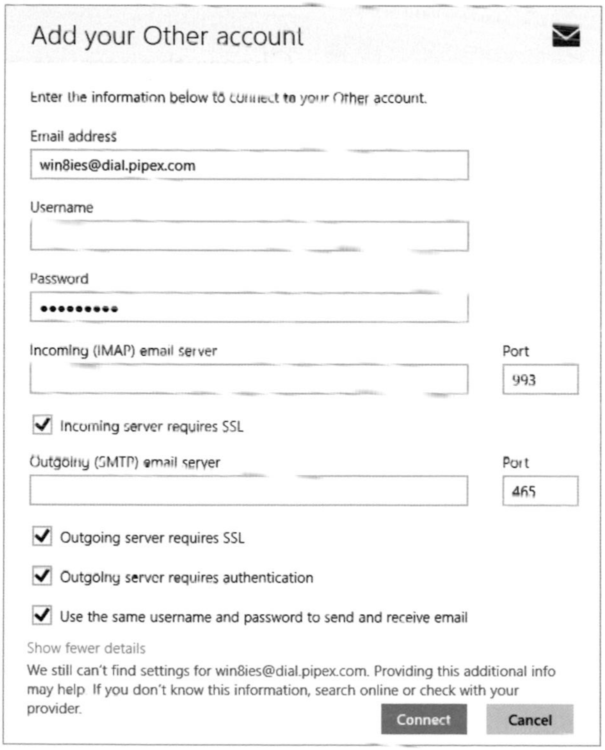
Add your Other account
Enter the information below to connect to your Other account.
Email address
win8ies@dial.pipex.com
Username
Password
Incoming (IMAP) email server
Port
993
Incoming server requires SSL
Outgoing (SMTP) email server
Port
465
Outgoing server requires SSL
Outgoing server requires authentication
Use the same username and password to send and receive email
Show fewer details
We still can't find settings for win8ies@dial.pipex.com. Providing this additional info may help. If you don't know this information, search online or check with your provider.
Connect
Cancel

Hot tip

Your ISP will provide you with the port and server addresses, or try searching on the Internet for email settings for your account type.

Don't forget

Mail provides the settings it thinks may apply. In fact, the ports for Dial.Pipex are 143 and 25 and the SSL options should be deselected. With these changes and with the servers addresses:

pop.dial.pipex.com
smtp.dial.pipex.com

Mail is able to make the connection.

The Mail Window

These are the main elements of the Mail window:

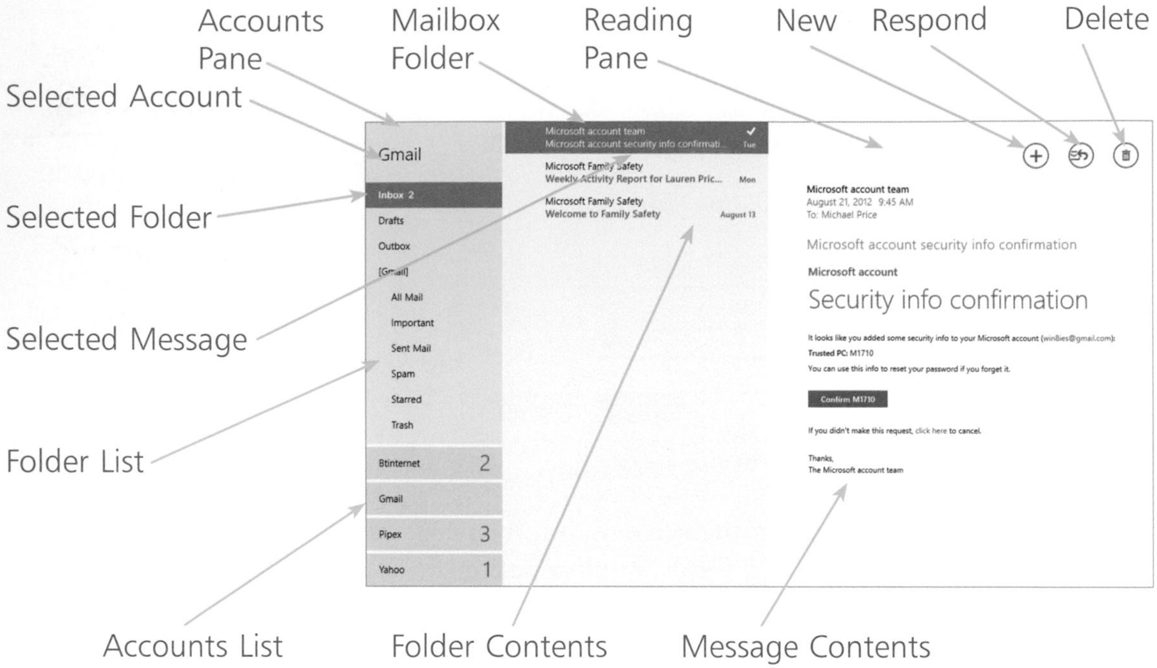

1. Right-click an empty portion of the window to display the App bar with its additional functions

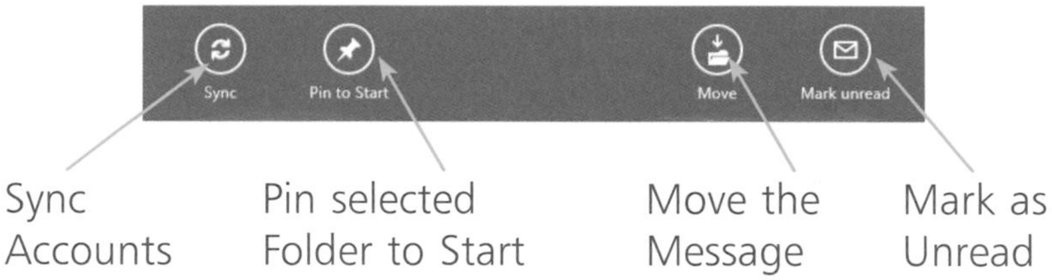

The Accounts list shows unread message counts and the Start screen tile for Mail shows the total new message count, plus a rotating extract of messages waiting.

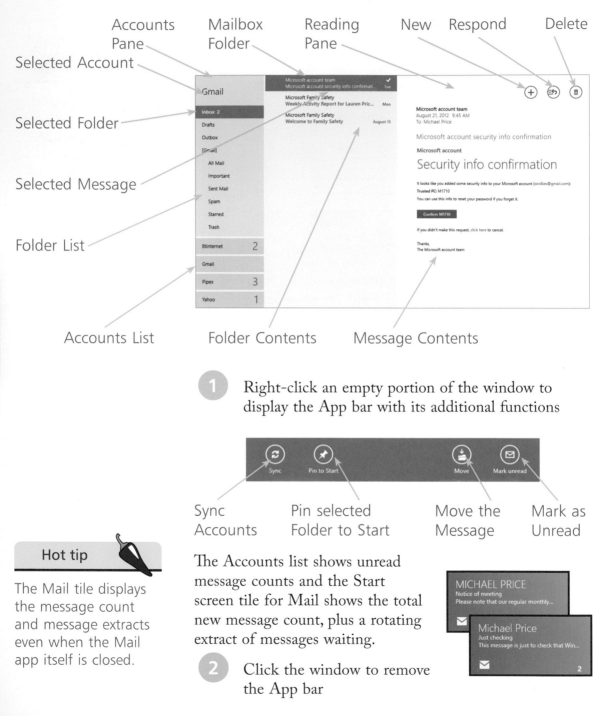

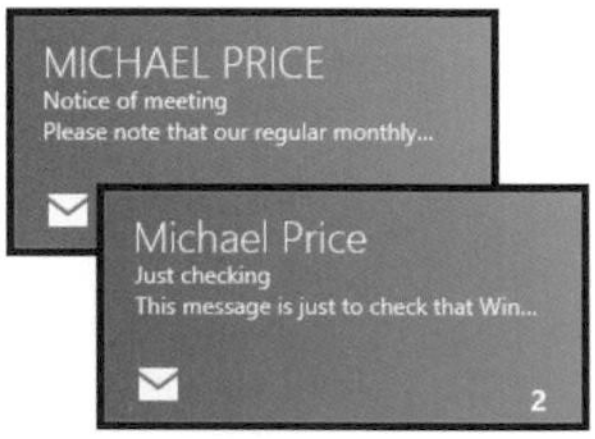

2. Click the window to remove the App bar

Hot tip

The Mail tile displays the message count and message extracts even when the Mail app itself is closed.

View Message

1. Select a message in the Folder pane and it displays in the Reading pane

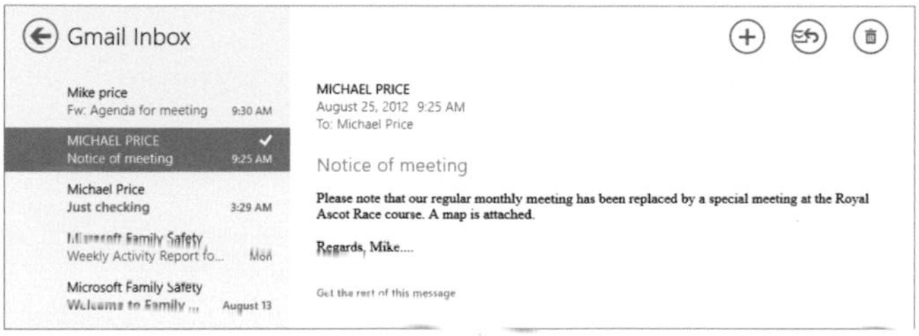

2. If there is an attachment, click Get the rest of this message and it will download

MICHAEL PRICE
August 25, 2012 9:25 AM
To: Michael Price
Notice of meeting
Ascot Race course. A map is attached.
Regards, Mike....

3. Click the Respond button and select Reply, then type your reply and click the Send button

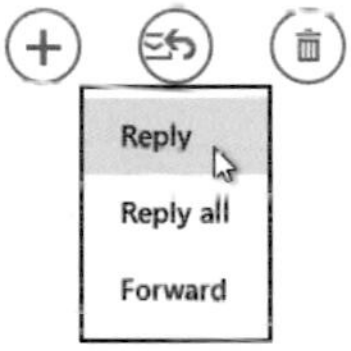

4. A copy is saved in the Sent folder for the account used to send the reply

Don't forget

Pictures can be embedded in the message. Other files such as documents can be saved or opened from the message.

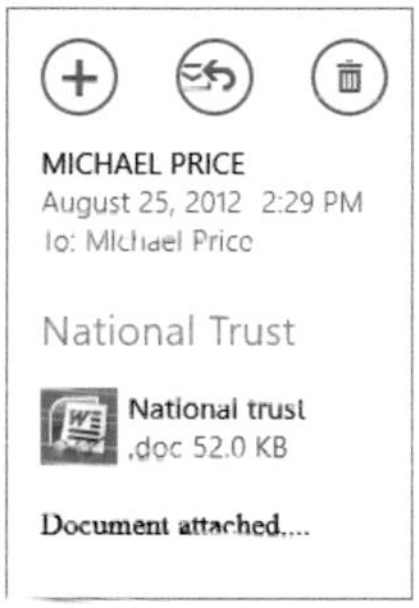

Hot tip

You can add people from your Contacts list (see page 148) and you can also switch the account used to send the reply.

People

Windows 8 allows you to collect details of all your contacts and make them available to apps such as Mail and calendar, using the new People app.

1. Click the People tile on the Start screen

2. Display the Charms bar and select Settings and then Accounts

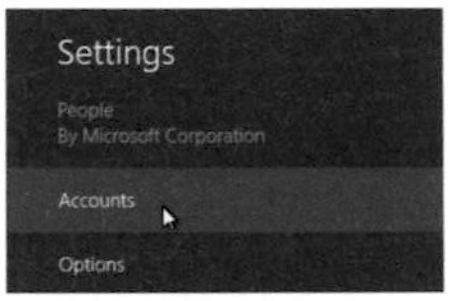

3. To start with there may be just your Microsoft account, which may initially have no contacts list associated with it

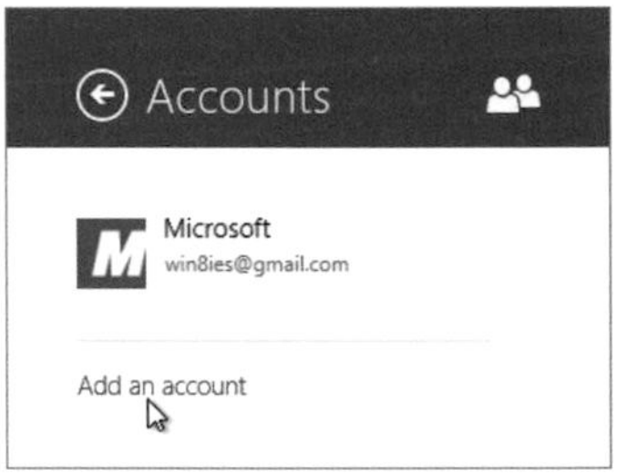

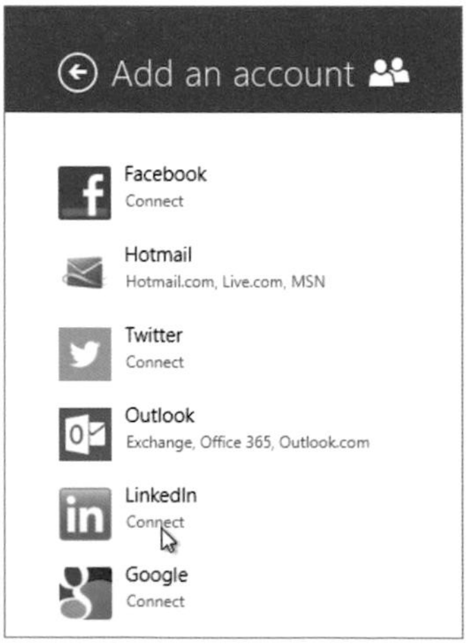

4. Click Add an account

5. Identify the types of account that have contacts that you may want to add

6. For example choose the LinkedIn account

Don't forget

The People app can manage all contacts associated with your email and personal networking, but you need to define which accounts to use.

Hot tip

Click the Connected to bar at the top of the window and the Accounts pane will be displayed immediately.

Hot tip

LinkedIn will be used as an example, but you'd follow a similar procedure for any of the account types.

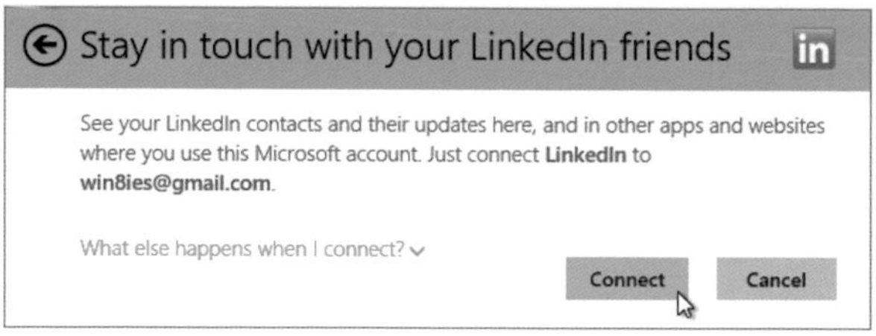
Stay in touch with your LinkedIn friends
See your LinkedIn contacts and their updates here, and in other apps and websites where you use this Microsoft account. Just connect LinkedIn to win8ies@gmail.com.
What else happens when I connect?
Connect
Cancel

7. Click Connect for your LinkedIn account

Connecting to a service
LinkedIn
Don't have an account?
Join Now
Grant Microsoft access to your LinkedIn Account
Only allow access if you trust this application with your LinkedIn network information
Email: win8ies@gmail.com
Password:
Forgot password?
Access Duration: Until Revoked change
Ok, I'll Allow It
Cancel
You can always revoke Microsoft's access through your settings page. By granting access you agree to the LinkedIn User Agreement and Privacy Policy

8. To grant access, enter your Email and Password for LinkedIn and click OK, I'll Allow It

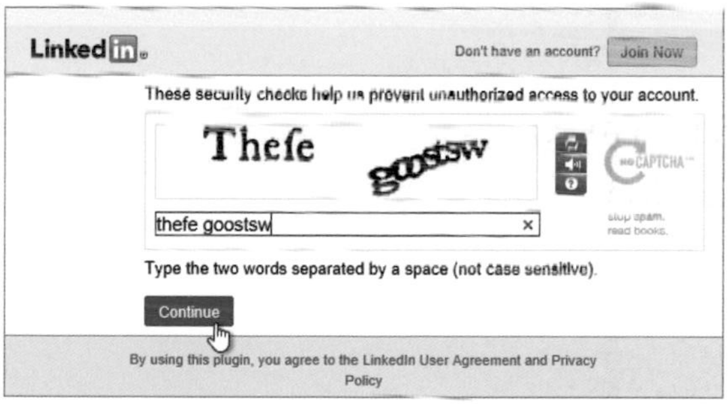
LinkedIn
Don't have an account?
Join Now
These security checks help us prevent unauthorized access to your account.
Thefe
goostsw
thefe goostsw
Type the two words separated by a space (not case sensitive).
Continue
By using this plugin, you agree to the LinkedIn User Agreement and Privacy Policy

9. Type the words as displayed (case doesn't matter) to validate the request and click Continue

Don't forget

To change the access settings, open the Accounts pane and select the account.

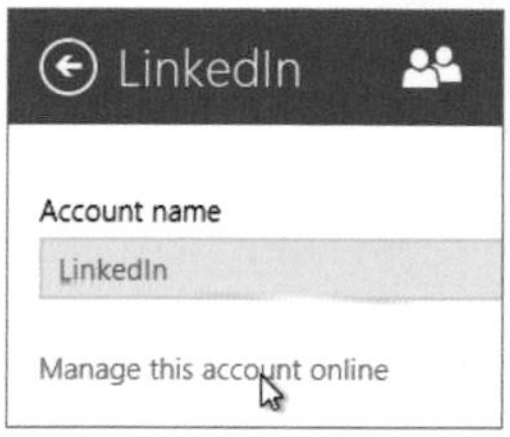
LinkedIn
Account name
LinkedIn
Manage this account online

Internet Explorer opens and you'll be given the option to change settings or remove the connection.

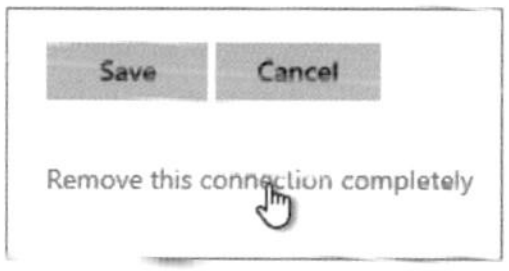
Save
Cancel
Remove this connection completely

Hot tip

The codes are not always easy to read, but you can click the buttons to display a new code or to request an audio prompt.

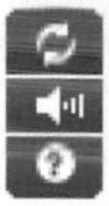

Viewing Contacts

The People app adds details of the contacts in your account.

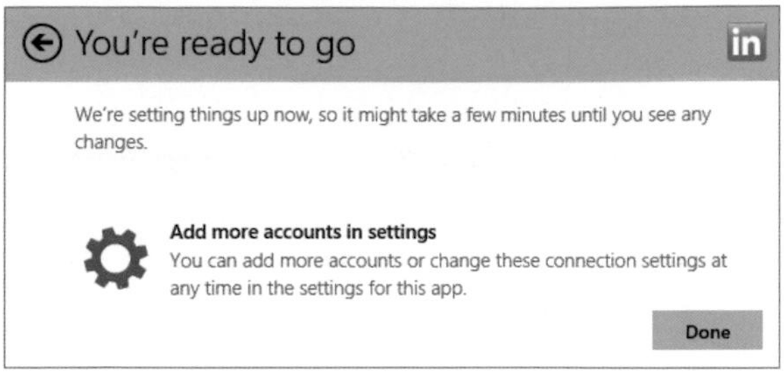

1. Switch to the People app to view the new details

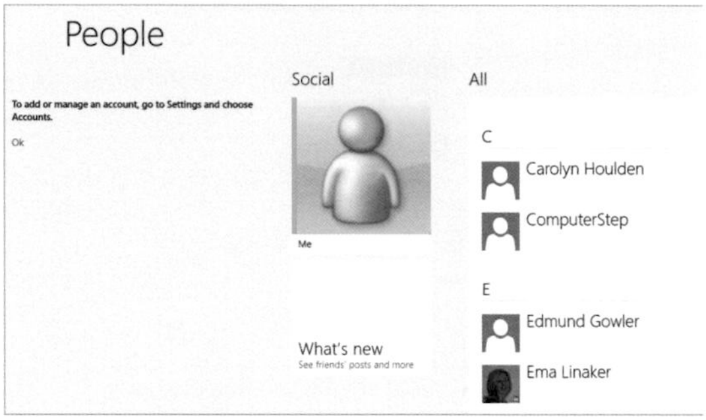

2. Using Windows 8 Snap, you can view your contacts beside another app such as Mail

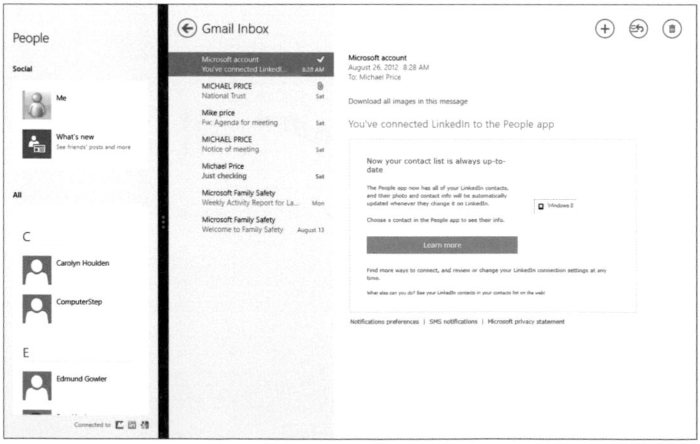

Hot tip

When you open the People app, you may see a note at the top of the window, to indicate that the app is fetching the latest details from your accounts.

Hot tip

The live tile for the People app shows images for some of your added contacts.

Don't forget

You'll need a higher resolution monitor to use the Windows 8 Snap function (see page 38) to place two apps side by side.

Managing Contacts

1. From the People app, select Settings from the Charms bar and click Options

2. Click the button to sort your contacts by last name, if desired

3. Hide contacts from some of your accounts, to reduce the number being displayed

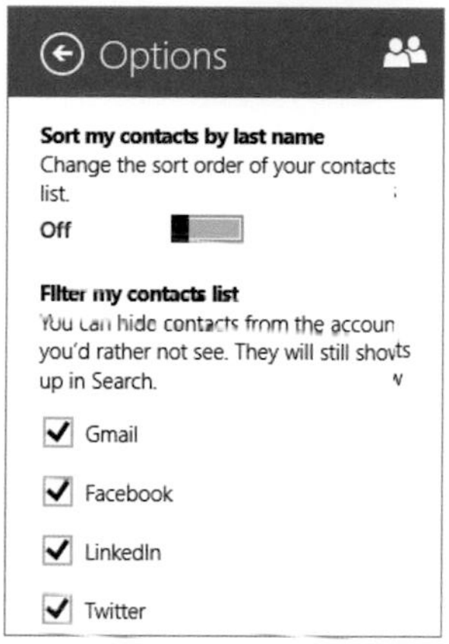

4. To work with a specific contact, click the entry

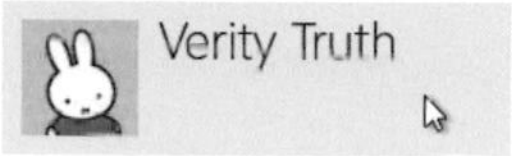

5. You can send an email, map the contact's address or view more details

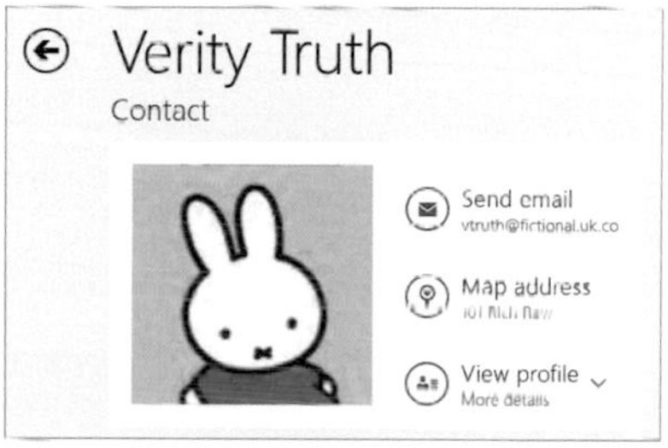

6. Right-click the details page to display the App bar

Pin to Start, mark as Favorite or Edit the contact's details.

Don't forget

If you right-click the Contacts page and select New from the App bar, you can enter the details for a new contact.

Hot tip

If you Edit the contact details, your changes will be shared with the originating account, the next time you Sync Mail and Contacts.

Create a Message

Don't forget

You can alternatively select the recipient from People and click Send Email (see page 147).

1. Select the email account, go to the Inbox and click New (or press Ctrl + N)

Gmail Inbox

2. A blank message form is displayed, ready for typing

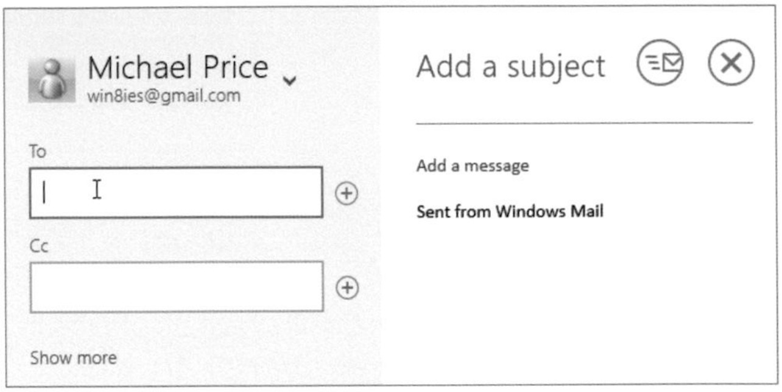

Hot tip

You can also click the Add button to add contact names from the People list.

3. Begin typing the contact name in the To box, then select the contact when it appears

4. Type the Subject for the message, add the message text and end with your name and email signature

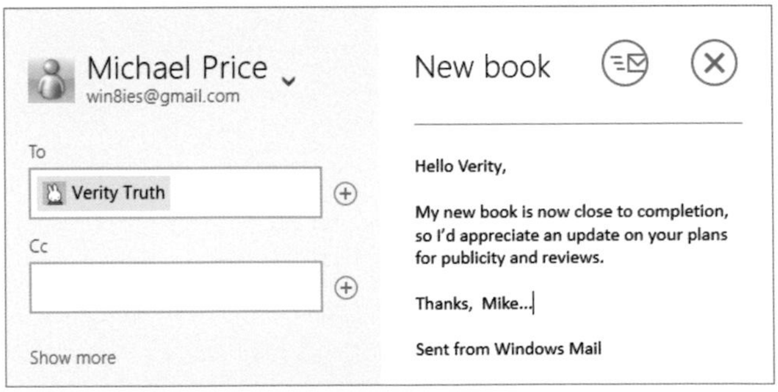
Michael Price
win8ies@gmail.com
To
Verity Truth
Cc
Show more
New book
Hello Verity,
My new book is now close to completion, so I'd appreciate an update on your plans for publicity and reviews.
Thanks, Mike...
Sent from Windows Mail

5. Add Cc (Carbon-copy) recipients, or click to Show more options

6. You can send Bcc copies and also set a priority

7. Right-click to display the App bar with further options

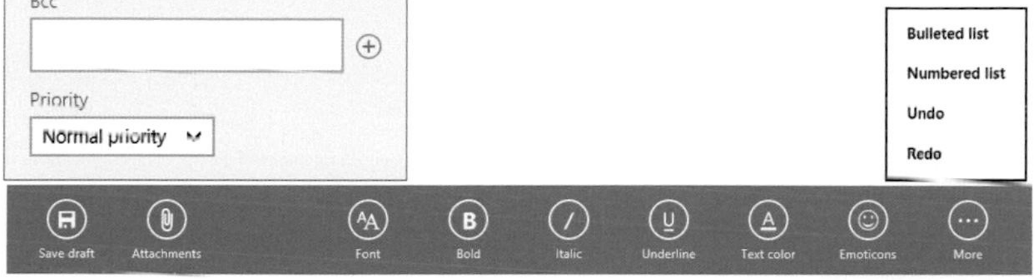

8. To see your email signature, display the Mail Settings, select Accounts and choose the sending account

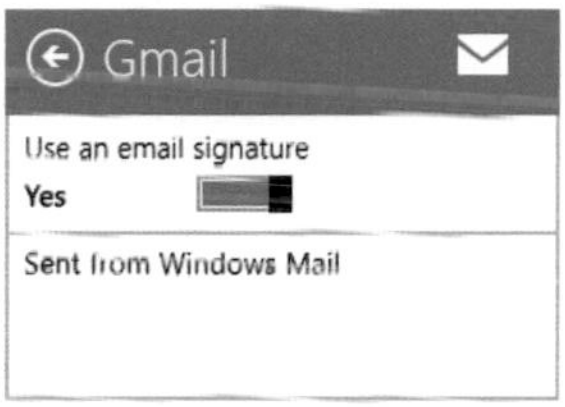

Note that any changes to the signature text will not affect the current message but will apply to future messages only.

9. Click the Send button to submit the message

A copy of the message is kept in the Sent folder for the sending account.

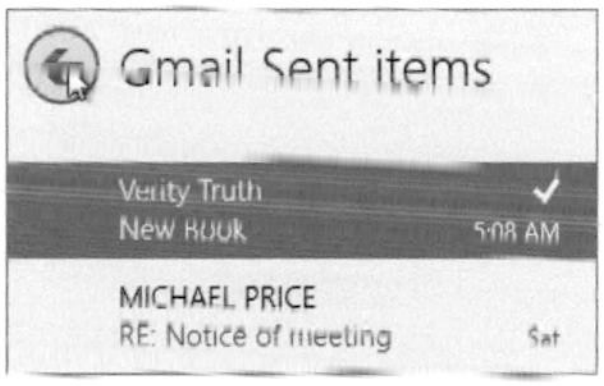

Should there be any problems with the email addresses used for the recipients, you may receive a message from the Mail Delivery subsystem describing the problem and explaining the reason.

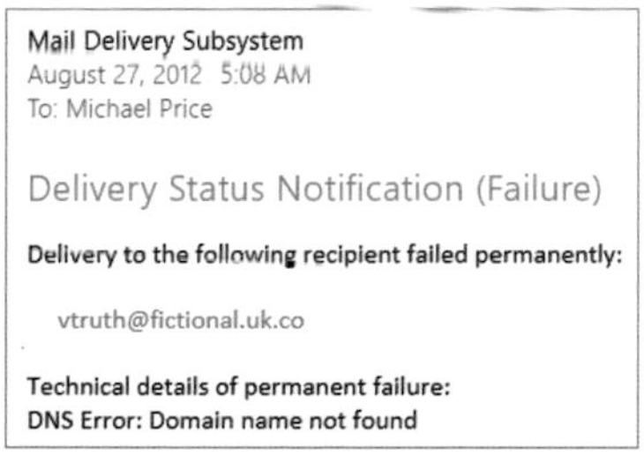
Mail Delivery Subsystem
August 27, 2012 5:08 AM
To: Michael Price
Delivery Status Notification (Failure)
Delivery to the following recipient failed permanently:
vtruth@fictional.uk.co
Technical details of permanent failure:
DNS Error: Domain name not found

In this case an invalid email address has an unknown domain name.

Hot tip

Recipients added using Bcc (Blind carbon-copy) will not be shown on the copies of the message that others receive.

Don't forget

Sometimes a message to a email address may fail, perhaps because the domain server is offline for a period. After several attempts, an error response message may be returned to you.

Calendar

Don't forget

Like Mail and People, the Calendar tile is live and shows events for the current day.

1. Switch to the Start screen and select the Calendar app

September 2012
Sunday
Monday
Tuesday
Wednesday
Thursday
Friday
Saturday
David Soul's birt...
Labor Day
Grandparents Day
Patriot Day
Stepfamily Day
International Da...
First Day of Autu...
Johnny Applesee...
Native American...
Michaelmas Day

2. The default view is Month, but you can change this

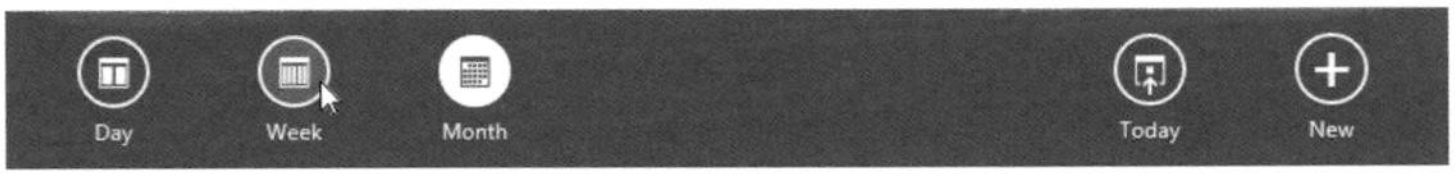

3. Right-click to display the App bar and select Week

September 2012
Sunday 23
Monday 24
Tuesday 25
Wednesday 26
Thursday 27
Friday 28
Saturday 29
First Day of Au...
Johnny Apples...
Native Americ...
Michaelmas Day

Hot tip

If you have a calendar associated with the email account used for your Microsoft account, its contents will be downloaded and kept in sync.

4. Select Day view and you'll normally see two days at the same time. Each day can be separately scrolled

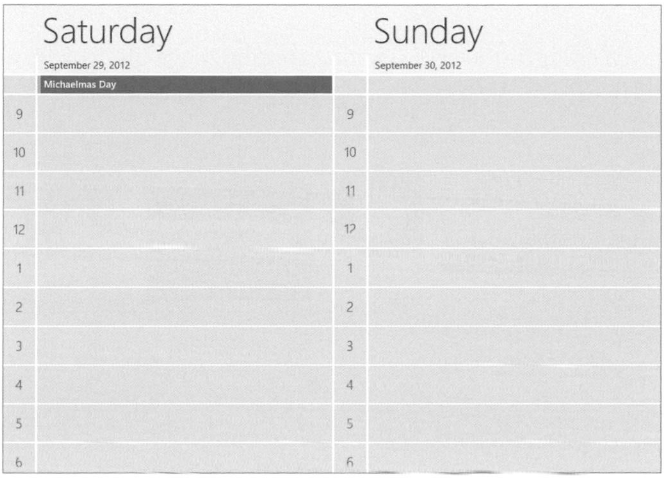

Saturday
September 29, 2012
Michaelmas Day
Sunday
September 30, 2012
9
10
11
12
1
2
3
4
5
6

5. On higher resolution monitors, 1920 x 1080 for example, the Day view will show three days at once

6. In any view, when you move the mouse, horizontal scroll arrows appear at the top of the screen

Don't forget

One click of the mouse (or a sideways swipe on a touch screen) will scroll the calendar one day, one week or one month, depending on the view you have set.

Instant Messaging

To set up Instant Messaging:

1. Select the Messaging app from the Start screen

2. Messaging starts up and displays a welcoming note from the Windows team

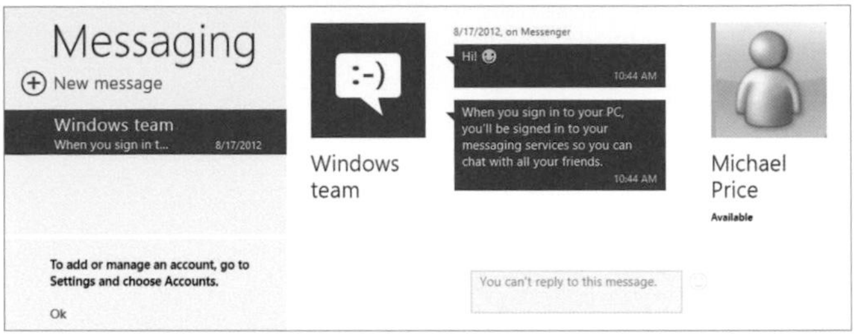

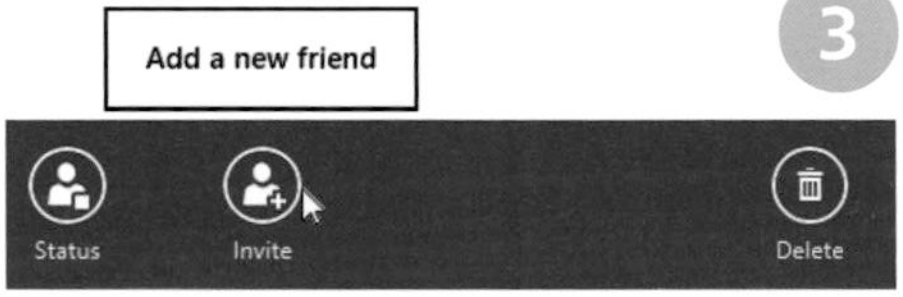

3. Right-click the window and select Invite from the App bar then click Add a new friend

4. Internet Explorer starts up and you can enter your new friend's email address, then press Next

5. Preview the invitation and then click Invite

Hot tip

Use your Microsoft account to exchange instant messages with friends who are online at the same time as you, using the Messaging app.

Don't forget

You are given the option to add an account, but currently only Messenger and Facebook accounts are supported.

Hot tip

Click View your privacy settings, to control how much information you will share and with whom.

6. Your friend will receive the invitation and can click Accept to allow communication via Messaging

7. The invitation will be confirmed

To communicate with your friend:

1. In Messaging, click the Plus button to check which friends are online

2. Choose your friend and begin a conversation

Hot tip

Your contacts can also view and change their privacy settings to ensure safe and secure communications.

Don't forget

You must both be online to carry out an instant messaging conversation.

Windows Live Mail

If you install the Windows Essentials (see page 22) you can use Windows Live Mail for your email accounts.

1. From the Start screen select Windows Live Mail, which starts up on the desktop

Windows Live Mail
Windows Live Messenger

2. If there's no email account already defined, Windows Live Mail prompts you for the details

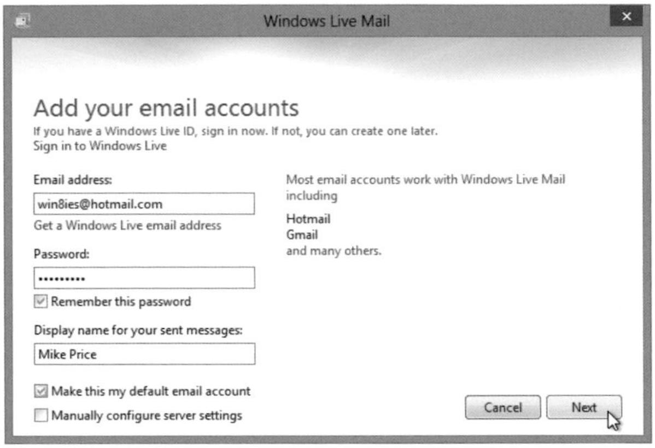
Windows Live Mail
Add your email accounts
If you have a Windows Live ID, sign in now. If not, you can create one later.
Sign in to Windows Live
Email address:
win8ies@hotmail.com
Get a Windows Live email address
Password:
Remember this password
Display name for your sent messages:
Mike Price
Make this my default email account
Manually configure server settings
Most email accounts work with Windows Live Mail including
Hotmail
Gmail
and many others.
Cancel
Next

3. Enter your email address, password and your name as you'd like it to appear on messages and click Next

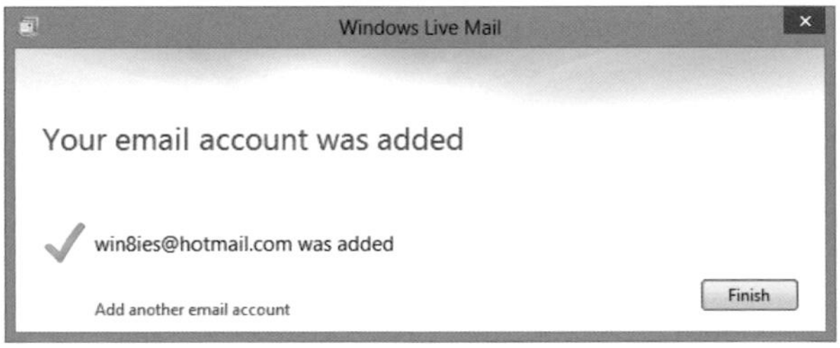

4. Windows will usually add the server details and you can click Finish (or Add another email account)

If Windows is unable to determine the details automatically, you may be asked to configure the server settings.

Hot tip

For Gmail accounts, you are directed to enable IMAP before continuing. For Yahoo accounts, you must have Yahoo Mail Plus.

Don't forget

Your ISP should give you addresses, port numbers and security options as required for the incoming and outgoing servers.

Windows Live Mail provides access to the mail folders for all your accounts, in four sections – Accounts, Folder contents, Reading pane and Calendar and Events.

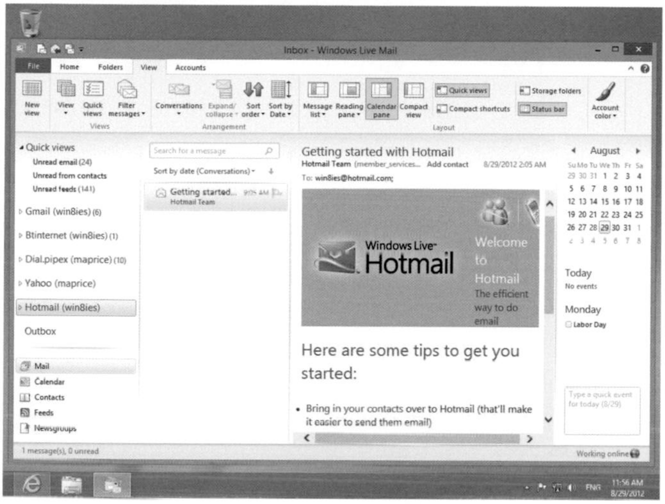

Don't forget

You can vary the layout to suit your requirements, using the View ribbon. For example, turn off the Reading pane, or select Compact view.

Quick View

As well as displaying the individual accounts, Windows Live Mail offers a consolidated view with, for example, unread emails from all the accounts in one combined list.

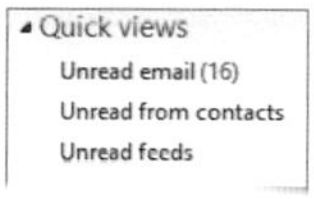

Shortcuts

There are shortcuts to switch the display between Mail, Calendar, Contacts, Feeds and Newsgroups.

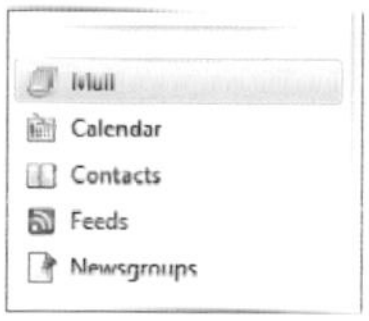

RSS Feeds

RSS feeds are updates to the contents of websites that change frequently, for example news services such as CNN. You would use Internet Explorer to find and subscribe to RSS feeds, as part of your online browsing. Windows Live Mail can identify and list the contents of feeds for which subscriptions have been created.

Hot tip

If you have the web address for a feed, you can subscribe to it directly from Windows Live Mail.

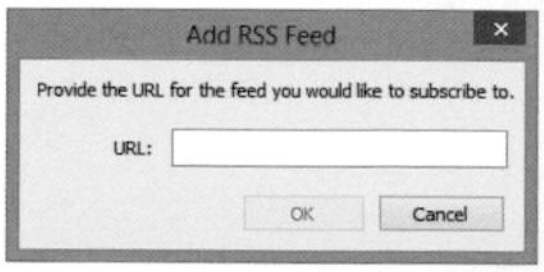

Newsgroups

Don't forget

Your ISP may provide a news server and there are others supported by special interest groups. Many news servers charge for access, but usually offer a free trial.

1. Open Windows Live Mail, select the Newsgroups shortcut and click Accounts, Newsgroups

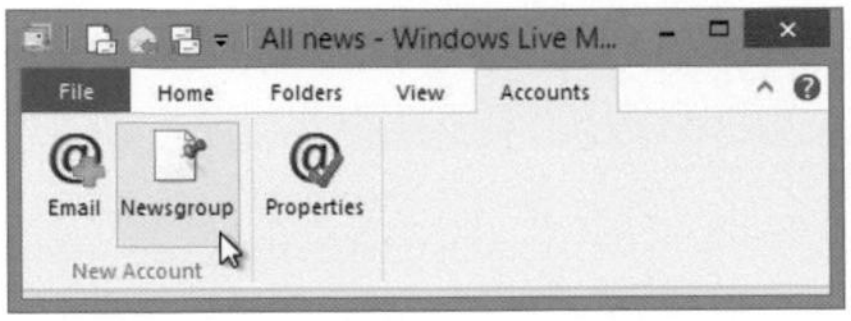

2. Follow the prompts to specify your user name and email address for posting to newsgroups

3. Enter the name of the News (NNTP) Server for example freenews.netfront.net

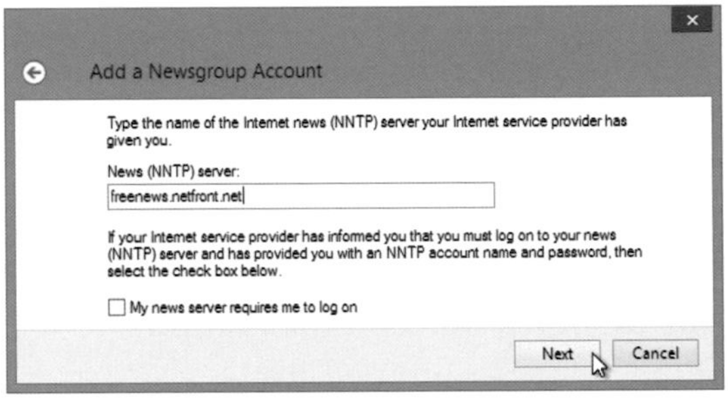

Hot tip

When you subscribe to a newsgroup, it is added to your account and can be treated like a mail folder. You can just read messages, or you can add your own comments.

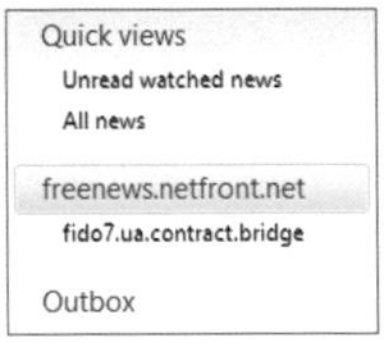

4. Download the newsgroups, search for topics of interest and Subscribe to newsgroups of interest

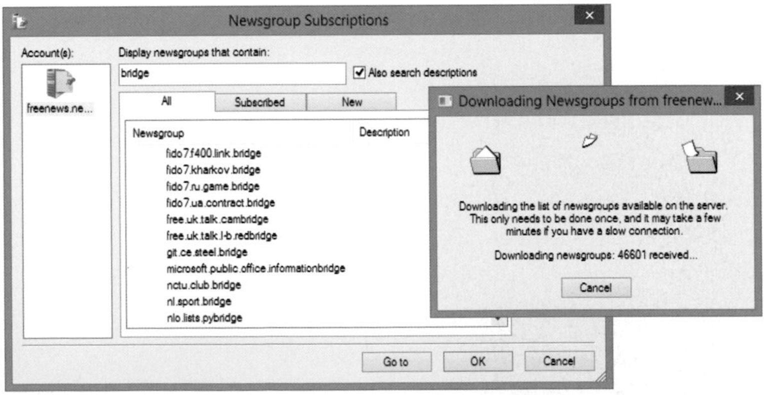

9 Internet

Windows 8 provides two versions of the Internet Explorer browser to help you navigate through the Web , with the full screen Windows 8 app and standard Desktop application. They both offer features such as tabbed browsing, favorites and support for RSS feeds.

158 Internet Connection
160 Browse the Web
162 Right-click Menu
164 Desktop Internet Explorer
166 Tabbed Browsing
168 Close Tabs
170 Add to Favorites
171 Pin Websites
172 Zoom Web Page
174 RSS Feeds

Internet Connection

Don't forget

During the installation or first time of use, you may be offered the option to Customize or Use express settings. Select the latter and let Windows set up the network for you.

Use express settings

If your computer is connected to your DSL router via an ethernet cable, the connections will usually be set up automatically when you install Windows 8, or the first time that you run a new computer with Windows 8 pre-installed. No interaction will be required.

If you have a wireless connection to your router, you'll be asked to provide the network key the first time, but connection will be automatic thereafter.

To review your network settings:

1. At the Start screen, type Control Panel and press Enter

2. From Network and Internet, click View network status and tasks. The Network and Sharing Center opens

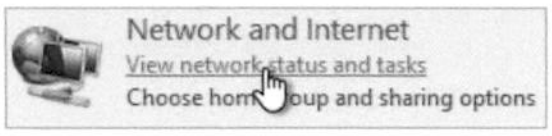
Network and Internet
View network status and tasks
Choose hom oup and sharing options

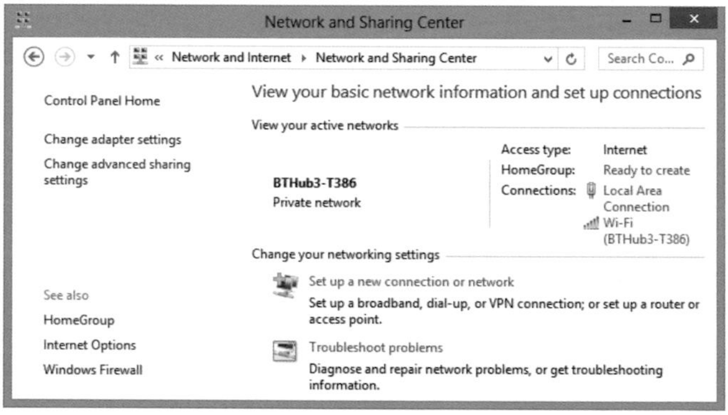

Don't forget

The connection to your router will be shown as a Private network, suitable for sharing files and printers. If you connect at the office or at an Internet cafe, you'd have a Guest or Public network and should avoid sharing files.

In this example, there are two connections – Local Area Connection (ethernet cable) and Wi-Fi (wireless). Either connection can provide access to the Internet.

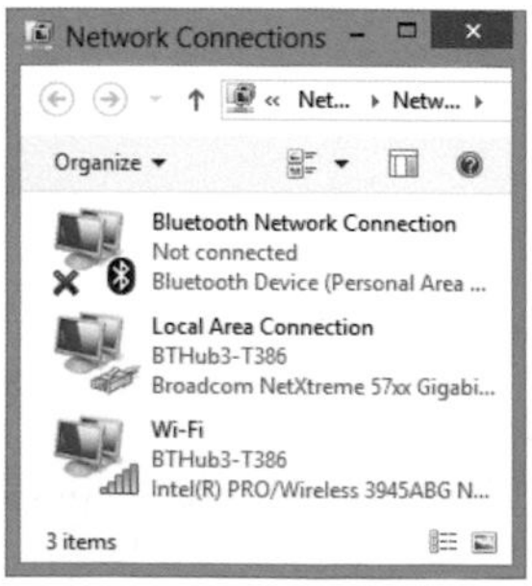

3. Click Change adapter settings to see more details of the connections available

To set up an Internet account directly from your computer:

1. In the Network and Sharing Center select the link to Set up a new connection or network

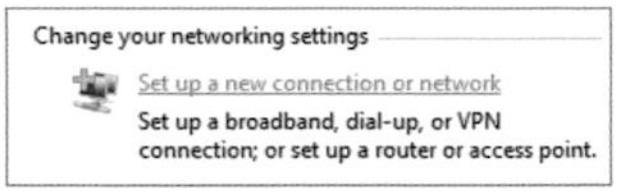
Change your networking settings
Set up a new connection or network
Set up a broadband, dial-up, or VPN connection; or set up a router or access point.

2. Choose Connect to the Internet to start the wizard which prompts for the connection type

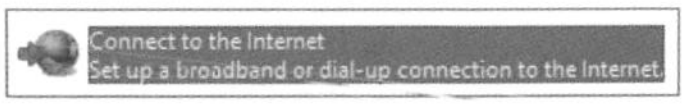
Connect to the Internet
Set up a broadband or dial-up connection to the Internet.

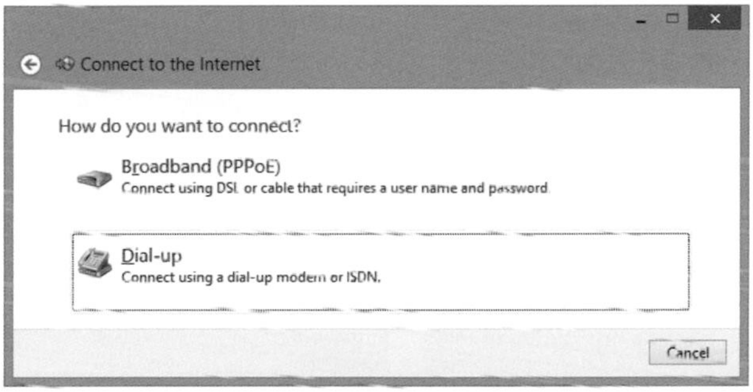
Connect to the Internet
How do you want to connect?
Broadband (PPPoE)
Connect using DSL or cable that requires a user name and password.
Dial-up
Connect using a dial-up modem or ISDN.
Cancel

3. Click the type, provide phone number (dialup only), account name, password etc and click Connect

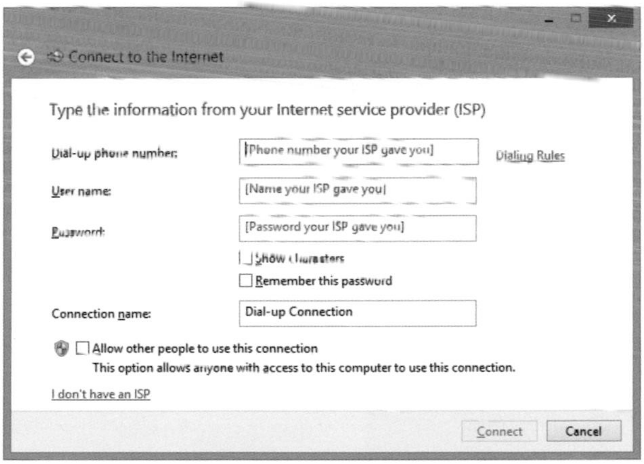
Connect to the Internet
Type the information from your Internet service provider (ISP)
Dial-up phone number:
[Phone number your ISP gave you]
Dialing Rules
User name:
[Name your ISP gave you]
Password:
[Password your ISP gave you]
Show characters
Remember this password
Connection name:
Dial-up Connection
Allow other people to use this connection
This option allows anyone with access to this computer to use this connection.
I don't have an ISP
Connect
Cancel

You can allow anyone who has access to this computer to use this connection, or keep it for your own use only.

Don't forget

If your network wasn't available at installation time, you can add a connection later.

Don't forget

If there's already an Internet connection, the wizard will tell you but allow you to continue and define a second connection, for example a dialup backup for your DSL connection.

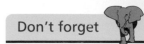

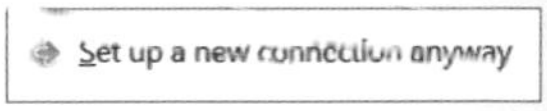
Set up a new connection anyway

Browse the Web

Windows 8 provides access to the Internet via a browser such as Microsoft's Internet Explorer v10.0. There are two versions – Windows 8 app and Desktop app.

1. Click Internet Explorer on the Start screen to open the Windows 8 app

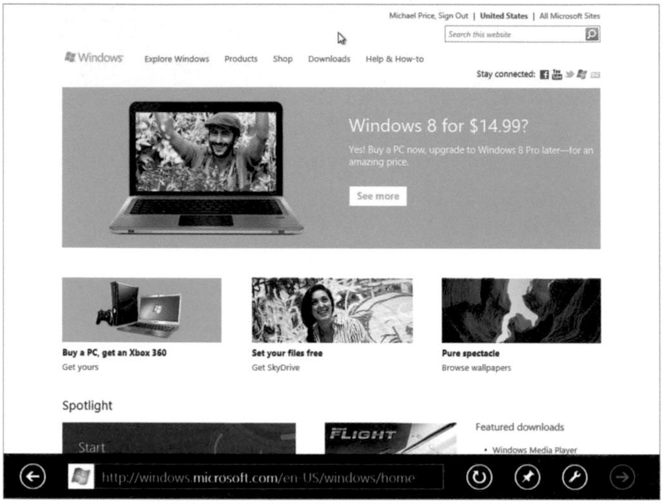

2. The app opens full screen displaying the App bar. This vanishes if you scroll the screen

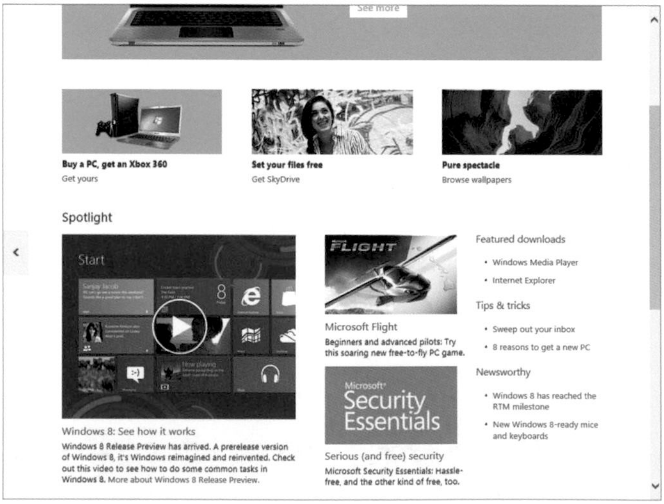

Don't forget

Windows 8 does give you the option to specify other browsers such as Mozilla, Opera or Chrome, as the default, but Internet Explorer is used for these examples.

Don't forget

You can scroll the screen with the mouse wheel, with the scroll bar that appears when you move the mouse, or by dragging on a touch monitor.

3 Right-click an empty part of the Internet Explorer window and the App bar reappears, in two parts – Tab switcher on top, and Navigation bar below

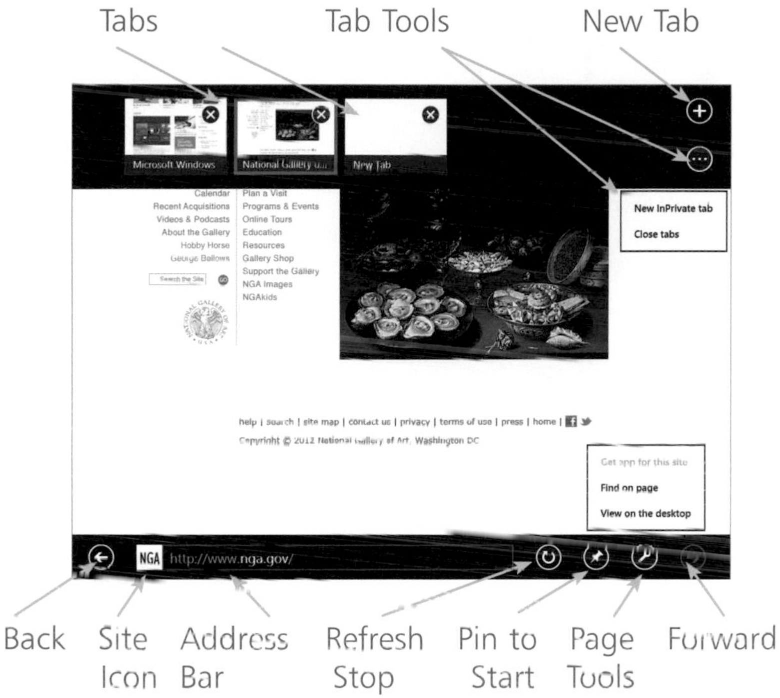

4 Click in the Address bar and begin typing and Internet Explorer will suggest possible web pages

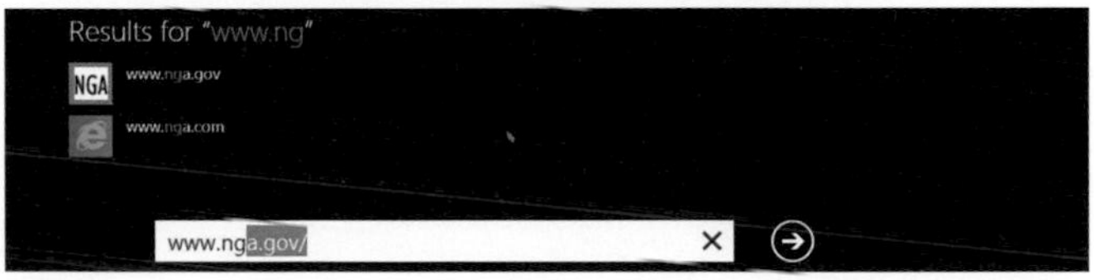

Don't forget

There's no Home page in the Windows 8 version. It will open the same tabs that you last had open, even after shutting down the system.

Hot tip

The Pin to Start option also provides an entry for Add to Favorites.

Don't forget

Internet Explorer keeps a history of the websites that you visit and will make suggestions based on those and upon the Favorites that you may have saved (see page 170). Pinned websites are also searched.

Right-click Menu

The right-click action can vary depending where you click.

Hot tip

The right-click action is one area where the Windows 8 Internet Explorer app performs differently from the Desktop version.

1. Right-click an empty part (where the mouse pointer remains as an arrow) to get the App bar

Microsoft Windows
CNN.com Internat...
National Gallery o...
NGA IMAGES
NGA Images is a repository of digital images of the collections of the National Gallery of Art. On this website you can search, browse, share, and download images. A standards-based reproduction guide and a help section provide advice for both novices and experts. More than 20,000 open access digital images up to 3000 pixels each are available free of charge for download and use. NGA Images is designed to facilitate learning, enrichment, enjoyment, and exploration.
Featured Image Collections
THE McCRINDLE GIFT
https://images.nga.gov/en/page/show_home_page.!

Don't forget

Hyperlinks direct you to other website locations. They can be associated with images, with graphics and with text.

2. Right-click an image with a hyperlink (where the mouse pointer becomes a hand) and a menu will be displayed

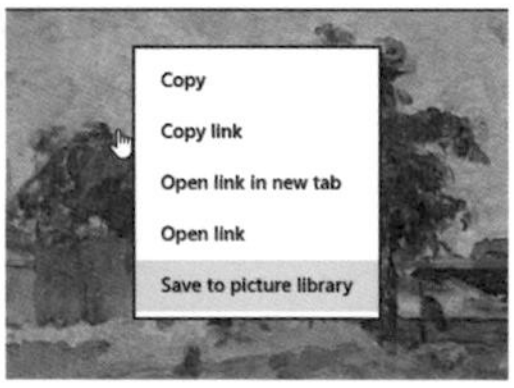
Copy
Copy link
Open link in new tab
Open link
Save to picture library

3. There's a slightly different menu displayed when you right-click text with a hyperlink (again indicated by a hand symbol)

Copy link
Open link in new tab
Open link
THE McCRINDLE GIFT

These right-click actions are quite unlike the results that you get with the Desktop Internet Explorer. To explore the differences, view the current web page on the Desktop:

4. Display the App bar, then click the Page tool and select the option View on the desktop

Get app for this site
Find on page
View on the desktop

The web page on the current tab in Windows 8 Internet Explorer is displayed in the Desktop Internet Explorer.

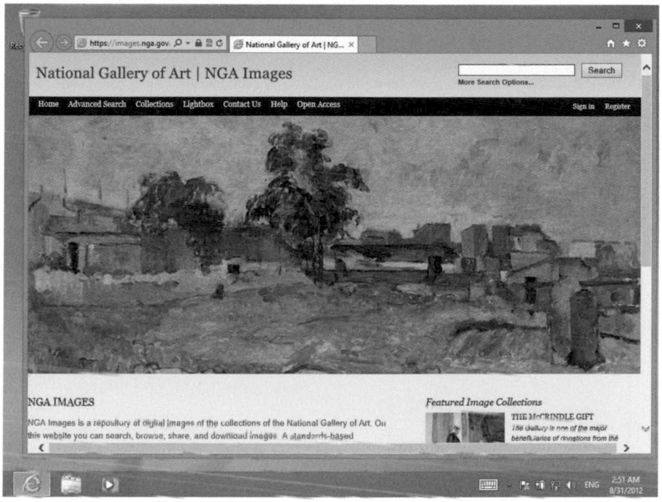

Don't forget

Only the active tab gets opened in the Desktop Internet Explorer, though you can add more tabs and switch web pages in the normal Desktop manner.

5. Right-click an empty part of the window, or one of the hyperlinks and you'll see no App bar, just menus

Plain Area | Patterned Area | Picture Hyperlink | Text Hyperlink

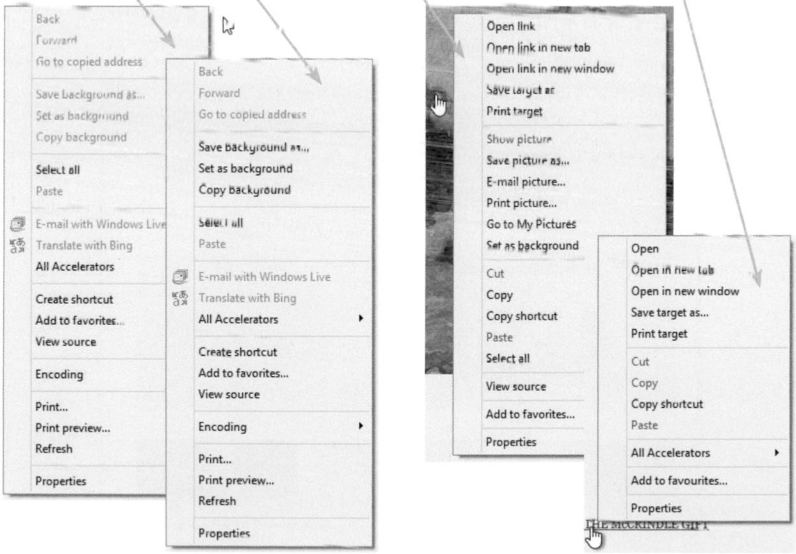

Don't forget

The Desktop Internet Explorer is a resizable window and contains all the elements (see page 55) you'd find in previous releases of Windows, including the comprehensive right-click menus.

Hot tip

With hyperlinks, the right-click menu gives options to open the link in a new window or in a new tab (see page 166).

Desktop Internet Explorer

Don't forget

The Internet Explorer tile on the Start screen opens the Windows 8 app, but you can open the Desktop version from the Taskbar.

Hot tip

You select one bar at a time and it is added and then marked with a tick. Select again to remove the tick and hide the bar. You can also set Show tabs on a separate row.

1. Click the Internet Explorer icon on the Desktop Taskbar

2. Internet Explorer opens the Home page in a window

Address and Search Bar

Tab Bar

Mini Toolbar

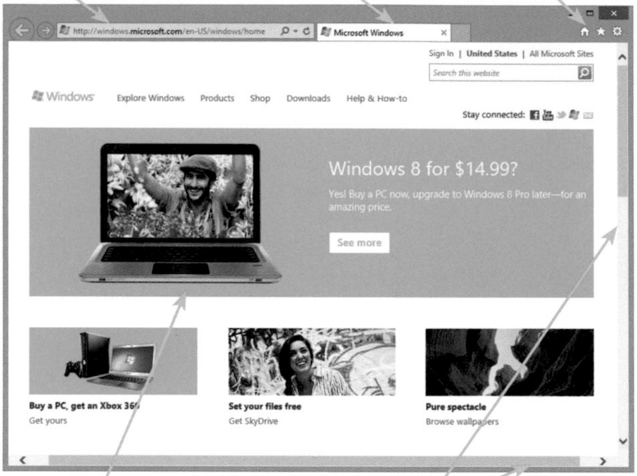

Web Page

Scroll Bars

3. Right-click alongside the Tab bar and click another bar, e.g. Favorites

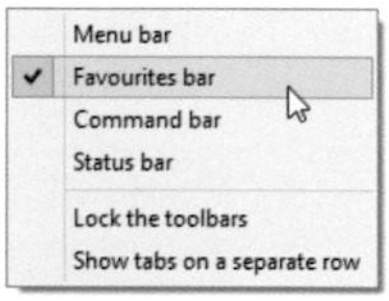

Back and Forward

Tab Bar

Menu Bar

Favorites Bar

Command Bar

Status Bar

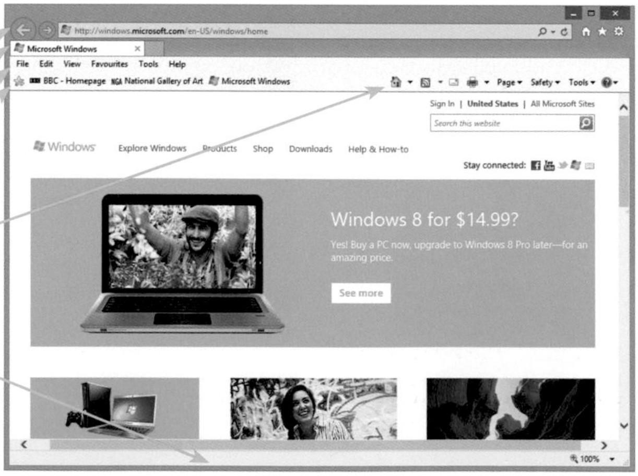

4 Click in the Address bar and Internet Explorer makes suggestions based on your previous visits

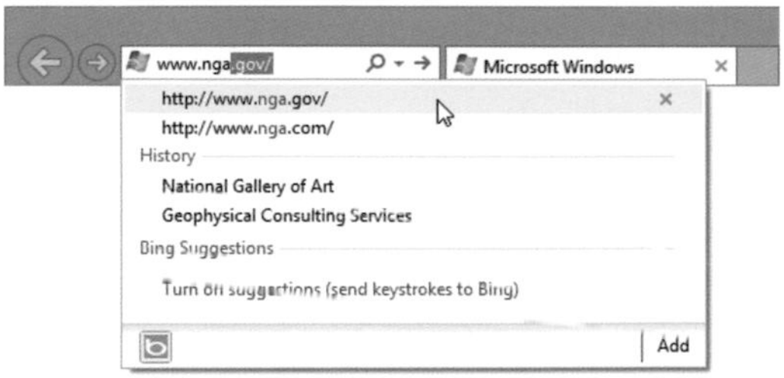
www.nga.gov/
Microsoft Windows
http://www.nga.gov/
http://www.nga.com/
History
National Gallery of Art
Geophysical Consulting Services
Bing Suggestions
Turn on suggestions (send keystrokes to Bing)
Add

5 Click a hyperlink to switch to that web page

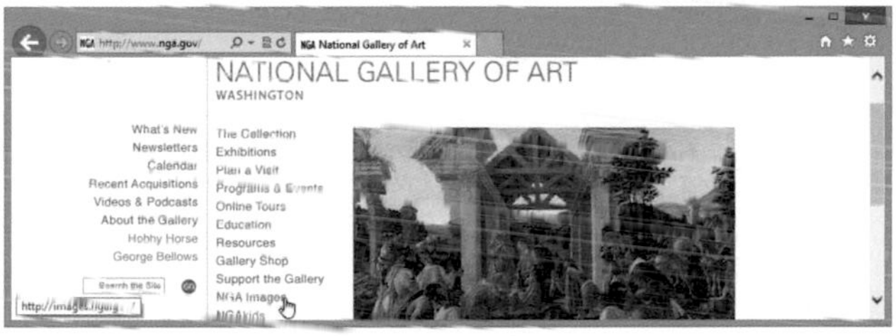

6 Click the Back and Forward buttons to review pages

7 Right-click the Back and Forward arrows, to see the list of recent visits and select any web page to go directly there

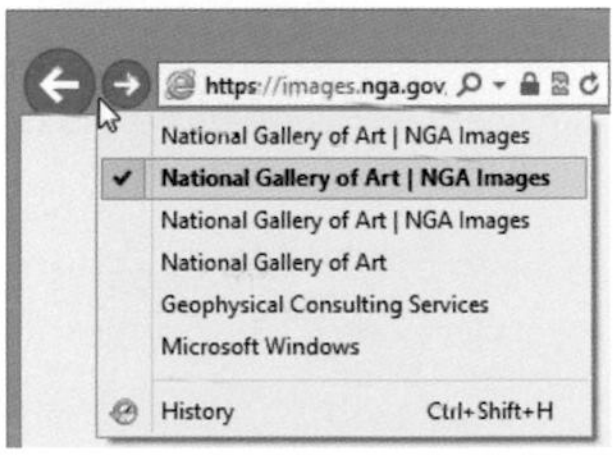

Don't forget

When you move the mouse pointer over a hyperlink and the hand symbol appears, you'll also see a box with the address that the hyperlink will direct you to.

http://images.nga.gov/

Don't forget

Navigating the web is intrinsically the same, but the tools do differ between the two versions of Internet Explorer.

Tabbed Browsing

Hot tip

The New Tab button gives you a blank tab where you can enter a URL on the address bar, or redisplay your previously viewed web pages.

Don't forget

You can use the same keyboard shortcuts in the Windows 8 IE app, to open a new tab, or to open a hyperlink in a new tab.

Using tabs allows you to explore websites without losing your place in the website you are currently visiting.

To open a web page in a tab:

1. Click the New Tab button or press Ctrl + T and the new tab is added and becomes the current tab

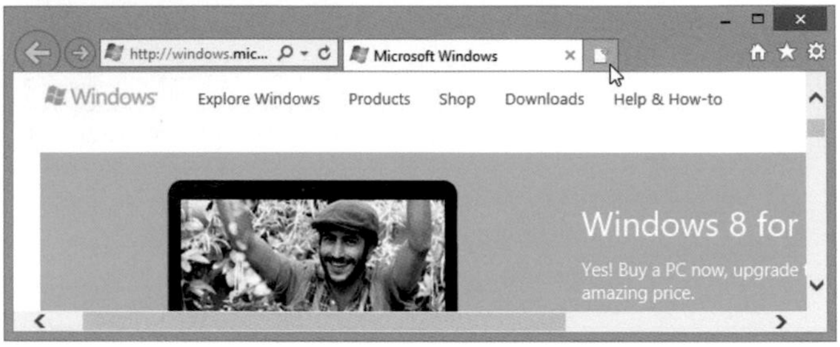

2. Type the web page address in the address bar (or select from the suggestions) and press Enter

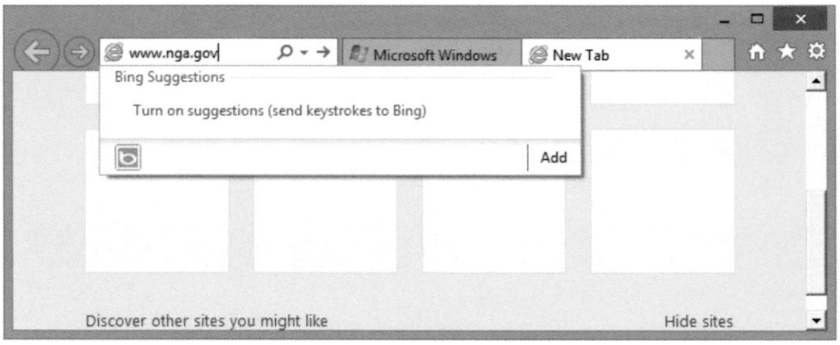

3. The new tab displays the required web page, with the previous web page still available on the other tab

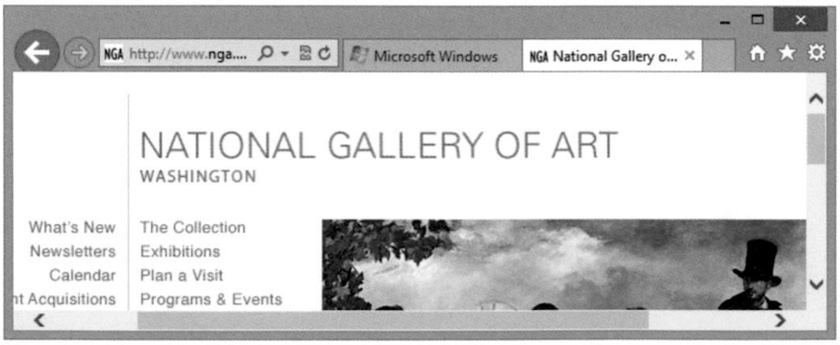

4. Right-click a hyperlink on the current web page and select Show Link on New Tab, or press Ctrl + Click

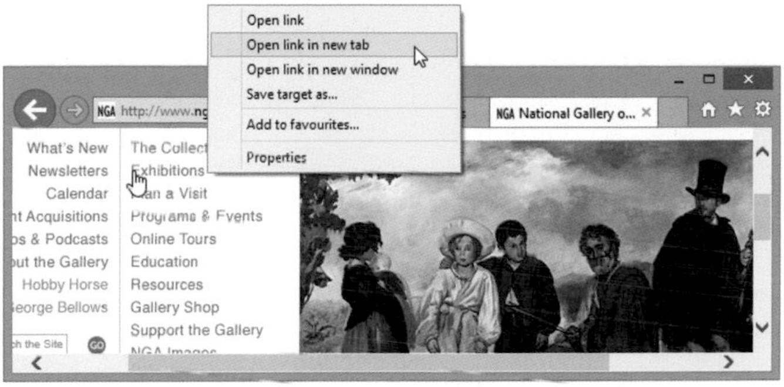

The new tab is added but the original tab remains displayed.

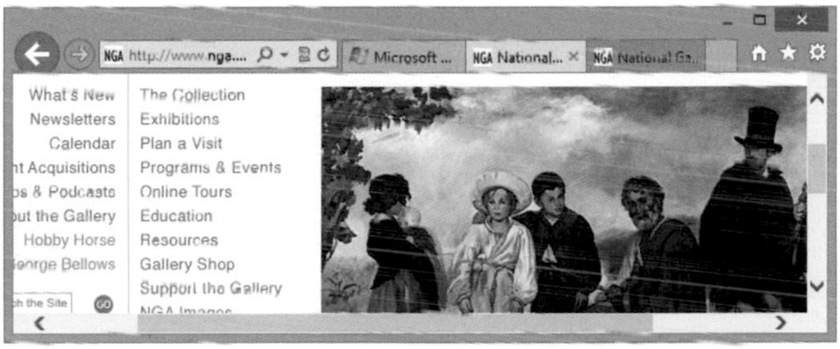

5. Click on the new tab to view the chosen web page

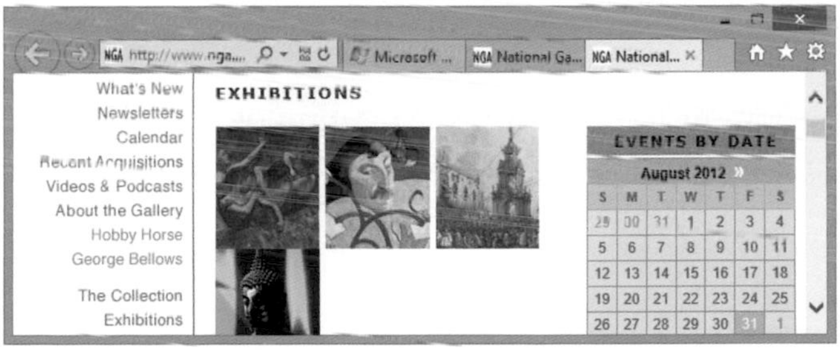

Scroll buttons are added if there are too many tabs to fit on.

Hot tip

If you press Ctrl + Shift + Click to select a hyperlink, it will display immediately in the new tab.

Don't forget

Hold the mouse over a tab, to see the full title of the web page that it displays.

Close Tabs

1. To close the current tab, click the X on the tab (or press Ctrl + W or press Alt + F4)

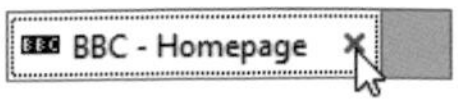

2. To close all the tabs except the current tab, press Ctrl + Alt + F4

3. To close the Internet Explorer session, click the X on the window title bar, or press Alt + F4, or click the title bar and select Close

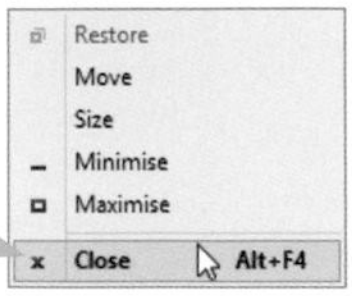

4. You could also right-click the taskbar icon and select Close window from the Jump list

5. However you close, if there's more than one tab open, you are prompted to select Close all tabs or Close current tab

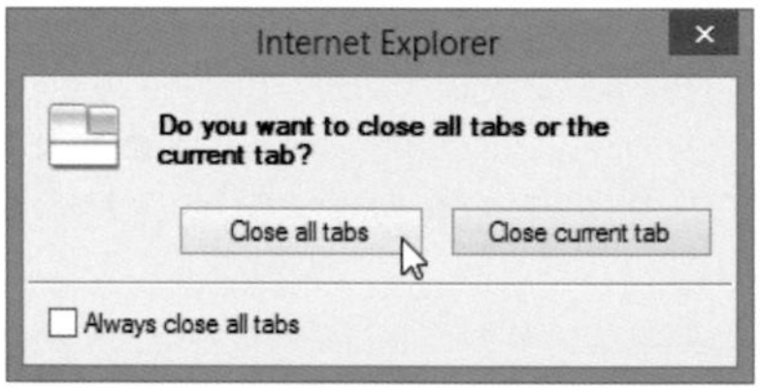

Hot tip

If you have a wheel mouse, click a tab on the tab row with the wheel to close that tab.

Hot tip

Click the "X" button to cancel, if you decide you do not want to close any of the tabs at this time.

If you close all tabs Internet Explorer closes. The next time you start Internet Explorer, you can reopen all those tabs.

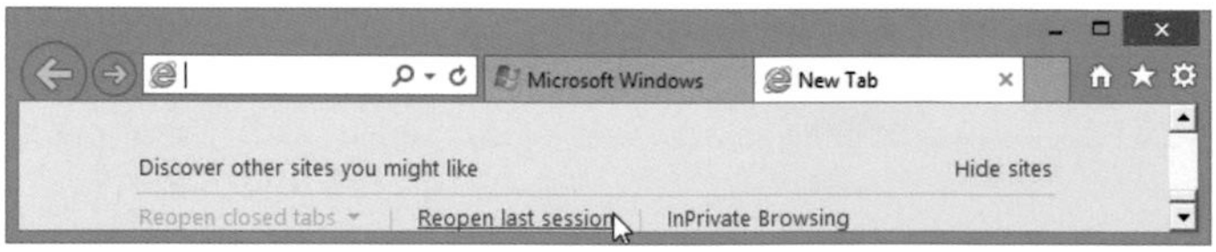

1. Open a new tab (see page 166) and select Reopen last browsing session

Don't forget

This is useful for continuing work in progress, but if you will need the same set of web pages at a later date, save them as a group favorite.

To open a web page in a new tab with the Windows 8 version of Internet Explorer, you can:

1. Click the Address bar, right-click a Pinned, Frequent or Favorite website and select Open in new tab

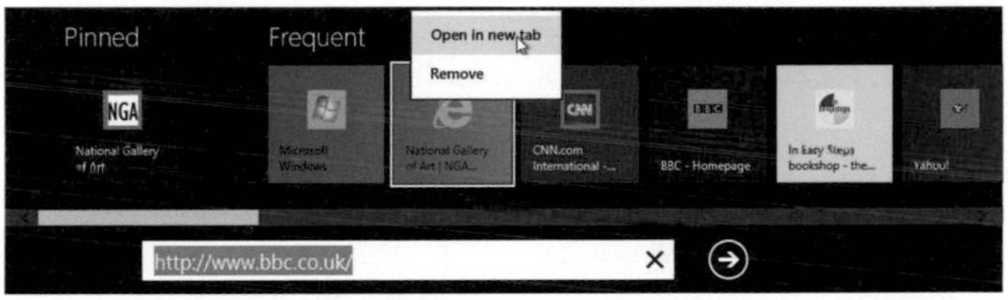

2. If you type an address, right-click the suggested page

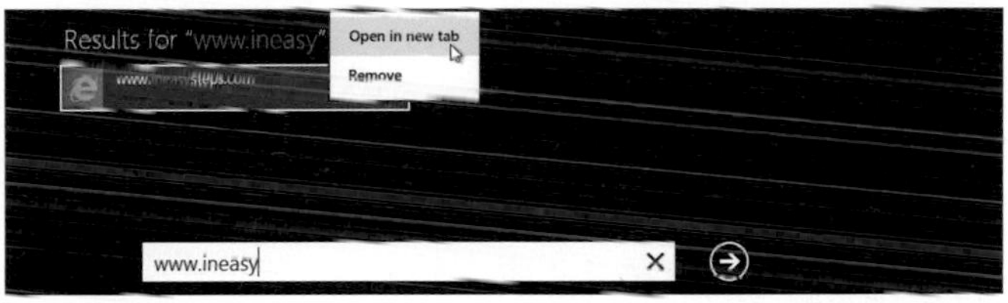

3. To close a tab, display the Tab bar and click X on the thumbnail (or click the thumbnail with the wheel)

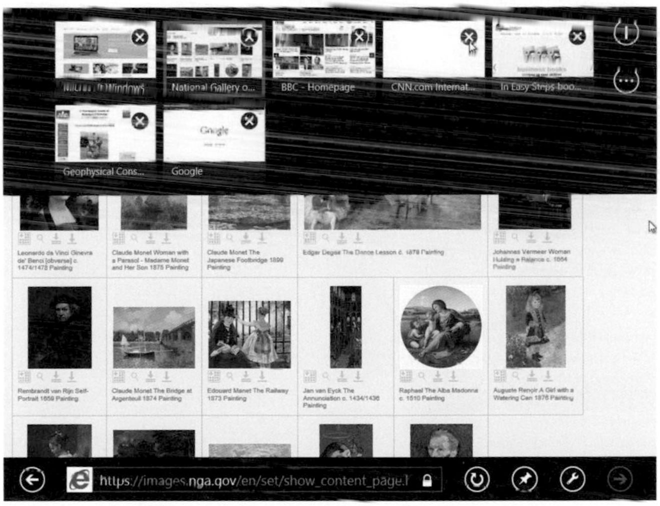

Don't forget

There aren't as many options for opening and closing tabs in the App version, but there are some useful shortcuts available.

Hot tip

Keyboard shortcut Ctrl + Alt + F4 will close all the tabs except the current tab, just as it does in the Desktop version. You don't have to display the Tab bar, though it does let you see the action.

Add to Favorites

When you visit a web page that you'll want to view again in future, you can save it as a Favorite.

1. With the web page displayed, click the Favorites button and then click Add to Favorites

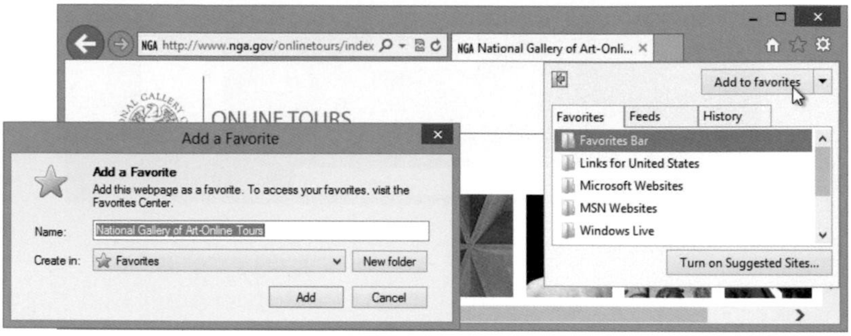
Add a Favorite
Add a Favorite
Add this webpage as a favorite. To access your favorites, visit the Favorites Center.
Name: National Gallery of Art-Online Tours
Create in: Favorites
New folder
Add
Cancel
Add to favorites
Favorites
Feeds
History
Favorites Bar
Links for United States
Microsoft Websites
MSN Websites
Windows Live
Turn on Suggested Sites...

2. Click Add to put the named entry in the main folder

3. To save the set of open tabs as a group, click the down-arrow and select Add Current Tabs to Favorites

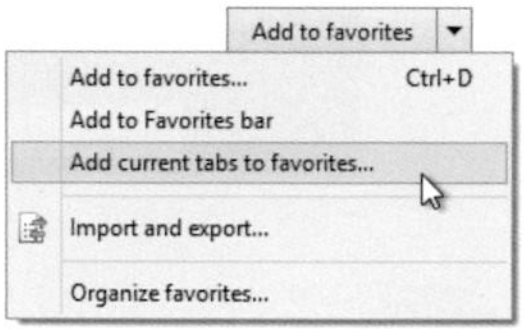
Add to favorites
Add to favorites... Ctrl+D
Add to Favorites bar
Add current tabs to favorites...
Import and export...
Organize favorites...

4. Provide a Folder Name for the group of tabs and click Add

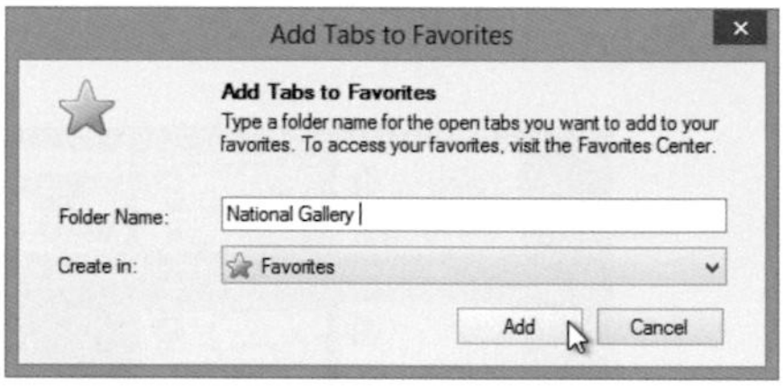

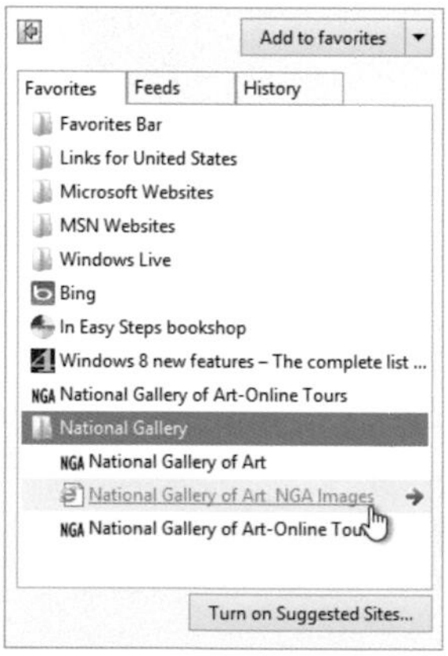

Favorites Center

To make use of the entries saved in your Favorites list:

1. Click the Favorites button, then select the whole tab group, a web page from within the group, or a web page saved individually

Beware

The button on the Favorites bar is used to Add to Favorites bar. This should be restricted to a limited number of entries, to avoid crowding.

Hot tip

To make favorites easier to identify, change the name, select a different folder from the list or create a new folder.

Hot tip

Click the arrow button to pin the Favorites Center to the window so that you can quickly view each of the entries in turn.

Pin Websites

Windows 8 IE can also add web pages to the same list of Favorites as the Desktop IE. To add a web page:

1. Display the web page and the App bar and select the Pin button, then click Add to favorites

2. When you next click the address bar to enter a web address, Favorites are listed alongside Frequent sites

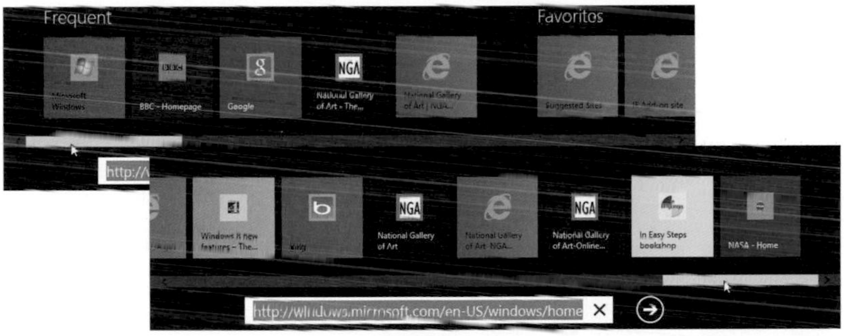

3. To see the latest Favorites, you must scroll to the end

4. Alternatively, select Pin to Start, accept or amend the website name, then click Pin to Start

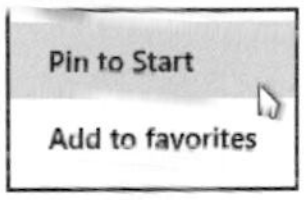

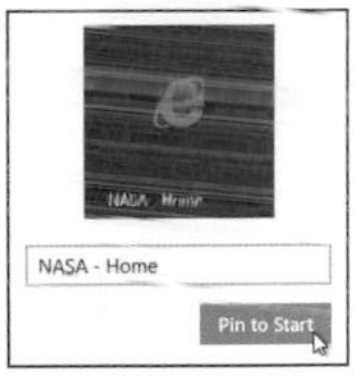

5. Your Pinned sites will appear first in the list of suggested websites

Don't forget

In the Windows 8 app there are no options to rename the Favorites or to organize them in folders or tab groups.

Don't forget

The websites that you Pin to Start will, of course, appear on the Start screen as a group of tiles, so you can start Internet Explorer with a Pinned site.

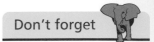

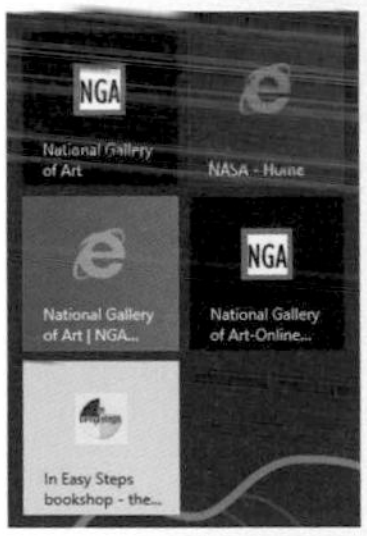

Zoom Web Page

You may find some web pages difficult to read, especially if you have your monitor set for high resolution. The Zoom feature provides an effective solution to this problem.

Hot tip

Values below 100% are useful to overview a large web page. Choose Custom to apply a specific zoom factor. You can specify any value between 10% and 1000%.

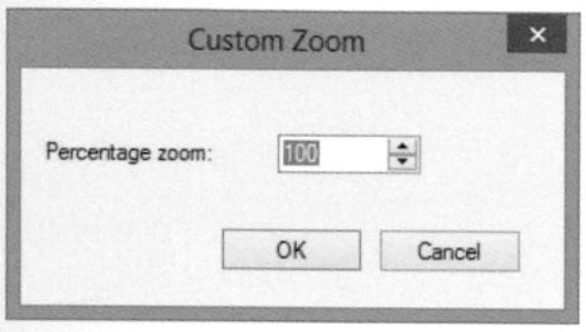

1. Click the Tools button on the Toolbar and select Zoom

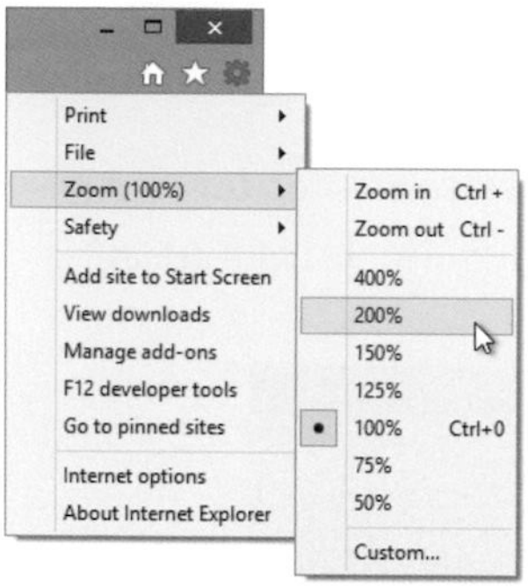

2. Choose a level, e.g. 200%

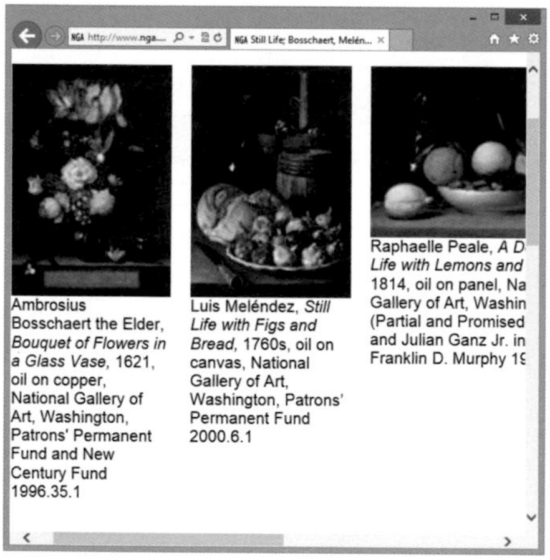

3. Press Ctrl + to Zoom in, 25% more each time

4. Press Ctrl - to Zoom out, 25% less each time

5. Press Ctrl 0 to return to the 100% level

Don't forget

Click the down arrow next to the Zoom button to display the Zoom menu and select the level required.

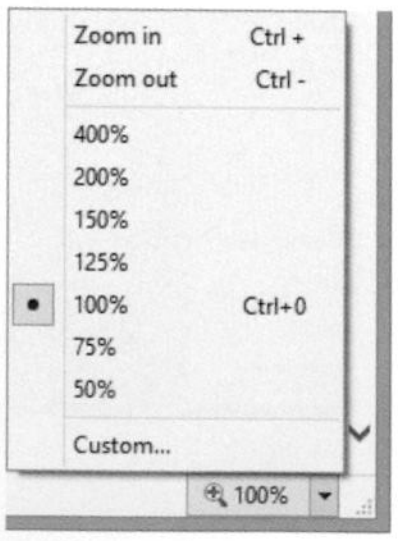

Zoom Button

If you enable the Comments bar, you'll find a Zoom button that makes it easier to apply changes.

6. Click the Zoom button repeatedly to cycle through the levels 125%, 150% and 100%

The Windows 8 Internet Explorer app will accept the same keyboard shortcuts, but there are no Zoom menus or button.

1. With full screen display always in effect, some web pages may not make full use of the display area

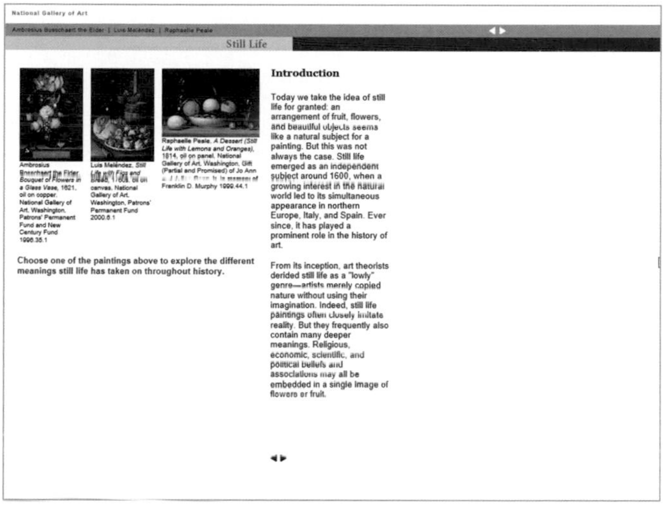
National Gallery of Art
Still Life
Introduction
Choose one of the paintings above to explore the different meanings still life has taken on throughout history.

2. Press Ctrl + two times to apply a zoom factor of 150% and the web page fills the screen

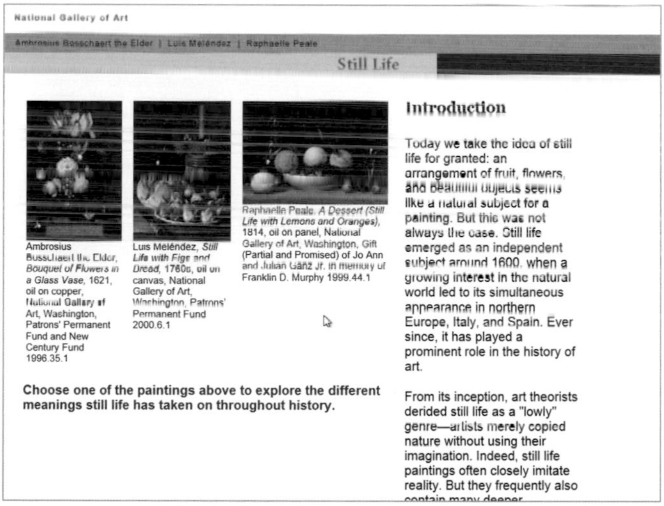
National Gallery of Art
Ambrosius Bosschaert the Elder | Luis Meléndez | Raphaelle Peale
Still Life
Introduction
Today we take the idea of still life for granted: an arrangement of fruit, flowers, and beautiful objects seems like a natural subject for a painting. But this was not always the case. Still life emerged as an independent subject around 1600, when a growing interest in the natural world led to its simultaneous appearance in northern Europe, Italy, and Spain. Ever since, it has played a prominent role in the history of art.
From its inception, art theorists derided still life as a "lowly" genre—artists merely copied nature without using their imagination. Indeed, still life paintings often closely imitate reality. But they frequently also
Ambrosius Bosschaert the Elder, Bouquet of Flowers in a Glass Vase, 1621, oil on copper, National Gallery of Art, Washington, Patrons' Permanent Fund and New Century Fund 1996.35.1
Luis Meléndez, Still Life with Figs and Bread, 1760s, oil on canvas, National Gallery of Art, Washington, Patrons' Permanent Fund 2000.6.1
Raphaelle Peale, A Dessert (Still Life with Lemons and Oranges), 1814, oil on panel, National Gallery of Art, Washington, Gift (Partial and Promised) of Jo Ann and Julian Ganz Jr. in memory of Franklin D. Murphy 1999.44.1
Choose one of the paintings above to explore the different meanings still life has taken on throughout history.

Press Ctrl 0 to return to the 100% zoom level.

Don't forget

If you have a particularly high resolution screen, you can increase default zoom factor from 100%. From the Internet Explorer app display the Charms bar and select Settings.

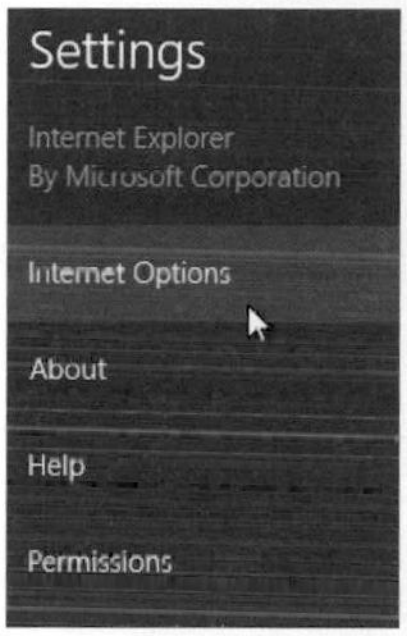
Settings
Internet Explorer
By Microsoft Corporation
Internet Options
About
Help
Permissions

Select Internet Options and adjust Zoom slider where you can set a value between 50% and 400% as the default. This only affects the Windows 8 Internet Explorer app.

Internet Explorer Settings
Zoom
150%

RSS Feeds

Hot tip

An RSS feed (also known as a web feed) is a means of collating updates to web pages so you can be made aware of changes without having to revisit the website.

Internet Explorer tells you whenever there's a feed available, if you enable the Command bar to see the Feeds icon.

1. If there are no feeds available, the button is grayed

2. When you switch to a web page that has a feed, the Feeds button changes color and a sound plays

3. Click the Feeds button and select the feed to view the reports it offers

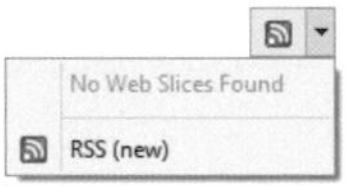

No Web Slices Found
RSS (new)

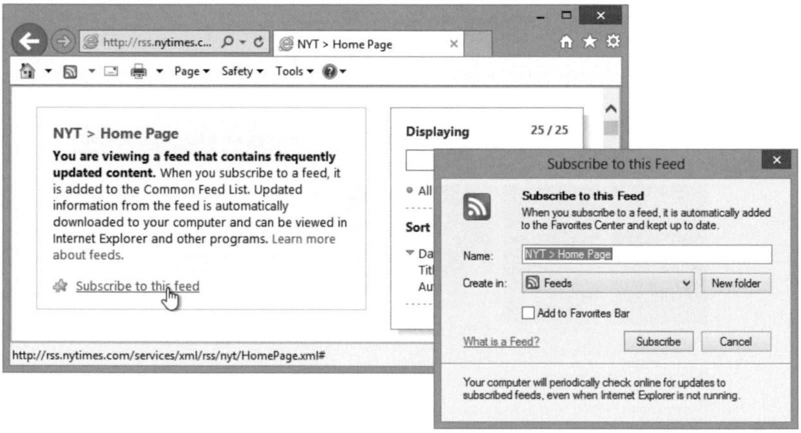

4. If the reports interest you, click Subscribe to this feed, then click Subscribe and you'll be able to view updated content in Internet Explorer or in Windows Live Mail (see page 154)

Don't forget

In the Windows 8 app you will see any feeds as suggested sites when you enter a web address and you can select a feed to review reports and subscribe.

10 Windows Games

Go to Xbox Games and the Windows Store, to find a variety of products to challenge and teach. You can record your scores and compare your results with other players.

Games in Windows 8

In previous releases of Windows, a good selection of games was included in the initial installation. In Windows 7, for example, you'd find the following in the Games folder:

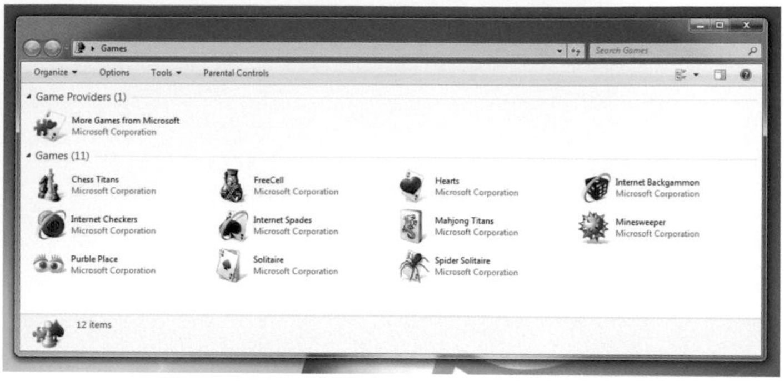
Games
Search Games
Organize
Options
Tools
Parental Controls
Game Providers (1)
More Games from Microsoft
Microsoft Corporation
Games (11)
Chess Titans
Microsoft Corporation
FreeCell
Microsoft Corporation
Hearts
Microsoft Corporation
Internet Backgammon
Microsoft Corporation
Internet Checkers
Microsoft Corporation
Internet Spades
Microsoft Corporation
Mahjong Titans
Microsoft Corporation
Minesweeper
Microsoft Corporation
Purble Place
Microsoft Corporation
Solitaire
Microsoft Corporation
Spider Solitaire
Microsoft Corporation
12 items

Associated with this folder was the Games Explorer, which helped you to get software updates and news feeds for the installed games. The Games Explorer also tracked wins, losses and other statistics.

You won't find these games in Windows 8. In fact there are no Desktop games actually installed with the system. However, Microsoft is integrating Xbox content and gaming services into Windows. There is a Games app which helps you find Xbox games, available from the Games section of the Windows 8 Store (see page 24), where you'll find many games available.

Xbox

Xbox is a video game console manufactured by Microsoft, first released in 2001. It is a sixth-generation gaming device designed to compete with Sony's PlayStation. The integrated Xbox Live service, launched in 2002, allows players to play games online with a broadband connection.

Hot tip

There are many third party games that are compatible with Windows and some of these will operate in the Windows 8 Desktop environment.

Don't forget

The Games app doesn't actually download games, but gives you a link to the Windows Store where you can purchase (if necessary) and download the app.

Games App

1. Click Games on the Start screen and the Games app launches, displaying an Xbox image as it loads

2. A selection of Xbox games for the PC is highlighted

xbox games
spotlight
Mahjong Classic
Minesweeper
Solitaire Collection
Pinball FX2
Wordament
Spelunky
Plants vs Zombies
Left 4 Dead 2
Rock Band Blitz

3. Select a game, e.g. Minesweeper, to see a description. Click Explore game for more details

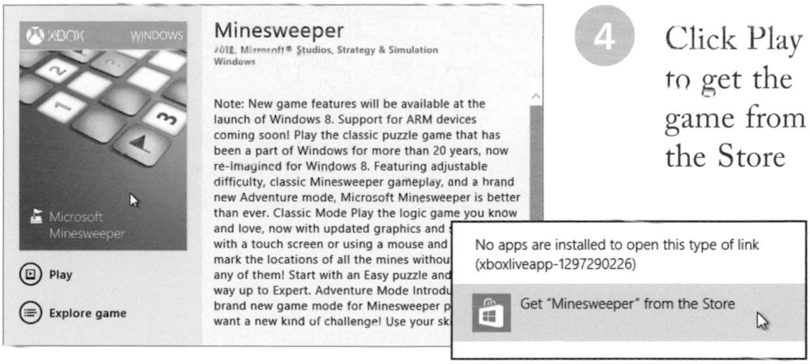
XBOX WINDOWS
Microsoft Minesweeper
Play
Explore game
Minesweeper
Windows
Note: New game features will be available at the launch of Windows 8. Support for ARM devices coming soon! Play the classic puzzle game that has been a part of Windows for more than 20 years, now re-imagined for Windows 8. Featuring adjustable difficulty, classic Minesweeper gameplay, and a brand new Adventure mode, Microsoft Minesweeper is better than ever. Classic Mode Play the logic game you know and love, now with updated graphics and
with a touch screen or using a mouse and
mark the locations of all the mines withou
any of them! Start with an Easy puzzle and
way up to Expert. Adventure Mode Introdu
brand new game mode for Minesweeper p
want a new kind of challenge! Use your sk
No apps are installed to open this type of link (xboxliveapp-1297290226)
Get "Minesweeper" from the Store

4. Click Play to get the game from the Store

Don't forget

The Games app allows you to discover and download games to your PC, record progress and achievements and compare results with your friends.

Hot tip

The first time you play, you are told that the app needs to be added and you get a link to the Store.

Minesweeper

Don't forget

The process that you follow to install and play Minesweeper is typical of the Xbox for PC games.

1. Select the link to Get Minesweeper from the Store to show the description and click the Install button

2. The game is installed and a tile is added to the Start screen

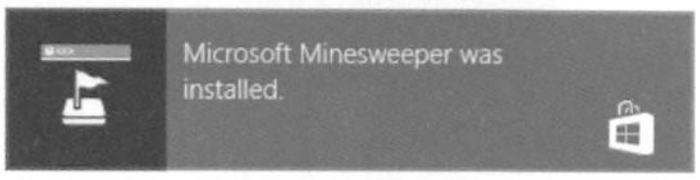

3. Select the tile to start the game

The first time you play, you'll get a gametag assigned to your Microsoft account, to identify you to other players.

4. Choose one of the game types, such as Easy 9x9 to get started, or a more advanced level later

Hot tip

You could also start the game from the Play button in the Game app, since you will now have installed the required app.

5 The game starts and the first time you play you get hints and prompts to explain how it works

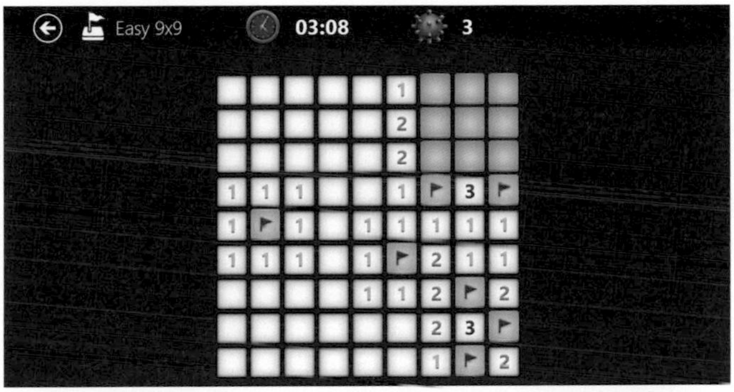

6 If you go wrong the results can be explosive

7 Get it right and you are treated to fireworks

Don't forget

You use the number to help deduce whether a square is safe to uncover. Right-click a suspect square to add a flag, or left-click a safe cell. On a touch screen, you would press for a flag or tap for a safe cell.

Hot tip

Your results are stored under your gametag and with the Game app you can create an avatar (a graphical representation of yourself), view your achievements and edit your profile.

Games at the Windows Store

Don't forget

The games that are highlighted and the numbers of apps shown will change frequently, but these examples illustrate the type of findings you can expect.

1. Open the Windows Store and scroll horizontally to the Games section to see the spotlighted selection

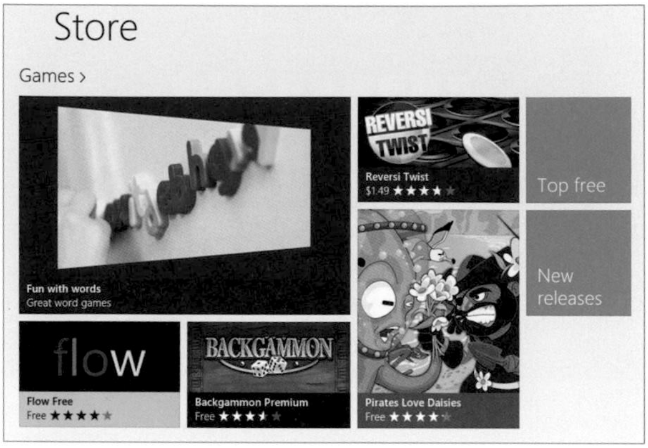

2. Click the Top free box to see a selection of the free games that are available (76 apps shown)

Top free in Games 76 apps
Games
Free
Microsoft Mahjong
Free
Doodle God Free
Free
Fruit Ninja
Free
Bubble Star
Free
Paint 4 Kids
Free
Microsoft Solitaire Collection
Free
Wordament
Free
Dark Arcana: The Carnival
Free

Hot tip

Many of the games shown in the Top free selection are also included in the New releases selection.

3. Press the back arrow to return to the Games section and click the box for New releases (95 apps shown)

New releases in Games 95 apps
Doodle Hangman Free
Free
Cake Tower
Free
Slide ur buddy
Free
Fantastic 4 In A Row Free
Free
Meduza
$1.49
Tetravex
Free
Escapa
Free
Bubble Wrap
Free
Puzzles
Free

Press the Back arrow to go back to the Games section.

4 Left-click alongside the Games section heading, to get a full list of Games (157 apps shown)

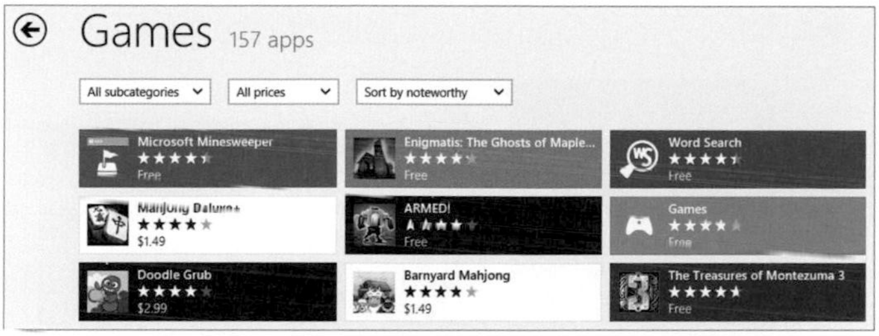

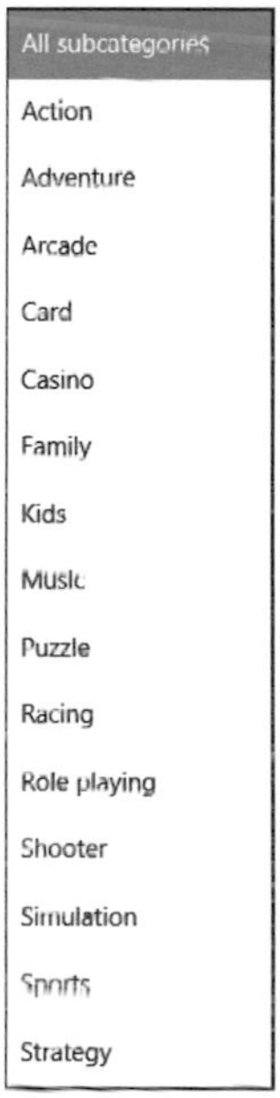

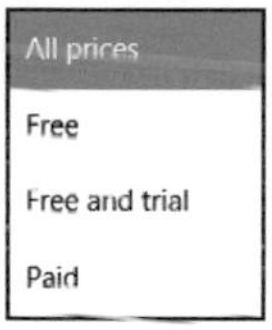

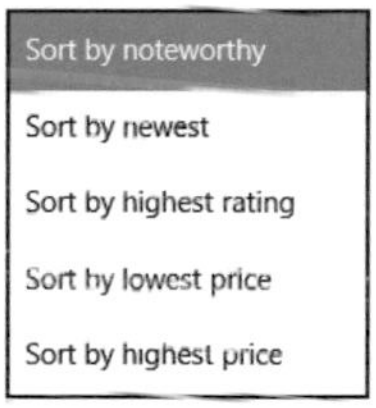

5 Click the down-arrows next to All sub-categories, All prices or Sort by noteworthy, to display the filter options

6 To find out what costs might be involved, choose All sub-categories, Paid and Sort by highest price

7 Games are sorted by the most expensive first, (33 apps shown, at $4.99 or less)

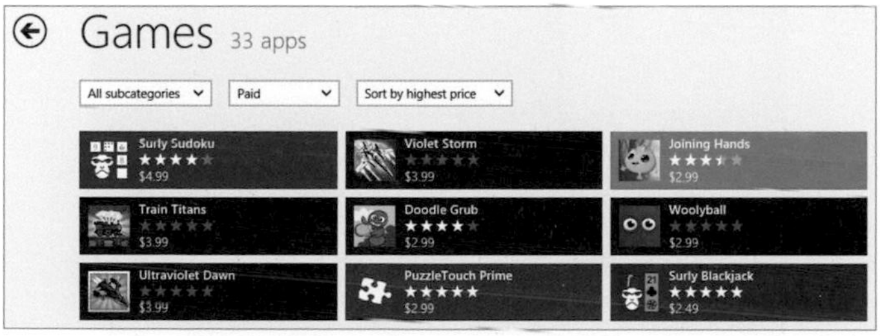

Don't forget

You can also select Search from the Charms bar and search the Windows Store for Games.

You get All categories (192 apps shown) but can choose the Games category (155 shown).

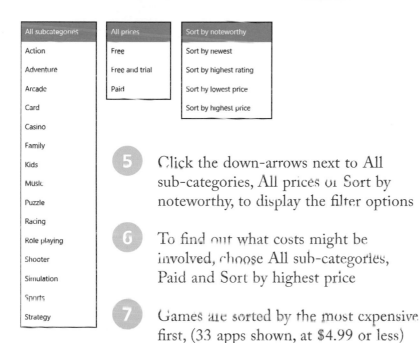

Microsoft Solitaire Collection

Don't forget

If you have enjoyed playing FreeCell or Spider solitaire in a previous release of Windows, you'll be pleased to find the Microsoft Solitaire Collection in the Store.

1. Select the app from the Store

2. Click the Install button to download the app

3. Select the app from the Start screen

4. The first time, you'll be asked to allow the app to access and update your Xbox Live info

5. The app loads up and offers you a choice of games (Klondike, Spider, FreeCell, Pyramid, TriPeaks) plus a daily challenge

Hot tip

By allowing access, you will have a record of the results for all the games you play and you can share your achievements with other players.

6. Scroll horizontally to review and select a theme

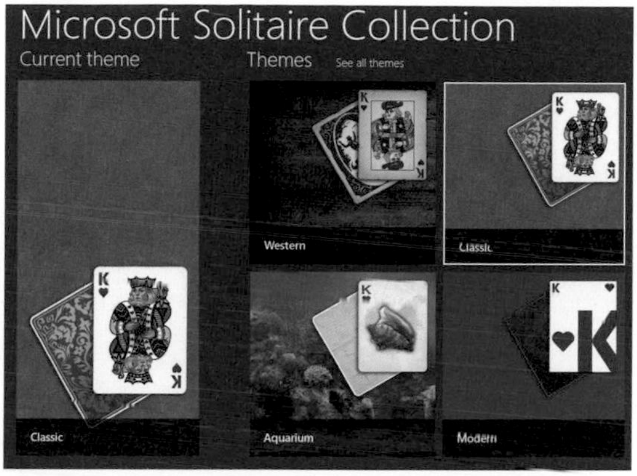

7. Scroll on to the How to play section

8. Select FreeCell for step by step guidance on playing

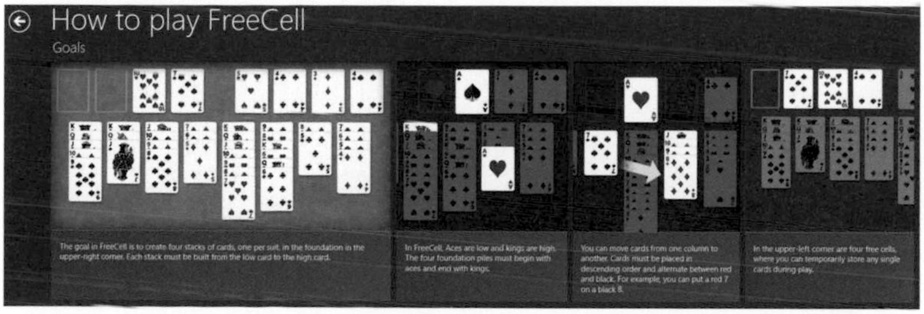

Don't forget

The Theme specifies the card deck style and the play area background for all of the games in the collection.

Hot tip

There are also Awards and Statistics areas, to keep a complete record of your results. You might even get yourself put on the Leaderboards.

Microsoft Mahjong

Don't forget

This game has three skill levels, with four puzzles for each, giving 12 in total. It can be played with keyboard, mouse or by touch.

1. Locate the app in the Store, and choose Install to download the app and add it to the Start screen

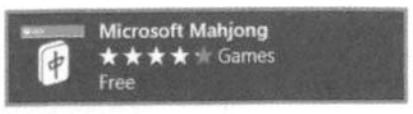
Microsoft Mahjong
Games
Free

2. The first time you run the app you are asked for permission to access your Xbox Live info

Let this app access your info?
Yes
No

3. Select Choose puzzle

4. You'll start with just one Easy choice puzzle available

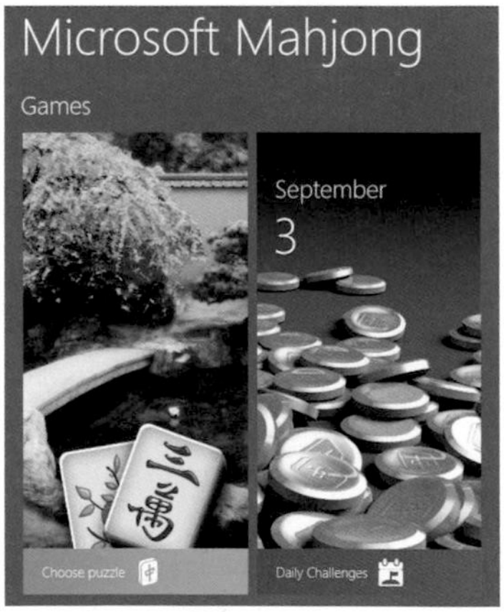

Hot tip

As with all the Xbox Live games, you get a record of your scores for all the puzzles and you can compare your results with other players.

5. Each time you complete a puzzle, the next one will be unlocked

6. Click matching pairs of free tiles to remove them

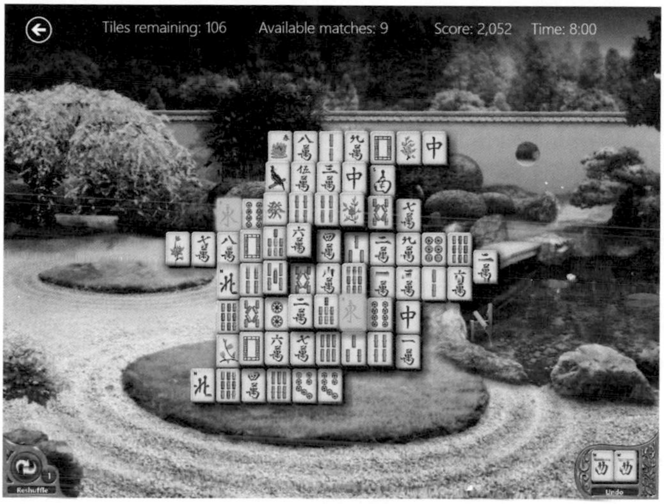

7. If you get stuck, press H for a hint and two matching tiles will flash

8. Fireworks are displayed when you complete the game and the next puzzle gets unlocked

9. Press the back arrow to go back to the main screen

10. Scroll horizontally and you'll find Themes, Awards, Statistics, Leaderboards and finally How to play, with tutorial, controls and tips and tricks

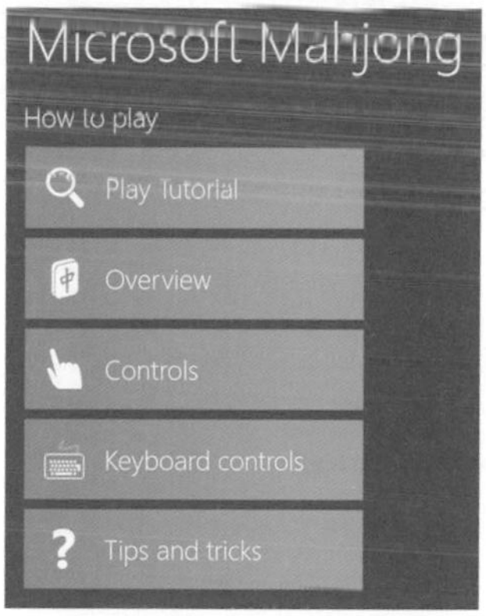

Don't forget

Right-click the play area and you'll see an App bar with buttons giving access to How to play, Pause, Hint and New game.

Hot tip

If there's a particular puzzle you like to relax with, select it and Pin it to the Start screen to make it easy to get.

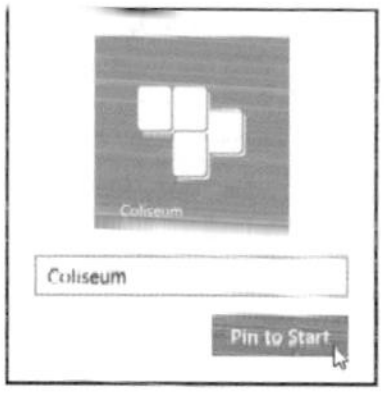

Word Games

Don't forget

Not all games are as complex as Mahjong and Solitaire. There are simple games that are easy and fun to play, for example Word Games.

1. Click Fun with words in the Games section of the Store

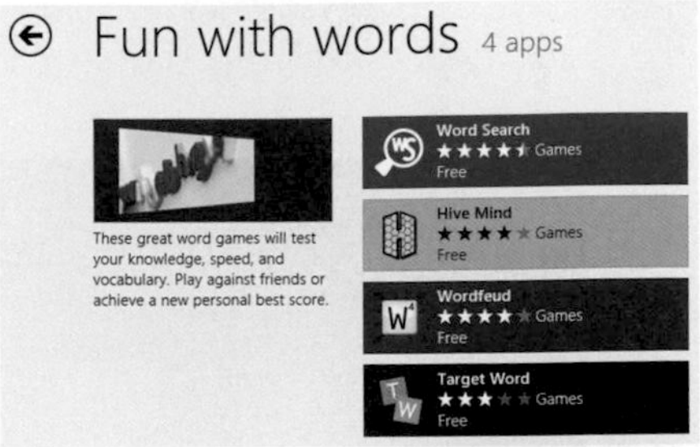

2. Select and install Wordsearch

3. Click Wordsearch on the Start screen

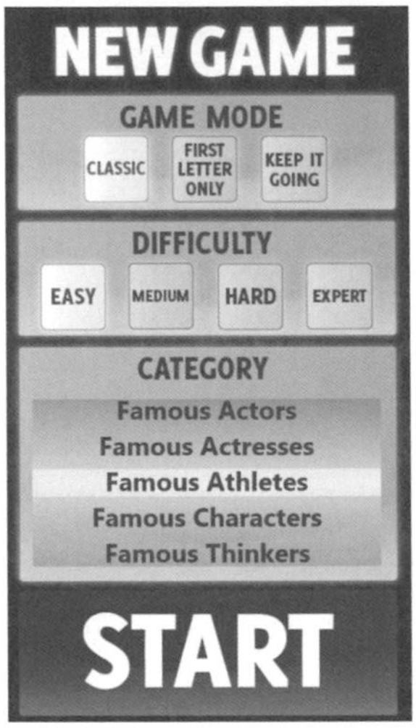

4. Select a game mode, the difficulty level and a category and click Start

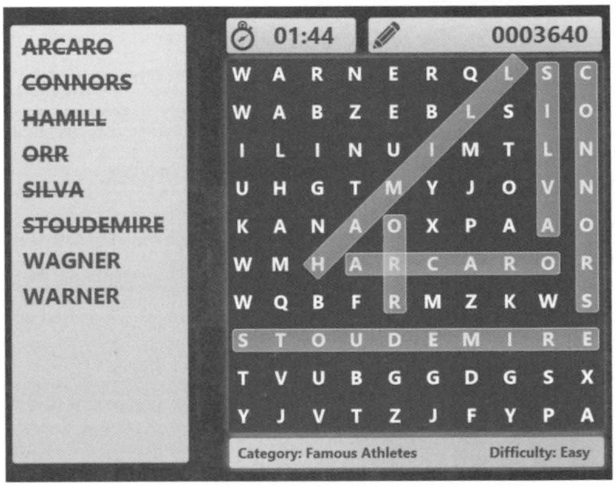

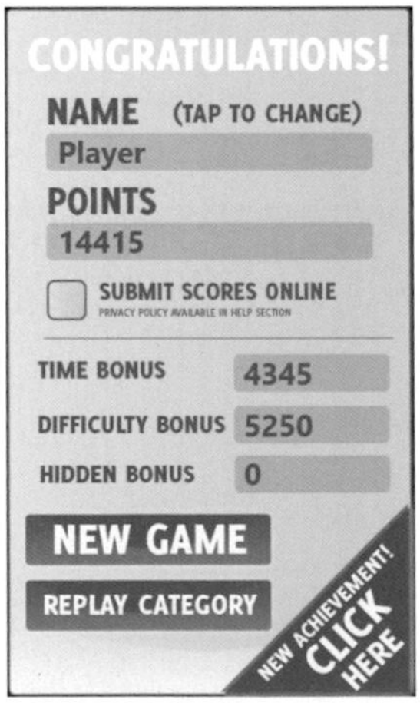

5. Locate the words in the panel

6. Even with a simple game, you can use the mouse keyboard or touch to select the letters that make the words

7. When you finish, you are offered the option to specify a player name and to submit your scores online

Hot tip

You don't have to worry about providing a name and recording your scores, unless you do like keeping track of your results.

11 Music and Pictures

With the sound card in your system, you can create recordings, play audio CDs and convert tracks to computer files to build and manage a music and sound library. You can also store and manage digital pictures and videos and create movies from your photos and video clips.

188 Sound Card and Speakers
190 Recording
192 Play Audio CD
194 Copy Tracks
195 Media Library
196 Music App
198 Digital Pictures
200 Viewing Pictures
201 Photos App
203 Windows Photo Viewer
204 Photo Gallery
206 Movie Maker

Sound Card and Speakers

Hot tip

The sound card on your system may be incorporated into the system board, or may be provided as a separate adapter card.

The sound card in your computer processes the information from programs such as the Music app or Windows Media Player and sends audio signals to your computer's speakers.

To review and adjust your sound setup:

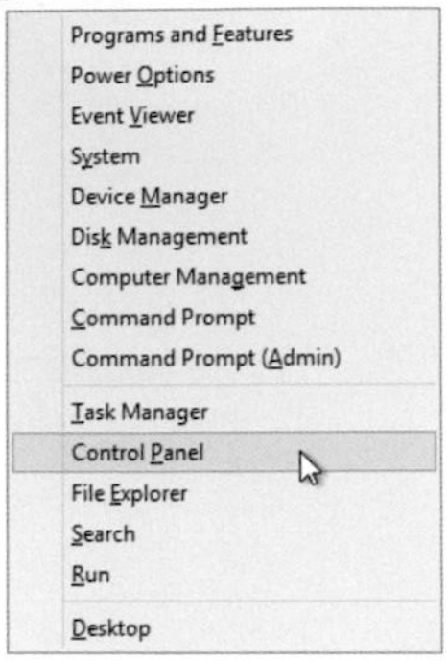

1. Press WinKey + X to open the Power Users menu and select Control Panel

2. Select Hardware and Sound and then Sound

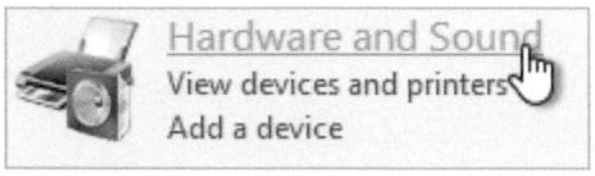

Sound
Change system sounds
Manage audio devices

4. Click the Playback tab, select the entry for speakers and click Configure

5. Select your speaker setup and click Test to check the speakers and then click Next to continue

Don't forget

Click Test to hear a sound from each speaker, or click an individual speaker to hear a sound from it, to ensure all speakers are working.

Choose your configuration
Select the speaker setup below that is most like the configuration on your computer.
Audio channels:
Stereo
Quadraphonic
Surround
5.1 Surround
5.1 Surround
Test

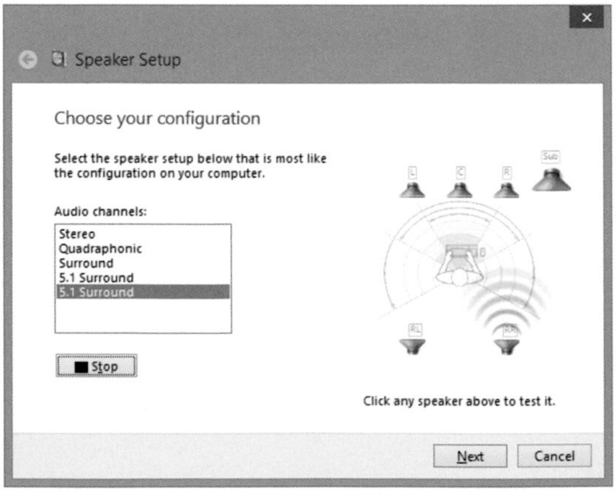
Speaker Setup
Choose your configuration
Select the speaker setup below that is most like the configuration on your computer.
Audio channels:
Stereo
Quadraphonic
Surround
5.1 Surround
5.1 Surround
Stop
Click any speaker above to test it.
Next
Cancel

6. Specify which speakers are present in your setup

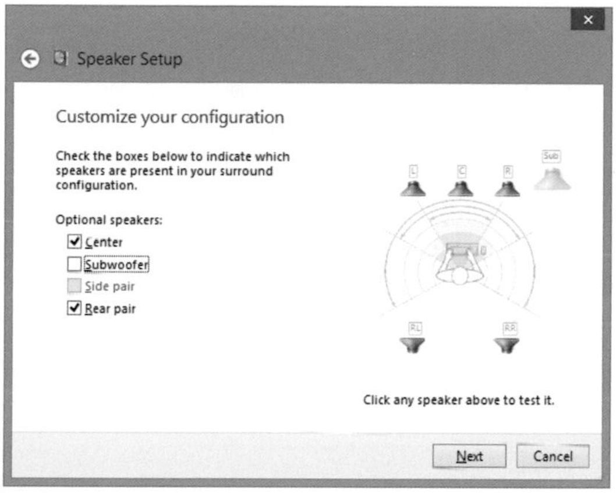
Speaker Setup
Customize your configuration
Check the boxes below to indicate which speakers are present in your surround configuration.
Optional speakers:
Center
Subwoofer
Side pair
Rear pair
Click any speaker above to test it.
Next
Cancel

7. Specify if speakers are full range versus satellite

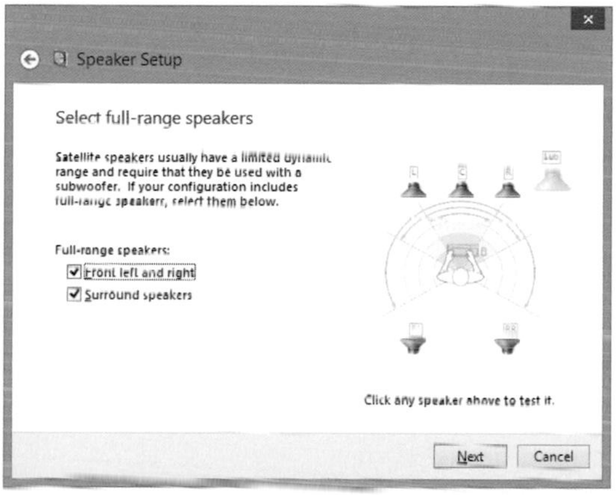
Speaker Setup
Select full-range speakers
Satellite speakers usually have a limited dynamic range and require that they be used with a subwoofer. If your configuration includes full-range speakers, select them below.
Full-range speakers:
Front left and right
Surround speakers
Click any speaker above to test it.
Next
Cancel

8. Click Finish to complete and apply the configuration

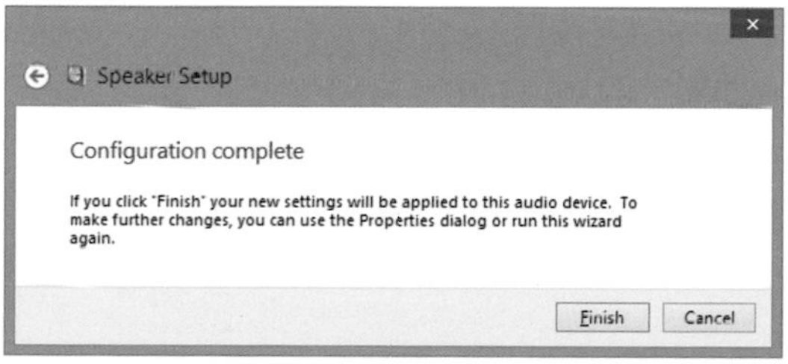
Speaker Setup
Configuration complete
If you click "Finish" your new settings will be applied to this audio device. To make further changes, you can use the Properties dialog or run this wizard again.
Finish
Cancel

Hot tip

If you have a laptop or tablet PC with built in speakers these will normally be stereo and full-range.

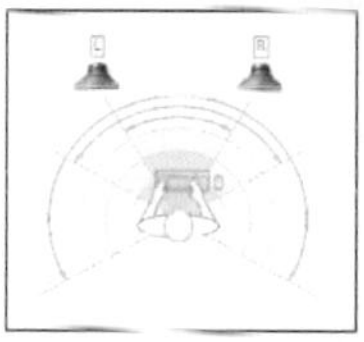

Don't forget

If you have a separate sound adapter, it may be installed with its own audio application programs to set up, configure and test the device features.

Recording

Don't forget

In this example, there are two microphones, one a headset and the other a webcam.

With a sound card on your system, you can make voice recordings from a microphone or other audio sources. To set up your microphone:

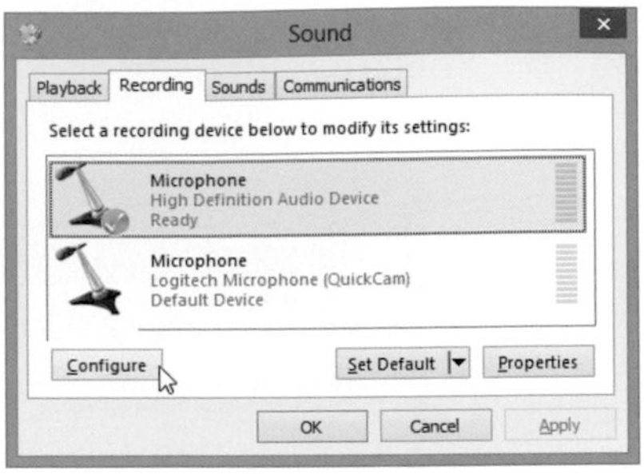

1. Open the Sound option from the Control Panel and click the Recording tab
2. Select the Microphone entry and click Configure

Don't forget

A headset microphone is the best choice if you are considering use of voice control.

3. Select Set up microphone and select the type you are using (headset, desktop or other kind)

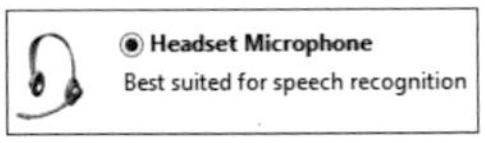
Headset Microphone
Best suited for speech recognition

4. You should set up your microphone according to the recommendations, to ensure clear and effective recordings

5. Read the sample text and follow the prompts to set up the microphone for the best recording

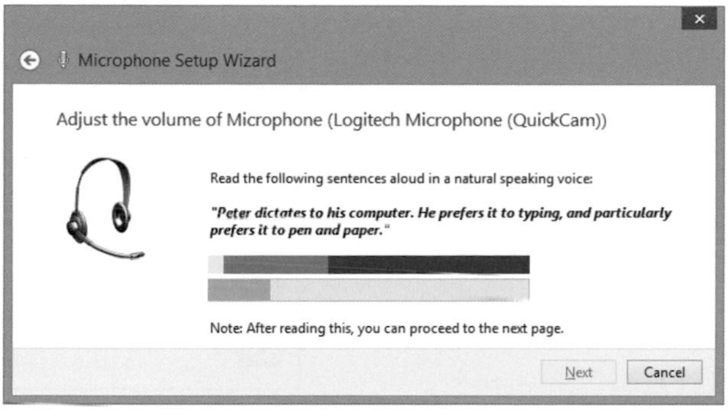
Microphone Setup Wizard
Adjust the volume of Microphone (Logitech Microphone (QuickCam))
Read the following sentences aloud in a natural speaking voice:
"Peter dictates to his computer. He prefers it to typing, and particularly prefers it to pen and paper."
Note: After reading this, you can proceed to the next page.
Next
Cancel

6. Your microphone is now set up. Click Finish

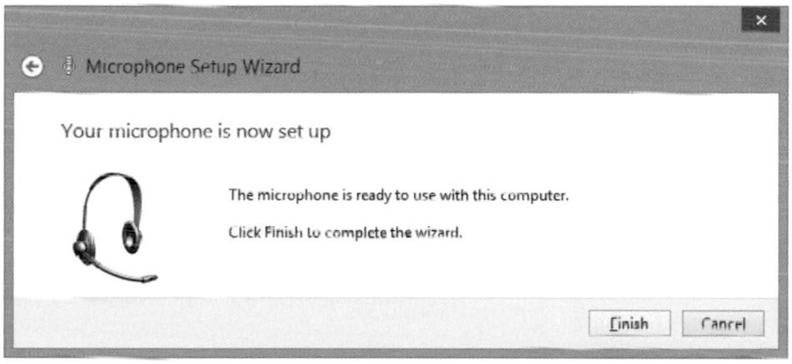
Microphone Setup Wizard
Your microphone is now set up
The microphone is ready to use with this computer.
Click Finish to complete the wizard.
Finish
Cancel

With the microphone set up, you can now use a program such as Audio Recorder from the Windows Store, to record and play audio notes. These can be stored on your Skydrive, so you can share them and access them from any computer.

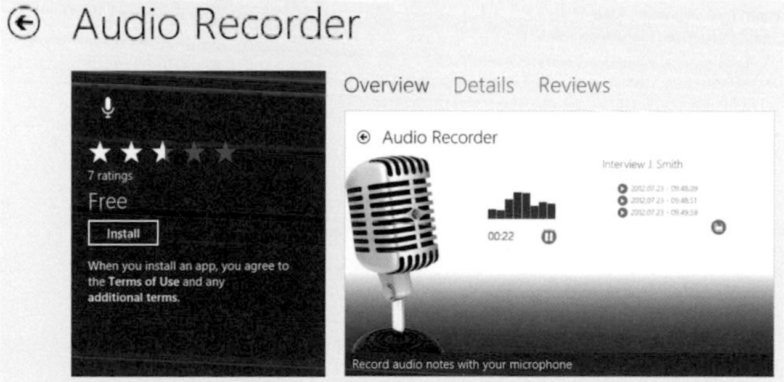
Audio Recorder
7 ratings
Free
Install
When you install an app, you agree to the Terms of Use and any additional terms.
Overview
Details
Reviews
Audio Recorder
Interview J. Smith
00:22
Record audio notes with your microphone

Don't forget

If there are problems with the level of recording, you may be asked to go back and try again, perhaps avoiding background noise.

Hot tip

Repeat the microphone configuration and take the Speech Tutorial, or train your computer to better understand your voice.

Play Audio CD

1. Insert an audio CD and close the drive

2. Windows recognizes the type of disc and prompts you (if a default action isn't yet defined)

DVD RW Drive (F:) Audio CD
Tap to choose what happens with audio CDs.

3. You can choose to Play audio CD (using Windows Media Player) or Take no action, whenever audio CDs are inserted

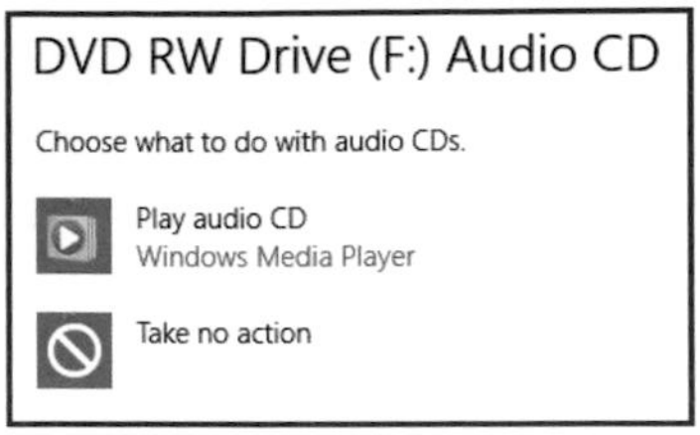
DVD RW Drive (F:) Audio CD
Choose what to do with audio CDs.
Play audio CD
Windows Media Player
Take no action

4. Click Play audio CD. Windows Media Player starts and the first time you must choose the settings

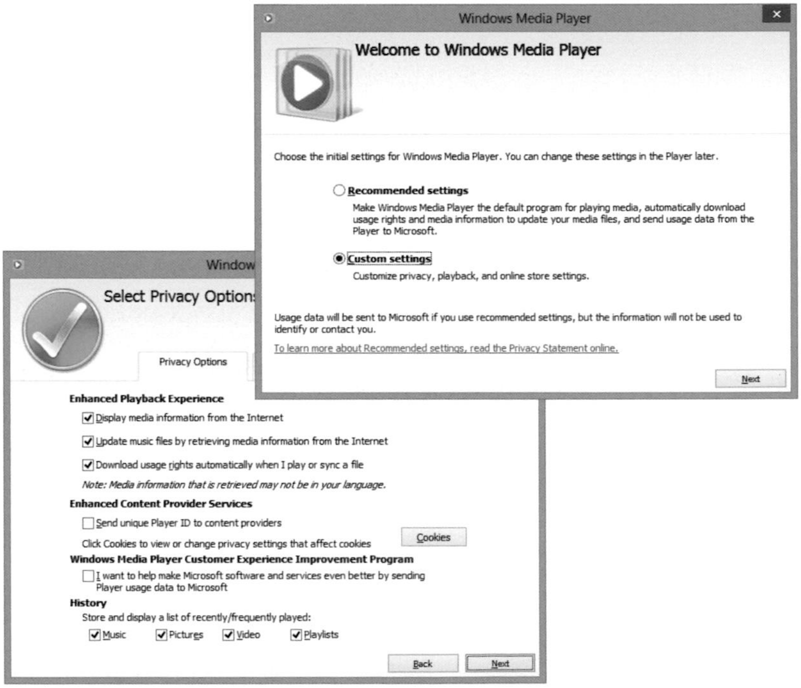
Windows Media Player
Welcome to Windows Media Player
Choose the initial settings for Windows Media Player. You can change these settings in the Player later.
Recommended settings
Make Windows Media Player the default program for playing media, automatically download usage rights and media information to update your media files, and send usage data from the Player to Microsoft.
Custom settings
Customize privacy, playback, and online store settings.
Usage data will be sent to Microsoft if you use recommended settings, but the information will not be used to identify or contact you.
To learn more about Recommended settings, read the Privacy Statement online.
Next
Select Privacy Options
Privacy Options
Enhanced Playback Experience
Display media information from the Internet
Update music files by retrieving media information from the Internet
Download usage rights automatically when I play or sync a file
Note: Media information that is retrieved may not be in your language.
Enhanced Content Provider Services
Send unique Player ID to content providers
Click Cookies to view or change privacy settings that affect cookies
Cookies
Windows Media Player Customer Experience Improvement Program
I want to help make Microsoft software and services even better by sending Player usage data to Microsoft
History
Store and display a list of recently/frequently played:
Music
Pictures
Video
Playlists
Back
Next

5. Click Custom settings to review and if necessary make changes to the Privacy options that are applied

Hot tip

You also use your sound adapter and speakers to play music from a CD or files that you download from the Internet.

Don't forget

If you accept the recommendations, Windows Media Player becomes the default for music files. Information about the music is downloaded and usage data will be sent to Microsoft.

6. Make Windows Media Player the default, or choose the file types that you want it to handle

Don't forget

Windows Media Player is the only option offered for playing CDs. However, to play music files there is a Music app (see page 196) you can use.

7. The CD begins to play and track data is added

8. Move the mouse over the window and click the Switch to Library button that appears, to see details

Windows Media Player
Unknown album (9/4/2012 9:56:22 AM) (F:)
Unknown album (9...
Unknown artist
Unknown genre
Retrieving media info for...
Windows Media Player
At the End of a Perfect Day (F:)
Play
Burn
Sync
Organize
Stream
Create playlist
Rip CD
Rip settings
Search
Album
#
Title
Length
Rip status
Contributing artist
Michael Price
Playlists
Music
Videos
Pictures
Other media
At the End of a Perfect Day (F
Other Libraries
Michael Price (premium-pc)
Lauren (premium-pc)
Audio CD (F:)
At the End of a Perf...
Chris de Burgh
World
1976
1 Broken Wings 3:10 Chris de Burgh
2 Round and Around 3:07 Chris de Burgh
3 I Will 3:31 Chris de Burgh
4 Summer Rain 4:01 Chris de Burgh
5 Discovery 2:55 Chris de Burgh
6 Brazil 3:14 Chris de Burgh
7 In a Country Churchyar... 3:58 Chris de Burgh
8 A Rainy Night in Paris 3:23 Chris de Burgh
9 If You Really Love Her, L... 4:01 Chris de Burgh
10 Perfect Day 4:01 Chris de Burgh
Chris de Burgh
01:16

Don't forget

The CD just provides the track numbers and the durations, but the CD is identified and the full artist and album details are downloaded.

Copy Tracks

1. Right-click Now Playing, select More Options, then click the Rip Music tab

2. For Format, choose the type of audio file (e.g. MP3)
3. Choose the Audio Quality (e.g. using bit rate 192 Kbps)
4. Start playing the CD and click the Rip CD button (it becomes Stop rip and then CD Already Ripped)

Broken Wings

Chris de Burgh

5. Each track in turn is copied, converted and saved

Windows Media Player
At the End of a Perfect Day (F:)
Play
Burn
Sync
Organize
Stream
Create playlist
Stop rip
Rip settings
Search
Album
#
Title
Len...
Rip status
Audio CD (F:)
Michael Price
Playlists
Music
Videos
Pictures
Other media
At the End of a Perfect Day (F
Other Libraries
Michael Price (premium-pc)
Lauren (premium-pc)
At the End of a Perf...
Chris de Burgh
World
1976
1 Broken Wings 3:10 Ripped to library
2 Round and Around 3:07 Ripped to library
3 I Will 3:31 Ripped to library
4 Summer Rain 4:01 Ripped to library
5 Discovery 2:55 Ripping (50%)
6 Brazil 3:14 Pending
7 In a Country Churchyar... 3:58 Pending
8 A Rainy Night in Paris 3:23 Pending
9 If You Really Love Her, L... 4:01 Pending
10 Perfect Day 4:01 Pending
Media changing...
00:00
Ripping: 6 tracks re...

6. Files will be saved by default in your Music folder

Beware

The higher the bit rate, the better the quality but the larger the file. As an estimate, a full audio disc copied at:

Bit rate	Needs
128 Kbps	57 MB
192	86
256	115
320	144

Don't forget

You can play the CD while tracks are being independently copied (at a multiple of the standard play speed – the whole CD may be completed before the first track finishes playing).

Media Library

The converted tracks will be saved in the specified location, (the Music folder), in an album under the artist's name.

To explore the albums stored on your hard disk and to play tracks from them:

1. Start the Windows Media Player and click the Library button to switch to the Library view

2. Choose how to display the contents of the Music library, e.g. by Album or by Artist

3. Double-click an artist to display their albums, then double-click one of the albums to start it playing

Don't forget

Type Windows media on the Start screen and press Enter. If you plan to use this often, you can Pin it to the Taskbar or the Start screen (see page 55).

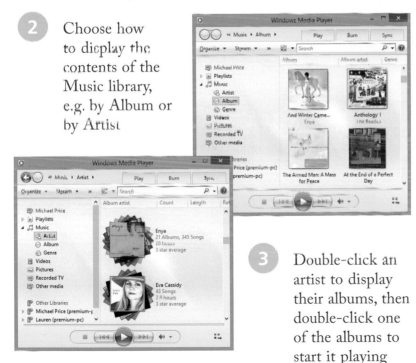

Hot tip

To include folders in Windows Media Player, you add them to the appropriate Windows Library, either Music, Pictures, Recorded TV or Videos.

Music App

Hot tip

If you want to play music on a tablet or netbook PC, you might prefer the simplicity of the Music app.

1. Select Music from the Start screen to launch this full screen app

Don't forget

The first display is the Now playing area, with featured songs. Scroll right to display the Xbox music and to view the Most popular selections.

2. By default, it opens with Xbox music, where you can sample music and purchase tracks if desired

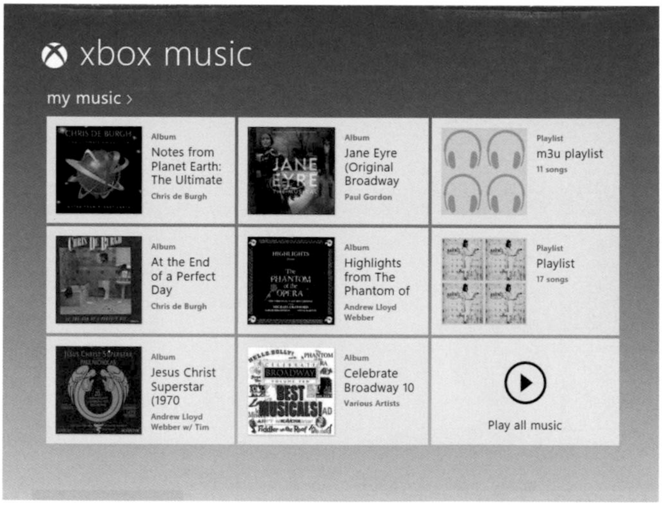

3. Scroll left and you'll find My music, with some of your recent albums and links to your playlists

4. Click the My music heading to list your albums. You can also arrange by Artists, Songs or Playlists

my music
137 albums arranged by
date added
albums
artists
songs
playlists
Play all music
Notes from Planet Earth: Th...
Chris de Burgh
rock
15 songs
At the End of a Perfect Day
Chris de Burgh
World
10 songs
The Phantom of the Oper...
Andrew Lloyd Webber
Classical
21 songs
Miss Saigon
London Theatre Orchestra and C
Musical
15 songs
Martin Guerre [London Ca...
Marcus Cunningham
Musical
22 songs
Les Misérables (1987 ori...
Claude-Michel Schönberg
Soundtrack
34 songs
La Cava
Oliver Tobias
Jesus Christ Superstar (197...
Musical
23 songs

5. Click an album and select Play album. The App bar gives you full control over the sequence

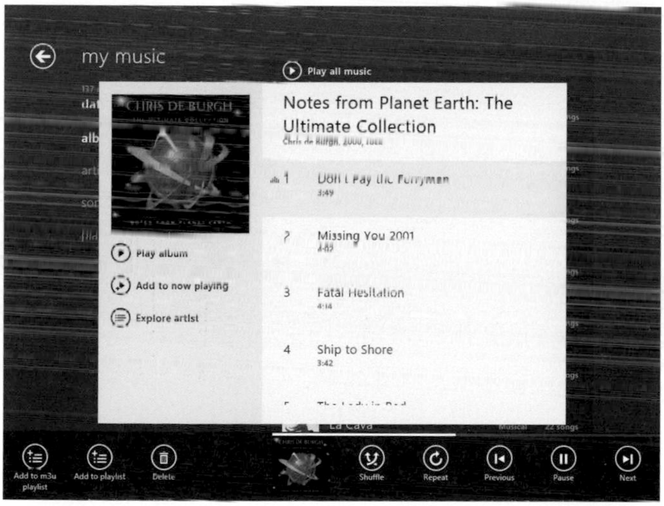

6. You can switch to other apps and the music will keep playing until the album completes

Don't forget

To start at My music, from the Music app, display the Charms bar and select Settings and then Preferences and for Start up view turn on Open my music when I start the app.

Hot tip

You can Snap the Music app to the side of the screen, if you want quick access to the controls, for example to click Pause when the phone rings.

Digital Pictures

There are a number of ways you can obtain digital pictures:

- Internet (e.g. art and photography websites)
- Scanner (copies of documents, photographs or slides)
- Digital Camera (photographs and movies)
- Email attachments and faxes

Website pictures will usually be stored as JPEG (.jpg) files, which are compressed to minimize the file size. This preserves the full color range but there is some loss of quality. Some images such as graphic symbols and buttons will use the GIF (.gif) format, which restricts color to 256 shades to minimize the file size. To copy a digital image from a website such as www.nga.gov:

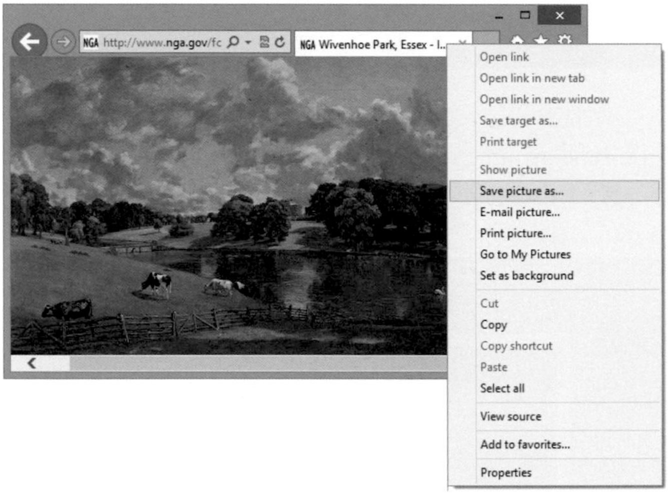

1. Right-click the image and select Save picture as...
2. Type a suitable file name and click Save

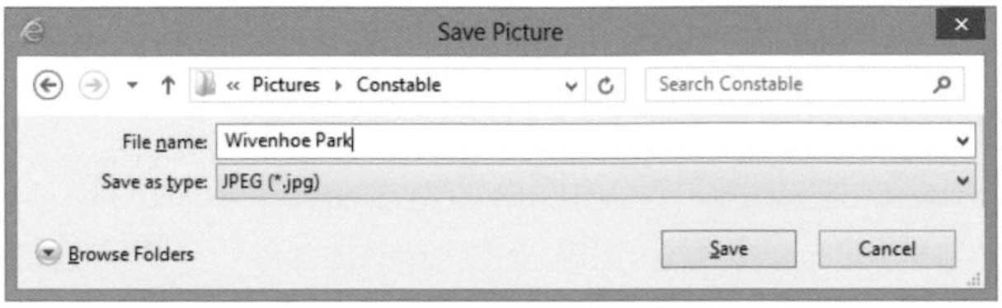

Don't forget

The Desktop Internet Explorer is used for these examples, but you can do similar actions with the Windows 8 Internet Explorer app, though you do get different menus (see page 162).

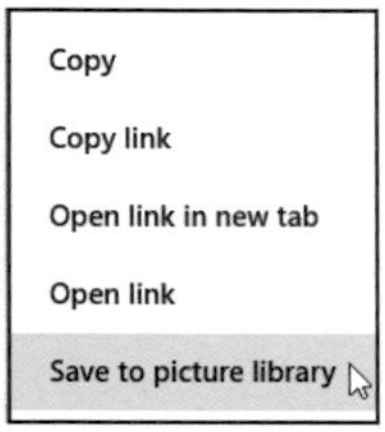

Hot tip

You can right-click and save the picture even when only part of it is visible on the screen.

Hot tip

Click Browse Folders to select a folder and create a subfolder, e.g. using artist name, to organize the saved images.

3. Select Start, Pictures and select the appropriate subfolder to list and view the saved images

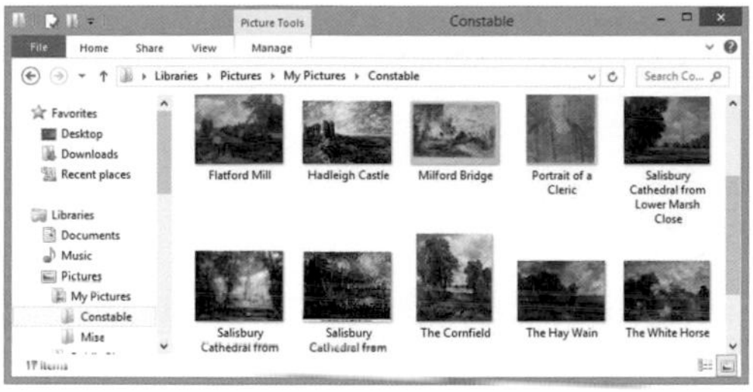

Websites may sometimes offer you the option to download higher quality images. For example, en.wikipedia.org/wiki/Flatford_Mill_(Scene_on_a_Navigable_River):

1. This entry shows Constable's Flatford Mill (Scene on a Navigable River) at a size of 350 x 279 pixels

2. Click the image and you'll see a preview 752 x 600, with a link to a full resolution image 2620 x 2090 pixels

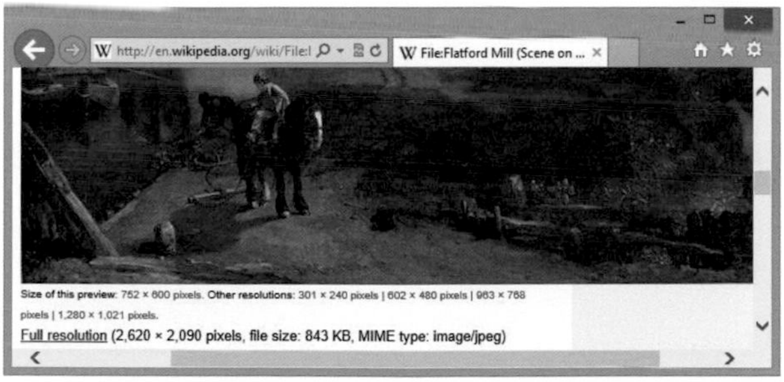

Hot tip

Windows 8 includes a number of picture viewers you can use to examine your downloaded pictures (see page 200).

Beware

Images downloaded from websites are usually copyrighted and provided for personal use only.

Viewing Pictures

Don't forget

You can explore your pictures in the library folder, or using one of the included apps.

1. Open the Pictures library in File Explorer, select View and choose Extra large icons or Preview pane

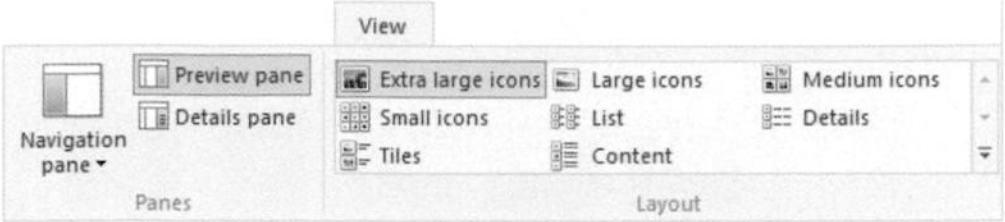
View
Navigation pane
Preview pane
Details pane
Panes
Extra large icons
Large icons
Medium icons
Small icons
List
Details
Tiles
Content
Layout

Hot tip

To make more space in the folder, click the Navigation pane button and turn off that pane.

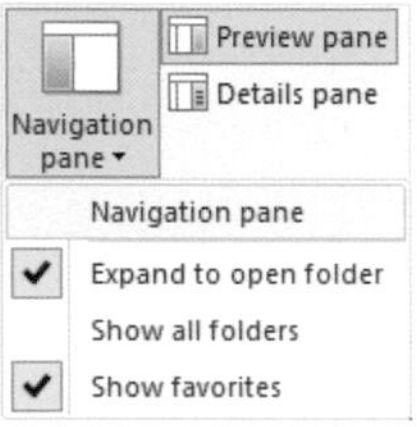

2. You can explore the folder or view specific pictures

Don't forget

The first time you double-click a file type, you may be asked to select an app, if no default has been previously defined.

3. To view a picture more closely, double-click to open it in the default app, or right-click and select an app, e.g. the Photos app

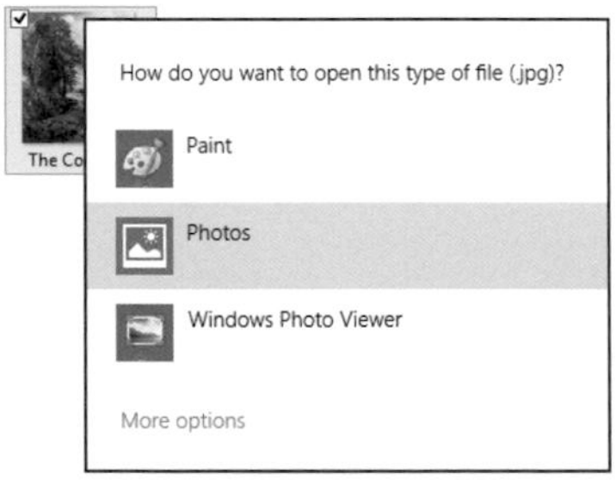

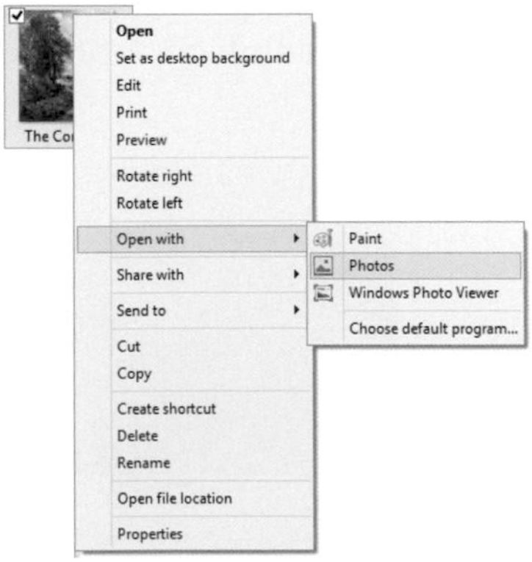
Open
Set as desktop background
Edit
Print
Preview
Rotate right
Rotate left
Open with
Share with
Send to
Cut
Copy
Create shortcut
Delete
Rename
Open file location
Properties
Paint
Photos
Windows Photo Viewer
Choose default program...

Photos App

1. The Photos app opens full screen with the picture

2. Left-click and select the back-arrow to see what picture sources Photos can access (with live displays)

3. Click the forward arrow for a live photo collage

Hot tip

Right-click to show the App bar and you can select Set as, to apply the image as a background screen or tile image.

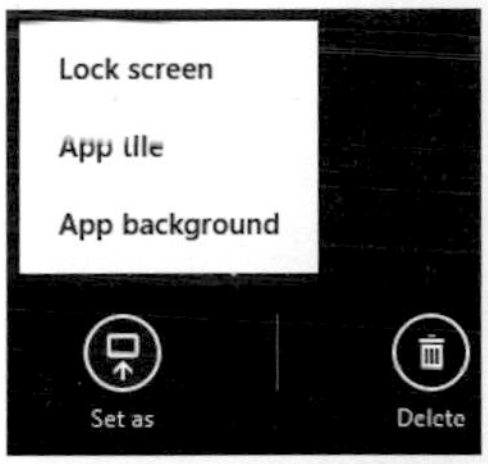

Don't forget

To review picture sources, display the Charms bar and select Settings then Options and you can choose which sources to keep active.

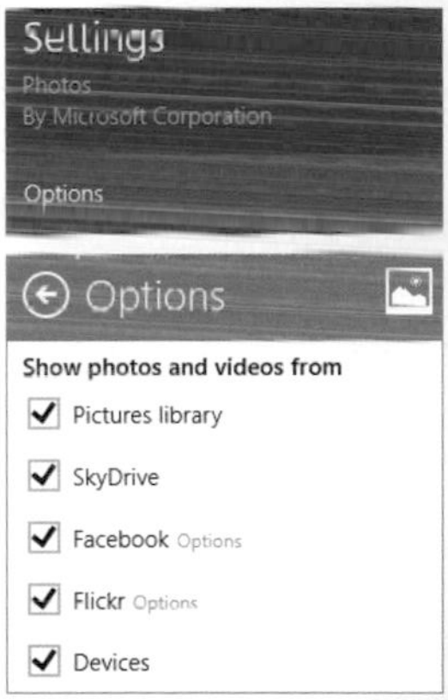

...cont'd

4 Select a source such as Pictures to see the folders

5 Select a folder and scroll horizontally to scan the full contents. Just a swipe is needed on a touch screen

6 Right-click to display the App bar and you can run a slide show with photos changing every few seconds

7 Select Import to transfer pictures from attached devices such as your camera or a USB storage device

Hot tip

If your pictures are mostly Portrait, you can Rotate your screen using Screen Resolution (see page 80) or motion detection if supported, then scroll vertically to view the contents.

Don't forget

Clicking Select all (or selecting one or more pictures) adds two options to the App bar, to Delete, or to Clear selection.

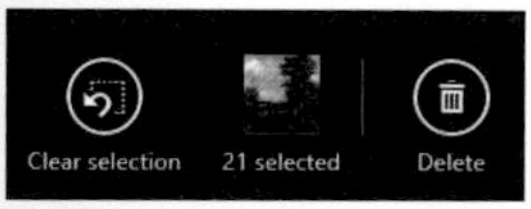

Windows Photo Viewer

The alternative to Photos app is Windows Photo Viewer. This is a Desktop application.

1. Choose to open a picture with Windows Photo Viewer and it starts up on the Desktop

2. Controls include Magnify, Actual size, Previous, Play slide show, Next, Rotate left, Rotate right and Delete

3. Click Play slide show to run a full screen slide show with the pictures

4. Right-click the window to display the menu and change the settings or Exit the slide show

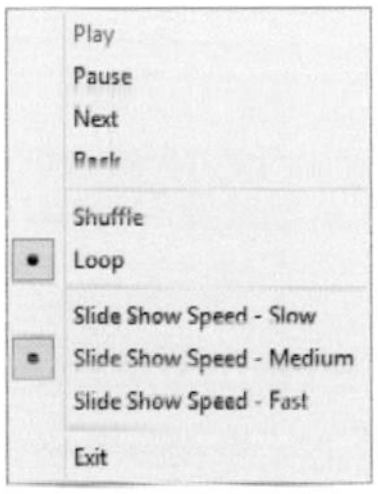

5. From the Menu bar, you can Print, Email or Burn picture files to CD or DVD

Note that when you Email pictures they will by default be attached as reduced size files.

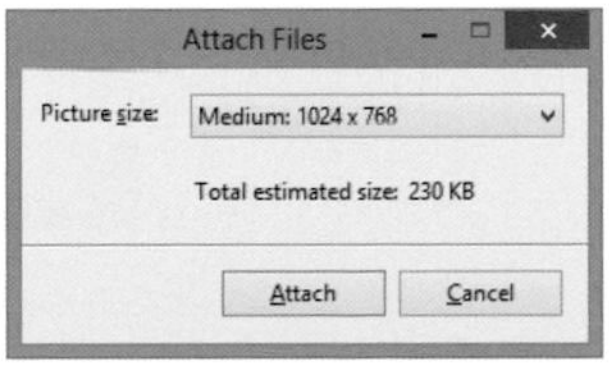

Don't forget

You can select Picture Tools in the Library folder and click the Slide show button to start Windows Photo Viewer and display your pictures.

Hot tip

You can change the size of file that is sent, or specify Original size.

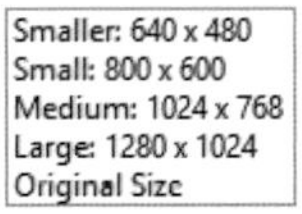

Photo Gallery

Don't forget

If you have installed Windows Essentials (see page 22) you'll have more choices for opening your picture files - Photo Gallery and Movie Maker (see page 206).

1. Right-click a picture file and select Open with and see two new options

2. Select the Photo Gallery entry. The picture is displayed in a minimal layout that is similar to the Windows Photo Viewer

3. Click Edit, Organize or Share, to display the full Photo Gallery, with tabs and ribbons giving access to all of the functions

Don't forget

Move the mouse over a picture icon and a preview image immediately appears.

1. Click each tab in turn to see the range of functions

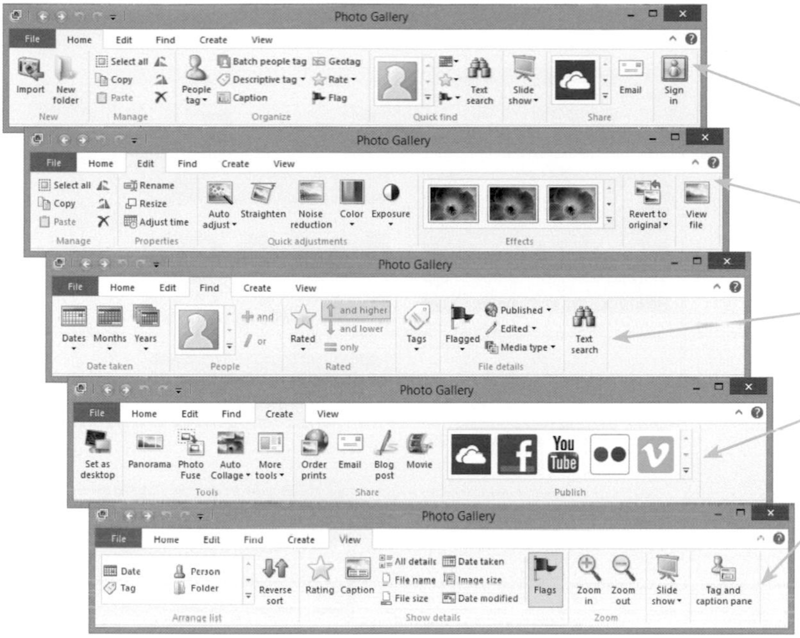

Don't forget

Highlighting some of the tab functions:

Home – Slide show and Import

Edit – Auto adjust and Effects

Find – search by Date, People and Tags

Create – make Collage, Movie and Panorama

View – Arrange list, Show detail, Zoom and Slide show

2. As these ribbons illustrate, Photo Gallery provides more powerful facilities for importing, editing, viewing and sharing pictures

3. Click File for functions such as Import, Include folder, Print, Burn a CD

4. You can also display the Properties of the selected picture or video files

5. When necessary, Minimize the ribbon to get more space

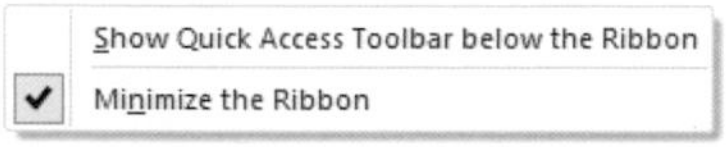
Show Quick Access Toolbar below the Ribbon
Minimize the Ribbon

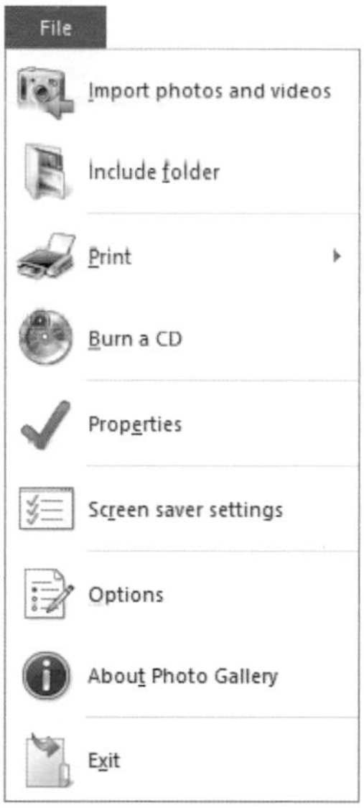

Hot tip

Photo Gallery deals equally well with the still photos and the videos that you take with your digital camera.

Movie Maker

Don't forget

Movie Maker helps you make more advanced movies from your videos and photographs, and publish them to YouTube, Facebook and other Internet locations.

1. Choose the items that you require from Photo Gallery and then select the Create tab and then Movie

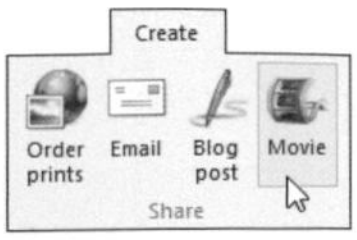

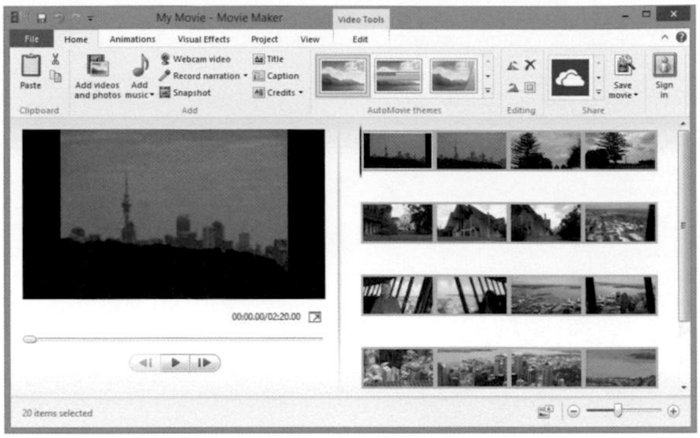

2. Choose an AutoMovie theme, then follow the prompts to add music

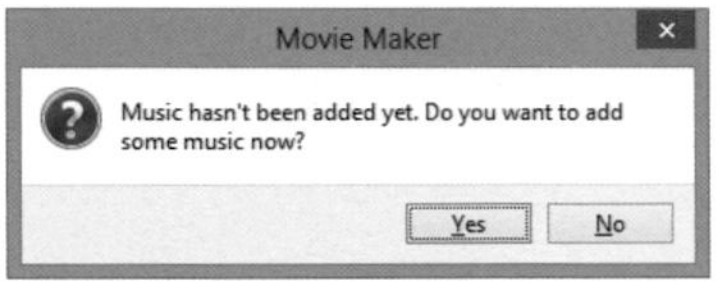

Hot tip

When you play the video file, you will find that there are several programs on your system that can handle the MP4 file type.

3. Click the arrow next to Save movie and choose the format, e.g. for Computer or Email

4. Follow the prompts to name, convert and save the movie as an MP4 video file

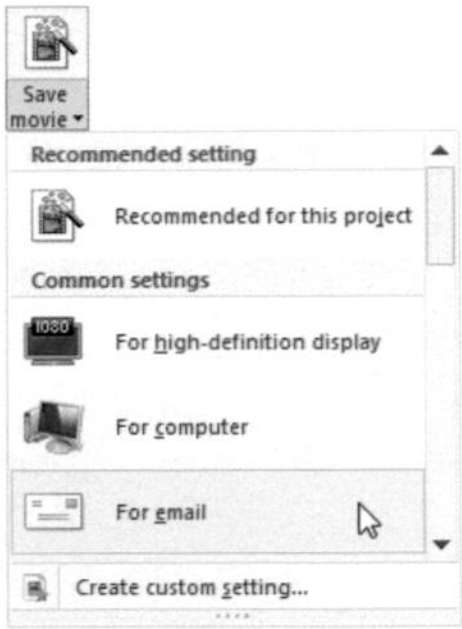

12 Networking

Create a home network, wired or wireless, to share drives, printers and Internet access. Windows 8 computers can create or join a HomeGroup. to share media libraries with other computers and devices on the network.

208 Create a Network
209 Network Classification
210 Create HomeGroup
212 Connect to Wireless Network
213 Join the HomeGroup
214 View Network Devices
215 View HomeGroup
216 Network and Sharing Center
218 PC Settings

Create a Network

Hot tip

Unlike devices that are attached directly to a computer, the devices on a network operate independently of one another.

You have a network when you have several devices that exchange information over a wire or over radio waves. The simplest network consists of one computer and a router that links to the Internet. You can add a second computer, to share Internet access and exchange information with the other computer. If the computers are Windows 8 (or Windows 7) based, a HomeGroup can help with sharing data.

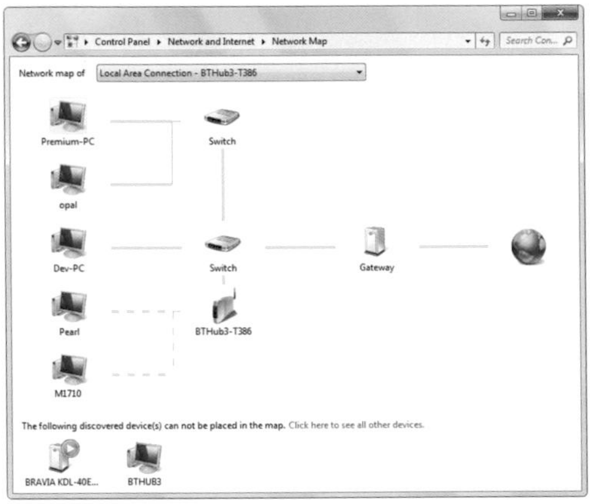

Hot tip

This network map is from the Windows 7 PC. There's no map in Windows 8, but it does show network computers and devices (see page 214).

To make the connections, your network will require:

1. Ethernet twisted-pair cables, for the wired portion
2. A router to manage the network connections
3. An Internet modem, which may be integrated with the router
4. An adapter for each computer (wired or wireless)

To implement your network, you'll need to carry out actions such as these:

- Install the necessary network adapters
- Establish the Internet Connection
- Set up the wireless router
- Connect the computers and start Windows

Don't forget

Windows 8 detects the presence of a network and will automatically set up the computer to participate and to create or join a HomeGroup (for a home networks only).

Network Classification

1. Install the network adapter (if required) and start up Windows (with no network connection)

2. Display the Charms bar and select Settings. The Network icon shows Unavailable

3. Add a cable between the adapter and the router and the Network shows as named and connected

Windows will detect the network and give it a default classification, but you can override its choice.

4. Click the Network icon, right-click the Network and click Turn sharing on or off

5. Choose No, for networks in public places

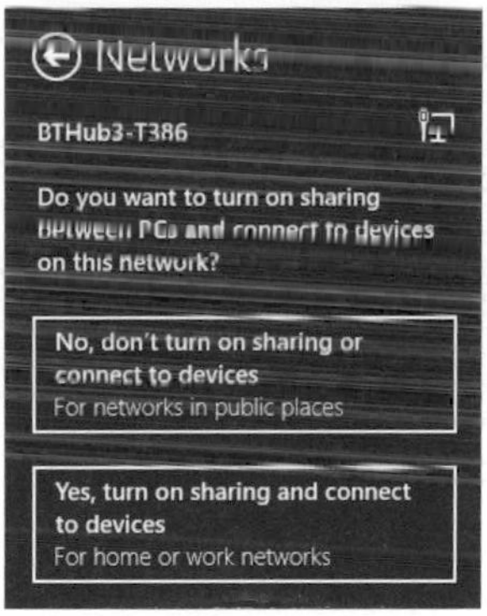

This gives a **Public network** for networks in places like coffee shops or airports, or for guests to access. HomeGroup is not available and network discovery is turned off.

6. Choose Yes for networks at home or at work

This gives a **Private network** for home or work networks or for known and trusted environments. The computer can join a HomeGroup and Network discovery is turned on.

Don't forget

Often, there will be a network adapter built into your computer. If not, you'll need to install an adapter card or add a USB adapter.

Hot tip

The classification is shown in the Network and Sharing Center (see page 216).

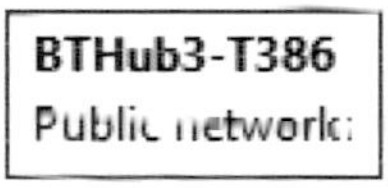
BTHub3-T386
Public network

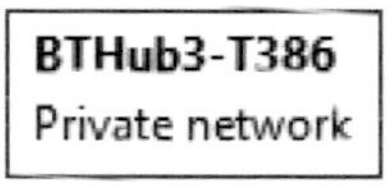
BTHub3-T386
Private network

Don't forget

Network discovery allows you to see other computers and devices on the network and allows other network users to see your computer. Turning Network discovery off hides your computer.

Create HomeGroup

If you set up a Private network and no HomeGroup has yet been established, you are given the option to create one.

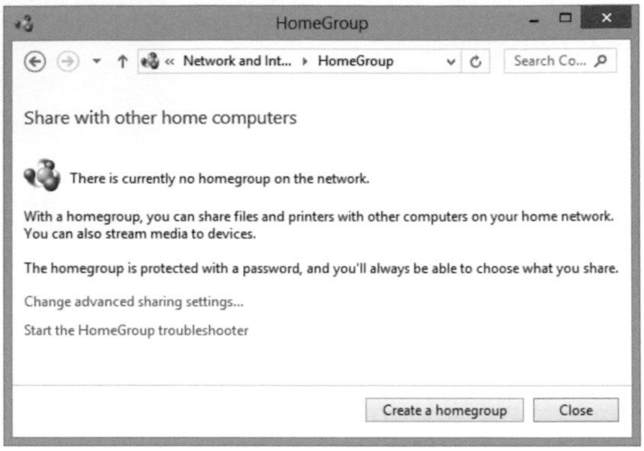

1. To confirm you want to share with other home computers, click Create a homegroup

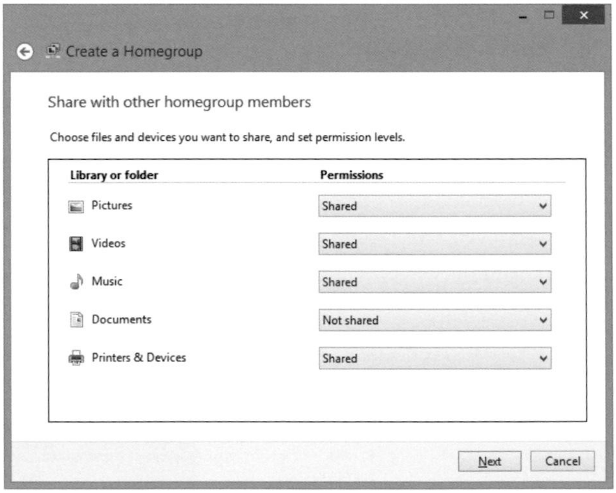

2. Specify what types of data or devices you want to share then click Next

By default, you'll share your Pictures, Music, Videos and Printers, but not your Documents. However, you can change any of these to Shared or Not shared, as desired.

Don't forget

If a HomeGroup has already been created on the network, you get the option to join that HomeGroup (see page 213).

Beware

If the other computers on your network are powered off or hibernating, a new computer might think there is no HomeGroup. In that case, just click Close.

Windows will automatically generate a secure password for the HomeGroup for you to share with other network users.

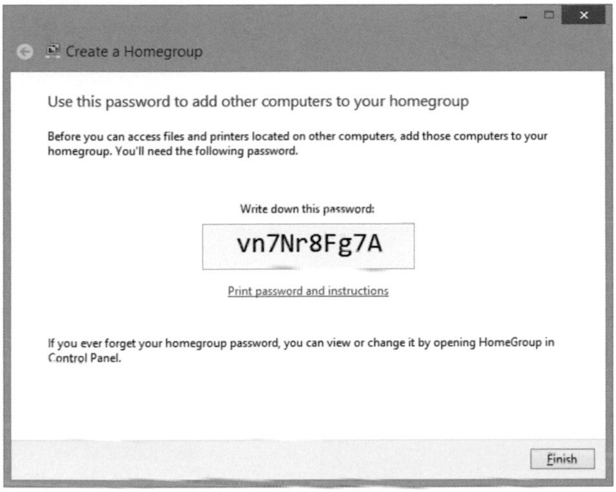
Create a Homegroup
Use this password to add other computers to your homegroup
Before you can access files and printers located on other computers, add those computers to your homegroup. You'll need the following password.
Write down this password:
vn7Nr8Fg7A
Print password and instructions
If you ever forget your homegroup password, you can view or change it by opening HomeGroup in Control Panel.
Finish

3. Make a note of the new password and click Finish

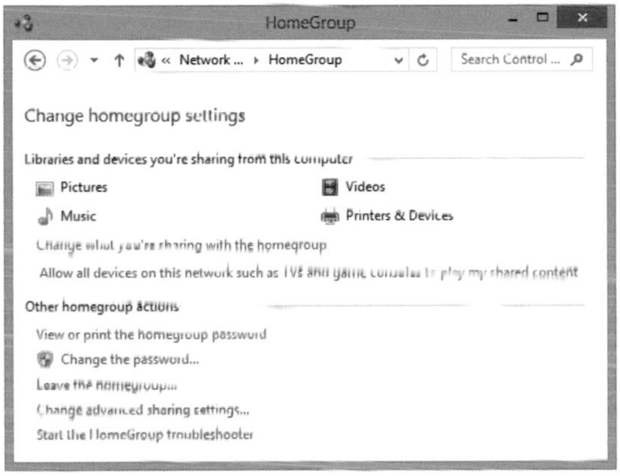
HomeGroup
Network ... HomeGroup
Search Control ...
Change homegroup settings
Libraries and devices you're sharing from this computer
Pictures
Videos
Music
Printers & Devices
Other homegroup actions
View or print the homegroup password
Change the password...
Change advanced sharing settings...
Start the HomeGroup troubleshooter

4. View the HomeGroup settings and make and changes if required. You can also view or print the password, or change it to a more memorable password

5. Click Close for the HomeGroup Settings and do remember to share the password with the other users

Don't forget

Windows uses a random combination of lower case, upper case and numbers. However, you can change the password to something more easily remembered, if you wish.

Hot tip

Note the option to allow all devices on the network, including TVs and games consoles, to access your shared content.

Connect to Wireless Network

1. Display the Charms bar, select Settings, note the Network icon indicates Available networks

2. Click the icon to display the connections and choose your main wireless network

3. Click in the box to Connect automatically and then click Connect

4. Enter the network security key for your wireless network and click Next

5. If this is the first time the computer has been connected to the network, you'll be asked to specify the network classification – Private or Public

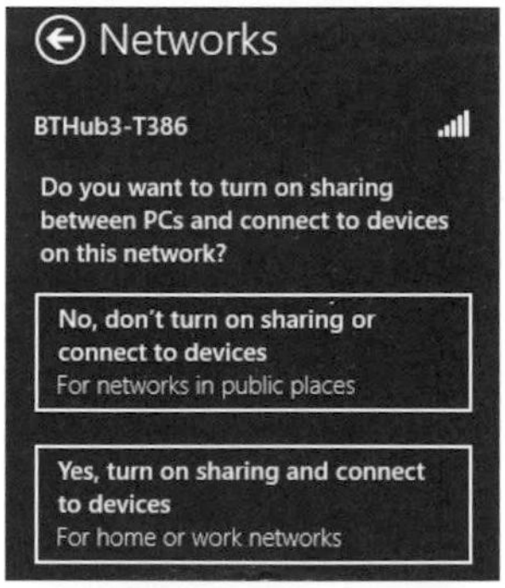

6. Your computer will now show as connected to the wireless network

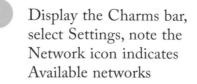

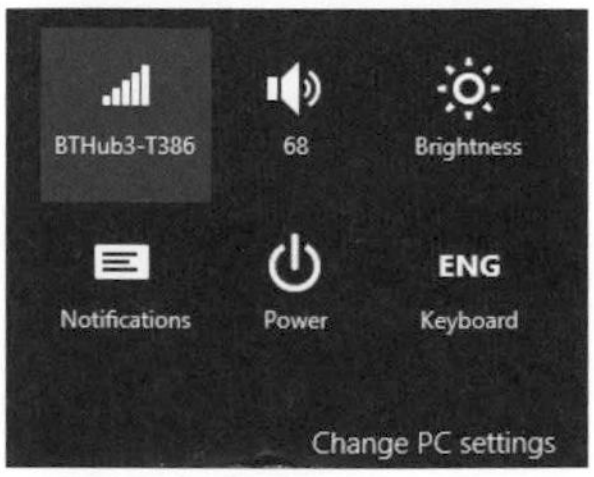

Don't forget

Cabled PCs usually get added automatically. When you bring a new wireless PC into the network, you'll need to set up the connection.

Beware

Your system may detect other wireless networks that are in the vicinity, so make sure to select the correct entry.

Don't forget

Your computer will now always connect to that network, when it comes into range. You can have numerous wireless connections defined, for example home, office and Internet cafe.

Join the HomeGroup

1. Windows tells you about the existing HomeGroup. Click Join now, or click Close if you are not joining

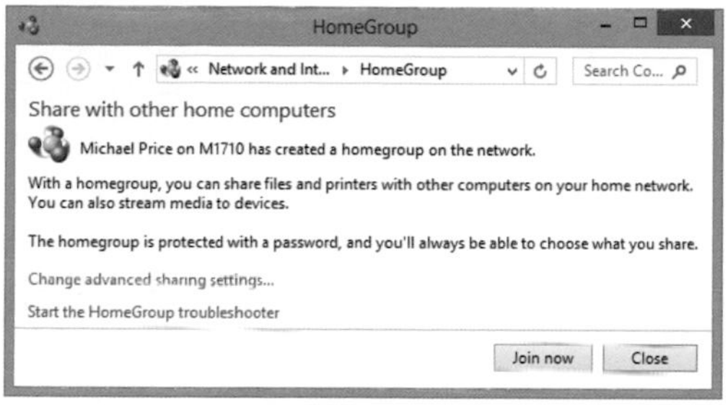
HomeGroup
Network and Int... ▸ HomeGroup
Search Co...
Share with other home computers
Michael Price on M1710 has created a homegroup on the network.
With a homegroup, you can share files and printers with other computers on your home network. You can also stream media to devices.
The homegroup is protected with a password, and you'll always be able to choose what you share.
Change advanced sharing settings...
Start the HomeGroup troubleshooter
Join now
Close

2. Choose the items you want to share and click Next

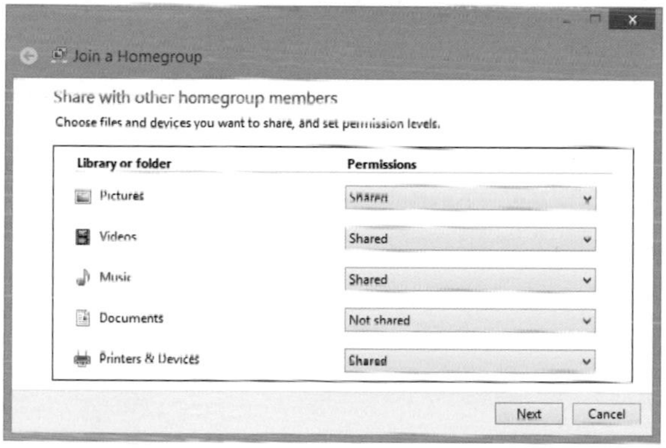
Join a Homegroup
Share with other homegroup members
Choose files and devices you want to share, and set permission levels.
Library or folder
Permissions
Pictures
Shared
Videos
Shared
Music
Shared
Documents
Not shared
Printers & Devices
Shared
Next
Cancel

3. Type the HomeGroup password and click Next

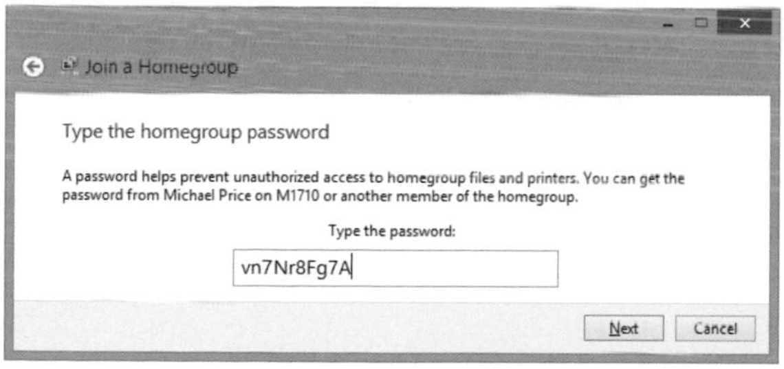
Join a Homegroup
Type the homegroup password
A password helps prevent unauthorized access to homegroup files and printers. You can get the password from Michael Price on M1710 or another member of the homegroup.
Type the password:
vn7Nr8Fg7A
Next
Cancel

4. Click Finish when prompted and you have joined

Don't forget

When you add a new cabled or wireless PC to a Private network, you may be invited to join the HomeGroup.

Beware

Windows may take a few minutes to set up sharing, so you should not shut down the computer until you are told that you have joined the HomeGroup.

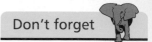

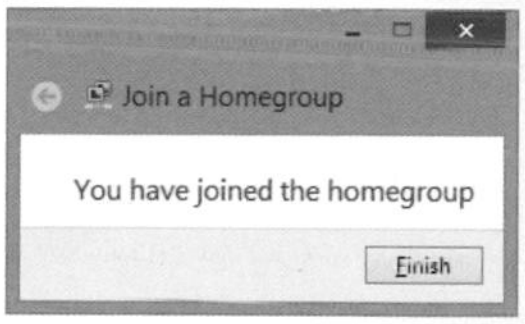
Join a Homegroup
You have joined the homegroup
Finish

View Network Devices

There's no Network map facility in Windows 8, unlike Windows 7 (see page 208). However, you can find a list of all the computers and other devices that are connected and active on your network.

Don't forget

You can also display the Charms bar, select Search and then select Settings, to carry out a Settings search.

1. Press WinKey + W to display Search Settings, type View network devices and select the entry for View network computers and devices

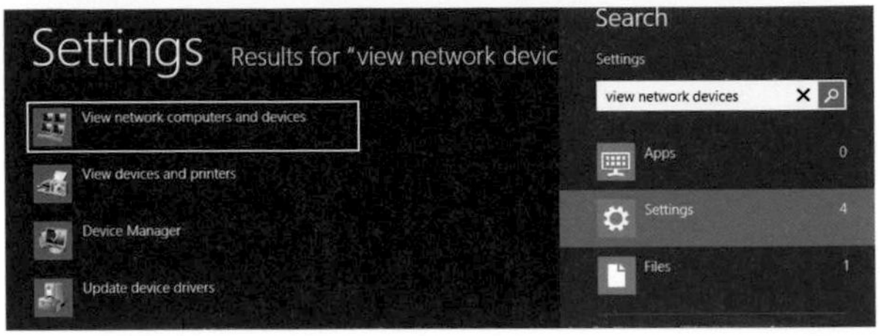

2. The File Explorer program opens on the Desktop with the Network category selected

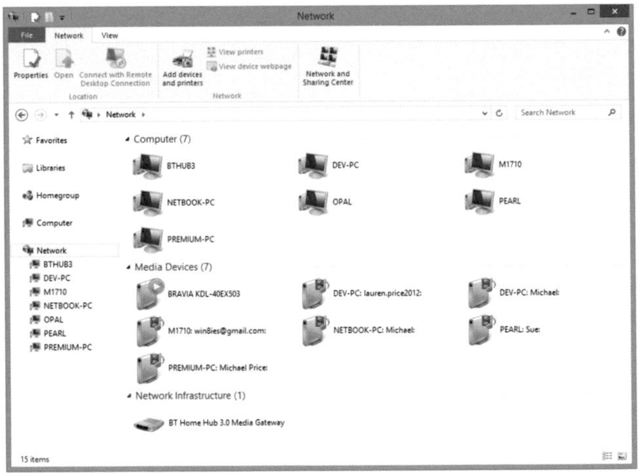

Don't forget

Alternatively, go to the Desktop, open File Explorer from the Taskbar icon and select the Network category.

3. This shows all the computers, network devices such as hubs, media devices such as Internet connected TVs and shared media libraries

4. Click the HomeGroup category to view its members

Hot tip

Only devices that are currently active will show up.

View HomeGroup

1. Open File Explorer and select HomeGroup to display the users on the network who are members

2. Expand the entries to see the computer names. You may have a user signed on at two or computers, or have more than one active user on one computer

3. Double-click a user's entry to see what libraries and devices are available for sharing

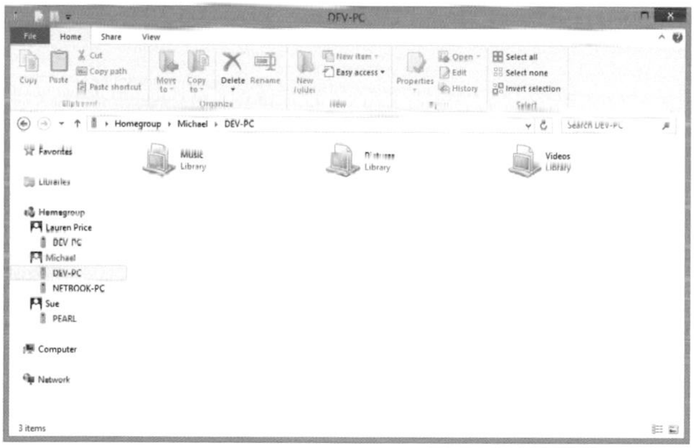

4. Double-click a library entry to explore its contents. You can access other users' libraries as if they were your own

Hot tip

If a computer on the network is powered off or hibernates, its entries are removed. When a computer is powered up, its entries are added. To ensure the display is up to date, right-click and select Refresh.

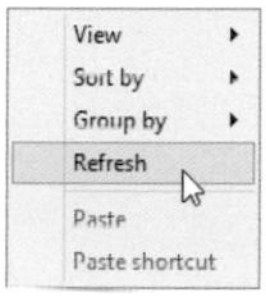

Hot tip

If you choose not to create the HomeGroup initially, you'll see the Ready to create option in the Network and Sharing Center.

Network and Sharing Center

Hot tip

Alternatively, open the Control Panel and click View network status and tasks.

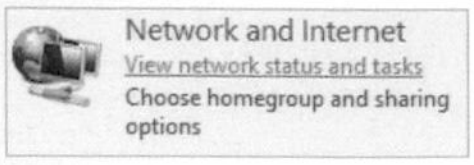

You can also right-click the Network icon on the Taskbar and select Open Network and Sharing Center.

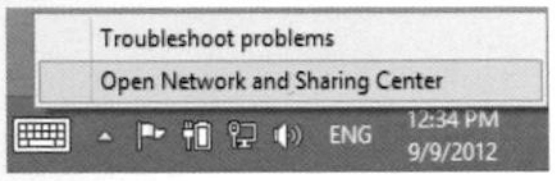

1. Display Search Settings, type Network center and select the entry for Network and sharing center

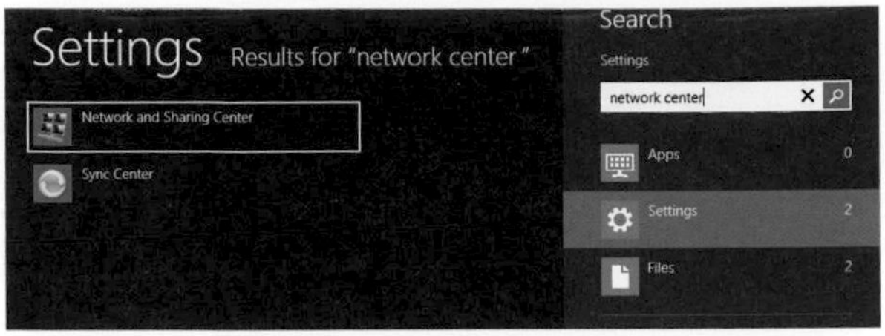

2. View the basic information for your active networks

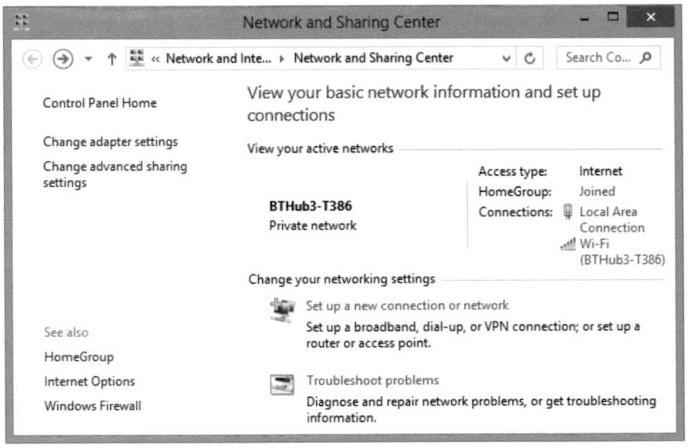

3. Click Change advanced sharing settings, to review the options for Private and for Public networks

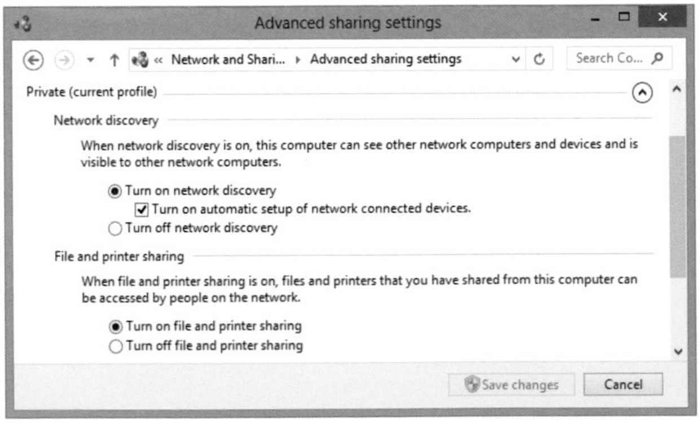

Hot tip

You'll see that Private networks usually have Network discovery and File and printer sharing turned on. For Public networks, these are usually turned off.

1. Click HomeGroup in the Network and Sharing Center, to view and change HomeGroup settings

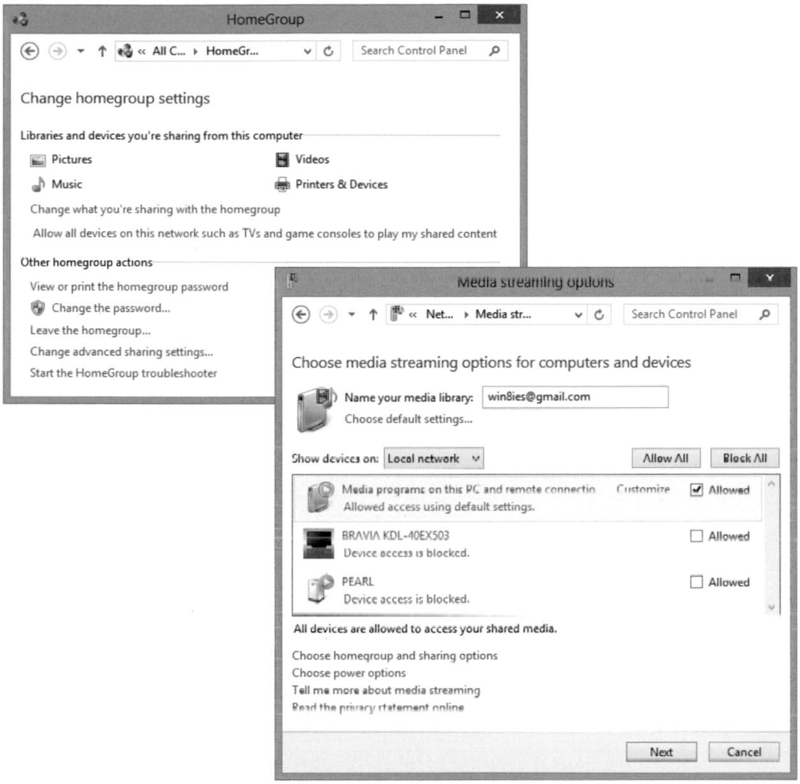

Hot tip

This panel is displayed when you create or join the HomeGroup. This link from the Network and Sharing Center allows you to revise your initial settings.

2. Click the link Allow all devices on this network, to choose media streaming options and click Allow All, then click Allow all computers and media devices

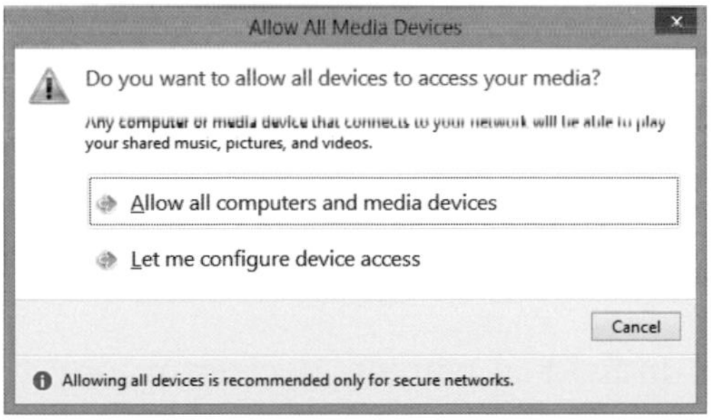

Beware

As noted, the option to allow all devices is recommended only for secure networks.

PC Settings

1. Open the Charms bar, select Settings and then click Change PC settings

2. Select the HomeGroup entry

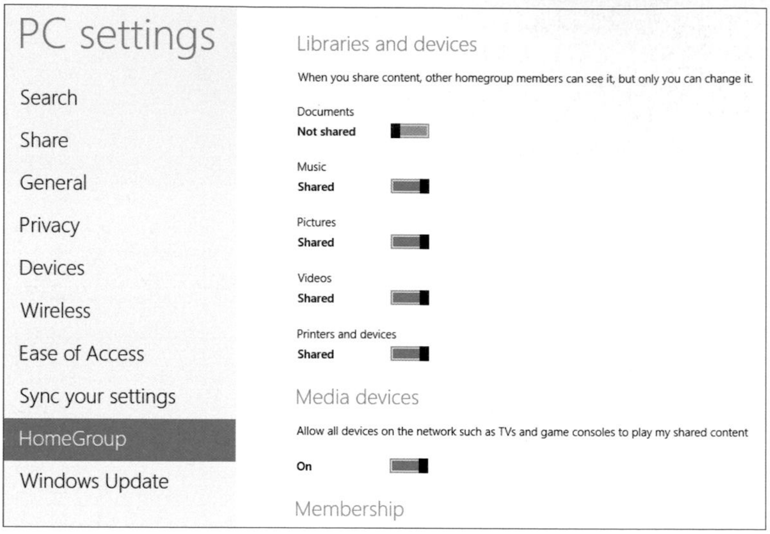
PC settings
Search
Share
General
Privacy
Devices
Wireless
Ease of Access
Sync your settings
HomeGroup
Windows Update
Libraries and devices
When you share content, other homegroup members can see it, but only you can change it.
Documents
Not shared
Music
Shared
Pictures
Shared
Videos
Shared
Printers and devices
Shared
Media devices
Allow all devices on the network such as TVs and game consoles to play my shared content
On
Membership

3. You can easily turn access on or off for the individual devices and libraries. The Membership section has the password and also a Leave HomeGroup button

4. Select Wireless for the associated settings

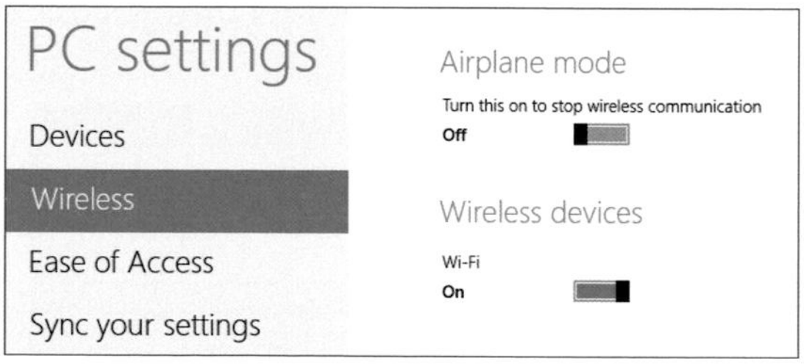
PC settings
Devices
Wireless
Ease of Access
Sync your settings
Airplane mode
Turn this on to stop wireless communication
Off
Wireless devices
Wi-Fi
On

5. Turn individual wireless devices on or off, or use the Airplane mode to control all wireless devices at once

Don't forget

You can also open Search Settings and look for entries related to HomeGroup.

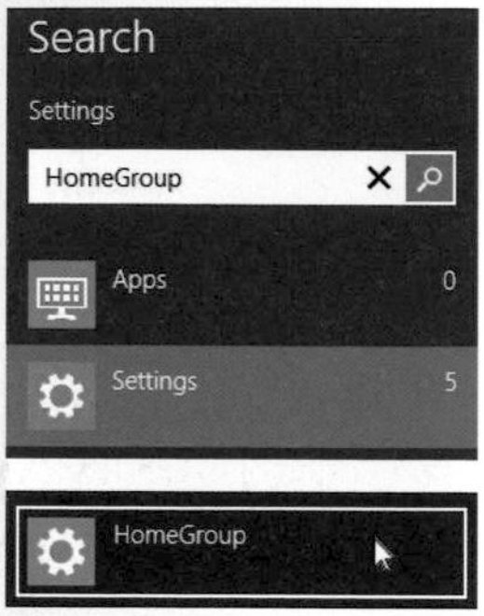

Hot tip

The individual wireless devices that you might find on your computer could include Wi-Fi, Mobile broadband and Bluetooth. Airplane mode switches all of them on or off with one click.

13 Security & Maintenance

Help and support is enhanced by online access to the latest information and there are other ways of getting useful advice. Windows Action Center keeps track of your system and a variety of system tools help protect your computer from hazards.

Windows Help

Most functions in Windows are supported by wizards, which make the tasks easier by providing prompts and suggestions. However, there is a comprehensive help system when you do need answers to questions.

Hot tip

You can also press F1 while at the Desktop, to open Windows Help and Support.

1. From the Start screen, type Help and press Enter

Apps Results for "help"
Help and Support

2. Windows Help and Support displays on the Desktop

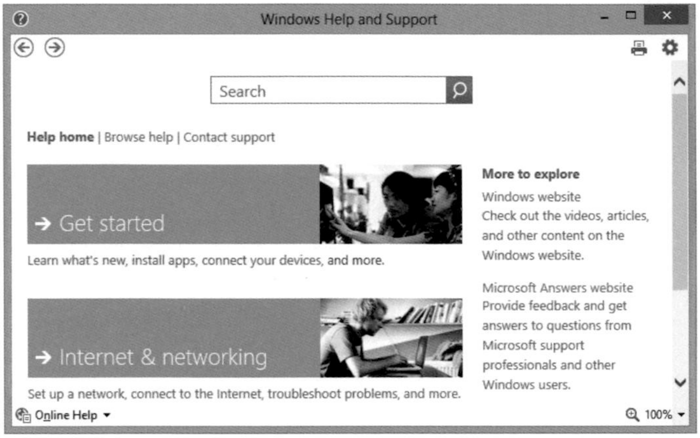
Windows Help and Support
Search
Help home | Browse help | Contact support
Get started
Learn what's new, install apps, connect your devices, and more.
Internet & networking
Set up a network, connect to the Internet, troubleshoot problems, and more.
More to explore
Windows website
Check out the videos, articles, and other content on the Windows website.
Microsoft Answers website
Provide feedback and get answers to questions from Microsoft support professionals and other Windows users.
Online Help
100%

3. You may see a message at the top of the screen saying you are not connected to the Internet

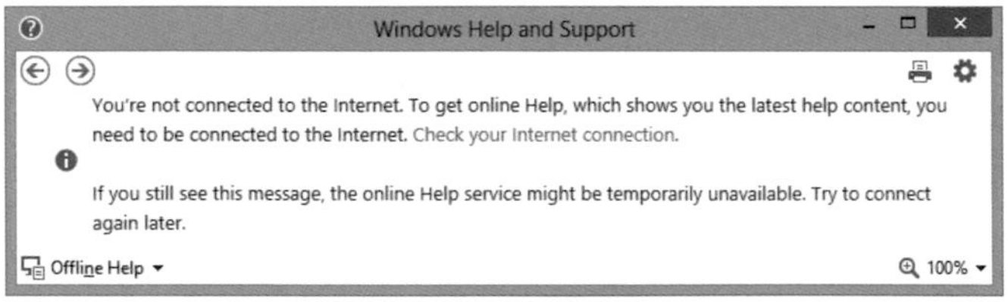
Windows Help and Support
You're not connected to the Internet. To get online Help, which shows you the latest help content, you need to be connected to the Internet. Check your Internet connection.
If you still see this message, the online Help service might be temporarily unavailable. Try to connect again later.
Offline Help
100%

Don't forget

If the online Help service is unavailable, it remains in Offline mode, but you will still get local help and support information.

4. Check your Internet connection

5. Restart Help and Support, or click the Offline Help button and select Get online Help, to be sure you get the most up-to-date help

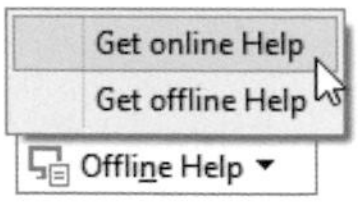
Get online Help
Get offline Help
Offline Help

6. Click Get Started to learn what's new in Windows 8

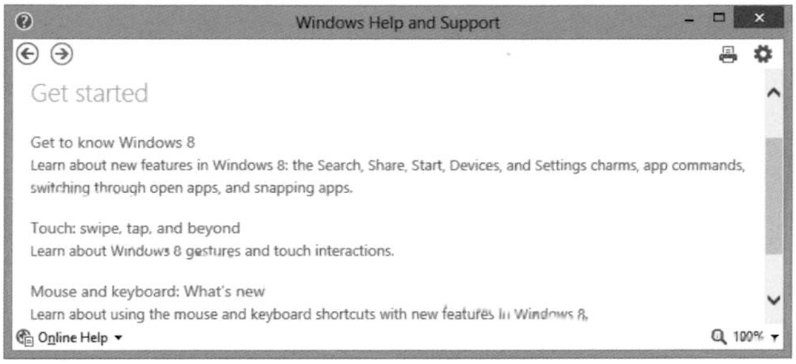
Windows Help and Support
Get started
Get to know Windows 8
Learn about new features in Windows 8: the Search, Share, Start, Devices, and Settings charms, app commands, switching through open apps, and snapping apps.
Touch: swipe, tap, and beyond
Learn about Windows 8 gestures and touch interactions.
Mouse and keyboard: What's new
Online Help
100%

7. Click Get to know Windows 8, to view new features

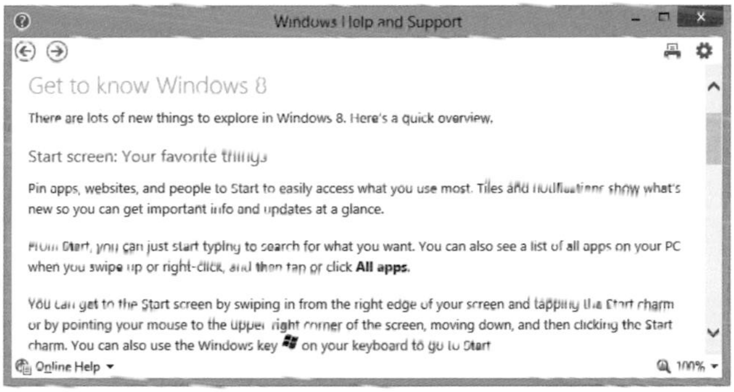
Windows Help and Support
Get to know Windows 8
There are lots of new things to explore in Windows 8. Here's a quick overview.
Online Help

8. Click the back arrow and select Touch: swipe, tap and beyond, to learn about Windows 8 gestures

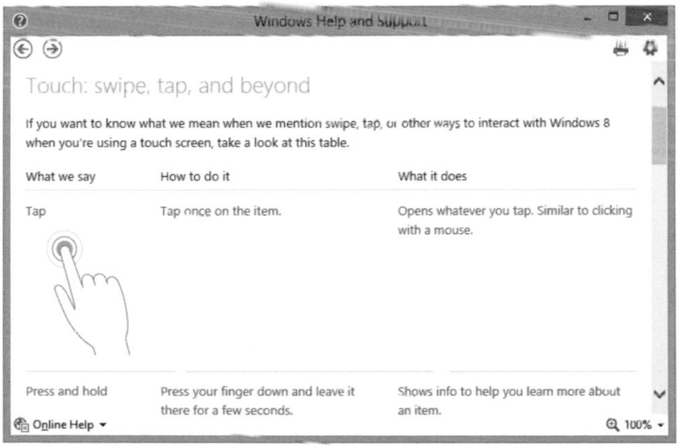
Touch: swipe, tap, and beyond
If you want to know what we mean when we mention swipe, tap, or other ways to interact with Windows 8 when you're using a touch screen, take a look at this table.
What we say
How to do it
What it does
Tap
Tap once on the item.
Opens whatever you tap. Similar to clicking with a mouse.
Press and hold
Press your finger down and leave it there for a few seconds.
Shows info to help you learn more about an item.
Online Help
100%

Don't forget

If the particular topic you want doesn't appear when you scroll the Help pages, type a suitable search phrase in the Search box and click the Find button.

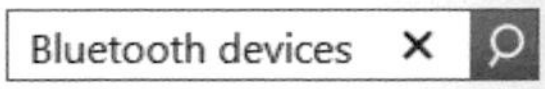
Bluetooth devices

Hot tip

In keeping with its Online status, the Help and Support information can be expected to change over time, so the contents you see on your system may differ.

More Support Options

If you can't find the answer you are seeking in the Help information, you can ask Support or other users for help.

1. In Windows Help and Support, click Contact support

Windows Help and Support
Help home | Browse help | Contact support
Contact support
If you didn't find the answer you were looking for, try these additional options.
General Windows support
Provide feedback and get answers to questions about Windows 8 from Microsoft support professionals and other Windows users in the Windows 8 forum.
Developer support
Find out about developing apps for Windows, samples, and get help from Microsoft support engineers and a global community of developers in the Windows Developer Center.
IT pro or enterprise support
More to explore
Windows website
Check out the videos, articles, and other content on the Windows website.
Microsoft Answers website
Provide feedback and get answers to questions from Microsoft support professionals and other Windows users.
Online Help
100%

Don't forget

The forum contains answers to questions about Windows 8, from the Microsoft support team and from other Windows users.

2. Click the link for the Windows 8 forum and review the questions and answers, or submit your questions

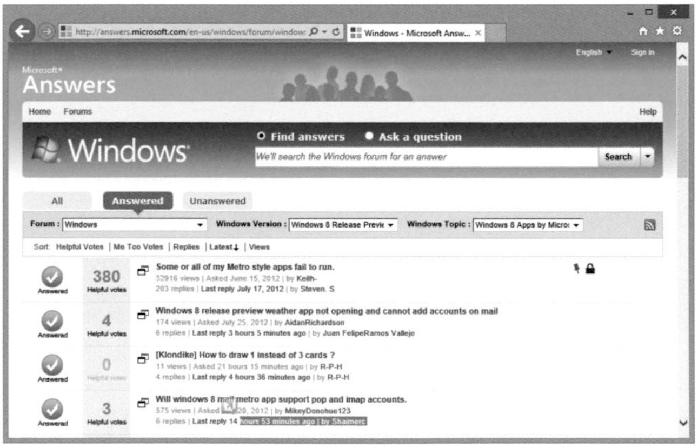

Hot tip

Show all Windows topics, or select a specific topic that you want to explore in more detail.

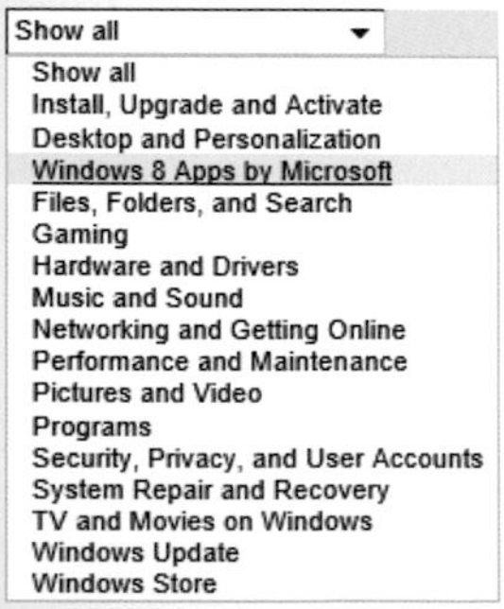
Show all
Show all
Install, Upgrade and Activate
Desktop and Personalization
Windows 8 Apps by Microsoft
Files, Folders, and Search
Gaming
Hardware and Drivers
Music and Sound
Networking and Getting Online
Performance and Maintenance
Pictures and Video
Programs
Security, Privacy, and User Accounts
System Repair and Recovery
TV and Movies on Windows
Windows Update
Windows Store

3. From Window Help and Support, click the link to explore the Windows website for articles and videos

4. Search your computer manufacturer's website for Windows 8-related updates and information

Product Solution Centers

Microsoft offers solution centers for many products, Windows 8 included. To view the list of solution centers:

1. Open http://support.microsoft.com and select the area of interest, or click More products for a full list

2. Select the topic and then the subtopic, e.g. Xbox & Games and PC Games

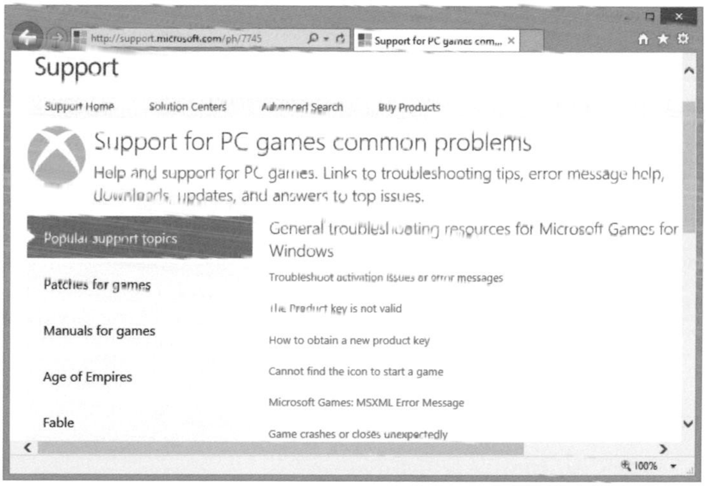

http://support.microsoft.com/ph/7745
Support for PC games com...
Support
Support Home
Solution Centers
Advanced Search
Buy Products
Support for PC games common problems
Help and support for PC games. Links to troubleshooting tips, error message help, downloads, updates, and answers to top issues.
Popular support topics
Patches for games
Manuals for games
Age of Empires
Fable
General troubleshooting resources for Microsoft Games for Windows
Troubleshoot activation issues or error messages
The Product key is not valid
How to obtain a new product key
Cannot find the icon to start a game
Microsoft Games: MSXML Error Message
Game crashes or closes unexpectedly
100%

3. Select a topic, for example, Patches for games or Manuals for games and explore the information

Don't forget

The solution centers, categories and topics listed will change from time to time, so you could revisit the website periodically.

Hot tip

Right-click the topic and select Open in new tab or Open in new window, to keep the Solution Center available.

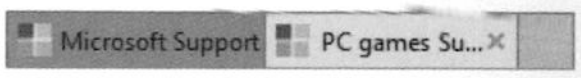

Windows Action Center

There are various security and maintenance features in Windows 8 and these are monitored in the Windows Action Center. You will be alerted by an icon in the notification area.

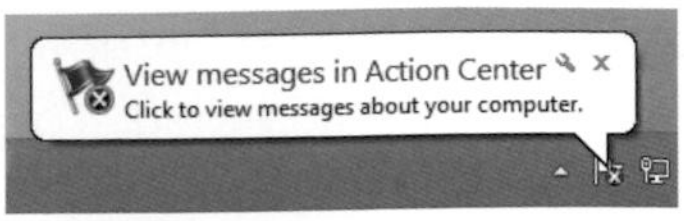

1. Click the icon to see the message summaries, then click Open Action Center

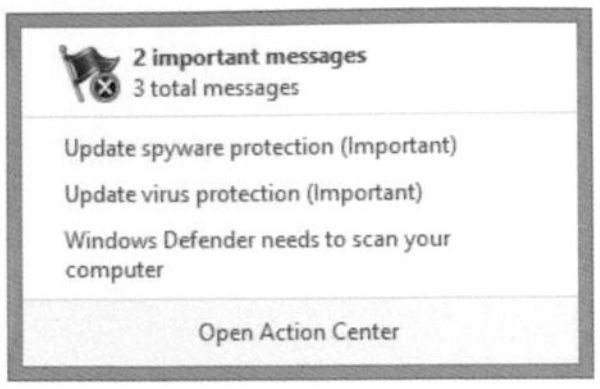

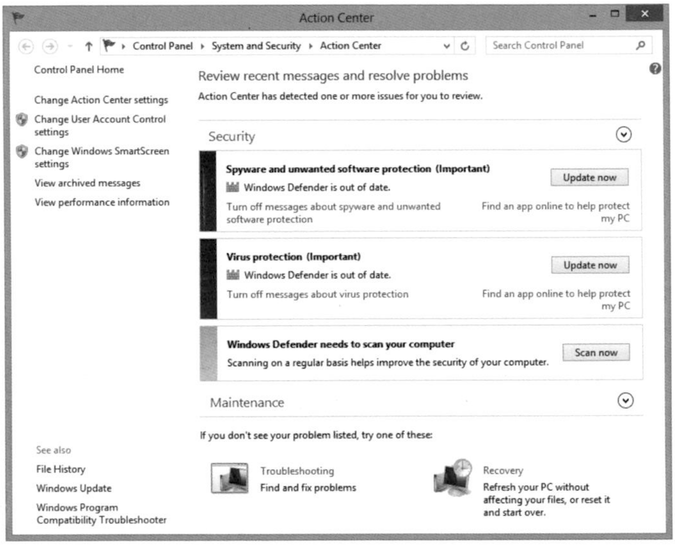

2. Action Center warns you when your spyware or virus protection needs installing or updating

3. You may be reminded to run a scan using Windows Defender, the software included in Windows

4. You will be reminded if there are problems you have not yet reported to Microsoft

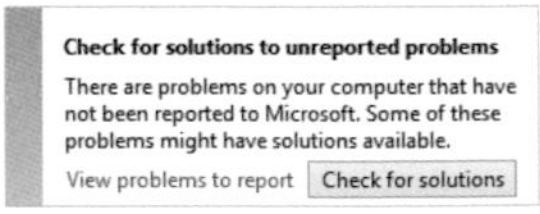

Check for solutions to unreported problems
There are problems on your computer that have not been reported to Microsoft. Some of these problems might have solutions available.
View problems to report
Check for solutions

5. Action Center also has links to Troubleshooters and to Recovery tools

Hot tip

You can also select Action Center by right-clicking the icon.

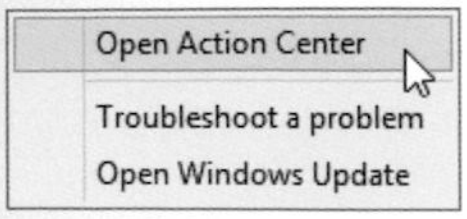

Alternatively, Search Settings on the Start screen and select Action Center.

Don't forget

Red shows important items that should be dealt with quickly, such as antivirus software. Yellow items are suggested tasks such as maintenance activities.

Program Compatibility

Windows 8 helps you deal with older programs.

1. Right-click the Alerts icon and select Troubleshoot a problem, then select Run programs made for previous versions of Windows

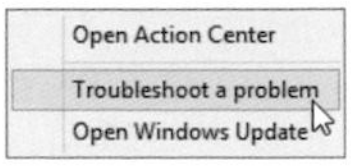
Open Action Center
Troubleshoot a problem
Open Windows Update

Programs
Run programs made for previous versions of Windows

2. Click Next to find and fix problems with running older programs in Windows 8

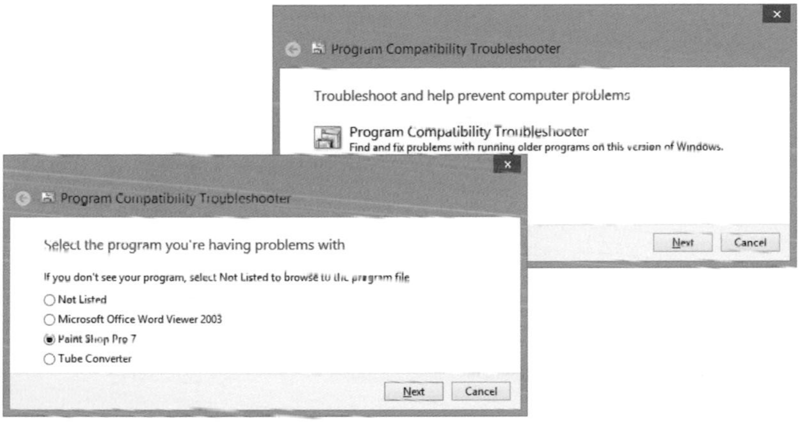

3. Select the program and Try recommended settings

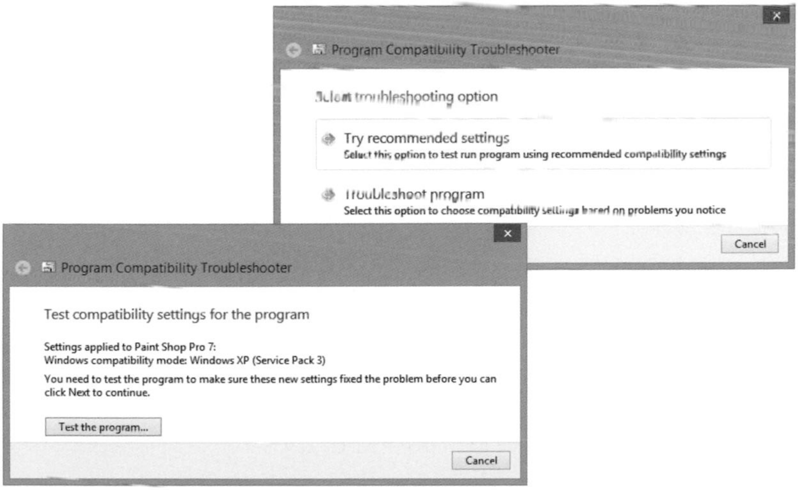

Hot tip

Alternatively, you can Search Settings for Compatibility, to locate and run the Compatibility troubleshooter.

Don't forget

You must test run the program, to see if the selected settings work, before you can continue and complete the troubleshooter.

Windows Firewall

Hot tip

To protect your computer from malicious software while it is connected to the Internet, you need Firewall software. This is included as part of Windows.

1. Open Control Panel, select System and Security and click Windows Firewall

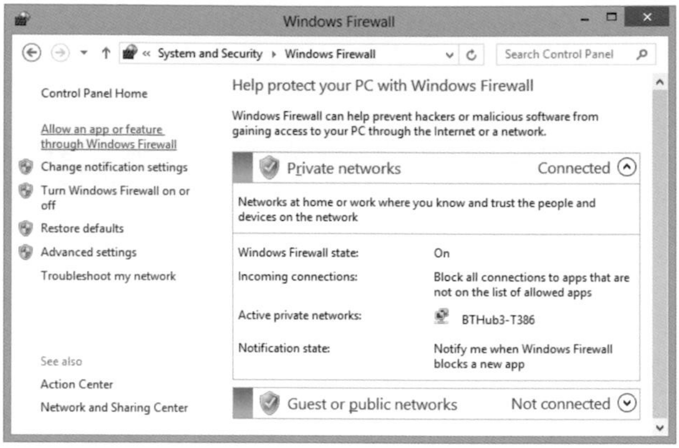

2. Click Allow a program or feature through Windows Firewall, to view the list of allowed programs

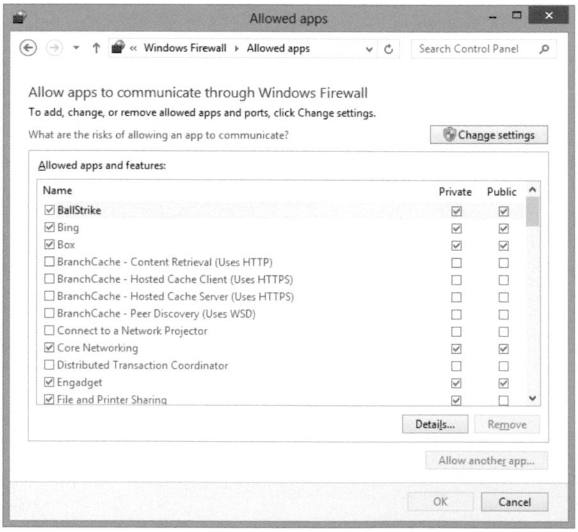

Don't forget

Programs may be added automatically when applications are installed, for example the Mail and Messenger apps.

3. Click Change settings to change or remove allowed features and apps and to enable Allow another app

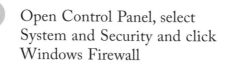

Windows Defender

1. On the Start screen, type Defend and select the Windows Defender program

2. Windows Defender opens to display the latest status

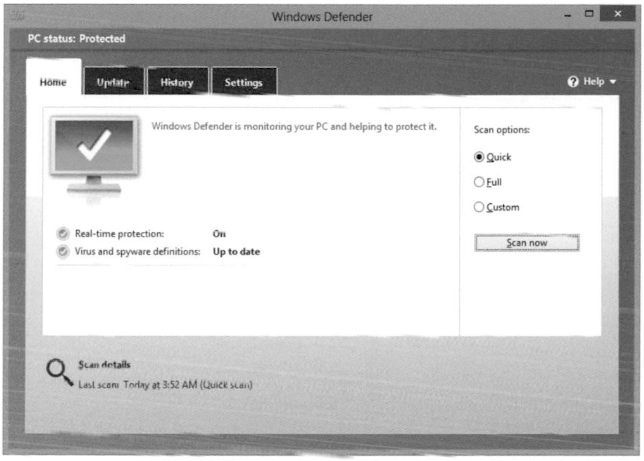

3. Click Scan now and Windows Defender will carry out a quick scan of your computer and report results

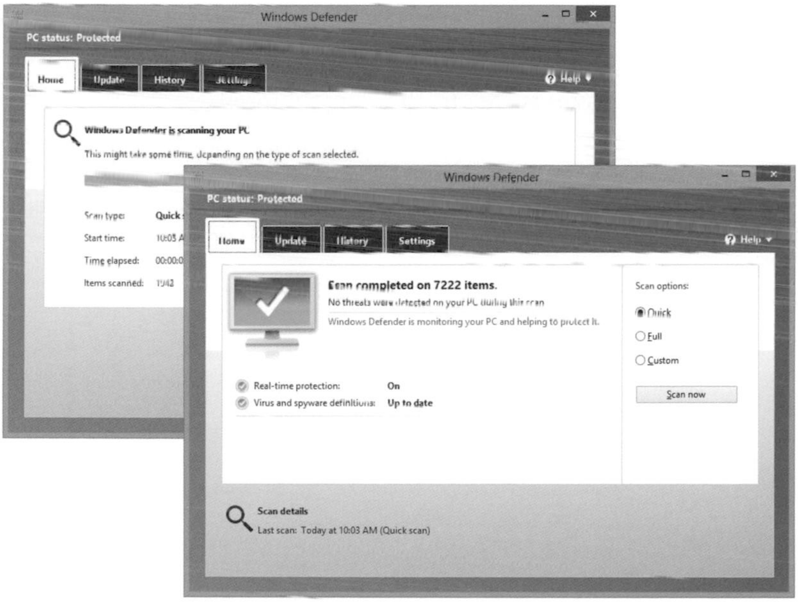

Don't forget

Windows Defender provides protection against malicious software such as viruses and spyware, so you do not have to install separate utilities.

Don't forget

The Action Center may also alert you and offer to run a scan.

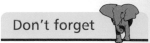

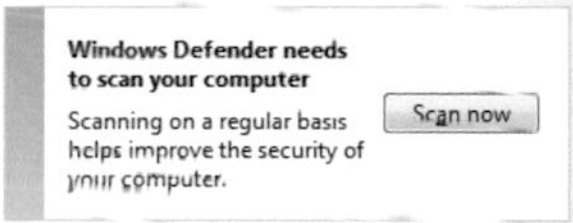
Windows Defender needs to scan your computer
Scanning on a regular basis helps improve the security of your computer.
Scan now

Hot tip

Windows Defender also alerts you when spyware attempts to install or run, or when programs try to change important Windows settings.

Windows Update

To review the process by which software updates are added to Windows:

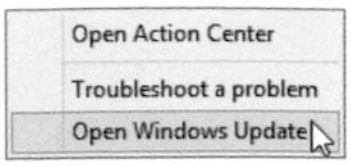
Open Action Center
Troubleshoot a problem
Open Windows Update

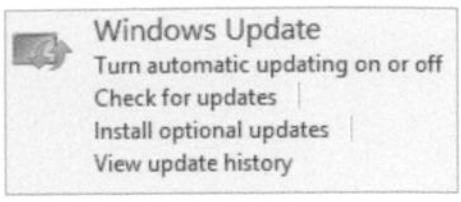
Windows Update
Turn automatic updating on or off
Check for updates
Install optional updates
View update history

1. Right-click the Alerts icon and select Open Windows Update, or select Control Panel, System and Security, Windows Update

2. Windows displays the status and gives a summary of the settings that are currently in effect

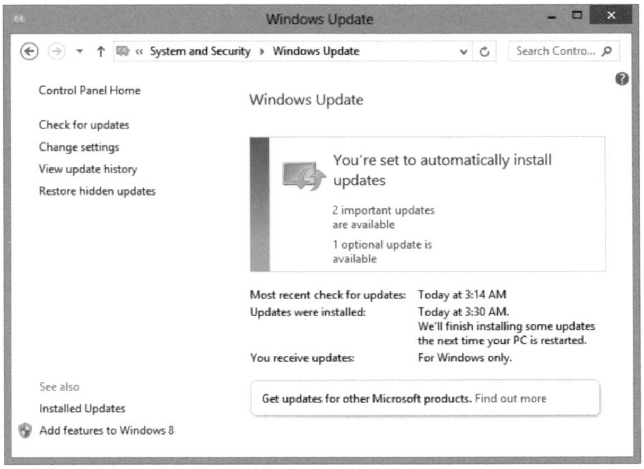
Windows Update
« System and Security ▸ Windows Update
Search Contro...
Control Panel Home
Check for updates
Change settings
View update history
Restore hidden updates
Windows Update
You're set to automatically install updates
2 important updates are available
1 optional update is available
Most recent check for updates: Today at 3:14 AM
Updates were installed: Today at 3:30 AM.
We'll finish installing some updates the next time your PC is restarted.
You receive updates: For Windows only.
Get updates for other Microsoft products. Find out more
See also
Installed Updates
Add features to Windows 8

3. Select the Change settings command to see the full list of settings, ready for any changes

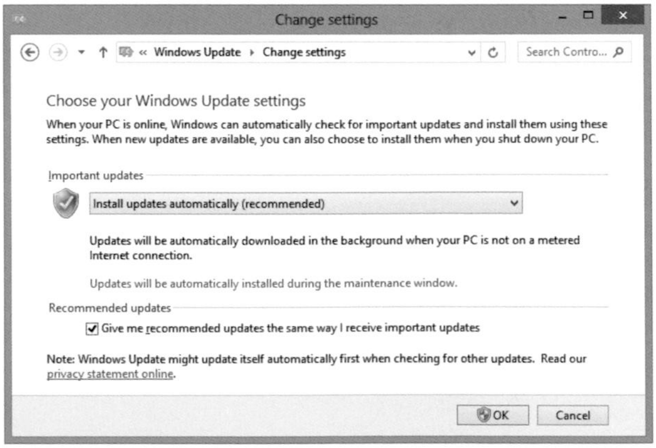
Change settings
« Windows Update ▸ Change settings
Search Contro...
Choose your Windows Update settings
When your PC is online, Windows can automatically check for important updates and install them using these settings. When new updates are available, you can also choose to install them when you shut down your PC.
Important updates
Install updates automatically (recommended)
Updates will be automatically downloaded in the background when your PC is not on a metered Internet connection.
Updates will be automatically installed during the maintenance window.
Recommended updates
Give me recommended updates the same way I receive important updates
Note: Windows Update might update itself automatically first when checking for other updates. Read our privacy statement online.
OK
Cancel

Hot tip

Updates are changes or additions that will help fix or prevent problems, enhance operation or improve performance.

Beware

If Windows Update is not switched on, you'll see an alert in the Notification area and a message in the Action Center.

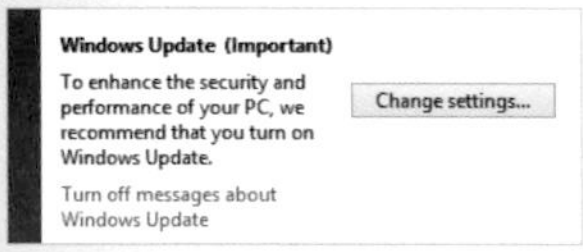
Windows Update (Important)
To enhance the security and performance of your PC, we recommend that you turn on Windows Update.
Change settings...
Turn off messages about Windows Update

4 Click the Important updates box and the list of options is displayed (with Automatic recommended)

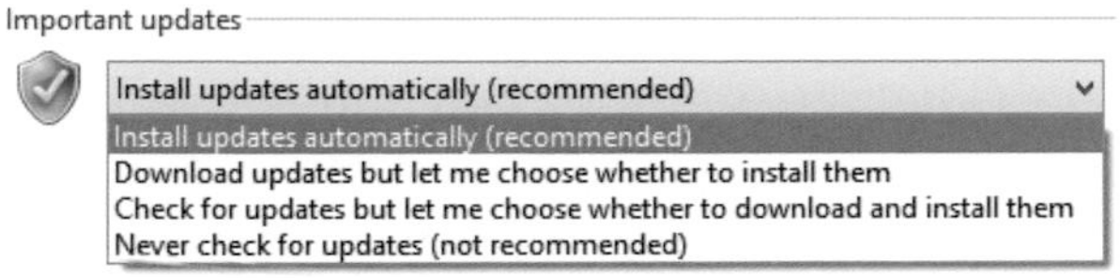

5 Click the link Install Updates automatically and you will see the Automatic Maintenance window

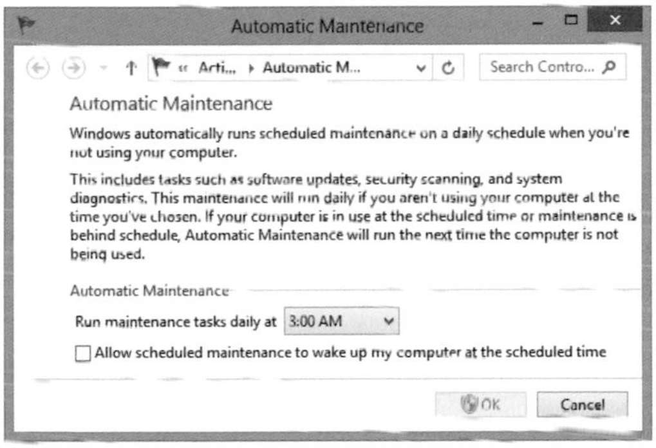

6 For the full screen Windows Update status, display the Charms bar, select Settings and Change PC Settings and click Windows Update

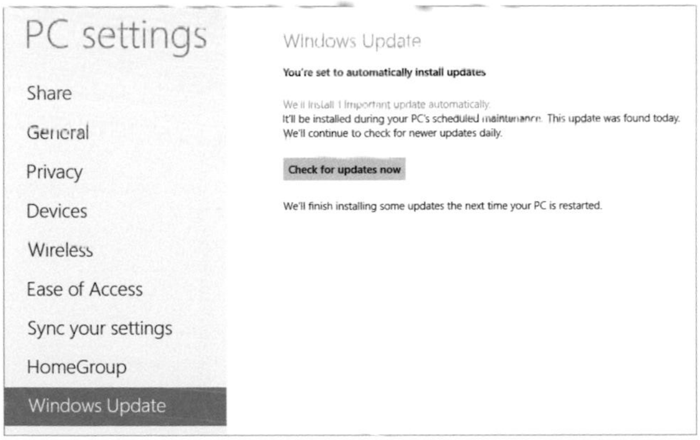
PC settings
Share
General
Privacy
Devices
Wireless
Ease of Access
Sync your settings
HomeGroup
Windows Update
Windows Update
You're set to automatically install updates
It'll be installed during your PC's scheduled maintenance. This update was found today.
We'll continue to check for newer updates daily.
Check for updates now
We'll finish installing some updates the next time your PC is restarted.

Don't forget

If you have an always-on broadband connection, you should allow Windows to apply updates automatically.

Hot tip

Updates are installed automatically at 3:00 AM unless you specify a different time. If the PC is not active at that time, updates are installed the next time you Shutdown.

Beware

The full screen Windows Update is for status display only and does not offer any facilities for changing settings etc.

System Restore

1. Open Control Panel, then System and Security and then click System

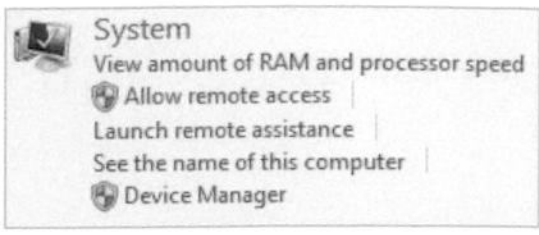

2. Select the System Protection entry

3. Click the System Restore button

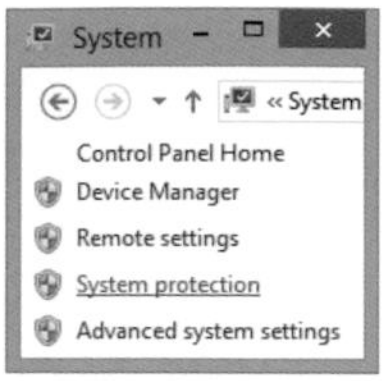

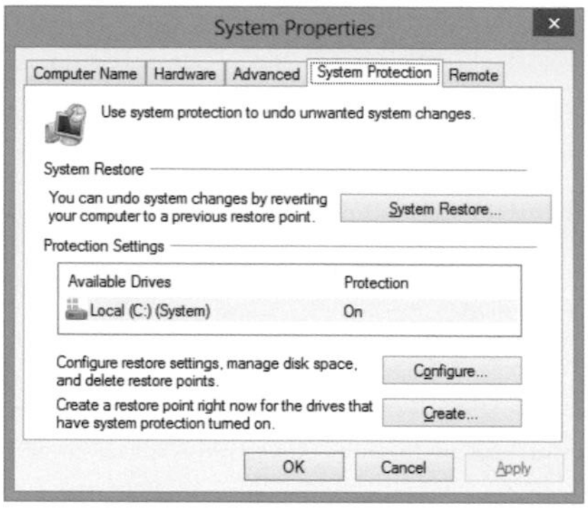

4. System Restore recommends the restore before the most recent change, but you can choose another one

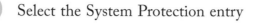

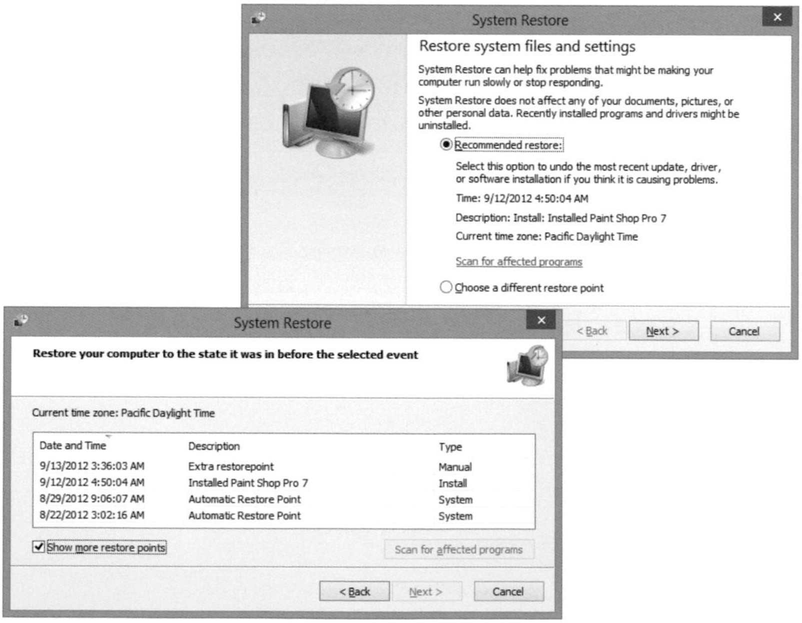

Don't forget

Problems may arise when you install new software or a new device. If uninstalling does not correct the situation, you can return the system files to their values prior to the changes.

Hot tip

Restore points are created every day and just before any significant change such as an installation or update. You can also open System Protection and create a restore point yourself.

Don't forget

Select a date and time that's prior to the problems and then click Next to restore the settings to that point in time.

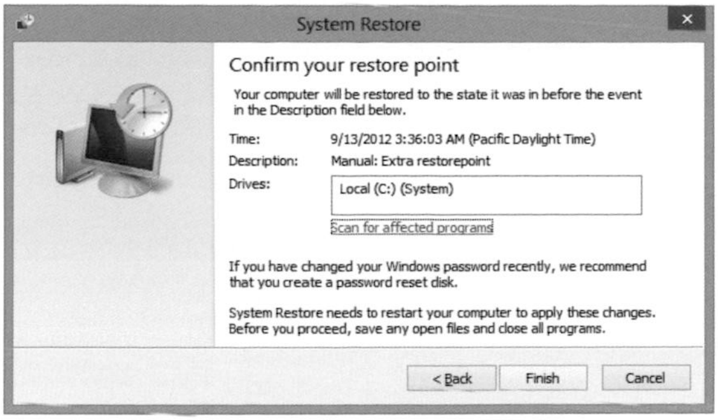

System Restore
Confirm your restore point
Your computer will be restored to the state it was in before the event in the Description field below.
Time: 9/13/2012 3:36:03 AM (Pacific Daylight Time)
Description: Manual: Extra restorepoint
Drives: Local (C:) (System)
Scan for affected programs
If you have changed your Windows password recently, we recommend that you create a password reset disk.
System Restore needs to restart your computer to apply these changes. Before you proceed, save any open files and close all programs.
< Back
Finish
Cancel

5 Click Finish to confirm your selected restore point

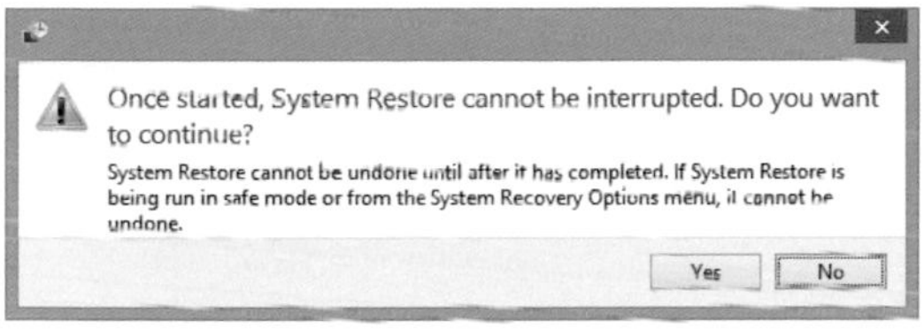

6 On restart, System Restore confirms restore

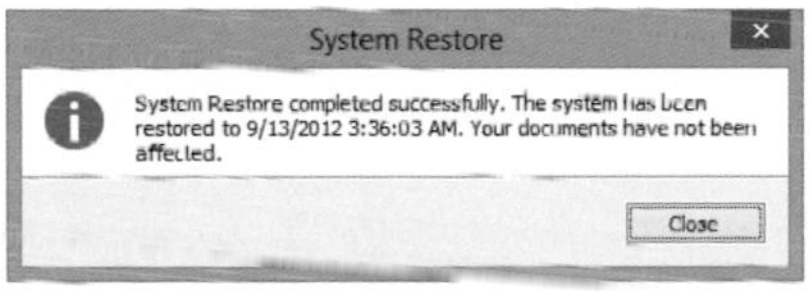

7 You can still run System Restore to undo the restore

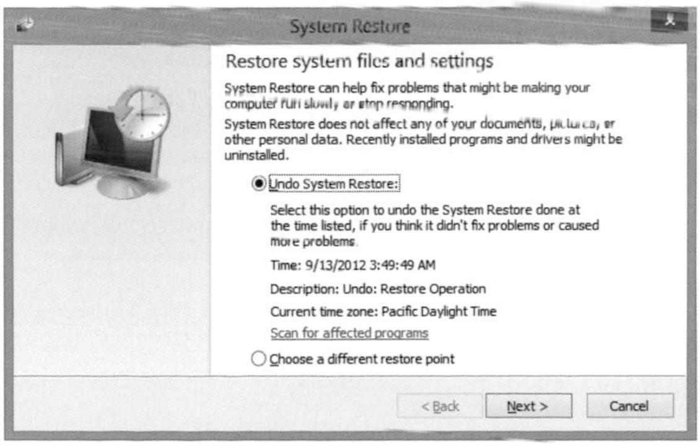

Don't forget

Once started, System Restore cannot be interrupted, though it can be undone (unless run from Safe Mode or the System Recovery Options menu).

Hot tip

If the selected restore point does not resolve your problems, you can undo the restore and try a different restore point.

File History

Don't forget

You can lose files accidentally, as a result of a virus, or due to software or hardware failure. To protect your data, you must keep copies of your files.

1. Open Control Panel, then System and Security and then click File History

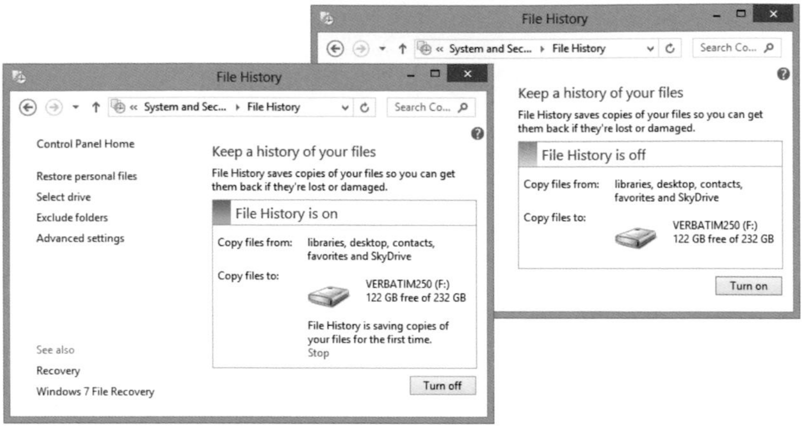

Hot tip

Backup copies are created every hour by default, but you can change the frequency. Backups are kept forever, but you can specify a time limit.

2. File History identifies an external or network drive to use for back up and you then select Turn on
3. An initial backup of your files is taken and regular backups of changes are carried out thereafter
4. Select a file in File Explorer and click the History button to see all its backups in a Player style display

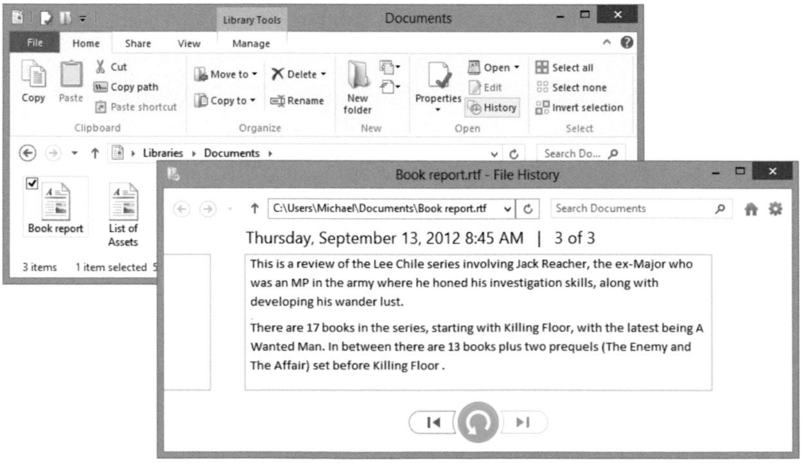

Don't forget

To browse through the backups, select File History and click Restore personal files.

Symbols

32-bit 14, 16–18
64-bit 14, 16–18

A

Account picture 66
Account type 88–89, 140–141, 144
Action Center 224
Activation 26
Add email account 140
Add Folder to library 92–93
Add tiles 68
Add to favorites 170
Adjust resolution 80
Administrator account 69, 88
Adobe Reader 54, 68, 85
All apps screen 123
App account 132
Application window 56
Apps. *See* Windows 8 apps
Apps switcher 37, 40, 44, 60
ARM processor 10, 16–17
Audio Recorder 191

B

Backup 232
Broadband 176, 218, 220
Browse the Web 160–161

C

Calculator 111
Calendar app 150–151
Change default program 120
Change user account 73
Charms bar 32
  Accounts 140, 144
  Devices and Printer 125
  Search 107, 130, 214
  Settings 41, 45
  Start screen 78
Class of network 209
Close
  Desktop app 40, 60
  File Explorer 103
  Internet Explorer 168
  Tab 168–169
  Window 55, 60, 168
  Windows 8 41–42
  Windows 8 app 40
Connect to network 208
Contact support 222
Contents pane 55, 95, 104
Copy files 97–98
Copy tracks 194
Create a network 208
Create folders and files 96
Create HomeGroup 210–211, 217
Create message 148–149

D

Delete files 99
Desktop
  Appearance 44
  Application window 56
  Auto-hide the Taskbar 48
  Charms bar 45
  Close Desktop app 60
  Display 44–45
  Lock the Taskbar 47
  Maximize window 55
  Menus and Dialogs 57
  Move window 58

E

F

G

Games in Windows 8 176
- Microsoft Mahjong 184–185
- Microsoft Solitaire Collection 182–183
- Minesweeper 178–179
- Windows Store 180–181
- Word Games 186

Group tiles 23, 35, 70–71
Guest account 89, 209
Guest network 158

H

Help and Support 220–221
- Contact support 222
- Product solution centers 223

HomeGroup
- Create 210, 217
- Join 208, 213, 217
- Leave 218
- Media streaming 217
- Password 211
- Settings 218
- View 215–216
- Windows 7 208

Home page 161, 164
Hotmail 140
Hotspots 13, 32–34, 44
Hyperlink 162–163, 165–167

I

Insert pictures 114
Install
- Desktop apps 22
- Windows 8 Apps 24–25

Instant Messaging app 152–153
Internet
- Browse the Web 160–161
- Close tabs 168–169
- Desktop Internet Explorer 164–165
- Ethernet connection 158
- Home page 161, 164
- Hyperlink 162–163, 165–167
- Set up connection 159
- Suggested websites 161
- Tabbed browsing 166–167
- Wireless connection 158

Internet Explorer 22, 46, 160
- RSS Feeds 174

J

Join HomeGroup 208, 210, 213, 217
Jump list 53, 168

K

L

Landscape orientation 81
Leave HomeGroup 218
Libraries
- Accessing folders 94
- Add folder 92–93
- Add to Start screen 69
- Navigation pane 91
- Save location 57

Live tiles 12, 31
- Turn off or on 67

Local account 21
Lock screen 12, 28, 41
- Personalize 63–64
- Quick status 64

Lock the Taskbar 47
Logon screen 28–30, 87

M

Mail app 139
- Add email account 140–141
- Create message 148
- Mail window 142
- View message 143

Manage apps 69
Manage contacts 147
Manage tiles 67
Manual restore point 230
Maximize window 55
Media library 195
Media streaming 217
Menus and Dialogs 57
Microsoft account 20
Microsoft Mahjong 184–185
Microsoft Net Framework 23
Microsoft SkyDrive 134–135, 191
Microsoft Solitaire Collection 182–183
Minesweeper 178–179
Modem 138, 208
Move files 97–98
Move tiles 71
Move window 58
Movie Maker 204, 206
Multiple monitors 13
Multiple user accounts 28
Multi-touch 10, 14, 17, 35
Music app 196–197

N

Name group 72
Navigation pane 55, 95, 104
- Computer 84
- Expand folder 85, 90, 98
- Libraries 90–91
- Options 105, 200

Network and Sharing Center 216–217
Networking
- Classification 209
- Create a network 208
- Create HomeGroup 210–211, 217
- HomeGroup password 211
- HomeGroup settings 218
- Join HomeGroup 208, 210, 213, 217
- Leave HomeGroup 218
- Media streaming 217
- Modem 138, 208
- Network and Sharing Center 216–217
- Router 138, 158, 208–209
- View HomeGroup 215
- View network devices 214
- Wireless network 212, 218
- Wireless router 158, 208

Network map
- Windows 7 208, 214

Newsgroups 156
New user account 86–87
Notepad 112
Notification area 46, 50
- System icons 50, 52

O

On-screen keyboard 46, 82
Organize files 84
Outlook 138, 140
Outlook Express 138

P

Paint 115–116
PC settings
- HomeGroup 218

PC Settings
- Delete history 40
- Ease of Use 77
- Personalize 63, 65–66
- Search 108
- Users 73–74, 76, 86–87
- Versus Control Panel 62

Windows Update 229
PDF files 124–125
Peek at Desktop 51
People app 144–145
Manage contacts 147
View contacts 146
Personalize
Account picture 66
Control Panel 78–79
Display settings 80–81
Ease of Access 82
Ease of Use 77
Landscape orientation 81
Lock screen 63–64
Picture password 74
PIN code 76
Portrait orientation 81
Start screen 65
Photo Gallery 204–205
Zoom 205
Photos app 201–202
Picture password 74–75
PIN code 76
Pin websites 171
Play audio CD 192–193
Portrait orientation 81
Power users menu 34, 62, 78, 188
Preview pane 104–105, 200
Private files 126
Private network 158, 209, 212, 216
Product solution centers 223
Program compatibility 225
Public folders 57, 90–91, 95, 126
Public network 158, 209, 212, 216

Q

Quick access toolbar 55–56, 95, 113
Quick status 64
Quick view 155

R

Reader 124–125
XPS files 124
Recording 190–191
Recovery tools 224
Requirements 14
Resize tiles 67, 123
Resize window 58
Restore point 230
Restore window 55
Router 138, 158, 208–209
RSS feeds 155, 174

S

Search app
Find apps 78
Settings 108
Using 107
Windows Store 111, 128, 130
Search box 22, 55, 106
Search Internet
File type 118
Search Settings 108
Select tiles 67
Set up connection 159
Show Desktop 51
Show hidden items 84
Shutdown 41
SkyDrive 126–127, 191
Sleep 41–42, 45, 63
Snap
Desktop window 59
Windows 8 app 12, 14, 38–39
Sound card and speakers 188–189
Copy tracks 194
Play audio CD 192–193
Recording 190–191
Standard account 88
Start app 36–37
Start button 13, 30–31, 41

Start menu 12–13, 30, 53
Start screen 12, 29, 44–45, 122
  Account picture 66
  Add tiles 68
  Apps bar 34, 123
  Find app 53, 107, 112
  Group tiles 70–71
  Hotspots 32
  Installed apps 23, 25
  Layout 31
  Lock 41, 64
  Move around 35
  Name group 72
  Personalize 65
  Pin app 54, 69, 110
  Power users menu 34
  Pre-install app 119
  Reader 124
  Select tiles 67
  Sign out 41
  SkyDrive 126
  Start app 36–37, 78, 84
  Store 24
  Thumbnail 32–33
  Unpin app 69
  User name 21, 30, 64
  Zoom 35
Start Windows 28–29
System drive 84
System icons 50, 52
System properties 11, 26, 34
System Restore 230–231
System Tray. *See* Notification area

T

Tabbed browsing 166–167
  Close tabs 168–169
Tablet PC
  ARM processor 10, 16–17
  Audio 189
  Settings 62
  Sign-on 76
  Touch 10, 35, 76
  USB 12
Taskbar 46–47
  Auto-hide 48
  Buttons 46, 49, 60
  Jump list 53, 168
  Location 49
  Properties 48–49
  Shortcuts 53
Tiles 12, 25
  Group 23, 35, 70–71
  Live 12, 31
  Manage 67
  Move 71
  Name group 72
  Resize 67, 123
Touch gesture 32, 36, 67, 151
Touch screen 16, 122
Troubleshooters 224

U

Unknown file types 117
Unlock the Taskbar 47
Unpin tiles 67
Upgrade Assistant 15
Upgrade Windows 15, 18
User folders 85, 90, 95

V

View contacts 146
View network devices 214
View pictures 200

W

Close 41–42
Contact support 222
Editions 16
Features 12–13
File Explorer 12
First logon 19
Help and Support 220–221
Hotspots 13, 32–34, 44
Local account 21
Lock screen 12, 28, 41
Logon screen 28–30, 87
Microsoft account 20
Multiple user accounts 28
Personalize Lock screen 63–64
Power users menu 34, 62, 78, 188
Product solution centers 223
Program Compatibility 225
Releases 10
Requirements 14
Search app 107
Search Settings 108
Shutdown 41
Sleep 41–42, 45, 63
Start 28–29
System properties 11, 26, 34
Touch gesture 32, 36, 67, 151
Touch screen 16, 122
Upgrade 10, 15, 18

Windows 7
Games 176
HomeGroup 208
Network map 208, 214
Personalize 79
Release 10–11
Removed Features 13

Windows 8. *See also* Windows
Activation 26
Applications 22
Editions 16–17
Features 12–13
Release 10–11
Requirements 14

Windows 8 apps
Add email account 140–141
Add tiles 68
All apps screen 123
Calendar 150
Group tiles 23, 35, 70–71
Install 24–25
Installed 123
Instant Messaging 152–153
Internet Explorer 160–161
Live tiles 12, 31
Mail 139
Mail window 142
Manage apps 69
Manage tiles 67
Move tiles 71
Music 196–197
Name group 72
People 144–145
Photos 201–202
Reader 124–125
Resize tiles 67, 123
Screen resolution 12, 14, 38, 80
Scroll tiles 35
Select tiles 67
SkyDrive 126–127, 191
Start 36–37
Tiles 12, 25
Unpin tiles 67
Windows Store 122

Windows 8 Enterprise 16
Windows 8 Pro 16
Windows Defender 19, 224, 227
Windows Essentials
Install 22–23, 110
Picture viewers 94, 204
Windows Live Mail 138, 154–155
Windows Firewall 19, 226
Windows key. *See* WinKey
Windows Live Mail 138, 154–155
Newsgroups 156
Quick view 155
RSS feeds 155
Windows logo key. *See* WinKey
Windows Mail 138
Windows Media Center 13–14, 16–17
Windows Photo Viewer 203
Windows RT

ARM processor 10, 16–17
Edition 16–17, 44
Release 10
Upgrade 18
Windows Store 12, 16
Audio Recorder 191
Books & Reference 129
Categories 128
Desktop apps 134–136
Games 176–177, 180–181
Local account 21, 29
Microsoft account 20, 30
Resolution 15
Search 111, 129–130
Spotlight 24
Updates 133
Windows 8 apps 110, 122, 131
Window structure 55
Windows Update 14, 19, 228–229
Windows Vista
Personalize 79
Upgrade 10–11, 15, 18
Windows XP
Release 10–11
Upgrade 15, 18
WinKey
Apps bar (+Z) 68, 123
Apps switcher (+Tab) 37
Charms bar (+C) 32
Desktop (+D) 31, 44
Lock (+L) 41
Power users menu (+X) 34, 62, 188
Searches (+F, +Q, +W) 107, 214
Settings pane (+I) 41, 45, 62, 108
Wireless connection 158
Wireless network 212, 218
Wireless router 158, 208
Word Games 186
WordPad 113

X

Xbox games 177
XPS files 124

Y

Yahoo Mail Plus 154
YouTube 206

Z

Zoom
Paint 116
Photo Gallery 205
Reader 125
Start screen 35, 71–72
Web page 172–173
Windows Store 128
Zoom slider 56